CRISIS MANAGEMENT: LEADING IN THE NEW STRATEGY LANDSCAPE

Fourth Edition

CRISIS MANAGEMENT: LEADING IN THE NEW STRATEGY LANDSCAPE

Fourth Edition

William Rick Crandall, Ph.D.
University of North Carolina, Pembroke

John A. Parnell, Ph.D.
University of North Alabama

John E. Spillan, Ph.D.
University of North Carolina, Pembroke

Copyright 2021
ISBN: 9798550555514
www.thecrisisbook.com
info@crisisbook.com

Crisis Management: Leading in the New Strategy Landscape (4e)

Abridged Table of Contents

Table of Contents

PREFACE

Since my graduate school years, I have been fascinated with the area of crisis management. In the late 1980s, the field was just emerging, and we had witnessed a trio of great calamities: the 1984 Bhopal, India, gas leak that killed thousands; the 1986 radiation accident at Chernobyl that killed thousands more; and in the same year, the tragic loss of the Space Shuttle *Challenger,* an unmistakable fireball in the sky that took the lives of seven American astronauts. Then, in 1989, while we were catching our breath, Exxon's supertanker, the *Exxon Valdez,* hit a reef off the coast of Alaska. The result was one of the most geographically dispersed oil spills ever, and a front-page example of crisis management gone astray. There were containment booms in the dock that could not be mobilized because that boat was under repair. There was the chief executive officer, Lawrence Rawl, who meant well but did not travel to the disaster site to address the situation directly. Oil spilled everywhere, creating a monstrous slick that sucked the life out of the environment. The ship's captain had consumed too many drinks and had illegally put the tanker under the leadership of a junior officer. The rest is history; the importance of crisis management was evident.

While developing this fascination for crisis management, I met John Parnell, a prolific writer with a passion for strategic management. Our discussions prompted the idea for a book that would address the field of crisis management within a strategic context. Another colleague, John Spillan, shared our growing interest in crisis management and was a logical choice for collaborating on this book.

Our diverse research backgrounds—human resource management, supply chain management, business strategy, international management, business ethics, and strategic marketing—influenced our growing interest in the field and, ultimately, our decision to write the book. We have lectured and presented research on crisis management topics in many countries, including Austria, Bolivia, Canada, Chile, China, Costa Rica, Egypt, Finland, Germany, Ghana, Guatemala, Kenya, Mexico, Peru, Poland, and the United Kingdom. We learned that crisis management approaches differ markedly across borders, and we began to consider the pros and cons of myriad perspectives on the field.

We were convinced that crisis management should not be just a response to an unfortunate event; it needed to be a management mindset practiced proactively and strategically. After many long discussions, the framework for the book emerged. Crisis management is a process, not a reactive event that is activated only occasionally. The four stages we propose should be incorporated into the strategic management process of the organization.

There are many others whose research influenced this project. You will find their names in the reference sections of this book. We are indebted to them for commitment to growing the discipline. I remember reading Larry Barton's first book on crisis management, *Crisis in Organizations,* and thinking, *I want to make this my research field*. As I read more on the topic, I noticed many other contributors to this growing management area. Ian Mitroff was an early contributor to the field and is still writing today. Others frequent contributors included Robert Bertrand, Arjen Boin, Steven Fink, Thierry Pauchant, Christopher Roux-Dufort, Paul Shrivastava, Denis Smith, and Karl Weick. Robert Hartley's manner of writing case studies of catastrophic events is the best I have ever seen. He concludes each case with practical lessons learned, a need for students and practitioners, and impatient researchers like the three of us. "Reframing Crisis Management," by Christine Pearson and Judith Clair, appeared in a 1998 issue of *Academy of Management Review.* This article influenced the prevailing perspectives on crisis management and helped advance the field as a legitimate academic discipline.

More recently, there have been many additional contributors to the field. Timothy Coombs has written extensively on the communication aspects of crisis management. He has also advocated crisis management as a necessary component for all organizations, referring to it as the organization's DNA. Other names continue to surface in the literature regularly, including Dominic Elliott, Sarah Kovoor-Misra, Patrick Lagadec, Christopher Lajtha, Maria Nathan, Matthew Seeger, Timothy Sellnow, and Robert Ulmer. You will find many more mentioned in the reference section at the end of each chapter. To these authors, we are grateful for what you have done to advance crisis management scholarship.

My co-authors and I would like to thank our wives, Susan, Denise, and Martha, who patiently put up with our obsession for researching and writing, which, translated, meant many hours in front of our computers. To you three, we are most grateful and appreciate your love and patience with us.

—*William "Rick" Crandall, Ph.D.*

Chapter 1: A Framework for Crisis Management

Learning Objectives

After reading this chapter, each student should be able to:

1. Define and describe an organizational crisis.
2. Explain the two primary functions of the crisis management team.
3. Identify and describe the four phases of the crisis management framework.
4. Distinguish between the internal and external landscapes.

Opening Chapter Case: Death in Room 225 - The Best Western Hotel Crisis - Part 1

It was supposed to be a restful night for Daryl and Shirley Jenkins in their guest room at the Best Western Hotel in Boone, North Carolina. On Monday, April 15, 2013, they visited relatives in the area. They were traveling with Shirley's brother, Gary Watts, and his wife, Patsye. The two couples dined at the local Cracker Barrel and planned to meet for breakfast the following morning, but Daryl and Shirley did not show up. Gary and Patsye asked the hotel to check their room. When the door was opened, Daryl and Shirley were found dead. Room 225 was hiding a mystery that would take authorities almost two months to unravel.

Background

Operating a lodging establishment is difficult. Changing linens and cleaning rooms are relatively straightforward procedures, but constant attention to detail is critical. For example, an unsuspected equipment malfunction can have a devastating impact on the business. Anything that can happen in a person's life can occur at a hotel. This case is about death, but it extends beyond Daryl and Shirley Jenkins.

On Friday, April 19, three days after Daryl and Shirley Jenkins perished, a sleepover birthday party was held at the hotel for 13-year-old Levi Solinkski. She and ten friends swam in the pool, ate cake in the lobby, and retreated to room 325 later that night. Several girls began to get sick. Some were vomiting, while others said they just did not feel well. One complained about the lights and noise. The party ended early, and most of the girls returned home (Leland, 2013). Perhaps there was a connection between the deaths in room 225 and the birthday party in room 325.

Requesting the Toxicology Reports

When the Jenkins' bodies were found, the fire and police departments conducted a preliminary investigation. There was no suicide note or evidence of a crime. When death is suspicious, a medical examiner is summoned to determine the cause. The local County Medical Examiner, Dr. Brent Hall, examined the bodies and sent blood samples to the state laboratory for analysis. He noted that both Daryl and Shirley had heart disease, and this alone, could have killed them, but simultaneous deaths from heart disease was highly unlikely. In his report to the lab, Dr. Hall asked for the toxicology samples to be tested for drugs, alcohol, and carbon monoxide. Such tests can be requested to be expedited—a reasonable request—especially if there is an environmental concern about the safety of a room that could be rented to others. But Dr. Hall did not request that the results be expedited (Leland, 2013).

Hotel management decided not to rent room 225 for six weeks until the cause of the deaths had been determined. On May 31, room 225 was rented again, but only after a contractor inspected the room and nearby facilities for safety. The first guest in the room reported no problems, but Dr. Hall had not yet received the toxicology results.

On Friday, June 7, Jeannie Williams and her 11-year old son, Jeffrey, checked into the hotel. They were initially assigned to another room but moved to 225 because of a strong cigarette smoke smell. Jeannie and Jeffrey were scheduled to pick up her daughter, Breanne, the following day from summer camp. Unfortunately, sometime during the night, Jeanne became critically ill, and Jeffrey died. Room 225 had claimed two more victims, but the cause remained a mystery.

The Unread Email

Email is a valuable management tool, but sometimes messages are overlooked, mistakenly deleted, or sent to a spam folder. An email with the toxicology results was sent to Dr. Brent Hall on Monday, June 3, three days *before* Jeannie and Jeffrey entered room 225. The report noted that Darryl and Shirley had died of carbon monoxide poisoning. For reasons unknown, Dr. Hall never read the email (Leland, 2013; 2016). If he had, Jeffrey Williams would probably not have perished.

Case Discussion Questions

1. What were your initial thoughts after you read the first paragraph of this case? Did your thinking gravitate to a specific cause of death?
2. Do you see any communication breakdowns in this case?
3. How can carbon monoxide deaths in a hotel be prevented?

Visualizing Crisis Management

What comes to mind when you think about crisis management? Perhaps you ponder the human and economic toll of the COVID-19 pandemic. Maybe you think of the scandal when German automaker, Volkswagen, installed software in vehicles exported to the United States with the goal of "fooling" emission standards testing equipment (ICM, 2016). Perhaps you think of the 2015 Blue Bell crisis that resulted in three deaths from consuming ice cream that contained Listeria monocytogenes, a form of deadly bacteria.

 In this case, listeria had been found in the production facility two years prior, but little had been done to prevent it from reoccurring (Elkind, 2015). Perhaps you envision a team of managers trying to deal with a fire that has destroyed the production facilities at a manufacturing plant. Indeed, fires remain one of the most prominent types of crises that managers must address.

The term, *crisis management*, invokes many images, but it is more than just a one-time response to an unfortunate event. **Crisis management** is a strategic process that begins long before the first crisis ever occurs in an organization. It is an activity that must be planned, both before and after the crisis event. This book offers a conceptual framework to help managers prepare more effectively for crisis events in their organizations.

The onset of crises in organizations is typical today. The COVID-19 global pandemic has changed how business leaders perceive, anticipate, and plan for crises. Some still assume that business interruption coverage covers their losses. Even so, financial losses that emanate to a catastrophe can be challenging to quantify, and companies are usually left to absorb those that stem from long-term damage to their brands and reputations. Moreover, in the case of COVID-19, most business interruption coverage did not help because the policies required physical damage; more than half specifically excluded viruses as well (Scism, 2020). While insurance can help organizations cover losses from many crisis events, it does not replace effective crisis management.

Many business leaders associate a crisis with far-reaching events that cause mass destruction and even causalities. Some crises damage multiple organizations, industries, or even entire economies, while the negative impact of others is felt by a single firm. For example, in 2013, a chicken found its way into an electrical sub-station at the Kahului Airport in Maui, Hawaii. A 30-minute power outage occurred and, although not serious, required passengers to disembark their aircraft using the older mobile stairways, causing flight delays (*Associated Press*, 2013). In 2016, a computer system meltdown at Southwest Airlines resulted in the cancellation of over 2000 flights over four days and cost the carrier tens of millions of dollars (Bachman & Schlangenstein, 2016). As these examples illustrate, a crisis need not be widespread to reap havoc on an organization. Leaders who fail to recognize the broad scope of crisis management can easily fall into the "it can't happen to us" trap. However, they may be closer to a disaster than they realize.

Setting the Context

Unfortunate events occur in the life of most organizations. The impact of crises—particularly those instigated by natural disasters—has increased exponentially with population growth. Between 1980 and 2019, 246 hurricanes, droughts, severe storms, floods, wildfires, and other disasters in the United States have exceeded $1 billion in costs. In total dollars, it costs firms, governments, and individuals $1.6 trillion. Hurricanes are the costliest by far, accounting for $928 billion. Because the southeast (where storms occur) is growing faster than other parts of the country, the costs for future storms will continue to increase (Ailworth, 2019).

There are two broad approaches to managing crises: (1) Try to keep them from occurring, and (2) mitigate the impact of the crisis when it does occur. Crisis management addresses these two approaches and is a field of growing interest because many managers now realize that their firms are not immune to those sudden, unexpected events that can put an organization into a tailspin and sometimes even out of business. This book for managers and students of crisis management. Leaders should engage in crisis planning and develop a crisis toolkit for organizational and professional success.

A Framework for Studying Crisis Management

Frameworks group or organize what we experience in organizational life. Here, we develop a framework that examines crisis management in four distinct phases, including internal and external dimensions, which we call landscapes. Our framework begins with a definition of the term. The word *crisis* is often used interchangeably with other terms, including disaster, business interruption, catastrophe, emergency, or contingency (Herbane, 2010). Numerous specific similar definitions have been proposed. Pearson and Clair's (1998) definition is cited often:

> *An organizational crisis is a low-probability, high-impact event that threatens the viability of the organization and is characterized by an*

ambiguity of cause, effect, and means of resolution, as well as by a belief that decisions must be made swiftly (p. 60).

The following implications of this definition should be highlighted:

- A crisis is a "low-probability" event. This characteristic makes planning for a crisis even more troublesome. Events that are not perceived to be imminent are hard to plan for, and managers are often not motivated to plan for such an event. The notion is, "Why should we plan for something bad if it probably won't occur anyway?" Many managers have asked the same question until they were confronted with a crisis.
- The reference to "ambiguity of cause" means that the origins and effects of the crisis might *not* be known initially. Paradoxically, the human instinct is to quickly point to simple reasons that may have caused the crisis, including human stakeholders such as managers or company owners who might have been negligent. As we will see throughout this book, multiple interrelated factors can lead to a trigger event that initiates a crisis.
- The ambiguity in this definition also implies that the means of resolving the crisis may be multifaceted. In other words, several viable options may be available for the crisis management team to use in its goal of mitigating the crisis.
- Certain aspects of managing a crisis may require swift decision-making. The failure to act decisively during the acute stage of the crisis can often intensify the ordeal.

Pearson and Clair's definition provides a starting point for understanding crisis management. However, the element of perception is also useful to consider. For example, Timothy Coombs (2015) proposed the following definition:

A crisis is the perception of an unpredictable event that threatens important expectancies of stakeholders related to health, safety, environmental, and economic issues. It can severely impact an organization's performance and generate negative outcomes (p. 3).

This definition emphasizes perception. A crisis is generally perceived to be a threat by the organization's stakeholders, the groups that influence and are influenced by the organization. Employees, customers, and the community in which the organization resides are considered stakeholders. Coombs infers that not all stakeholders will perceive that a crisis is occurring. A product defect detected by consumers, but not by individuals inside the company, is an example of the incongruity that can occur. Nonetheless, a crisis has occurred because the event has impacted negatively, at least one group of stakeholder's perceptions. Recognizing this distinction is important because there are occasions when managers sometimes deny that a crisis is occurring (Sheaffer & Mano-Negrin, 2003).

Consider General Motors' (GM) denial that anything was wrong with its Corvair automobile (Nader, 1965). In this early-1960s well-documented example of a corporate crisis, consumers and the media claimed that the Corvair automobile became unstable when going into a turn. Several accidents involving fatalities had already occurred because of this structural problem. GM maintained that the problem of instability resulted from driver error, not a defect in the car. This denial by GM that a problem even existed resulted in a massive public image problem for the company. It even launched the career of consumer crusader, Ralph Nader (Hartley, 1993).

This book follows the crisis definition guidelines offered above. We build on the definition offered by Pearson and Clair in 1998, but we also include the perspective offered by Coombs. To paraphrase Pearson, Clair, and Coombs, we offer the following definition as a reference point throughout the book:

> A **crisis** is an event that has a low probability of occurring, but should it happen, can negatively impact the organization. The cause of a crisis and the appropriate response may not be apparent; nonetheless, it should be resolved as quickly as possible. Finally, the crisis impact may not be initially evident to all the relevant stakeholders of the organization.

A critical characteristic of a crisis that it rarely "just occurs" without warning. Instead, many preconditions or vulnerabilities usually exist that form a breeding ground for the crisis. Put differently, crises have a life cycle, and understanding what occurs before a crisis commences is essential to preventing it.

Some management scholars investigate similar issues under the realm of "error management." Errors in organizations are unintended deviations from established goals and standards that can lead to either positive or negative consequences (Frese & Keith, 2015; Lei, Naveh & Novikov, 2016). Like crises, errors are often, but not always, avoidable.

The Life Cycle of a Crisis

Researchers typically examine a crisis sequentially to understand its evolution. One approach includes four stages: preconditions, the trigger event, the crisis itself, and the aftermath.

Preconditions. Smith (1990) was one of the first to point out that a set of smaller events typically interact before a crisis occurs. This combination of events eventually leads to a significant occurrence, commonly called the "trigger event" (Roux-Dufort, 2009; Smith, 1990), which causes the actual crisis to commence. For example, the trigger event at Union Carbide's Bhopal India plant in 1984 was water entry into a gas storage tank that subsequently caused the tank's temperature to rise. The resulting pressure increase forced the dangerous gas, methyl isocyanate (MIC) to escape into the air, resulting in the deaths of thousands of innocent civilians who lived nearby. However, responsibility for the crisis cannot be attributed solely to those involved with that step in the crisis because numerous preconditions contributed to the origin of the accident. These included shutting down a refrigeration system, failing to reset the tank temperature alarm, operating with a non-functioning gas scrubber, and not repairing an inoperative flame tower designed to burn off toxic gases (Hartley, 1993).

Trigger Event. The trigger event is the point where the crisis escalates and upsets the healthy equilibrium of the organization. The firm has been functioning normally up to this point, but preconditions brewing "beneath the surface" have led to the trigger event, which ultimately sets the crisis in motion. Some might equate it to the point "where all hell breaks loose" or "the straw that broke the camel's back" (Crandall, 2007).

The Crisis. The escalation of the crisis produces the most significant impact and damage to the organization and its stakeholders. Potential stakeholders include employees, management, owners/stockholders, customers, those who use social media outlets, suppliers, the local community, and government regulators. Damage can be extensive during this acute stage of the crisis and can significantly affect the business or organization's operating continuity.

Post-crisis. After the acute phase of the crisis is over, management should reflect on the event and identify changes that can prevent or mitigate the effects of future crisis events (Kovoor-Misra & Nathan, 2000; Smith & Elliott, 2007). For example, after the first cyanide poisoning of extra-strength Tylenol, Johnson & Johnson switched to a tamper-proof container. After the second poisoning in 1986, Johnson & Johnson made additional changes and manufactured the product as a caplet, a non-penetrable material that cannot be degraded by cyanide.

Strategic Orientation

In many instances, crisis events in organizations are addressed with a short-term, reactive perspective. When a crisis occurs, specific individuals in an organization—perhaps those on an established crisis management team—convene to minimize the damage and present a positive image to the public. Any preparations for dealing with such crises often focus on effective communications and public relations. In contrast, organizations constantly face strategic challenges. They must adapt to their changing business environments and modify their strategies to survive and remain competitive. In doing so, their managers tend to adopt a long-term perspective on strategic planning.

Between the extremes of short-term organizational crises and long-term, strategic challenges (i.e., substantial problems) are obstacles to organizational success that are not always easy to classify. Indeed, distinguishing between a crisis and a strategic challenge may be difficult. Consider these potential scenarios, all of which are based on actual events that have occurred over the last several years:

- A supplier in another country produces a product that turns out to be defective, and the product is assembled as a component into a domestically manufactured product. The final product fails, and in the process, kills three people. Is this a crisis or a strategic challenge? The answer is both. It is a crisis because there has now been a loss of life due to a defective product. It is a strategic challenge because the supplier might have been selected solely for its ability to manufacture the component product at a low cost.
- A labor union stages a mass boycott of certain products that are sold by domestic companies but manufactured overseas. The message from the protest is that these products have caused the loss of domestic jobs. The boycott causes revenue loss for the companies that manufacture and retail these products. In a few cases, vandalism occurs in retail store properties that offer the products. Is this a crisis or a strategic challenge? Again, it is both. It is a crisis because of the sudden and unexpected loss of revenue for the companies involved. Furthermore, the damage and public apathy are of concern and require swift and effective decisions. It is a strategic challenge because the products are made overseas for cost reasons.
- A prominent pharmaceutical company expands its product line to address the health needs of baby boomers (i.e., born between 1946 and 1964), a market viewed as a significant revenue source in the years to come. Several new drugs are approved and introduced to the market. After a few years, however, one of the drugs is linked to deadly heart disease. The pressure to withdraw the drug is put firmly on the pharmaceutical company. Is this a crisis or a strategic challenge? Once again, it is both. It is a crisis because stakeholder attention is questioning the credibility of the drug and, indirectly, the company's credibility.

A significant repercussion could result from this event, and swift decisions are required. It is also a strategic challenge because the drug was in the firm's long-term arsenal of products that would be popular and produce revenue for the next 20 years.

- A major corporation establishes a performance-based compensation plan for its managers. As hoped, performance appears to have improved, even though the local economy has been struggling. For seven quarters, two managers receive performance-based bonuses based on meeting the compensation plan's performance indices. However, both managers have been "cooking the books." They are eventually fired, and the company is fined by regulators. During the ordeal, the company receives negative publicity because of the ethical lapse. Is this a crisis or a strategic challenge? Of course, the answer is both. The crisis aspect was manifested by the reputational and financial damage the company suffered. This dilemma also has roots as a strategic challenge. The decision to set up a bonus plan based on performance was not necessarily a poor decision. Indeed, most managers in both service and manufacturing industries are compensated in part on performance. However, some compensation plans are set up in such a way that they can invite unethical management decisions.

- Finally, many grocery stores and restaurant chains have been sourcing shrimp from Thailand, a country known for slavery in the supply chain. As a result, the affected companies are now facing intense social media criticism. These companies were not aware that slavery existed in their supply chains but discovered it only after several investigative reports were aired in the media. Is this a crisis or a strategic challenge? Again, the answer is both. The crisis is severe in that human rights violations have occurred, and boycotts are commencing. However, the situation is also strategic, in that these companies decided to source shrimp from Thailand. Supply chain decisions involving sourcing are strategic and can have long-term ramifications.

Because of the link between crises and strategy, planning for crises should be a part of the strategic management process. While traditional crisis management approaches often identify this function as a separate planning process, crisis planning should not exist in a vacuum but should intertwine with strategic planning. This theme is common throughout the book.

Previous Crisis Management Frameworks: Classifications of Crises

Early crisis management frameworks examined the types of crises organizations encounter. In their work on presenting corporate policy during a crisis, Marcus and

Goodman (1991) identified three types of crises: accidents, product safety & health incidents, and scandals. Pearson and Mitroff's (1993) framework identified seven crisis families: economic attacks, environmental accidents, occupational health diseases, psycho events (e.g., terrorism, sabotage, product tampering), damage to reputation, informational attacks, and breaks (e.g., recalls, product defects, computer breakdowns). In a similar crisis family arrangement, Myers (1993) offered a framework of crises consisting of natural disasters (e.g., floods, hurricanes), environmental events (e.g., aircraft accidents, contamination events, explosions), and incited incidents (e.g., arson, sabotage, vandalism).

Coombs (2006) has offered this framework and classified crises as follows:

- *Attacks on organizations*: Computer hacking or tampering, rumors, product tampering, workplace violence, and terrorism. The common theme is that the attacks originate from outside the organization. However, not all attacks are external. A disgruntled employee can initiate an attack as well, particularly in a workplace violence episode.
- *When things go wrong*: Defective products are caused by company error, loss of key personnel, industrial accidents, transportation problems, and stakeholder challenges (when an outside group accuses the company of wrongdoing). Often, these types of crises arise because of operational problems in the company.
- *When the organization misbehaves*: Not addressing known risks, improper job performance leads to an accident, legal and regulatory violations. An ethical breach has occurred.

In an assessment of crisis categories that could occur on US college or university campuses, Mitroff, Diamond, and Alpaslan (2006) identified seven types of crises:

- *Criminal activities*: These include the 2007 Virginia Tech massacre incident, when a student, Seung-Hui Cho, went on a shooting rampage and killed 32 people is an example.
- *Informational crises*: This group of crises includes identity theft, fraud, and confidentiality problems.
- *Building safety issues*: This category includes discoveries of mold in buildings.
- *Athletic scandals*: Many of these have occurred at universities in the United States and include unethical practices by coaches and illegal payments to athletes.
- *Public health problems*: COVID-19 is a prime example, but this category also includes food safety issues in restaurants and supply chains.

- *Unethical behavior/misconduct*: Examples include plagiarism, record tampering, and fraud.
- *Financial crises, natural disasters, legal/labor disputes, and reputation problems*: Natural disasters such as hurricanes put the safety of many people in a small area at risk.

As these examples illustrate, cries often occur in clusters, further complicating the response effort. Recognizing this fact can be useful when preparing for crises.

Using a framework for classifying crisis events into families is a useful way to organize what we experience. It is impossible to prepare for every crisis that might occur, but preparing for several families of crises is feasible (Mitroff, 1989). In this book, we present a framework of crisis families that consider the internal and external landscapes of the organization's environment. First, we must acknowledge that crisis events also occur in stages.

Previous Crisis Management Frameworks: Stages of Crises

Frameworks have also been developed to address the various stages of a crisis. Most frameworks that emerged in the 1990s followed a three- or four-stage approach to analyzing the life of a crisis. A crisis is more than just an event. It is a life cycle phenomenon with a birth, an acute stage—the crisis—and aftermath, a time of learning and reflection. Table 1.1 overviews various frameworks.

The most basic framework is the simple three-stage approach that follows a pre-crisis, crisis, and post-crisis format. Smith (1990) offered a three-stage format consisting of a pre-crisis period, the crisis of management; a crisis period, the operational crisis; and a post-crisis stage, the crisis of legitimation. Once the crisis is underway, the organization manages the crisis as best it can during the operational crisis stage. This stage is characterized by building a supportive climate among the key players involved. Unfortunately, the crisis of legitimation stage can include scapegoating other individuals or the organization, as well as the government and the media. The scapegoating process involves attributing blame for the crisis to various stakeholders.

Richardson (1994) offered a three-step framework like the one proposed by Smith. The pre-crisis/disaster phase focuses on prevention by addressing the threats that can trigger a crisis. The crisis impact/rescue stage is the occurrence of the actual crisis. During this period, management should seek to mitigate the crisis and offer support to those affected by it. The recovery/demise stage involves restoring stakeholder confidence in the organization.

Table 1.1 Frameworks for Crisis Management

3-Stage Framework General	3-Stage Framework Smith, 1990	3-Stage Framework Richardson, 1994	4-Stage Framework Myers, 1993	4-Stage Framework Fink, 1996	5-Stage Framework Pearson & Mitroff, 1993	This Book: 4-Stage Framework Crandall, Parnell, & Spillan, 2019
Before the Crisis ➡	Crisis of management	Precrisis/ disaster phase	Normal operations	Prodromal crisis stage	Signal detection	Landscape survey
					Preparation/ Prevention	Strategic planning
During the Crisis ➡	Operational crisis	Crisis impact/ rescue phase	Emergency response	Acute crisis stage	Containment/ Damage limitation	Crisis management
			Interim Processing	Chronic crisis stage		
After the Crisis ➡	Crisis of legitimation	Recovery/ demise phase	Restoration	Crisis resolution stage	Recovery	Organizational learning
					Learning	

Four-Stage Frameworks

By adding a stage, the four-stage frameworks offer a more detailed approach. Myers (1993) offered a four-stage approach that begins with the normal operations stage when prevention practices are established. In this stage, operations are normal, but preparations are made to address a crisis event should one occur. The second stage, emergency response, encompasses the activities during the first hours following the onset of the crisis. The third stage, interim processing, represents an intermediate phase where temporary procedures are established until normal operations can resume. Restoration, the final stage, focuses on the organization's transition back to normal operations.

Fink (1996) also proposed a four-stage framework beginning with the prodromal stage. This stage occurs before the full-blown crisis and contains warning signs that signal a crisis may be imminent. During this stage, the crisis is preventable if the warning signs are heeded. The acute crisis stage follows and includes the sudden onset of the event. Problems are most noticeable by outsiders during this stage. Next, the chronic crisis stage is less dramatic in appearance but is still significant since the organization is attempting to address the episode's lingering damages. The final stage is the resolution when the organization returns to its pre-crisis existence.

Five-Stage Framework

Unlike the previous four-stage frameworks, Pearson and Mitroff's (1993) five-stage crisis framework provides an even more comprehensive approach to understanding the stages, including:

1. **Signal detection**: The warning signs that precede a crisis occur in this stage. Becoming adept at signal detection is a mindset and a skill, that organizations need to embrace.
2. **Preparation/prevention:** This stage involves forming a crisis management team and a plan for addressing those crises that may occur. Crisis management is approached systematically and continuously to the point where it resembles science. The goal is to prevent as many crises as possible and effectively manage the ones that do occur.
3. **Containment/damage limitation:** This stage is where the actual management of the crisis occurs. The intent is to contain the crisis to the greatest extent possible and mitigate the event and minimize organizational and stakeholder damage.
4. **Recovery:** In this stage, attempts are made to resume activities as much as feasible. The recovery will often proceed in stages as well. Short-term recovery aims to get the system back online and achieve a minimally acceptable level of service. Long-term recovery follows as operational activities are restored to their pre-crisis level. Some organizations leverage the recovery process to raise their capabilities and performance. An example would be a company that experiences a fire in its production facilities. After the fire, the rebuilt facility is usually better equipped technologically than the old one.
5. **Learning:** This stage involves reflecting on what managers can learn from the crisis. The emphasis is not on searching for scapegoats and blaming others, although a response is often encouraged in a litigious society. Instead, the focus is on improving current operational problems and preventing future ones.

Our Framework for Crisis Management

Figure 1.1 presents another framework for crisis management, the one adopted in this book. We draw from previous scholarship and add another dimension, the existence of the internal and external landscapes that engulf the organization. The internal landscape exists within the organization and consists of the employees and the organizational culture of the organization. It is the human side of the company that exhibits the strengths and weaknesses of the organization.

The external landscape resides outside of the organization and includes all stakeholders with some vested interest in the organization but are not directly part of it. The external landscape includes customers, government regulatory agencies, consumer advocacy groups, industry associations, social media activists, the local community, suppliers, and the media. It also includes non-stakeholders that can impact company operations such as terrorist groups or even a jealous spouse of an employee. The external environment can also have broader forces, such as weather events, other natural disasters, a downturn in the economy, or a pandemic like COVID-19.

Figure 1.1 A Framework for Crisis Management

	Landscape Survey	Strategic Planning	Crisis Management	Organizational Learning
The Internal Landscape	What crisis threats exist INSIDE of our organization?	How can our organization plan for potential crisis events?	How should we manage our INTERNAL stakeholders during a crisis? ← Crisis	What can our organization learn from this crisis?
The External Landscape	What crisis threats exist OUTSIDE of our organization?	What planning has been done outside of our organization to help us prepare for potential crisis events?	How should we manage our EXTERNAL stakeholders during a crisis?	What learning is taking place outside of our organization in relation to the type of crisis we just experienced?

The progression of stages in the crisis management process follows a four-phase sequence. Figure 1.1 illustrates this framework in the form of a two-by-four matrix. The landscape survey is followed by strategic planning, then crisis management, and finally, the organizational learning stage. These stages can overlap to some extent.

Landscape Survey: Identifying the Crises Threats

The framework begins with the landscape survey, shown on the far-left side of the figure. The top half of the landscape survey looks at processes that management needs to evaluate within the organization. Identifying the strengths and weaknesses that exist in the organization is one such process. Such weaknesses indicate areas where the company may be vulnerable to a crisis. Enthusiasm for crisis management planning is another critical element to gauge. Some organizations are highly prepared for crisis events, whereas others are more complacent (Pearson & Mitroff, 1993). The degree of enthusiasm for crisis management is also a function of the organization's culture (Stead & Smallman, 1999), its ethical environment, and the diligence with which the company enforces its safety policies.

The bottom portion of the landscape survey focuses on events occurring outside of the organization, the external landscape. Industry vulnerability is a paramount consideration. For example, companies in the chemical industry are concerned about chemical leaks. Food manufacturers focus on health-related crises such as an *E. coli* outbreak. Within the hotel and lodging industry, the physical safety of guests is a significant concern. The location of a hotel, for example, in coastal areas, can create vulnerabilities based on flooding, earthquakes, and potential tsunamis (Henderson, 2005).

For companies operating across international borders, the host country's degree of political stability is an important consideration. Another critical factor is the general attitude of the host country toward a multinational corporation's (MNC) home country. Any heightened tensions that may exist between these two stakeholders can lay the groundwork for a potential crisis. Globalization's implications are also important. Outsourcing to other countries, occurs at the expense of a significant stakeholder - the home country's manufacturing employees. For example, manufacturing operations that leave the home country for cheaper labor in a developing country often leave a wake of unemployed workers back in the home country. Such moves typically do not sit well with local stakeholders such as labor unions and communities that experiencing job losses.

The technological advancements within an industry must also be considered part of the external landscape. For some industries, technology can lay the groundwork for a crisis. In the commercial airline industry, the smooth functioning of all technological systems on an aircraft (avionics) is essential for a safe flight. Also, airline reservation systems must run correctly, lest there be a massive cancellation of flights. In other industries, technology is essential but not necessarily life-threatening—yet can still be the source of a significant crisis. Retail chains rely on information technology to communicate and manage their field units. A malfunction in such a system will create a crisis, but not physically harmful to employees or customers.

Strategic Planning: Preparing for Potential Crises

In this book, we acknowledge the long-range goals of strategic planning. Strategic planning occurs primarily in the organization's internal landscape and seeks to prevent crises when possible and mitigate their effects should a crisis occur. Crisis planning begins with forming the **crisis management team (CMT).** The team acts as the management unit that prevents a crisis from arising or directs the organization through the crisis. One of the team's tasks is to periodically assess potential crises that may occur to the organization. For example, school districts for all grade levels, as well as colleges and universities, should plan regularly for a dysfunctional student who may become violent. Fires and other crises might require rapid building evacuations.

Crisis management teams also formulate **crisis management plans (CMPs)** that provide general guidelines for managing a crisis (Coombs, 2006). Such policies include who should address the media and procedures for managing specific crises that are unique to the organization. In other words, these guidelines address the organization's potential crises. During the strategic planning stage, some teams will conduct mock disasters to test the organization's crisis management response.

Managers can learn a lot about crisis prevention by staying abreast of industry trends. Governments often regulate industry activity to prevent crises. For example, the Federal Aviation Administration (FAA) and the Transportation Security Administration (TSA) work to ensure safety in the commercial air travel industries. Almost all industries create additional standards through associations that govern accepted practice.

Crisis Management: Handling the Acute Stage of the Crisis

We view crisis management as the stage where the organization is managing a specific crisis event. During this stage, efforts focus on addressing the crisis and resuming operations as quickly as possible. This process involves managing the various primary and secondary stakeholders. Primary stakeholders typically include owners, employees, customers, local communities, and suppliers (Wheeler & Sillanpää, 1997). Secondary stakeholders include any other groups that have some interest in the organization. For example, People for the Ethical Treatment of Animals (PETA) has an interest in companies that use animals for laboratory research. A crisis can result when such a group takes an activist stand against a company that uses animals for this purpose.

Stakeholders can also be divided into internal and external groups. Internal stakeholders include the owners, management, and employees. External stakeholders include customers, suppliers, the local community, various government entities, and special interest groups. Within the internal landscape, the crisis management process leverages management expertise to address issues related to the owners and employees during the crisis. The external landscape looks at how the organization manages the remaining stakeholders that exist outside of the firm.

Organizational Learning: Becoming More Effective

After the crisis, management should identify lessons learned. **Organizational learning** is more likely when managers evaluate the response quickly before they forget about the details. During the "forgetfulness" stage, the organization has returned to normal operations, and managers become less motivated to evaluate and learn from the crisis (Kovoor-Misra & Nathan, 2000).

Learning should focus on (1) what can be done to mitigate the impact of a similar crisis in the future or prevent it altogether. Management might discover that it handled some processes correctly, but mishandled others. Pearson and Clair (1998) suggested

that such an evaluation be examined in terms of degrees of success and failure. For example, an organization may succeed in resuming operations promptly but fail at protecting its reputation. Learning to examine failures on management is a necessary ingredient in being more proactive in the future (Carmeli & Schaubroeck, 2008). Instead of learning from a crisis, some organizations do not heed the lessons and repeat the mistakes. On the other hand, learning organizations change policies and procedures when necessary and apply that new knowledge to future crisis events.

In the external landscape, regulators often reevaluate and renew their directives after a crisis, especially as the general public "demands action." Indeed, the airline industry has changed dramatically in terms of safety regulations after America's worst terrorist incident on September 11, 2001. Government regulations are often implemented or upgraded after a crisis, usually to increase stakeholder safety. Stakeholders outside the organization may also change their outlooks after a crisis. At a minimum, they will be more aware and compassionate toward the organization. The Virginia Tech massacre on April 16, 2007, resulted in the deaths of 32 people and the gunman. After the incident, a wave of sympathy and solidarity spread among many citizens throughout the country and even worldwide. Simultaneously, some stakeholders were also critical of the university, questioning whether specific measures could have been taken to prevent or mitigate the crisis. Indeed, in 2012, a jury found the university negligent for not warning students promptly of the threat of an active shooter on campus (Lipka, 2012).

Figure 1.2 – Overview of the Book

	Landscape Survey		Strategic Planning		Crisis Management		Organizational Learning	
The Internal Landscape	**Chapter 4:** A Strategic Approach to Crisis Management				Crisis →	**Chapter 7:** Taking Action When a Crisis Strikes	**Chapter 9:** The Importance of Organizational Learning	**Chapter 10:** Ethics in Crisis Management
		Chapter 2: The Crisis Management Landscape	**Chapter 3:** Sources of Organizational Crises	**Chapter 5:** Forming the Crisis Management Team and Writing the Plan	**Chapter 6:** Organizational Strategy and Crises				
The External Landscape						**Chapter 8:** Crisis Communications		**Chapter 11:** Emerging Trends in Crisis Management

Overview of the Book

This book is organized around the crisis management framework previously introduced.

Chapter 1 - A Framework for Crisis Management

This chapter outlines the framework presented in the book. Figure 1.2 overviews the progression of the remaining chapters.

Chapter 2 - The Crisis Management Landscape

This chapter begins our survey of the strategic landscape that can be a breeding ground for many crises. The focus is on six trends that are common across most cultures and business environments.

Chapter 3 - Sources of Organizational Crises

In this chapter, we explore the sources of crises from several perspectives. First, an external environment analysis is presented from the political-legal, economic, social, and technological perspectives. The external environment is critical to analyze because many crisis events emerge from the volatility of these four environmental sectors. Crises are also viewed from the industry and organizational life cycle perspectives because different life cycle stages have unique vulnerabilities.

Chapter 4 - A Strategic Approach to Crisis Management

In this chapter, we outline the strategic planning process and its link to crisis anticipation and prevention. One of the key themes of the chapter is the need to incorporate crisis management into the organization's strategic management process. As such, some of the traditional tools used in strategic planning, such as the SWOT analysis, can help assess crisis vulnerability.

Chapter 5 - Forming the Crisis Management Team and Writing the Plan

The essence of crisis planning is forming the crisis management team (CMT) and then writing the crisis management plan (CMP). This chapter provides guidelines for both tasks. The composition of the CMT is discussed, including the essential qualities of team members. Components of the CMP are overviewed, and a template is provided at the end of this book. We conclude by offering guidelines for crisis management training.

Chapter 6 - Organizational Strategy and Crises

This chapter links the organization's strategy to its crisis vulnerability at the corporate and business levels. Corporate strategies address the growth trajectory of the firm and the specific industries in which the firm operates. Business strategies address competitive issues; we use Porter's cost leadership-differentiation dichotomy to illustrate the crisis impact of business strategies. Strategic choices at both levels influence the types of crises the organization may encounter. The chapter ends with a discussion on strategic control and how it relates to crisis planning.

Chapter 7 - Taking Action When a Crisis Strikes

This chapter explores the tactical responses to a crisis. The response consists of three phases—the initial impact, the crisis as it unfolds, and the post-crisis activity—each with unique decision points. Decision-making and evaluation are important during each phase.

Chapter 8 - Crisis Communication

One of the most critical challenges of crisis management is effective communication with both internal and external stakeholders. This chapter presents guidelines for maneuvering in this complex arena of crisis communications. Navigating the maze of social media is essential, as it can make a crisis travel fast and far. We provide examples of social media crises guidelines for leveraging social media.

Chapter 9 - The Importance of Organizational Learning

This chapter focuses on the need to learn from the crisis event. Organizational learning does not come naturally; however, the push to get the organization back to normal operations often supersedes the need to reflect on preventing future crises. This chapter examines the potential learning areas in each of the four stages of the crisis management framework. Barriers that can impede learning are discussed, as well as approaches to building a learning organization.

Chapter 10 - Ethics in Crisis Management

This chapter examines how executive misbehavior is the root cause of many organizational crises. The reasons why ethical blunders take place are examined. This chapter discusses how organizational culture can be changed to reduce the likelihood of an ethics-based crisis.

Chapter 11 - Emerging Trends in Crisis Management

This chapter examines the future of crisis management. Emerging trends are identified in each of the four stages of the framework: landscape survey, strategic planning, crisis management, and organizational learning.

Summary

The field of crisis management is growing in scope and sophistication. We acknowledge these changes by recognizing that crisis management should be a part of the organization's strategic management effort. Drawing on the work of others, we employ a crisis management framework that utilizes a two-by-four matrix that recognizes four phases of the crisis management process. We also underscore the importance of acknowledging the internal and external landscapes within each phase.

Discussion Questions

1. Why is it essential to understand crisis management in terms of its four different stages?
2. Identify a recent crisis event that occurred where you work. Discuss the different stages of the crisis in terms of:
    *   **Landscape Survey**- Were there any events in your organization that might have contributed to the crisis? What events outside of your organization might have contributed?

- **Strategic Management-** Did your organization have any plans in place to address this type of crisis? Were there any industry controls or government regulations in place to prevent this type of crisis?
- **Crisis Management-** How well did your organization respond to the crisis? Did any outside agencies or stakeholders help your organization manage it?
- **Organizational Learning-** What lessons did your organization learn from the crisis? Did any industry or regulatory changes occur when it ended?

Chapter Exercise

As a class, determine the following:

1. What events could happen to the class that would constitute a crisis? Write these on the board and then seek a consensus as a class on the top five crisis events. Focus on these as you proceed to the next step.

2. What crisis plans are available that could address each of these five potential crises? Distinguish between resources that are available inside the classroom and those that exist outside of the classroom.

Closing Chapter Case: Death in Room 225 - The Best Western Hotel Crisis - Part 2

Room 225 was a deathtrap. Daryl and Shirley Jenkins, and now young Jeffrey Williams, had died in that room. Jeffrey's mother, Jeannie, was left fighting for her life at the local hospital. Investigators were to determine if Jeffrey and Jeannie also succumbed to carbon monoxide poisoning, and if so, how and why. The toxicology report was completed and emailed on Monday, June 3. Jeffrey died four days later. Why were the results seemingly ignored?

The Elusive Carbon Monoxide Readings

Connecting the dots between Daryl and Shirley's deaths and Jeffrey William's death meant identifying the source of the carbon monoxide that had been in room 225 the night Jeannie and Jeffrey were there. Initial testing of the room indicated that no gas was present, but when the swimming pool heater was on, the presence of carbon monoxide soared! The swimming pool heater caused gas vapors to enter room 225.

Investigators ultimately identified a corroded pipe above the swimming pool ceiling with large holes. The pipe was supposed to carry carbon monoxide from the swimming pool heater to outside the building where it would dissipate. Instead, the holes in the pipe were leaking gas into room 225, which was located directly above the ceiling where the pipe was housed. The link had now been established, but why was the heater leaking in the first place?

A Swimming Pool Heater

Room 225 had a fireplace, which created a warm respite for cold winters in the chilly mountains of North Carolina. However, the gas pipe from the swimming pool heater was part of the air system that was also connected to the fireplace. Hence, carbon monoxide leaked from its original pipe from the swimming pool heater into the air duct system, and ultimately, that gas entered the guest room via the fireplace.

So how did the swimming pool heater enter this story? It was moved from another hotel, a Sleep Inn, owned by Appalachian Hospitality Management in 2011. The work was performed by hotel employees and required a permit, but one was not sought. Also, the employees were not licensed to do the work (Wood, 2014b). A carbon monoxide detector was required near the heater according to the owner's manual but was never installed.

Ironically, the heater did pass inspection in February 2012 when it was converted from propane to natural gas. The inspection was carried out by the town of Boone and included issuing a permit. What is not known is if the corroded pipe was also inspected; Boone officials did not comment (Leland, 2013).

Missed Opportunities and the Problem of Causation

When examining a crisis management case, there is a natural human inclination to find someone to blame. This tendency is driven by **heuristics**, decision-making rules that take the guesswork out of our thinking. For example, we may carry a cause-effect cognition in our thinking that says, "bad stuff" happens because of a single cause, and if one eliminates the reason, the "bad stuff" will not occur. This thinking may stem from childhood when we were taught right from wrong. Touch fire, get burned. For example, as a young person, we learn if we overeat something we like, get sick, or disobey a rule or law, there will be negative consequences.

Heuristics are useful because they reinforce simple cause-effect relationships and help us make quick decisions, but many crises have complicated explanations. Unlike the legal system, which may follow a single-cause paradigm in lawsuits, a crisis management perspective often reveals a more complicated pattern of cause and effect. The Best Western Hotel case is an example, as many stakeholders missed opportunities to stop the accidental deaths of Daryl and Shirley Jenkins and Jeffrey Williams.

To begin, when the hotel was built in 2000, combustible gas monitors were installed in the guest rooms with fireplaces instead of carbon monoxide detectors. This error was not discovered until after the three accidental deaths had occurred (Leland, 2013). They might have been prevented by this observation alone.

The hotel missed an opportunity to prevent the tragedy when it permitted unlicensed workers to move the swimming pool heater (Leland, 2016; Wood, 2014a). Why were the workers unlicensed? Why was the required carbon monoxide detector never installed? How could a swimming pool heater with leaky gas pipes pass inspection? Indeed, the pool heater passed an inspection performed by the town of Boone, an agency that was supposed to prevent such accidents (Wood, 2014a).

Another missed opportunity occurred when the local police and fire departments did not conduct carbon monoxide testing immediately after Daryl and Shirley Jenkins were found dead under suspicious circumstances. The deaths had clues to an environmental cause, and yet, this option of inquiry was not pursued initially.

Perhaps Dr. Brent Hall could have acted. Dr. Hall had served the community well for over 20 years and was the one who ordered the toxicology reports early on, but he was under intense scrutiny (Leland, 2013). What about the Chief Medical Examiner's office in Raleigh, which took so long to process the results? A toxicology report usually takes about 15 minutes to complete, but the report from the Medical Examiner's Office took over 40 days (Leland, 2013). Perhaps there is some blame here but recall that Dr. Hall did not request that the results be "expedited." Does this implicate Dr. Hall?

What about hotel management? Damon Mallatere was president of Appalachian Hospitality Management (AHM) when the swimming pool heater was moved. However, the hotel had a culture of cost-cutting and delaying needed repairs (Oakes, 2016). Could this culture have contributed to the gas leak that killed three hotel guests?

In the final analysis, multiple stakeholders contributed to the unfortunate outcome. All the stakeholders mentioned previously received their due scrutiny in the media and the courtroom, but in the end, only one was deemed responsible.

The Final Outcome

The assignment of ultimate blame, even when there is collective blame, is a reality in the world of crisis management. In the end, Damon Mallatere, the president of AHM, was arrested. For the crisis management student, this realization is important. Damon Mallatere did not cause the accidental deaths, but he was the one considered legally responsible.

In January 2014, Damon Mallatere was charged with three counts of involuntary manslaughter, which could have sent him to prison. The problem for prosecutors was that he was not personally involved in converting and maintaining the faulty swimming pool heater and its associated pipe system. That work was performed by others and even approved by the town of Boone. Still, from a legal perspective, Mallatere was to be the target in a case full of collective blame.

The defense strategy was to issue a guilty plea, but on behalf of AHM, not Mallatere himself. The plea was accepted, and in an unusual twist of events, the hotel was put on trial. In the end, the court ordered that AHM be dissolved. Mallatere would not go to jail, but the firm he managed would no longer exist. A $16.5 million-dollar settlement was reached with the two families involved, and other lawsuits remain unresolved (Oakes, 2018).

Closing Comments

The Best Western case is troubling, as even employees of the hotel were concerned about cost-cutting. District Attorney Seth Banks commented that employees interviewed by police maintained that, "upper-level management cut corners at the hotel to save money, thereby jeopardizing the safety of hotel guests. Requests for repairs were frequently denied because of the costs" (Oakes, 2016).

In a comment shared with the local newspaper, the *Watauga Democrat*, Best Western issued a curious statement: "Best Western denies liability for these matters, but its heartfelt thoughts and prayers are with the family and friends of those affected." (Oakes, 2018). Such a statement represents a denial of responsibility. To a crisis management student, one must read between the lines and recognize that nobody at Best Western International wanted the outcome that occurred. Nonetheless, heuristics suggest that a villain should be identified and punished. It is convenient to charge the hotel with cost-cutting measures that endangered guests. Indeed, businesses make cost-cutting decisions are made every day. However, no reputable business owner wants to put a guest at risk either. The outcomes of a guest's fatality or injury far outweigh the cost savings of a single decision. Managers want to be profitable and must be to operate their businesses.

Nonetheless, as crisis management students, we must acknowledge that Cost-cutting decisions can still compromise worker and customer safety, even if no harm was intended. Whether intentional or not, *cost-cutting can kill people*. There is nothing wrong with lowering expenses per se, but extraordinary care must be taken to ensure that doing so does not place employees, customers, or others in harm's way.

Case Discussion Questions

1. In the arena of college and professional sports, head coaches cen be fired for activities that were conducted by their assistants. What examples can you identify where this has occurred? Was there evidence of collective blame?

2. What evidence of cost-cutting have you seen where you work? Has any of it compromised safety? If so, how?

References

Ailworth, E. (2019, May 10). Growth fuels size of catastrophes. *Wall Street Journal*, p. A3.

Associated Press, (2013, February 27). Chicken causes power outage at Maui. Retrieved December 22, 2018, from http://www.hawaiinewsnow.com/story/21415577/chicken-causes-power-outage-at-maui-airport/

Bachman, J., & Schlangenstein, M. (2016, August 8). Southwest tries to squash its tech bugs. *Bloomberg Business*, 23-24.

Carmeli, A., & Schaubroeck, J. (2008). Organizational crisis-preparedness: The importance of learning from failures. *Long Range Planning*, *41*, 177-196.

Coombs, W. (2006). *Code red in the boardroom: Crisis management as organizational DNA.* Westport, CT: Praeger.

Coombs, W. (2015). *Ongoing crisis communication: Planning, managing, and responding* (4th ed.). Thousand Oaks, CA: Sage.

Crandall, W. R. (2007). Crisis, chaos, and creative destruction: Getting better from bad. In *Re-discovering Schumpeter four score years later: Creative destruction evolving into "Mode 3" (E.G. Carayannis & C. Ziemnowicz, eds.).* MacMillan Palgrave Press.

Elkind, P. (2015, October 1). How Blue Bell blew it. *Fortune*, *172*(5), 122-126.

Fink, S. (1996). *Crisis management: Planning for the inevitable.* New York: American Management Association.

Frese, M., & Keith, N. (2015). Action errors, error management, and learning in organizations. *Annual Review of Psychology, 66,* 661-687.

Hartley, R. (1993). *Business ethics: Violations of the public trust.* New York: John Wiley.

Henderson, J. (2005). Responding to natural disasters: Managing a hotel in the aftermath of the Indian Ocean tsunami. *Tourism and Hospitality* Research, *6*(1), 89-96.

Herbane, B. (2010). Small business research – time for a crisis-based view. *International Small Business Journal, 28*(1), 43-64.

ICM, (2016). *ICM Annual Crisis Report: News Coverage of Business Crises in 2015*. Retrieved December 19, 2016, from http://crisisconsultant.com/crisis-intel-reports/

Kovoor-Misra, S., & Nathan, M. (2000, Fall). Timing is everything: The optimal time to learn from crises. *Review of Business, 31*–36.

Lei, Z., Naveh, E., Novikov, Z. (2016). Errors in organizations: An integrative review via level of analysis, temporal dynamism, and priority lenses. *Journal of Management, 42*(5), 1315-1343

Leland, E. (2013, December 13). Why did Jeffrey Williams die? *The Charlotte Observer*. Retrieved July 4, 2018, from https://www.charlotteobserver.com/news/special-reports/nc-medical-examiners/jeffrey-williams/article9093218.html

Leland, E. (2016, March 28). DA says Boone Best Western was a 'deathtrap': Plea deal reached in carbon monoxide deaths. *The Charlotte Observer*. Retrieved December 22, 2018, from https://www.charlotteobserver.com/news/local/article68649217.html

Lipka, S. (2012, March 23). Jury's verdict against Virginia Tech sends strong messages to colleges. *Chronicle of Higher Education, 58*(29), p. A32.

Marcus, A., & Goodman, R. (1991). Victims and shareholders: The dilemmas of presenting corporate policy during a crisis. *Academy of Management Journal, 34*(2), 281–305.

Mitroff, I. (1989, October). Programming for crisis control. *Security Management,* 75–79.

Mitroff, I., Diamond, M., & Alpaslan, C. (2006). How prepared are America's colleges and universities for major crises? *Change, 38*(1), 60–67.

Myers, K. (1993). *Total contingency planning for disasters: Managing risk . . . minimizing loss . . . ensuring business continuity.* New York: John Wiley.

Nader, R. (1965). *Unsafe at any speed.* New York: Grossman.

Oakes, A. (2016, March 28). Plea deal reached in Best Western deaths case. *Watauga Democrat.* Retrieved August 25, 2018, from https://www.wataugademocrat.com/news/plea-deal-reached-in-best-western-deaths-case/article_5d4a2ac4-f50a-11e5-a470-5fc2f57d100a.html

Oakes, A. (2018, January 22). Best Western death lawsuits reach $16.5 million total in settlements. *Watauga Democrat.* Retrieved August 25, 2018, from https://www.wataugademocrat.com/news/best-western-death-lawsuits-reach-million-total-in-settlements/article_80c229aa-ff21-5d41-ac02-86236238264c.html

Pearson, C., & Clair, J. (1998). Reframing crisis management. *Academy of Management Review, 23*(1), 59–76.

Pearson, C., & Mitroff, I. (1993). From crisis prone to crisis prepared: A framework for crisis management. *Academy of Management Executive, 7*(1), 48–59.

Richardson, B. (1994). Socio-technical disasters: Profile and prevalence. *Disaster Prevention & Management, 3*(4), 41–69.

Roux-Dufort, C. (2009). The devil lies in details! How crises build up within organizations. *Journal of Contingencies and Crisis Management, 17*(1), 4-11.

Scism, L. (2020, July 1). Firms hit by Covid want insurers to pay. They won't. *Wall Street Journal,* pp. A1, A10.

Sheaffer, Z., & Mano-Negrin, R. (2003). Executives' orientations as indicators of crisis management policies and practices. *Journal of Management Studies, 40*(2), 573–606.

Smith, D. (1990). Beyond contingency planning: Towards a model of crisis management. *Industrial Crisis Quarterly, 4*(4), 263–275.

Smith, D., & Elliott, D. (2007). Exploring the barriers to learning from crisis: Organizational learning and crisis. *Management Learning, 38*(5), 519-538.

Spillan, J., & Crandall, W. R. (2002). Crisis planning in the nonprofit sector: Should we plan for something bad if it may not occur? *Southern Business Review, 27*(2), 18–29.

Stead, E., & Smallman, C. (1999). Understanding business failure: Learning and un-learning lessons from industrial crises. *Journal of Contingencies and Crisis Management, 7*(1), 1–18.

Wheeler, D., & Sillanpää, M. (1997). *The Stakeholder Corporation: A Blueprint for Maximizing Stakeholder Value.* London: Pittman Publishing.

Wood, J. (2014a, January 10). Mallatere pleads not guilty, posts $40,000 bond. *High Country Press.* Retrieved August 29, 2016, from https://www.hcpress.com/front-page/mallatere-pleads-not-guilty-posts-40000-bond.html

Wood, J. (2014b, April 30). Injunction issued against former maintenance workers employed at Best Western hotel during CO deaths. *High Country Press.* Retrieved August 29, 2016, from https://www.hcpress.com/news/injunction-issued-against-former-maintenance-workers-employed-at-best-western-hotel-during-co-deaths.html

Chapter 2: The Crisis Management Landscape

	Landscape Survey	Strategic Planning	Crisis Management	Organizational Learning
The Internal Landscape	**Chapter 4:** A Strategic Approach to Crisis Management		Crisis	
	Chapter 2: The Crisis Management Landscape	**Chapter 3:** Sources of Organizational Crises	**Chapter 5:** Forming the Crisis Management Team and Writing the Plan	**Chapter 6:** Organizational Strategy and Crises	**Chapter 7:** Taking Action When a Crisis Strikes	**Chapter 9:** The Importance of Organizational Learning	**Chapter 10:** Ethics in Crisis Management
The External Landscape					**Chapter 8:** Crisis Communications	**Chapter 11:** Emerging Trends in Crisis Management

Learning Objectives

After reading this chapter, each student should be able to:

1. Explain how modern slavery has entered the supply chain and how it can contribute to a crisis.
2. Identify and describe the four characteristics of a transboundary crisis.
3. Describe the factors that make terrorism an ongoing threat to organizations.
4. Discuss how social media can intensify a crisis.
5. Describe how human error and decision-making can contribute to the formation and escalation of a crisis.
6. Discuss the global implications of environmental damage and sustainability concerns as they relate to crisis events.
7. Identify and describe the ways globalization has contributed to the escalation of crisis events.
8. Identify and describe the strategies companies can use to address modern slavery in the supply chain.

Opening Chapter Case: When Slavery Hits the Supply Chain[1] – Part 1

Modern slavery is an uncomfortable topic, but with increased globalization, forced labor has crept into the supply chains of many multinational companies (Eckes, 2011). **Forced labor** (i.e., **modern slavery**) occurs when four conditions are met: (1) the worker is controlled by the employer through some form of mental or physical abuse; (2) the worker is dehumanized and treated like a commodity; (3) the worker's freedom of movement is restricted; and (4) the worker is subject to economic exploitation, usually due to high recruiting fees and underpayment (Crane, 2013).

Although the number of slave workers across the globe is difficult to determine, the International Labor Organization estimates 40.3 million victims of modern slavery worldwide, including 24.9 million victims of forced labor and 5.4 million victims of sexual exploitation. The others work in various supply chains and are concentrated in agriculture, food processing, fishing, manufacturing of textiles, garments, electronics, mining, and domestic employment (Drumea, 2011; International Labor Organization, 2017).

Outsourcing refers to shifting production or other business activities to other companies and can be domestic or global. The outsourcing boom in the 1980s created global supply chains that moved production to less developed countries with cheaper labor (Ballinger, 2011). Big-box retail chains flourished during this growth period, promoting less expensive, but often lower quality items (Shell, 2009). The resulting competition among retailers and brands accelerated the move to push production overseas. The working conditions in the new factories often included tedious labor and long hours. Many critics referred to these facilities as **sweatshops**, a hazardous work environment with exploitative business practices (Kennel, 1996).

Outsourcing to Asia raised concerns among many social activist stakeholders, especially labor unions, whose leadership complained that cheap labor in developing nations was destroying domestic jobs (Shell, 2009). These arguments gained support when Donald Trump was elected President of the United States in 2016 and began to address trade concerns with China, Mexico, and other nations. However, a *Fortune* article more than a decade earlier suggested a more severe problem, declaring that many of the workers in these factories were indentured servants (Stein, 2003). The existence of sweatshops in global supply chains did not concern many business leaders because the working conditions for laborers were often better anyway. However, the possibility of slavery in global supply chains--with *involuntary* work arrangements--changed the conversation.

---

[1] This case is based on Crandall, Parnell & Crandall (2015).

Why Companies Outsource to Developing Countries

Companies typically outsource production to developing countries for three reasons:

1. Low Labor Costs. Lower labor costs are a key motivator and can promote production efficiency, which makes outsourcing all but essential, especially in global industries where consumers are price conscious.

2. Ability to Scale Up or Down. Outsourcing to developing countries gives the sourcing company access to suppliers that can increase or decrease production quickly. Apple's production of the iPhone during the 2010s illustrates this phenomenon. While the lower labor costs are attractive for all firms, outsourcing enabled Apple to raise a factory on short notice and scale it back quickly as needed (Duhigg & Bradsher, 2012).

3. Reduced Social Costs. Sourcing to developing countries can reduce the social costs typically incurred by companies in developed countries or their home countries. **Social costs** include taxes and expenses associated with pollution control, employee welfare, sustainability initiatives, safety requirements, and other forms of regulatory compliance.

How Slavery Enters the Supply Chain

To comprehend how a migrant worker becomes a modern slave, one must understand worker migration patterns. Figure 2.1 summarizes this process. Each box in the figure represents a company and is labeled as an ITO (input, transformation, output) unit. All companies require inputs (raw materials, employees, equipment, and cash) to make (transformation) products and services (outputs). The company or ITO, at the far right of the figure, is the main sourcing company.

Migration Patterns

A migrant usually leaves home in search of economic opportunity and, in extreme cases, safety from war or terrorism. Migrant workers are at a severe disadvantage because they typically do not speak the language or understand local customs in the nations they enter. They often lack official documentation and are unfamiliar with the different legal environment, making them easy targets for exploitation. The most vulnerable migrants are poor and uneducated and must use a labor broker or agent to secure a job (Andrees, 2008). Moreover, they come from depressed or corrupt nations such as Myanmar and Uzbekistan (Crane, 2013). The migration pattern is depicted at the bottom of Figure 2.1 as the prospective worker crosses the border searching for work.

Labor-intensive industries offer the most attractive opportunities for firms to reduce costs through outsourcing. Hence, they are most prone to modern slavery and include agriculture, mining and extraction, construction, domestic work, and low-skill manufacturing (Crane, 2013). High-profile cases of forced labor and worker abuse have also occurred in the shrimp industry in Thailand (*The Economist*, 2015), the crawfish industry in the US (Greenhouse, 2012), and Apple's iPhone supply chain (Simpson, 2013).

Figure 2.1 – How Slavery Enters the Supply Chain

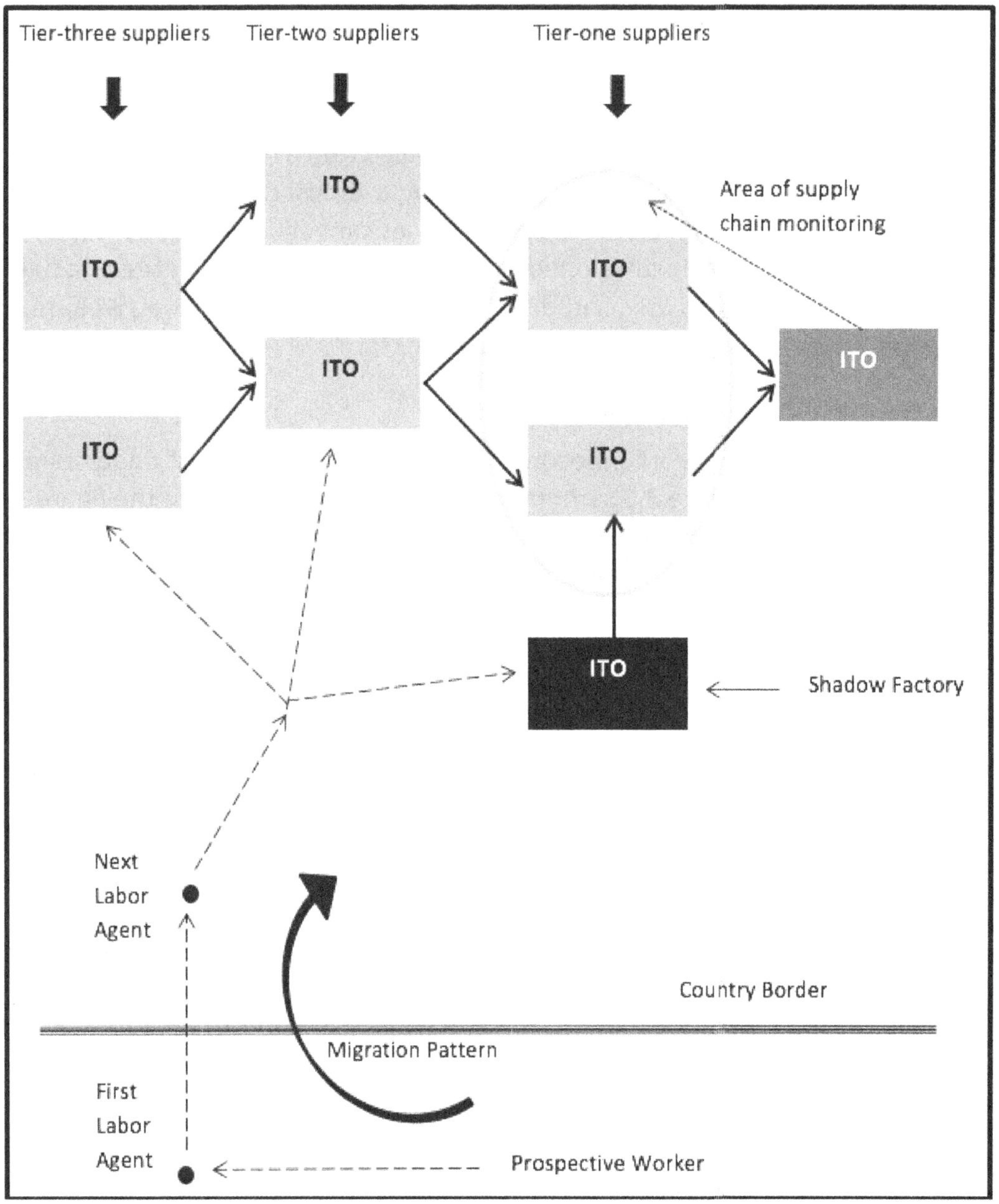

Labor Agents

As shown in Figure 2.1, the prospective worker often encounters at least two labor agents in the job search. The first agent recruits the worker out of the country, promising a good job elsewhere, often with false or misleading information. Workers most prone to these types of labor agents are often poorly educated and come from extreme poverty (Crane, 2013). Fees charged to the worker are exceedingly high; however, they accept the fees and move on because they are desperate for work.

After crossing the border, the prospective worker is met by a second labor agent who demands additional payments for which the worker is not prepared. These additional fees force the worker to become an indentured servant. Debt bondage—an arrangement where the worker pledges their labor against a loan of money—is the most common form of slavery in the world (Bales, 2004). However, because the labor agent's deceitful fees are now loans, the worker is said to be serving *involuntarily* and could be subject to exploitation, including confinement and violence (LeBaron, 2014a).

Suppliers

The principal sourcing firm depicted at the far right of Figure 2.1 is often a multinational corporation (MNC) such as a major retailer or clothing brand. The figure illustrates that this ITO has outsourced work to two tier-one suppliers, which are sourced by other tier-two and tier-three suppliers (i.e., suppliers of the suppliers). In general, as products move into deeper tiers in the supply chain, the sourcing firm loses control over the suppliers. The consequences of this transition can be profound. Consider the 2013 Rana factory collapse in Bangladesh that killed over 1100 workers; the factory was a tier-two textile supplier to a tier-one supplier that had outsourced part of the work. Several well-known brands were surprised to find their labels being made in that factory because they had not authorized the work at Rana (LeBaron, 2014b).

The term shadow factory has been used to describe these types of suppliers hired to augment either the capacity or some production process needed by the original tier-one supplier. In the garment industry, labor-intensive activities such as beadwork, sewing, and dying are often subcontracted to unregistered shadow factories (LeBaron, 2014b). Following Figure 2.1, the second labor agent may move the new worker to a shadow factory, or a tier-two or tier-three supplier. These types of suppliers are not monitored like tier-one suppliers; in many instances, they are often not monitored at all. As Figure 2.1 depicts, the sourcing ITO may have a monitoring system in place, but this system only oversees its tier-one suppliers. Other suppliers lie outside of this oversight region and become fertile areas for modern slavery.

The Role of Discount Retailers

Cost containment is an essential factor in any business, but it is most prominent in retail, especially in the discount sector. Consumers seek low prices, and successful discounters deliver. Many pressure manufacturers to lower costs, thereby heightening the incentive to outsource. In some cases, the ripple effect can create an environment conducive to lower labor standards (Bonacich & Hamilton, 2011; Chan, Pun, & Selden, 2013).

Textile and other manufacturers must be aware of modern slavery and the organizational crises that can result. Also, the retailers that sell these brands are vulnerable as well because social stakeholders demand accountability for their supply chains. Crisis management is not just about managing the interests of the organization. It is also about ensuring the integrity of supply chains and the organizations that function along those chains.

Case Discussion Questions

1. Why are certain industries such as agriculture, mining, construction, domestic work, and low-skill manufacturing more prone to modern slavery?
2. What types of crises could erupt for retailers and clothing brands that discover slavery in their supply chains?
3. Is it possible for a global organization to achieve, with certainty, a slavery-free supply chain? Explain.

Introduction

An organizational crisis can emanate from many actions (and inactions) of decision-makers. Although some crisis events are entirely beyond management control, most crises emanate from human activity. The crises that evolve are unexpected and can have serious negative repercussions. Preparation is essential. As stated in Chapter 1, a crisis is

an event that has a low probability of occurring, but could negatively impact the organization.

The September 11, 2001, terrorist attacks on New York City's World Trade Center (WTC) buildings and the Pentagon in Washington, DC collectively represent one of the most prominent crises in recent history. In addition to massive human and property losses, this crisis directly affected organizations located in and around the WTC. The COVID-19 pandemic that gripped the world in 2020 represents another prominent crisis, resulting in countless deaths and economic destruction. COVID-19 affected organizations differently; many experienced significant financial distress, some did not survive, and some benefitted from the abrupt changes in consumer habits and demand patterns.

However, terrorism and pandemics represent only a small percentage of organizational crises. Other types include fires, natural disasters, industrial accidents, workplace violence, extortion attempts, product or company boycotts, and negative publicity. Common crises related to the information age include computer system sabotage, copyright infringement, identity theft, and counterfeiting. Counterfeit goods account for between $250 billion and $600 billion in annual sales globally, most of which originate in China (Chu, 2015). Social media can also transform an adverse event into an organizational crisis under certain circumstances.

This chapter begins our study of crisis events by examining what we call the **crisis management landscape**. Important trends are identified that occur continuously throughout the global environment. In our discussion, we overview and link these trends to crisis management.

Figure 2.2 – Trends in the Crisis Management Landscape

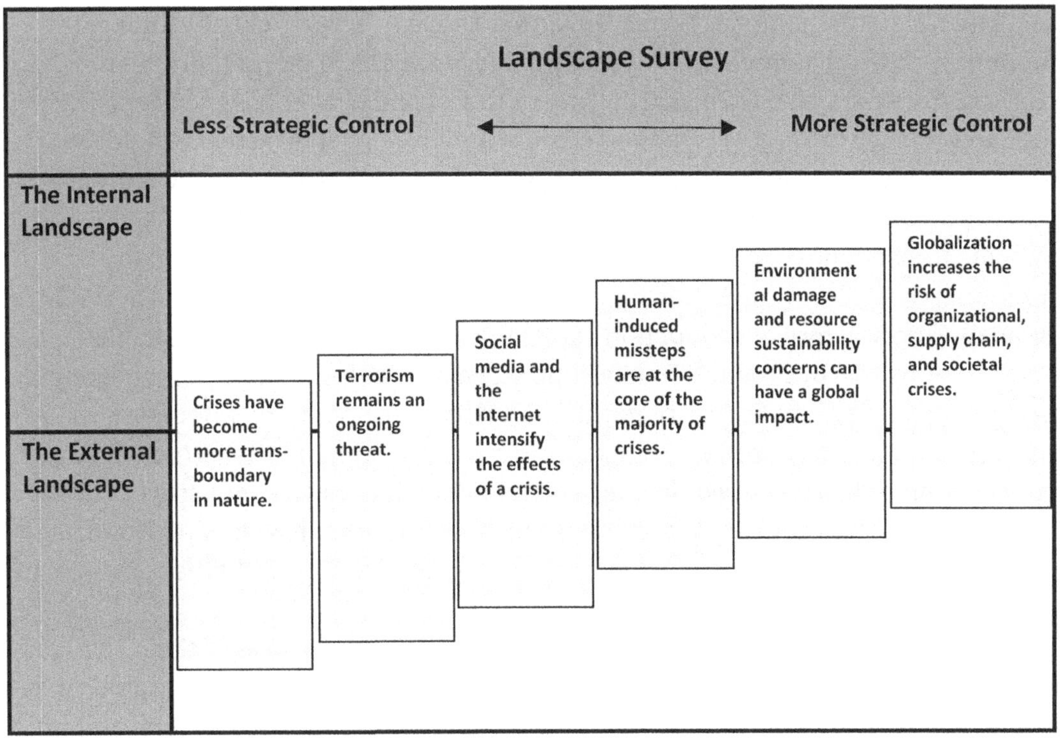

The Crisis Management Landscape

Six trends in the crisis management landscape, ranging from less to more controllable, are identified in Figure 2.2. Trends on the left side of the figure are less manageable, while those on the right can often be addressed with effective strategic planning. They also shift upward as they move from left to right, indicating that the internal environment becomes a stronger factor in the origin of these crisis events.

Crises Have Become More Transboundary in Nature

The world of crisis management is changing and broadening with the addition of transboundary threats. A **transboundary crisis** often lacks a sense of urgency. This dimension, along with a transboundary threat perception, can lead policymakers to develop different decision-making strategies (Hermann & Dayton, 2009). Transboundary crises are more than just a threat to people and organizations. They complicate the definition of a crisis because they deal with the spread and implications of events that occur across borders. Transboundary crises are interconnected with complex infrastructures linked with globalization. Events such as cyber-attacks, pandemics like COVID-19, and other pandemics, terrorism, and massive migration constitute major transboundary crises that impact many geographic areas of the world (European Societal Security Research Group, 2018). One of the critical challenges in addressing transboundary crises or threats is managing data and utilizing it effectively. Relevant data that becomes useful information can lead to effective decision-making and mitigate the impact of transboundary threats (Hermann & Dayton, 2009).

Managing transboundary crises can be complicated. Typically, we think of an organizational crisis as having distinct geographical boundaries. An industrial accident, a fire, or an unexpected loss of production capability can render a company unable to meet customer needs. But today's fragile supply chains that focus on lean management and global suppliers can make an organizational crisis transboundary, affecting stakeholders in multiple countries. For example, the 2011 tsunami that struck Japan interrupted supply chains worldwide, particularly in the automotive industry. Disruptions were most acute among Japanese firms like Toyota, Nissan, and Honda and affected production lines of carmakers based in the United States and other parts of the world (Shappell, 2012).

Transboundary crises are especially challenging to manage because of their complexity. According to crisis scholar Arjen Boin (2009), they (1) cross geographical boundaries, (2) cross-functional boundaries, (3) cross traditional time barriers, and (4) involve a tightly woven web of critical infrastructures.

1. A transboundary crisis crosses geographical boundaries

Transboundary crises transcend geographical barriers that extend far beyond the confines of a single organization. For example, in August 2003, what appeared to be an insignificant power utility malfunction was mishandled by authorities in Ohio, culminating into a significant blackout affecting millions of citizens in the northeastern United States and the Canadian province of Ontario (Lagadec, 2009). Severe weather and natural disasters can occur in one part of the world and wreak havoc in another part because of the impact on supply chains. Pandemics such as the SARS (Severe Acute Respiratory Syndrome) and COVID-19 epidemics can reap havoc well beyond human suffering.

The occurrence of natural disasters is also a function of geography. Earthquakes, for example, occur near fault zones. In the United States, active fault zones exist in California and along the New Madrid seismic zone, encompassing southeastern Missouri, northeastern Arkansas, and western Tennessee. Unusual weather patterns such as typhoons and cyclones can be especially devastating in developing countries ill-equipped to manage them. A tsunami is another natural phenomenon that can have widespread impact. On December 26, 2004, an earthquake off Sumatra's coast in Indonesia triggered a tsunami that killed almost 250,000 people in South Asia (Cheung & Law, 2006). Recently, in 2018, another earthquake with a magnitude of 7.5 and a tsunami devastated Palu, Indonesia. The tsunami swept away buildings and killed thousands of people (Karnini, 2018).

A transboundary crisis can affect significant resources over a more localized geographic area. In the United States, consider the impact of Hurricane Ike on the highly automated refinery industry in the Gulf of Mexico, a region responsible for about 20% of the nation's oil-producing capacity (Lee & Thurman, 2008). When the storm hit in August 2008, refineries "shut in" operations to minimize damage to oil-producing facilities. After the storm passed, production slowly resumed, but not fast enough to offset gas shortages in major cities such as Nashville, Tennessee; Atlanta, Georgia; and Charlotte, North Carolina. Panic-buying and high prices intensified the shortages.

In Europe, transboundary crises take on added complexity as effects of the events often traverse country borders. An incident in one corner of Europe can affect the entire continent (Boin, Rhinard, & Ekengren, 2014). For example, the Chernobyl explosion in 1986 in Ukraine sent radiation across many countries in Europe. More recently, the terrorist attacks in Paris, France were linked to extremists residing in the Molenbeek neighborhood of Brussels, Belgium (Barnes et al., 2016). One of the most widespread transboundary crises to face the European Union (EU) in recent years is the flood of refugees from war-torn Syria, Iraq, and Afghanistan. The refugee movement intensified in 2015, when over 1 million asylum claims were submitted to EU countries, including

441,800 to Germany alone (Damoc, 2016). Managing this crisis remains an ongoing challenge, in part, because it is difficult for EU authorities to confirm that individuals filing for asylum are not terrorists themselves.

Problems in the supply chain can easily translate into organizational crises. For example, Egyptian cotton has been touted as the highest quality cotton for bed sheets and bathroom towels. Egyptian cotton accounts for only about one percent of global cotton production and Welspun India commanded premium prices for its Egyptian cotton sheets and towels. But in 2016, an investigation revealed that Welspun had used non-Egyptian cotton for about two years. Walmart, Target, and other retailers immediately pulled Welspun products from their shelves. Welspun responded by announcing an investigation into its supply chain, claiming no knowledge of the problem (Nassauer & Rana, 2016).

2. A transboundary crisis crosses functional boundaries

Transboundary crises can cross-functional boundaries and threaten multiple life-sustaining systems and infrastructures (Ansell, Boin, & Keller, 2010). Put another way, the responsibility for managing a transboundary crisis may be spread across multiple organizations, some of which may not be closely related. For example, both British Petroleum (BP) and various US government agencies managed the BP oil spill in the Gulf of Mexico. Likewise, the response to Hurricane Katrina was managed by multiple stakeholders in both the private sector—those businesses that sustained damage—and government agencies at the local, state, and federal levels. What makes the crisis response difficult is that stakeholder response is often loosely coupled with other stakeholders, making coordination more complex (Ansell et al., 2010).

Transboundary crises can challenge the capabilities of government agencies within a single country, but when the crisis spans multiple countries, more complex arrangements must be made in advance. For example, the EU has installed various agencies to plan for and manage transboundary crises. In a 2010 planning council, five core threats were identified: (1) international crime networks, (2) terrorism and radicalization, (3) cyber threats, (4) border security, and (5) crises and disasters (Boin et al., 2014). As a result, EU nations must prepare and manage crisis events as a coalition of countries acting together, not as separate entities.

Transboundary crises can also emerge as a "package of disasters" (Green, 2004, p. 61), such as combining a severe weather event and a natural disaster. In Japan, the 2011 tsunami strike was a trio of disasters consisting of an earthquake first, followed by a tsunami and a nuclear calamity. Developing countries are especially vulnerable to these types of crises, resulting in high fatalities (Spillan, Parnell, & Mayoro, 2011). For example, a civil war may trigger a famine, or a natural disaster may instigate a flood of refugees as people are forced to leave their ravished homes. The wars in Mozambique illustrate how heavy rains and flooding can decimate an already damaged country (Green, 2004).

3. A transboundary crisis crosses time boundaries

Transboundary crises do not have definitive beginning or ending points. Instead, they can have deep roots in their origins, and their effects can linger for many years. Global climate change, oil spills, and the 9-11 WTC attacks are examples of how time is blurred in a transboundary crisis (Ansell et al., 2010).

One of the themes of this book is the extensive impact social media can have on a crisis. Indeed, many crises may have origins in an obscure event that becomes public via an outlet such as YouTube. Long after the crisis appears to have ended, remnants can still be played and viewed on social media. Such is the case with singer Dave Carroll's now-famous *United Breaks Guitars* video. Carroll and his band flew from Canada to the United States in March 2008 when they observed baggage handlers throwing their guitars while waiting for their connecting flight in Chicago. Carroll's guitar was damaged, and he sought compensation from United Airlines. The airline refused, prompting him to write a song about his dilemma and posting it on YouTube (https://www.youtube.com/watch?v=5YGc4zOqozo). The incident proved to be a public embarrassment for the airline (Grégoire, Tripp, & Legoux, 2011). This example constitutes a transboundary crisis in part because the video is still available.

4. A transboundary crisis involves a tightly woven web of critical infrastructures

Much of contemporary society consists of interlinking critical infrastructures. For example, the power grid that provides electricity for parts of the United States and Canada is tightly networked (Wachtendorf, 2009). As previously noted, a malfunction in Ohio can affect the power supply in Ontario, Canada. Another example is the now-famous Y2K computer bug. In the early days of computer technology, programmers would save valuable computer storage space by using only the two digits for the year (e.g., 99 instead of 1999). The Y2K bug concern occurred because a computer rolled over to 2000 might inadvertently interpret the date as 1900, which might also read 00. It was unclear how computer systems would function when this occurred. Some even interpreted the event as apocalyptic, signaling the end of human existence (Stallard, 1999).

During the years leading up to 2000, a vast amount of work was completed to alleviate this potential problem. In many instances, companies used the **Y2K** crisis as an opportunity to overhaul their operating systems. The Y2K bug proved to be uneventful, however, due in part to efforts invested in preparing for the worst. However, the cultural phenomenon occurring concurrently, particularly in the United States (Schaefer, 2004), was profound. Speculation was brewing in the late 1990s that the 2000 rollover would produce worldwide catastrophes. Although they did not materialize, this example illustrates how computer systems have created a tightly woven global web of critical infrastructures.

The fight against terrorism in the EU is another example of how infrastructures across boundaries are affected. One of the problems in this fight has been the coordination of efforts across various law enforcement agencies. While terrorism is a global problem, law enforcement still operates at the local level; hence, sharing valuable information about the names and location of suspected terrorists is not widely available (Walt, 2016). When the identities of potential terrorists are held only at the local law enforcement level and not shared across the EU, a valuable resource for fighting future attacks is lost. We discuss terrorism in more detail in the next section.

COVID-19: The Definitive Transboundary Crisis

The causes and impacts of most crises are often difficult to unravel until after the affected organizations return to normal—or establish a new normal. The COVID-19 pandemic illustrates this point. COVID-19 (also called the coronavirus) emanated from China in late 2019. By mid-2020, it had spread throughout the world, taking countless lives and reaping economic destruction. It will take several years before the human and organizational effects of a dramatic crisis like COVID-19 are fully understood, and the response can be evaluated in a comprehensive manner.

COVID-19 is a different kind of organizational crisis for several reasons. Because it stems from a contagious and potentially deadly illness, COVID-19 has affected entire societies and industries, not just one or a few organizations. The magnitude of its impact in human and economic terms is well beyond what is typically required to refer to an event as a crisis, requiring many organizations to rely directly on government assistance to survive. Moreover, the event created massive uncertainty, as it took epidemiologists, physicians, and scientists months to learn about the virus, its transmission, treatment options, and requirements for resuming organizational life safely.

The COVID-19 pandemic created a wide range of crises for organizations. When the virus moved through Wuhan and other parts of China in late 2019, many Western firms that relied on Chinese suppliers were unable to obtain need parts and finished goods. When the virus took hold in Europe and the United States in early 2020, many firms could not function because of sick employees, decreased demand for their products or services, or both. Some firms were prevented from operating due to public health concerns. Many restaurants and retailers were ordered to temporarily close or curtail their operations while authorities sought to contain the spread of the virus. Revenues for airlines and hotels all but vanished, as many citizens were strongly advised to—and often prevented from—traveling.

Although most organizations suffered in the short term, some performed well and even thrived due to the pandemic. Amazon and  other online retailers were positioned well to serve the needs of customers who were unable to shop in physical stores. Netflix enjoyed an increase in subscribers, as many Americans were unable or unwilling to leave home. Zoom Video Communications experienced a tenfold increase in demand for its telecommuting, teleconferencing, and distance education services as organizations searched for ways to make their employees productive at home.

The long-term effects of the COVID-19 pandemic remain unclear. Analyzing other crises that occurred during the past several decades can help strategic managers plan more effectively and evaluate changes that might make their firms more resilient in the event of a future pandemic.

Terrorism Remains an Ongoing Threat

Terrorism has always been a threat to entities throughout the world. Today, however, threats emanate from a variety of sources and are often directed towards business interests. Criminal cartels target business executives throughout Latin America. Tribal gangs attack oil refineries in Nigeria. Kidnap, and ransom networks exist in the Philippines. Criminal mafias exist in Russia and some of the former Soviet republics. Modern pirates prey on ships sailing near Somalia (Wernick & Von Glinow, 2012).

Historically, terrorist acts were motivated by political ideals rather than religious ones (Pedahzur, Eubank, & Weinberg, 2002). Since the early 1990s, however, terrorism has changed on at least three fronts. First, the number of victims per attack has increased because suicide bombers can move into crowded areas before detonating their explosives, often suicide vests, thereby increasing the number of casualties exponentially. Second, religious extremists are behind most assaults (Perliger, Pedahzur, & Zalmanovitch, 2005). Finally, the targets of terrorist attacks are not confined to traditionally troubled regions such as the Middle East. For example, the 1993 bombing of the World Trade Center in the US signaled that terrorism with Middle Eastern ties had struck close to home. Because the perpetrator was a US citizen, the 1995 bombing of the Alfred P. Murrah Federal Building in Oklahoma City destroyed Americans' long-held notion that terrorism only originates from abroad. The events of September 11, 2001, reinforced the ongoing threat of global terrorism.

The Geographic Factor in Terrorism

Modern terrorists often attack in urban areas because they represent the state's financial, political, and cultural centers (Perliger et al., 2005). Striking an urban target inflicts a psychological as well as a physical wound to the local area. It can maximize the number of casualties that can be inflicted with a single blow. Given the high concentration of businesses and government offices in urban areas, crisis management plans should include terrorist contingencies. Industries like destination tourism are highly vulnerable.

Destination tourism is affected when terrorists seek to instill fear in potential tourists, reducing the number of visitors to a site. Many events, such as wars, localized diseases, and terrorist attacks, can affect tourism in a specific area (Glaesser, 2005). Terrorism puts geographic restrictions on a region, even if the region is relatively peaceful. For example, Jordan is a relatively safe country, but its Middle Eastern location subjects it to variations in tourism revenue due to terrorism concerns (Ali & Ali, 2010).

From a business perspective, hotels have been an unfortunate target for terrorist attacks, particularly on the international front. From July 2013 to June 2014, there were 87 terrorist attacks on hotels worldwide (Fanelli, 2016). Especially at risk are hotels with American brand names and those that cater to Western visitors, particularly in Islamic cultures (Bergen, 2015). Several notable hotel terrorist attacks include:

- The November 9, 2005, bombings in Amman, Jordan targeted three American brands, the Grand Hyatt, Radisson, and Days Inn. The attacks were linked with al Qaeda and resulted in the deaths of 60 people (Bergen, 2015);
- The September 20, 2008, attack on the Marriott Islamabad Hotel in Pakistan which killed 56 people and injured 270 (Fanelli, 2016);
- The November 26, 2008, attack on tourist destinations in Mumbai, India, including two luxury hotels, resulted in 166 fatalities (Wernick & Von Glinow, 2012);
- The June 26, 2015, attack on the beach behind the Hotel Riu Imperial Marhaba in Tunisia killed 37 people, most of whom were European tourists. A lone gunman carried out the attack with Islamic State of Iraq and Syria (ISIS) affiliations (Addala & El-Ghobashy, 2015).
- The July 12, 2019, attack on the Asasey Hotel in Mogadishu, Somalia killed at least 26 people. The attack commenced with a suicide car bomb that destroyed the entrance gate and permitted four gunmen to enter the building (Guled, 2019).

Hotels are targets for terrorists because they symbolize Western affluence and culture. They also represent soft targets that can yield mass causalities (Neumayer &

Plümper, 2016). Unfortunately, devastating attacks such as these can help recruit aspiring terrorists to a movement (Wernick & Von Glinow, 2012).

Business leaders in the West revisited their views about terrorism after the attacks of September 11, 2001. In one day, the need for organizations to anticipate, prepare for, and respond to these potential events became clear (Greenberg, Clair, & Maclean, 2002). For some businesses, the attack resulted in both the tragic loss of employees and a loss of critical facilities and data (Greenberg, 2002). Many organizations decimated by this attack never reopened. While the companies in the World Trade Center's (WTC) Twin Towers were affected directly, thousands of other businesses were indirectly affected. Supply chains were interrupted, important information networks were destroyed, clients were lost, and business travel—at least in the short run—was severely curtailed. The events of September 11 sparked the worst disruption of global tourism since World War II and triggered a temporary slowdown in the world's economy (Ali & Ali, 2010). Its tumultuous effects on organizational and economies throughout the world have since been rivaled only by the COVID-19 pandemic.

Preparing for Terrorism

Preparing for terrorist attacks is not an easy task for either the small business owner or the sizeable corporate management team. While the probability of being the target of a direct hit from a terrorist attack is low when compared to other crisis events, the aftermath of an attack is more likely to impact business continuity. These impacts include a decline in revenue due to reduced consumer demand and the restrictions governments may place on the movements of people, goods, and money across borders (Wernick & Von Glinow, 2012). A direct terrorist attack remains a concern.

Most organizations in developed nations depend on government entities for protection from terrorist attacks. Following the September 11 terrorist attack on the WTC, the US government created the first Department of Homeland Security. Scholarly research on the effectiveness of combating terrorism followed as well, including three new journals. An online journal, the *Journal of Homeland Security and Emergency Management,* was launched in 2003 (Nickerson, 2011). In 2008, *Critical Studies on Terrorism* was launched, and one year later, *Behavioral Sciences of Terrorism and Political Aggression* commenced. Because terrorism is unlikely to disappear, crisis management teams should prepare for this threat, understanding that it could intensify in the years to come.

Social Media and the Internet Intensify the Effects of a Crisis

The Internet can facilitate a crisis, or it can even trigger one directly (González-Herrero & Smith, 2008). It can set the stage for a crisis by permitting individuals to spread negative information about an organization rapidly and over a broad geographical region at little or no expense. Consumers can discuss their negative experiences with products and services on discussion forums, Facebook, in YouTube videos, on blogs, and all forms of social media.

Social Media

An early example illustrates the power of social media concerned Proctor & Gamble (P&G) and its disposable diaper product Dry Max Pampers. The product was introduced in March 2010 as the "driest and thinnest" nappy ever. Many parents complained about the product via blogs, claiming it caused their babies to develop a rash. A Facebook page with 6,000 followers appeared and claimed children were developing chemical burns from the product (Birchall, 2010). P&G was quickly thrown into crisis management mode and was soon inviting mothers to their corporate headquarters in Cincinnati, Ohio, to discuss their concerns. The extent to which the product caused harm is not the only issue. From a crisis perspective, if one consumer *believes* the product caused the problem and communicates it via social media, others may agree, even without medical confirmation (Birchall, 2010).

Social media's ability to facilitate a crisis is enhanced by the lack of oversight on online material because editorial filters often associated with print journalism do not exist in social media, a problem Facebook and Twitter have experienced since the mid-2010s. (Hunter, Wassenhove, & Besiou, 2016). Opinions, whims, and anger can be expressed in social media outlets in real time.

Fake News

The Internet has also become a haven for **fake news**—references to events that appear to be accurate but are either misleading or entirely false. The term should not be confused with satirical news, which is purposely meant to be amusing, but not intended to confuse readers about the facts. The Onion News network would be an example of this type of satirical outlet (Alvarez, 2016). Fake news can benefit the originator by increasing the number of clicks to a website or may be employed to influence an election or another event (Rash, 2016).

Fake news has always existed under other names but was not as impactful until social media provided the engine for rapid, efficient proliferation to a broad audience. Early American newspapers were tools of political parties that frequently printed mistruths about their opponents. **Yellow journalism** reporting that was sensationalized and often entirely fabricated—was common in the 19th century. Yellow journalism can help sell newspapers and even influence political elections (Stoffers, 2017).

The 2016 and 2020 US presidential campaign cycles included a plethora of fake news reports. In August 2016, one story claimed that Hillary Clinton was selling weapons to ISIS. In November 2016, another reported that hundreds of paid protestors had been transported to an anti-Trump rally in Texas (Stoffers, 2017). Neither story was true, but many people both believed these stories and shared them on their Facebook pages.

The editorial effects of fake news can be subtle. Even when a fake news story is debunked as untrue, future stories may—intentionally or inadvertently—reference it as support. For example, false, negative reports about an individual or an organization create a broader, negative aura, often leading to more explicit references in future stories to "a series of negative allegations" or "previous concerns" about an entity. In this respect, fake news can inflict damage in the public arena, even when the stories are proven false.

Combatting fake news is complicated. Many of the "fact-checking" sites that ostensibly evaluate the accuracy of news are run by organizations with political motives, leaving one to wonder who fact-checks the fact-checkers. In a fast-paced world, it is almost impossible for consumers to separate fact from fiction, especially when a fake news story is mostly true.

The advent of fake news is troubling for crisis managers because it demonstrates the public's inability to distinguish accurate news reports from inaccurate ones and the indirect, adverse effects a fake news item can have even after it has been discredited. Managers must recognize how fake news can damage organizations, and they must prepare accordingly. A strong, positive social media presence can help, but there is no perfect solution.

Internet Woes

The Internet can also be the trigger point for a crisis, one example being a highly motivated hacker community (González-Herrero & Smith, 2008). Experts estimate there are 1.5 million cyber-attacks each year, or about 4,000 per day. Most do not penetrate company firewalls, but a few do, about 1.7 per week (Fugazy, 2016). Several types of hacking can occur. A denial-of-service attack causes the organization's website either to slow down or to stop functioning altogether. Such an attack can lead to a sizable loss of revenue, like shutting down the store for the duration of the attack. Hacking can also occur in the form of security breaches in which customer database information is stolen and identity theft, a crisis that can create significant problems for both a company and its customers.

For example, more than 150 million personal records were breached in health-care company hacks between 2009 and 2018. As a result, hospitals are prompting medical device manufacturers to enhance cyber defenses of their Internet-connected healthcare products. In some instances, they have even cancelled orders and rejected bids for devices that lack the appropriate safety features (Evans & Loftus, 2019).

Another malicious attack occurs when a copycat website emerges that mimics a legitimate organization's website (González-Herrero & Smith, 2010). Such sites can cause unsuspecting customers to send money and private credit card information to scammers who secure revenue from victims but do not deliver the goods. A growing cybersecurity industry is emerging to combat these issues directly.

Finally, an alternate trigger point caused by the Internet occurs when a website malfunctions for a technical reason. When service is unavailable, customers cannot place their orders, and the company's revenue stream is interrupted. The impact can be significant for brick-and-mortar businesses but even more so for organizations that rely solely on online revenue.

Human-Induced Missteps Are at the Core of the Majority of Crises

Since 1994, the Institute for Crisis Management (ICM) has been tracking the types of crises that strike organizations. The ICM has tracked over 791,000 negative news stories in its 2018 annual report and found that 22.0% of all reported crises were directly attributable to mismanagement, followed by discrimination (14.3%), sexual harassment (9.4%) and labor disputes (9.4%) (ICM, 2018). Crises in the latter three categories are often associated with questionable management practice as well. Hence, most of these crises need not occur in the first place. Unlike externally induced crises such as hurricanes or natural disasters, **human-induced crises** often emanate from top management (Carroll & Buchholtz, 2014; Hartley, 1993). When lower-level employees are not sure how to react in a specific ethics-related situation, they look to their leaders for guidance. Therefore, crises can emerge when ethics is lacking with supervisors and top management. Chapter 10 is devoted to the intricate link between ethics and organizational crises. The remainder of this section examines human-induced crises stemming from workplace violence, human error, normal accident theory, and sloppy management.

Workplace Violence

Human-induced crises include various forms of workplace misbehavior. Griffin and Lopez (2005) coined the term **bad behavior** to refer to actions that can harm the organization and its members (p. 988). They further classified bad behavior into four categories: deviance, aggression, antisocial behavior, and violence.

Workplace deviance includes behavior that violates the accepted norms of the organization. Organizational deviance is composed of actions taken against the company and includes leaving early, wasting resources, stealing, and sabotaging equipment.

Interpersonal deviance is directed toward another individual in the workplace and can include verbal abuse, gossiping, and sexual harassment (Diefendorff & Mehta, 2007).

Workplace aggression is assertive and threatening behavior directed toward a person or an object but is nonphysical. Consider a terminated worker who verbally threatens her supervisor. Management should always be concerned about verbal threats because they can precede physical assault.

Antisocial behavior is a set of actions that can produce physical, economic, psychological, or emotional harm (Robinson & O'Leary, 1998). This behavior occurs when an employee is not sociable and disrupts organizational norms (Griffin & Lopez, 2005).

Workplace violence exists when behavior becomes physical (O'Leary-Kelly, Griffin, & Glew, 1996). Of the behaviors described by Griffin and Lopez, workplace violence generates the most attention in the crisis management field. Three recent examples provide evidence as to why it is so essential to be aware of this dysfunctional behavior of in an organizational setting:

- In August 2015, a disgruntled ex-employee of WDBJ-TV7 News fatally shot two former colleagues while broadcasting a story live (Marszalek, 2016).
- In December 2015, a young couple, Syed Farook and his wife, Tashfean Malik, fatally shot 14 of his colleagues at a Christmas party in California. It was later revealed that the couple sympathized with radical Islam (Powell, 2015).
- In February 2016, a disgruntled employee who worked as a painter fatally shot three people where he worked at a Kansas lawn care equipment manufacturing company (Bonczyk, 2016).

There has been an abundance of research on workplace violence. A personality profile for a potential killer in the workplace has been identified, new training and security procedures have been enacted in organizations, and better screening devices are in place to identify applicants who may be prone to violence.

One area of training that has received considerable attention on college and university campuses is active shooter education. Students, faculty, and staff are trained on responding if an individual with a firearm is actively discharging a weapon on the campus. For example, at Southern Methodist University, extensive training is provided to employees and students on lockdown plans, building assessment surveys (to map out lockdown areas), and conducting active shooter drills (Morris, 2014). In the private sector, additional emphasis on the human resource management function has been encouraged. These include encouraging employees to speak up and voice concerns about workplace safety and violence, forming safety committees, and using behavioral-based interviewing to hire new employees (Bonczyk, 2016).

Human Error and the Normal Accident Theory Problem

In addition to unethical decisions and bad behaviors, human-induced crises also include employee or operator errors, which are major contributors to industrial accidents. Errors of this kind may occur when the work environment is both complex and **tightly coupled**. Charles Perrow (1999) suggested that such a scenario can lead to a **normal accident**. Tight coupling considers the interdependence that exists among departments, units, teams, and other groups within an organization. The higher the interdependence (i.e., the more departments depend on other departments to function), the more tightly the departments are coupled. A department that can function independently from other departments in an organization is loosely coupled. For example, in a restaurant, the service staff and the cooking staff are tightly coupled because one group cannot function without the other. If the chef and several cooks suddenly became ill, a significant crisis would ensue, and the restaurant might have to close, albeit temporarily. However, the relationship between the cooks and the cleaning staff of dishwashers is more loosely coupled. The restaurant can survive if there is a shortage of dishwashers, even if the cooks must take over this function for a short time.

This example focused on the notion of interdependence within an organization. However, the concept of coupling also involves entities outside of the organization, which has increased with partnerships and strategic alliances. Some of the organization's suppliers are more tightly coupled with the company than others. Tightly coupled suppliers must be available to make regular deliveries with the full order and in a timely fashion if the business is to perform well. In a restaurant, food suppliers are tightly coupled to the organization, whereas suppliers of paper and cleaning goods, although important, are more loosely coupled. A crisis can develop when an entity within or outside the organization is temporarily incapacitated. The other groups aligned with that unit are now also part of the crisis. For example, in a just-in-time (JIT) work system, if a major supplier cannot make the delivery, the assembly line will shut down because there is very little slack built into the system. If the delay continues, the company may have to suspend operations temporarily. This example is not hypothetical; it occurs whenever there is a substantial disruption in a supply chain. Major industrial fires, earthquakes, terrorism, wars, and tsunamis can initiate a crisis of this sort because these events can disrupt supply chains. Indeed, in today's JIT-oriented society, supply chains are vulnerable due to the tight coupling among supply chain partners (Zsidisin, Ragatz, & Meinyk, 2005).

Perrow's (1999) original contributions to normal accident theory addressed technologies that create complexity and tight coupling for users who operate these technologies. In such a situation, an employee error can create a major crisis. Perrow (1999) believed that user errors of this sort were inevitable in certain facilities, such as chemical and nuclear power plants (Choo, 2008). The March 28, 1979, near-meltdown of a reactor at the Three Mile Island nuclear power facility outside of Harrisburg, Pennsylvania, illustrates how a normal accident might evolve (Hopkins, 2001). In this incident, nuclear plant operators could not explain what triggered the accident and what to do about it (Barton, 2001). The plant met the conditions that Perrow (1999) had outlined; it was complex and tightly coupled. The sheer complexity of the facility made it difficult to identify actions needed to remedy the problem. The plant was tightly coupled in that changes in one subsystem would affect the rest of the system as well. One of the primary means used by operators to control the rising temperature in the reactor core was to shut down high-pressure cooling pumps (Hopkins, 2001). Ironically, leaving pressure pumps on would have alleviated the problem, a tight coupling phenomenon.

More recently, on September 15, 2018, deadly gas explosions occurred in three towns north of Boston, the magnitude of which made it difficult to secure the area. Experts and first responders visited thousands of homes to turn off gas mains because no cause of the explosions was readily available (Sanchez & Chavez, 2018). Although this example has its roots in technology, it is also a case study on how human error can intensify a crisis.

Sloppy Management

Before Perrow's (1999) normal accident theory, Turner (1978) maintained that human-induced crises are caused by what he called **sloppy management**. Whereas Perrow (1999) blamed human error on technological factors, Turner (1978) attributed it to poor management and the systems in which they function. One of the characteristics of poor management is the failure to heed warnings from previous problems (Hopkins, 2001). In other words, managers saw warning signs but were in denial and failed to act, eventually triggering a crisis. The September 11, 2001, terrorist attack on the World Trade Center in New York City has been framed in this light (9-11 Commission, 2004). Poor management has also been linked with groupthink, a phenomenon whereby groups seek to appear united and cohesive but, ultimately, make poor decisions (Janis, 1982). Failing to heed warnings can be a by-product of groupthink because nobody in the group wants to be perceived as an alarmist.

Choo (2008) suggests that managers often do not heed these warnings because of epistemic blind spots, risk denial, and structural impediments. An epistemic **blind spot** occurs when warnings are not acted on because individuals selectively interpret information to align with current beliefs. For example, before Enron's bankruptcy in

2001, Enron's board evaded the warnings that surfaced about how the firm was accounting for its assets and holdings on its financial statements. The board viewed this type of disclosure was just a normal part of conducting business (Choo, 2008).

Unlike blind spots where the warning is missed, **risk denial** is a mindset that acknowledges the reality of the signal, but the norms and culture of the organization do not dictate a response. This denial is perplexing because so many crises could have been averted if the appropriate decision-makers had acted on clear warnings. Unfortunately, many managers share the proverbial "it can't happen to us" mentality, whereby the organization is impermeable, and crises only strike other firms.

Structural impediments prevent management from acting on warnings because of structural imperfections within the organization. Unlike risk denial, when the warnings are acknowledged but not considered significant, structural impediments hinder warnings from being addressed at all, even when management believes they are legitimate. Choo (2008) cites the example of a five-year-old boy who was admitted to a hospital for elective neurosurgery. Despite the surgery going well, the boy developed complications and seizures. Unfortunately, no single physician was designated to oversee the boy's case. The patient care was established with a research physician, a neurological resident, a neurosurgeon, and an attending physician at the hospital, but nobody officially took ownership of the case (Snook & Connor, 2005). Eventually, the boy's condition worsened to the point where he stopped breathing. In this example, everyone agreed that the warnings were serious, but the structure of the situation meant that nobody oversaw the case, a prescription for a crisis.

While Choo (2008) helps explain why some legitimate warnings are ignored, resolving this problem is not easy because many signs are not substantiated. In a large organization, someone always seems to be predicting doom or calamity. Leaders must be sufficiently skilled and experienced to distinguish between warnings based on fact and those based on speculation or even fake news.

Environmental Damage and Sustainability of Resources Can Trigger a Global Impact

Two separate but related issues can result in environmental concerns. **Sustainability** seeks economic growth while ensuring that natural resources are available for the next generation of users (Stead & Stead, 2004).

Before April 2010, the *Exxon Valdez* oil spill was the poster child for an oil company's worst environmental and public relations nightmare. In 1989, the *Exxon Valdez* tanker hit a reef in Alaska's Prince William Sound, spilling over 10 million gallons of oil. Although there was no loss of human life, the loss of animal and birdlife was extensive, and the negative press was daunting. The company's untested crisis management plan assumed that a spill could be contained in five hours. Unfortunately, due to bureaucratic and weather delays, efforts to contain the spill were not implemented for two days (Hartley, 1993). The onslaught of media coverage was negative and intense for Exxon.

BP surpassed Exxon in terms of severity on April 20, 2010, when its deep-water oil well was in the final stages of being capped. A surge of gas emerged from the seabed and blew past the containment apparatus supposed to suppress it. The resulting blast killed 11 workers and caused the most massive offshore oil spill in US history (Crooks, Pfeifer, & McNulty, 2010). The accident and recovery efforts were quickly known worldwide, and BP remained in the headlines for months afterward. During the capping of the oil well, viewers on the Internet could watch in real-time as efforts were made to stop the flow of oil, a phenomenon that reinforced the power of the Internet and social media.

Some managers may think that environmental crises only occur in large manufacturing companies or those that process oil. However, service industries are also under scrutiny. McDonald's experienced an environmental challenge in the early 1990s when critics noted how excessive packaging created unnecessary waste at landfills. The company met voluntarily with Environmental Defense Fund (EDF) members for over a year to discuss alternatives (Sethi & Steidlmeier, 1997). The result was a significant revamping of packaging practices that reduced the Styrofoam used and placed McDonald's in a favorable light among environmentalists, at least temporarily. What could have been a potential public relations crisis was handled proactively by the company, with cost savings to the firm as an added benefit (Sethi & Steidlmeier, 1997). Industry leaders like McDonald's are often targets of efforts designed to promote an environmental agenda.

Another large firm, Walmart, has also taken strides to promote sustainability. Walmart is gravitating towards the model of circular economies, which considers the total movement of a product through its life cycle (Kaplan, 2017). This includes examining all cost factors and social benefits as a product moves from its birth, usage, and ultimately its retirement from consumption.

Crises and sustainability are linked in two ways (Crandall & Mensah, 2008). First, a sudden environmental crisis can impair the sustainability of specific resources in the long term. For example, an oil spill can negatively influence the long-term survivability of the seafood industry in the affected area. The 2010 BP oil spill in the Gulf of Mexico and the 1989 *Exxon Valdez* spill off the coast of Alaska illustrate this scenario and depict events that are both sudden and unexpected. In the second scenario, the events occur slowly and methodically. Indeed, the steady growth of a firm (and on a larger scale, a society) can gradually deplete renewable resources faster than they are being replenished. It is these slower types of economic growth that are of importance in sustainability. Water, air, and land are noticeable resources that some firms have not always used responsibly. For example, shrimp farms in Thailand have destroyed many coastal mangrove forests. Coastal mangrove systems protect shorelines from storms and tsunamis, thus preventing erosion (Kelly, 2012).

Sustainable development is likely to become even more newsworthy in the future as continued attention focuses on the depletion of renewable resources. Companies and even countries perceived to be detractors to sustainable development will be viewed negatively, leading to an array of public relations crises. Emerging countries have been the target of criticism because they are often unwilling or unable to effectively address sustainability issues (Parnell, Spillan, & Lester, 2010).

Concern for the environment remains a high priority in the crisis management landscape. Indeed, the examples depicted in our discussion are not designed to identify individuals or firms in a positive or negative light. Evaluating a firm's sustainability efforts is usually a complex endeavor that lies outside of the scope of this discussion. From a crisis perspective, companies must not only work to prevent environmental damage, but they should also portray to the public their efforts to be champions of sustainable development. Indeed, companies are evaluated to a large extent in terms of how much they support or ignore sustainability management (Coombs, 2010). Municipalities, states, and entire countries should protect the environment and ensure that resources are available for future generations.

Globalization Increases the Risk of Organizational, Supply Chain, and Societal Crises

Globalization refers to the growing economic interdependence among nations. Although debates abound concerning the extent to which its effects are positive or negative, globalization is undeniable. In practice, it creates both positive and negative outcomes. One conclusion is clear: globalization has created an environment in which crisis events are more likely to occur.

Global outsourcing is a strategy associated with the proliferation of globalization. This term refers to contracting out a firm's peripheral, non–revenue-producing activities to organizations in other nations primarily to reduce costs. In other words, "it is the process of having suppliers provide goods and services that were previously provided internally. Outsourcing involves substitution, the replacement of internal capacity, and production by that of a supplier" (Blackstone, 2013). Put differently, global outsourcing implies that production was formally in-house, but is now performed elsewhere (Dolgui & Proth, 2013). Many of those suppliers are now in emerging or less developed countries (LDCs) with global outsourcing.

The extent to which a firm is involved globally affects its crisis exposure, but the link is complicated. Ceteris paribus, involvement in global markets can *reduce* political and economic risk by reducing reliance on a single nation or region. However, participation in countries and markets prone to crises can *increase* risk. For example, with myriad production facilities and approximately 140,000 employees in over 90 countries, Proctor and Gamble's geographical diversification enables the firm to survive crises induced by country- or region-specific factors such as war, political upheavals, currency devaluations, or catastrophic weather events. In contrast, LAN Airlines operates primarily in Peru, Chile, and nearby nations. As a result, LAN is particularly susceptible to external triggers associated with South America. During Europe's financial crisis in the early 2010s, companies with a substantial European presence like McDonald's, Heineken, and GlaxoSmithKline engaged in contingency planning. They took other preventive measures, such as reducing local Euro holdings, to limit their exposure, especially in struggling nations like Greece, Italy, and Spain (Fuhrmans & Cimilluca, 2012).

In the discussion that follows, we focus primarily on global outsourcing's impact on crisis events. The scope of the coverage looks at outsourcing's relation to operational control problems, fragile supply chains, reputational crises, and the movement toward bringing production back to the host country, a process known as reshoring.

Operational Control Problems

An organization loses some control over business functions when it allows other organizations to perform them. Arrangements such as strategic alliances, partnerships, and outsourcing—particularly across borders—can make an organization susceptible to the political, legal, cultural, and other influences that affect its partners. Union Carbide's Bhopal, India, disaster was one of the first crisis events to illustrate what can happen when partners in other countries fail to maintain the same standards as those in the home country. In 1984, gas leaked from a methyl isocyanate (MIC) tank at a Union Carbide plant in Bhopal, initially killing more than 2,500 people and injuring another 300,000. The plant was jointly owned and operated by parties in India (49%) and by Union Carbide (51%). Inadequate safety practices, equipment failures, and careless operating procedures contributed to the disaster that ensued when water accidentally entered Tank 610, which held the deadly gas (Hartley, 1993).

Herein lies the heart of the dilemma: outsourcing relinquishes control of production (Zsidisin, Meinyk, & Ragatz, 2005). Outsourcing can be beneficial when the outsourcer has expertise in the field and is better equipped to perform a task. Still, cultural differences between partners can create a gap between the anticipated and actual quality. Clarifying specifications in purchasing contracts can reduce—but not always eliminate—the problem of quality deviances. Other issues may not be addressed in an outsourcing relationship, such as maintaining the outsourced facility in terms of cleanliness and equipment functioning abilities. In other words, purchasing contracts usually consider the final product, but not necessarily the functional capabilities of the production facility.

The accident at Bhopal illustrates how a push for globalization and outsourcing can be devastating. Safety standards were unmet in the manufacturing of the deadly MIC gas. Control of these standards and equipment maintenance at the plant were in the Indian owners' hands, under an elaborate arrangement called Union Carbide (India) Limited (Sethi & Steidlmeier, 1997). In retrospect, one might liken this situation to giving a toddler a loaded handgun. Laissez-faire decentralization is inappropriate in less developed countries when safety and environmental degradation are at stake" (Hartley, 1993).

Another crisis threat looms for many companies with long and complicated supply chains – slavery. As the chapter case illustrates, supply chains in specific industries such as agriculture, mining, construction, domestic work, and low-skill manufacturing can hide forced labor (Crane, 2013). This crisis is humanitarian, reputational, and economic in scope. While no reputable firm in a developed country would condone slavery in its supply chain, the drive to expand and lower costs coupled with the complexity of second- and third-tier suppliers can unknowingly lead to this outcome.

The Problem of Fragile Supply Chains

Two sub-trends have been occurring in the world's supply chains. The first is global outsourcing; the second is the movement toward lean management and its accompanying emphasis on leaner supply chains and single-sourcing (Crandall, Crandall, & Chen, 2015). Both trends make supply chains more vulnerable to external shocks that can interrupt a firm's supply lines. When companies carry less inventory, interruptions in the supply chain due to a crisis can grind production to a standstill.

Single sourcing is another essential practice in many firms. Unfortunately, when a company's main vendor experiences a crisis, the companies it supplies will be affected as well. The same is true with vendors that provide daily deliveries. An interruption in the delivery schedule can halt production immediately. For a dramatic example of the impact of a crisis on a single supplier, consider the fire that took out the main production facilities of Philips Electronics in early 2000. Philips supplies radio-frequency chips (RFCs) to cellular phone makers. The crisis caused a $400 million revenue loss for the telecommunications company, Ericsson, and eventually led to its exit from the mobile phone sector altogether (Rice & Caniato, 2003).

Cisco, the San Jose, California-based provider of networking and communication systems, appears to understand the risks of supply chain disruptions because 95% of its production is outsourced (Harrington & O'Connor, 2009). Because most of its supply chain is global, the company has adopted a program to shift from single sourcing (a common practice with many companies) to multiple sourcing. Indeed, such planning was essential when on May 12, 2008, a 7.9 magnitude earthquake hit the Sichuan province of China, a region at the heart of Cisco's supply chain for that part of Asia.

Reputational Crises

Many American firms—including Nike and Walmart—have been fighting crises such as negative publicity and boycotts resulting from their ties to countries where labor costs are much lower. Walmart critic Arindrajit Dube suggested that the company's comparatively low wages emanating from outsourcing result in an annual wage loss in the retail sector of almost $5 billion. Hollywood's Robert Greenwald produced a movie about the giant retailer—*WALMART: The High Cost of Low Price*—chronicling the plight of an Ohio-based hardware store when Walmart moved to town (York, 2005). The net effect of this sentiment against Walmart is unclear, and not all press has been negative. As Jason Furman of New York University notes, Walmart's economic benefits cannot be ignored; the retailer saves its customers an estimated $200 billion or more on food and other items every year (Mallaby, 2005). Its presence also forces rivals to become more competitive, which also benefits consumers.

Nike experienced an immediate image crisis on February 20, 2019, when Duke University basketball star Zion Williamson suffered a right knee sprain after his left shoe came apart. The crisis erupted immediately on social media and was amplified by some high-profile fans, including former US President Barack Obama, who was sitting courtside. A written statement from Nike read, "We are obviously concerned and want to wish Zion a speedy recovery. The quality and performance of our products are of utmost importance. While this is an isolated occurrence, we are working to identify the issue" (Bruell, 2019). Nike shares fell 1.1% the following day, but the negative effect was not longlasting.

Public opposition to outsourcing can harm public sentiment and weaken customer loyalty for firms directly or indirectly involved. As an industry leader, Walmart is often the brunt of criticism from politicians, activists, and union leaders. Detractors contend that the retailer giant's aggressive negotiating tactics eventually decimate domestic manufacturers and send American jobs overseas (Fishman, 2006). Some critics charge that Walmart seeks to destroy small businesses in the communities in which it operates (Edid, 2005; Quinn, 2000). However, others cite positive influences, noting such factors as job creation and the benefits of low prices to consumers (Etter, 2005; Morillo, McNally, & Block, 2015; York, 2005).

Outsourcing from firms in the United States has shifted many domestic jobs overseas. Consider the case of India. Former General Electric (GE) CEO Jack Welch was instrumental in one of India's earliest partnerships. Welch first met with the Indian government in 1989, and GE formed a joint venture to develop and market medical equipment with Wipro Ltd. in 1990. By the mid-1990s, much of GE's software development and maintenance activities had shifted to Indian companies. GE Capital Services (GECIS) established the first international call center in India in 1999. GE sold 60 percent of GECIS for $500 million in 2004, freeing it to compete against IBM, Accenture, and Indian firms. In 2005, India received more than $17 billion from foreign corporations seeking to outsource various jobs (Solomon & Kranhold, 2005). The number of legal outsourcing firms in India has grown since the mid-2000s, with annual revenues currently exceeding $1 billion (Srivastava, 2014). The advantage is clear: reduced operational costs. A legal project in India can cost a fraction of what it would in the United States or another developed nation (Gogel, 2016).

The pressure to reduce prices by lowering operational costs can be overwhelming, especially in discount retail industries dominated by big boxers. Global competition has forced firms like Best Buy, Home Depot, Target, and Walmart to cut costs, and global outsourcing is an attractive option. However, outsourcing can create negative publicity. Television commentator Lou Dobbs has long charged that corporate greed is behind job losses because a firm chooses to outsource jobs overseas (Dobbs, 2004).

While it is convenient and simplistic to invoke the "corporate greed" argument, the reality is far more complex. In the long run, critics must acknowledge that consumer demand is what generates revenues, and consumers want low prices (Shell, 2009). Many retailers contend that to offer low prices, they must pay their employees less and outsource to reduce costs. But while outsourcing benefits customers through lower prices, it also feeds the notion that the retailers minimize the number of domestic employees and drive wages down. Hence, consumer decision-making triggers organizational action. Despite the enthusiasm for global outsourcing among many businesses, some advocates view manufacturing costs differently, as the next section illustrates.

The Reshoring Movement

Whether the production is offshored (i.e., the organization produces abroad) or outsourced (i.e., the organization contracts with other firms to produce in other nations), the total, long-term costs of shifting production to another country can be challenging to calculate. There is a **reshoring** movement afoot among US-based manufacturers to shift production back to the United States.

Harry Moser and other consultants maintain that the costs of global outsourcing should follow a total cost of ownership approach (Markham, 2011). This approach calculates all costs associated with making and transporting the product back to the US. These costs include risk factors such as currency valuations, the stability of the country where outsourcing occurs, the loss of business due to poor quality, the economic stability of the supplier, and loss due to lack of innovation. More traditional costs such as transportation and holding costs, damage to products while en route and duty fees should also be considered.

Reshoring simplifies the supply chain by shortening the distance between the home country and the outsourced manufacturer, which is usually located in a developing country due to the lower wages associated with making the product. Reshoring also increases supply chain visibility and product launch speed while lowering supply chain complexity, disruptions, shipping expenses, and corruption that can occur in distant supply chains (Moser & Kelly, 2016).

One factor that also must be considered is the convergence of labor rates across the globe. As labor costs rise in China and other popularly outsourced countries, the playing field levels when one compares the total cost of ownership in each country. In 2004, total manufacturing costs in the US were 13.5% higher than in China. However, in 2014, the cost differential was only 4.5% (Owen, 2016). Some of China's neighbors, such as Viet Nam and Laos, now offer lower production costs.

Another factor in favor of reshoring is identifying quality control problems when the source is from an overseas vendor. One estimate is that a defective product originating overseas could translate into 12 weeks of faulty products in the supply chain pipeline (Owen, 2016). The time length of the inbound logistics is why defective products can get stockpiled in the supply chain. For example, if a product is manufactured in China, it must travel through China, then through a port, followed by several weeks at sea. Once the product reaches the destination country, it must be unpacked, put on a rail, and then trucked to the market (Hutchins, 2015). Resources are also needed to isolate the cause of the product defect, which will likely raise transportation costs. With reshoring, suppliers are in the same country, so language and culture problems are averted, and transportation costs are reduced. The COVID-19 pandemic illustrates this phenomenon, although the problem was not product quality per se. By the time products manufactured in China during late 2019 arrived in the US, consumers were concerned about potential transmission of the disease. In essense, they deemed the products defective.

While the reshoring movement suggests that organizations take a closer look at long-term costs and risks associated with shifting production to another country, each situation is different. Outsourcing or offshoring are viable, cost-effective alternatives for many organizations. Nonetheless, firms should consider how such decisions affect their ability to manage crises due to supply chain and other complexities.

As we can see, globalization and global outsourcing strategies have spawned many crisis threats. Firms typically outsource to suppliers in emerging countries to reduce costs. As Shell (2010) contends, however, what is often at stake is more than just lower costs, but quality, safety, environmental responsibility, and human dignity.

Summary

This chapter examined six significant trends in the crisis management landscape, each of which contributes to the proliferation of crisis events that organizations must face. For each trend, a tradeoff exists between the external environment and the degree of influence that management can exert in its strategic planning efforts. The ever-changing landscape has introduced the transboundary crisis issues that continue to be even more challenging. Crisis managers can no longer focus only on traditional crisis events such as fires, accidents, and fraudulent activities. They must be aware of the broader landscape across borders. The speed of information exchange and the authenticity of information have made the manager's job even more complicated. Transboundary crises, along with the 24/7 news and information cycle, have prompted managers to think differently and constantly revise and renew their view of the domestic and global landscape. Management has the most strategic influence in its decisions to undertake globalization initiatives, but the least amount when addressing transboundary crises. Understanding these trends is useful as we examine the origins of crises, the topic of the next chapter.

Discussion Questions

1. What is a transboundary crisis? What are the four characteristics of a transboundary crisis? What are some examples of a transboundary crisis?
2. How should companies prepare for acts of terrorism? How much preparation is too much? Explain.
3. How does social media add to the severity of a crisis? Provide examples.
4. What types of human-induced crises have occurred where you work? Cite some examples of workplace violence, normal accidents, and poor management?
5. What is a "normal" accident? What conditions contribute to this type of accident?
6. What is sustainable development? How is it linked to crisis events?
7. How has globalization contributed to an increase in crisis events?
8. What can companies do to decrease the risk of a crisis involving global outsourcing?

Chapter Exercise

The six trends in this chapter have been carefully researched to reflect the latest factors that lead to organizational crises. Although the trends are discussed individually, they overlap as well. In this exercise, the class should form groups representing each of the six trends discussed in the chapter.

Each group should create a list of examples of crises that originate from its respective trend; this part can be done outside of class. Post lists in the classroom so that members of all six groups can view each group's examples. Once the class has reconvened, identify the examples that overlap into other categories. For example, a transboundary crisis can also have roots in globalization.

For each of the examples that overlap other trends, discuss as a class how an organization can exert more effective strategic control to prevent or mitigate a future crisis of that type.

Closing Chapter Case: When Slavery Hits the Supply Chain – Part 2

In the opening case to this chapter, we learned that businesses are under considerable pressure to keep their costs low because their consumers demand it. Otherwise, consumers are free to price shop and move their purchasing to other companies. This pressure has resulted in a proliferation of outsourcing to developing countries, as companies search for the lowest means possible to secure the products they need.

Given this background, the result is that cost pressure from companies in developed nations is passed along to their suppliers in developing countries. This means the manufacturers in these countries must find ways to lower their costs continually, a problem that often puts human rights and plant safety at risk. Furthermore, it can lead to the movement of slave labor into some of these factories.

The high degree of global interconnectedness common in many enterprises today emanates from the concept of comparative advantage, the idea that certain products may be produced more cheaply or at a higher quality in countries because of advantages in labor costs or technology (Parnell, 2021). Even if one nation enjoys an absolute advantage over another in most areas, the weaker nation must participate in some forms of business to develop economically and employ its citizens. Firms in these nations tend to produce in areas where the absolute advantage is lowest. All nations benefit economically from such an arrangement, but there is a downside.

Government leaders often seek to foster comparative advantage at the national level. Many developing countries lack the infrastructure and technology to compete on factors other than costs, so they promote policies that encourage the production of

58

goods for developed markets. This approach has been common in China and other parts of Asia and often includes currency manipulations to drive costs down even further. To promote low costs, governments have incentives to maintain low labor standards. Critics call this practice the race to the bottom (Chan & Peng, 2011). While there are valid arguments for such an approach, it can also engender an environment conducive to forced labor (see Figure 2.3).

Figure 2.3 – The Race to the Bottom Simplified

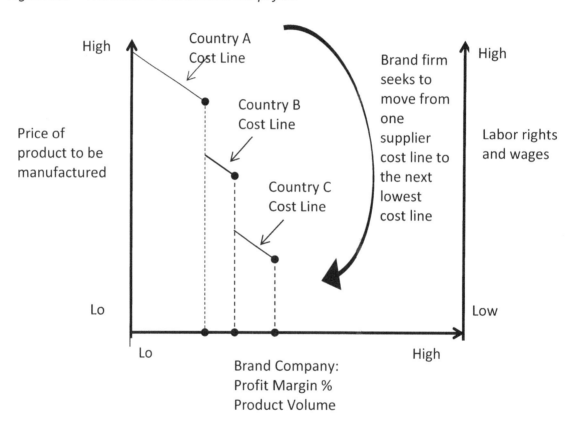

As Figure 2.3 illustrates, countries in developing countries exhibit cost lines regarding the production of goods. For example, Country A has a moderately high cost line, including a corresponding high level of labor rights and wages for factory workers. The cost line of Country B is lower than in Country A. Although this may increase profits or sales for the brand company, the corresponding labor rights and wages for factory workers are reduced. Country C has the lowest cost line, meaning that it can produce the same product as Country A or B at a lower cost. However, the tradeoff is that labor rights and wages for factory workers are lowest among the three countries.

Brand companies, particularly in electronics, garments, and household appliances, look for suppliers that offer the lowest per-unit price. The cost lines in this figure are on a per-country basis to illustrate the competition among developing countries to attract orders from brand companies. Because cost is typically the determining factor for the brand, countries must compete by reducing labor rights, including wages from their employees. Shell (2010) paints a bleak picture of the process:

> When competition is mostly about price, innovation too often takes a back seat to cost-cutting. Laying off workers and hiring cheaper ones is one sure way to enhance the bottom line. Another is to scour the world for low-wage workers, especially those in countries with lackluster enforcement of environmental and worker rights regulations. (p. 209)

Combating Modern Slavery

Modern slavery is an uncomfortable reality in the supply chains of many facilities in developing countries. Firms that outsource overseas are now moving out of the awareness stage of learning what is going on at tier-one, tier-two, and tier-three. It is no longer for a company in a developed country to claim ignorance. The next stage will involve companies addressing the problems that accompany modern slavery. Three implications are clear.

1. Stakeholders expect companies that outsource to developing countries to maintain the integrity of their supply chains. Large companies must satisfy multiple stakeholders. At a minimum, the stakeholder approach assumes that a firm's managers seek to collectively satisfy its employees, customers, and suppliers (Freeman, 1984). However, expanding the notion of stakeholders to include political and social groups has also been advocated (Byerly, 2012; Carroll & Buchholtz, 2012). This realization brings into account the developing countries, labor unions, and non-government organizations (NGOs) that have a vested interest in providing suitable employment for workers. Certainly, subcontractors in overseas countries should be considered as a stakeholder group that warrants attention. The inescapable reality is that multinational firms must be aware of their responsibilities with tier-one suppliers, and those at second and third tiers, and even beyond.

Indeed, some social critics would advocate that businesses not source at all to developing countries. However, this viewpoint is not realistic. Companies that pull back from overseas outsourcing could put themselves at a competitive disadvantage in the global market. Also, not sourcing to developing countries could lead to a loss of jobs, particularly for low-skilled workers struggling to survive. Companies must confront the question: How do we make sourcing overseas a legitimate strategy, and how do we understand and prevent worker abuse through sweatshops and forced labor?

Basic ethical considerations suggest that organizations are obliged to confront modern slavery as it exists within their supply chains. Ignoring the actions of their suppliers have contributed to the problem. Firms have an ethical responsibility to investigate their suppliers appropriately and only work with those committed to alleviating forced labor. Doing so is not always an easy task, but it is a critical and necessary one.

Companies can no longer say they did not authorize a supplier in a developing country, which is what some MNCs reported when the Rana factory collapsed in Bangladesh. Stakeholders now expect that successful MNCs should be able to monitor their supply chains at tier-two and tier-three.

2. Tier-one monitoring alone is insufficient. Companies must scrutinize tier-two and tier-three suppliers as well. While supply chain monitoring is warranted, efforts must not be solely focused on evaluating only tier-one suppliers. The core problems are more likely to exist with suppliers at tier-two and beyond because tier-one suppliers are more closely scrutinized. Their managers know that problems in their facilities can easily translate into a lost contract. Extra preparation for factory inspectors is common. Indeed, employees may even be coached as to what to say when the monitors ask questions (Frank, 2008).

Also, it is not enough for a company to go through the motions of monitoring without improving the integrity of the supply chain. Frank (2008) describes a low-end strategy used by some companies that used monitoring to disqualify questionable suppliers that should never have been used. Monitoring was simply a way to eliminate that supplier after several contracts, so another cheap supplier could be found.

3. Outsourcing to developing countries must include partnering with responsible NGOs and suppliers. The company is not expected to withdraw from sourcing to developing countries; indeed, this would be counterproductive to stakeholders in those countries. Instead, companies must begin to view their suppliers as strategic partners. Enacting corporate codes of conduct and monitoring systems for suppliers are standard practices in many supply chains, but using these tools wisely is essential.

Although such codes of conduct for suppliers are noteworthy, they are not effective unless they are enforced. Indeed, such regulations inevitably require capitalization and more labor resources on the part of overseas suppliers, but companies seeking a contract with a supplier rarely permit unspecified price increases. The company cannot have it both ways (Hoang & Jones, 2012). Put differently, codes of conduct, coupled with companies in the race to the bottom, can often harm the very workers they are supposed to help. This uncomfortable reality must be addressed.

There is a workable solution, however. If companies want to enforce supplier codes of operations, they must examine their supply partners more long-term. This approach shifts the paradigm from the arms-length contract arrangements that typically exist with many suppliers in developing countries. Ultimately, this means that companies will need to work with responsible NGOs and suppliers to improve the conditions of those working in the factories. Of course, considerable cost savings are still possible, but company resources may be required if the supplier operates as a long-term strategic partner.

Conclusion

There are four reasons why crisis managers should address the modern slavery in supply chains in some developing countries. First, slavery is unethical and an affront to human dignity. Second, products produced under duress could be inferior due to the adverse working conditions placed upon the workers. Third, companies that have slavery in their supply chains will suffer reputational harm, including possible consumer boycotts. Finally, the socially conscious investment stakeholder group is growing, and these groups want to see companies doing all they can to prevent slavery in their supply chains. Indeed, crisis management and prevention must exist on an international spectrum.

Case Discussion Questions

1. While consumers pressure companies to maintain low prices, most would not condone any form of slavery in their supply chains. Why is this such a challenge to discount retailers?
2. Discuss how slavery can enter a supply chain, even when suppliers are monitored at the tier-one level.
3. NGOs can help companies rid their supply chains of modern slavery. Identify and discuss NGOs that work to reduce slavery in the workplace.

References

Addala, R., & El-Ghobashy, T. (2015, June 27). Attack on Tunisian hotel leaves dozens dead; At least one gunman storms a beach resort, killing sunbathers; Islamic State claims responsibility for attack. *Wall Street Journal (Online)*.

Ali, S., & Ali, A. (2010). A conceptual framework for crisis planning and management in the Jordanian tourism industry. *Advances in Management, 3*(7), 59–65.

Alvarez, B. (2016). Public libraries in the age of fake news. *Public libraries*, *55*(6), 24-27.

Andrees, B. (2008). *Forced labour and trafficking in Europe: How people are trapped in, live through and come out.* Geneva: International Labour Office.

Ansell, C., Boin, A., & Keller, A. (2010). Managing transboundary crises: Identifying the building blocks of an effective response system. *Journal of Contingencies and Crisis Management, 18*(4), 195–207.

Bales, K. (2004). *Disposable people: New slavery in the global economy.* Berkeley, CA: University of California Press.

Ballinger, J. (2011). Sweatshop workers as globalization's consequence: How civil society can help. *Harvard International Review, 33*(2), 54-59.

Barnes, J., Norman, L., & Steinhauser, G. (2016, April 8). Belgium arrests key suspects in Brussels Attacks; Mohamed Abrini has been one of Europe's most-wanted terrorist suspects since Paris attacks in November. *Wall Street Journal (Online)*.

Barton, L. (2001). *Crisis in organizations II.* Cincinnati: South-Western.

Bergen, P. (2015, November 15). Why terrorist target hotels. CNN.com. Retrieved December 25, 2016, from http://www.cnn.com/2015/11/20/opinions/bergen-hotels-targeted-terrorists/

Birchall, J. (2010, May 27). Criticism that spread like a rash. *Financial Times,* p. 10.

Blackstone, J. (2013). *APICS Dictionary (14th ed.).* APICS – The Association for Operations Management, Chicago, IL.

Boin, A. (2009). The new world of crises and crisis management: Implications for policymaking and research. *Review of Policy Research, 26*(4), 367–377.

Boin, A., Rhinard, M., & Ekengren, M. (2014). Managing transboundary crises: The emergence of European Union capacity. *Journal of Contingencies and Crisis Management, 22*(3), 131-142.

Bonacich, E. & Hamilton, G. (2011). Global logistics, global labor, in Hamilton, G., Petrovich, M. & Senauer, B. (eds.). *The Market Makers.* Oxford, England: Oxford University Press, 211-230.

Bonczyk, K. (2016). Three keys to reducing workplace violence risks. *Claims Magazine, 64*(4), 22-24.

Bremmer, I. (2016, May 10). These 5 facts explain why Europe is ground zero for terrorism. *Time.com.* Retrieved February 1, 2017, from http://time.com/4268579/brussels-attacks-islamist-terrorism-isis/

Byerly, R. (2012). Combating modern slavery: What can businesses do? *Journal of Leadership, Accountability and Ethics, 9*(5), 25-33.

Bruell, A. (2019, February 22). Nike feels pain as a sneaker fails. *Wall Street Journal,* p. B3.

Carroll, A., & Buchholtz, A. (2012). *Business & society: Ethics, sustainability, and stakeholder management (8th ed.).* Mason, Ohio: South-Western Cengage Learning.

Carroll, A., & Buchholtz, A. (2014). *Business & society: Ethics and stakeholder management (9th ed.).* Cincinnati: Thompson South-Western.

Chan, C., & Peng, Z. (2011). From iron rice bowl to the world's biggest sweatshop: Globalization, institutional constraints, and the rights of Chinese workers. *Social Service Review, 85*(3), 421-445.

Chan, J., Pun, N., & Selden, M. (2013). The politics of global production: Apple, Foxconn and China's new working class. *New Technology, Work and Employment, 28*(2), 100-115.

Cheung, C., & Law, R. (2006). How can hotel guests be protected during the occurrence of a tsunami? *Asia Pacific Journal of Tourism Research, 11*(3), 289–295.

Choo, C. (2008). Organizational disasters: Why they happen and how they may be prevented. *Management Decision, 46*(1), 32–45.

Chu, K. (2015, December 7). Fight against fakes gets trickier. *Wall Street Journal,* pp. B1, B2.

Coombs, T. (2010). Sustainability: A new and complex "challenge" for crisis managers. *International Journal of Sustainable Strategic Management, 2*(1), 4–16.

Crandall, R., Crandall, W., & Chen, C. (2015). *Principles of supply chain management (2nd ed.)*. Boca Raton, FL: Taylor and Francis.

Crandall, W., & Mensah, E. (2008). Crisis management and sustainable development: A framework and proposed research agenda. *International Journal of Sustainable Strategic Management, 1*(1), 16–34.

Crandall, W. R., Parnell, J. A., & Crandall, R. E. (2015). Modern slavery in the supply chain: An uncomfortable reality. *Proceedings* of the 2015 Conference of the Academy of International Business – Southeast, Savannah, GA.

Crane, A. (2013). Modern slavery as a management practice: Exploring the conditions and capabilities of human exploitation. *Academy of Management Review, 38*(1), 45-69.

Crooks, E., Pfeifer, S. & McNulty, S. (2010, October 7). A sea change needed. *Financial Times,* p. 9.

Damoc, A. (2016). Fortress Europe breached: Political and economic impact of the recent refugee crisis on European states. *Annals of the University of Oradea, Economic Science Series*, *25*(1), 20-29.

Diefendorff, J., & Mehta, K. (2007). The relations of motivational traits with workplace deviance. *Journal of Applied Psychology, 92*(4), 967–977.

Dobbs, L. (2004). *Exporting America: Why corporate greed is shipping American jobs overseas.* New York: Time Warner.

Dolgui, A., & Proth, J. (2013). Outsourcing: Definitions and analysis. *International Journal of Production Research*, *51*(23-24), 6769-6777.

Drumea, M. (2011). Stopping forced labor. *Economic, Management and Financial Markets, 6*(2), 839-842.

Duhigg, C., & Bradsher, K. (2012, January 21). How the US lost out on iPhone work. *The New York Times*, p. A1.

Eckes, A. Jr., (2011). The seamy side of the global economy. *Global Economy Journal, 11*(3), 1-26.

Edid, M. (2005). *The good, the bad, and Walmart.* Ithaca, NY: Cornell University Institute of Workplace Studies.

Etter, L. (2005, December 3–4). Gauging the Walmart effect. *Wall Street Journal,* p. A9.

European Societal Security Research Group (2018). Retrieved October 7, 2018, from http://www.societalsecurity.eu/wp/slides/what-is-a-transboundary-crisis/

Evans, M., & Loftus, P. (2019, April 13). Hospitals warn on device security. *Wall Street Journal*, pp. B1, B4.

Fanelli, C. (2016). Protecting hotel industry businesses from liability for terrorist attacks. *Real Estate Finance*, *32*(4), 147-153.

Fishman, C. (2006). *The Walmart effect: How the world's most powerful company really works—and how it's transforming the American economy.* New York: Penguin.

Frank, T. (2008, April). Confessions of a sweatshop inspector. *The Washington Monthly*, 34-37.

Freeman, R. (1984). *Strategic management: A stakeholder approach*. Boston: Pittman Publishing Company.

Fugazy, D. (2016). Websites hacked, corporate data leaked, identities stolen. *Mergers & Acquisitions*, *51*(9), 18-28.

Fuhrmans, V. and Cimilluca, D. (2012, June 1). Business braces for Europe's worst. *Wall Street Journal*, pp. B1, B2.

Glaesser, D. (2005). *Crisis management in the tourism industry.* Oxford, UK: Butterworth-Heinemann.

Gogel, R. (2016, July 7). Top 3 trends to watch in legal outsourcing. *Huffington Post*. Retrieved July 5, 2017, from http://www.huffingtonpost.com/robert-gogel/top-3-trends-to-watch-in_b_10856942.html

González-Herrero, A., & Smith, S. (2008). Crisis communications management on the Web: How Internet-based technologies are changing the way public relations professionals handle business crises. *Journal of Contingencies and Crisis Management, 16*(3), 143–153.

González-Herrero, A., & Smith, S. (2010). Crisis communications management 2.0: Organizational principles to manage in an online world. *Organizational Development Journal, 28*(1), 97–105.

Green, W., III. (2004, Fall). The future of disasters: Interesting trends for interesting times. *Futures Research Quarterly, 59*–68.

Greenberg, D., Clair, J., & Maclean, T. (2002). Teaching through traumatic events: Uncovering the choices of management educators as they respond to September 11th. *Academy of Management Learning and Education Journal, 1*(1), 38–54.

Greenberg, J. (2002). September 11, 2002: A CEO's story. *Harvard Business Review, 80*(10), 58–64.

Greenhouse, S. (2012, July 25). C.J.'s Seafood fined for labor abuses. *The New York Times*, p. B6.

Grégoire, Y., Tripp, T., & Legoux, R. (2011). When your best customers become your worst enemies: Does time really heal all wounds? *New Insights, 3*(1), 27–35.

Griffin, R., & Lopez, Y. (2005). "Bad behavior" in organizations: A review and typology for future research. *Journal of Management, 31*(6), 988–1005.

Guled, A. (2019). Islamic extremist attack on Somali hotel leaves 26 dead. *AP News*, https://apnews.com/8f881d89ea05421e92fff3ea5f857088.

Harrington, K., & O'Connor, J. (2009). How Cisco succeeds. *Supply Chain Management Review, 13*(5), 10–17.

Hartley, R. (1993). *Business ethics: Violations of the public trust.* New York: John Wiley.

Hermann, M., & Dayton, B. (2009). Transboundary Crises through the Eyes of Policymakers: Sense Making and Crisis Management. *Journal of Contingencies and Crisis Management, 17*(4), 233-241.

Hoang, D., & Jones, B. (2012). Why do corporate codes of conduct fail? Women workers and clothing supply chains in Vietnam. *Global Social Policy, 12*(1), 67-85.

Hopkins, A. (2001). Was Three Mile Island a "normal accident"? *Journal of Contingencies and Crisis Management, 9*(2), 65–72.

Hunter, M., Wassenhove, L., & Besiou, M. (2016). The new rules for crisis management. *MIT Sloan Management Review, 57*(4), 71-78.

Hutchins, R. (2015, September 21). Homebound manufacturing. *The Journal of Commerce,* 14A-16A.

Institute for Crisis Management (ICM) (2019). *ICM Annual Crisis Report*. Retrieved September 9, 2019, from https://crisisconsultant.com/wp-content/uploads/2019/05/ICM-Annual-Crisis-Report-for-2018_Issued-30-May-2019.pdf.

International Labor Organization, (2014, May). Forced labor, modern slavery, and human trafficking Retrieved September 10, 2019, from https://www.ilo.org/global/topics/forced-labour/lang--en/index.htm.

Janis, I. (1982). *Groupthink: Psychological studies of policy decisions and fiascoes.* Boston: Houghton Mifflin.

Kaplan, S. (2017, Winter). Walmart's journey to sustainability. *Rotman Magazine*, 26-31.

Karnini, N. (2018, September 29). Indonesian tsunami and quake devastate coast. *USA Today*. Retrieved July 28, 2019, from https://www.usatoday.com/story/news/2018/09/29/indonesian-quake-and-tsunami-devastates-coast-killing-least-384/1470177002/.

Kelly, S. (2012). Succumbing to shrimp. *The Environmental Magazine, 23*(3), 32-33.

Kennel, P. (1996, August 21). The sweatshop dilemma. *The Christian Science Monitor, 88*(187). Retrieved July 25, 2019, from https://www.csmonitor.com/1996/0821/082196.opin.opin.2.html

Lagadec, P. (2009). A new cosmology of risks and crises: Time for a radical shift in paradigm and practice. *Review of Policy Research, 26*(4), 473–486.

LeBaron, G. (2014a). Reconceptualizing debt bondage: Debt as a class-based form of labor discipline. *Critical Sociology, 40*(5), 763-780.

LeBaron, G. (2014b). Subcontracting is not illegal, but is it ethical? Business ethics, forced labor, and economic success. *Brown Journal of World Affairs, 20*(11), 237-249.

Lee, G., & Thurman, E. (2008). Southeast retail deals with gas shortage. *Women's Wear Daily, 196*(68), p. 17.

Mallaby, S. (2005, November 29). Walmart: A progressive dream company, really. *Fayetteville Observer,* p. 11A.

Markham, D. (2011). Reshoring initiative challenges assumptions about overseas cost advantages. *Metal Center News, 51*(13), 4–6.

Marszalek, D. (2016). A year after shootings, WDBJ alum says local TV needs to toughen up. *Broadcasting & Cable, 146*(29), 25.

Morillo, J., McNally, C., & Block, W. (2015). The real Walmart. *Business and Society Review, 120*(3), 385-408.

Morris, L. (2014). Three steps to safety: Developing procedures for active shooters. *Journal for Business Continuity and Emergency Planning, 7*(3), 238-244.

Moser, H., & Kelley, M. (2016). Reshoring creates opportunities for US fastener makers, distributors, and users. *American Fastener Journal, 32*(5), 44-47.

Nassauer, S. & Rana, P. (2016, August 25). Are your sheets 'Egyptian cotton'? *Wall Street Journal*, pp. B1, B2.

Neumayer, E. & Plümper, T. (2016). Spatial spill-overs from terrorism on tourism: Western victims in Islamic destination countries. *Public Choice, 169*, 195-206.

Nickerson, R. (2011). Roles of human factors and ergonomics in meeting the challenge of terrorism. *American Psychologist, 66*(6), 555–566.

O'Leary-Kelly, A., Griffin, R., & Glew, D. (1996). Organization-motivated aggression: A research framework. *Academy of Management Review, 21*(1), 225–253.

Owen, C. (2016). New thinking and making the case for reshoring. *Product Design & Development*, 71(8), 6-7.

Parnell, J.A. (2020). *Strategic Management: Theory and Practice (6th edition)*. Solon, OH: Academic Media Solutions.

Parnell, J., Spillan, J., & Lester, D. (2010). Crisis aversion and sustainable strategic management (SSM) in emerging economies. *International Journal of Sustainable Strategic Management, 2*(1), 41–59.

Pedahzur, A., Eubank, W., & Weinberg, L. (2002). The war on terrorism and the decline of terrorist group formation: A research note. *Terrorism and Political Violence, 14*(3), 141–147.

Perliger, A., Pedahzur, A., & Zalmanovitch, Y. (2005). The defensive dimension of the battle against terrorism: An analysis of management of terror incidents in Jerusalem. *Journal of Contingencies and Crisis Management, 13*(2), 79–91.

Perrow, C. (1999). *Normal accidents: Living with high risk technologies.* Princeton, NJ: Princeton University Press.

Powell, B. (2015, December 18). Terror's new face. *Newsweek*, 165(22), 12-15.

Powell, B. (2016, October 21). The new ISIS crisis. *Newsweek*, 167(15), 26-33.

Quinn, B. (2000). *How Walmart is destroying America.* Berkeley, CA: Ten Speed Press.

Rash, W. (2016, December 7). Fake news brings life-threatening consequences in national capital. *eWeek.* Retrieved January 20, 2016, from http://www.eweek.com/cloud/fake-news-brings-life-threatening-consequences-in-national-capital.html

Rice, J., & Caniato, F. (2003). Building a secure and resilient supply network. *Supply Chain Management Review, 7*(5), 22–30.

Robinson, S., & O'Leary-Kelly, A. (1998). Monkey see, monkey do: The influence of work groups on the antisocial behavior of employees. *Academy of Management Journal, 41*(6), 658–672.

Sanchez, R. & Chavez N. (2018, September 15). 'It looked like Armageddon': Massachusetts governor declares state of emergency after deadly blasts, *CNN.* Retrieved July 22, 2019, from https://www.cnn.com/2018/09/14/us/massachusetts-explosions-fires/index.html

Schaefer, N. (2004). Y2K as an endtime sign: Apocalypticism in America at the fin-de-millennium. *Journal of Popular Culture, 38*(1), 82–105.

Seidenberg, S. (2014, July). New ABA principles provide starting point for businesses to eliminate forced and child labor. *ABA Journal.* Retrieved July 22, 2019, from http://www.abajournal.com/magazine/article/new_aba_principles_provide_starting_point_for_businesses_to_eliminate_force

Sethi, S., & Steidlmeier, P. (1997). *Up against the wall: Case in business and society* (6th ed.). Upper Saddle River, NJ: Prentice Hall.

Shappell, B. (2012). Falling Sun. *Business Credit, 114*(3), 10–12.

Shell, E. (2009). *Cheap: The High Cost of Discount Culture.* New York, NY: Penguin.

Simpson, C. (2013, November 7). An iPhone tester caught in Apple's supply chain. *Bloomberg Business.* Retrieved June 24, 2015, from http://www.bloomberg.com/bw/articles/2013-11-07/an-iphone-tester-caught-in-apples-supply-chain

Snook, S., & Connor, J. (2005). The price of progress: Structurally induced inaction. In W. H. Starbuck & M. Farjoun (Eds.), *Organization at the Limit* (pp. 178–201). Oxford, UK: Blackwell.

Solomon, J., & Kranhold, K. (2005, March 23). In India's outsourcing boom, GE played a starring role. *Wall Street Journal,* pp. A1, A12.

Spillan, J. E., Parnell, J. A., & de Mayoro, C. A. (2011). Exploring crisis readiness in Peru. *Journal of International Business and Economy, 12*(1), 57–83.

Srivastava, S. (2014, January 10). India is the place for legal outsourcing: Pangea3 MD. *Forbes India.* Retrieved July 5, 2017, from http://www.forbesindia.com/article/close-range/india-is-the-place-for-legal-outsourcing-pangea3-md/36877/1

Stallard, M. (1999*). Y2K: Mass hysteria or prophetic event?* Faculty Forum, Baptist Bible Seminary, Clarks Summit, PA. Retrieved December 23, 2016, from http://our-hope.org/blog/wp-content/uploads/2009/10/y2k.pdf

Stead, W., & Stead, J. (2004). *Sustainable strategic management.* Armonk, NY: ME Sharpe.

Stein, N. (2003, January 20). No way-out competition to make products for Western companies has revived an old form of abuse: Debt bondage. *Fortune, 147*(1), 102-108.

Stoffers, C. (2017, January 9). Fake news fooling millions! *The New York Times,* pp. 6-7.

The 9-11 Commission. (2004). *The 9-11 Commission report: Final report of the National Commission on Terrorist Attacks Upon the United States.* Washington, DC: Government Printing Office.

The Economist, (2015, March 14). Slavery and seafood: Here be monsters. Retrieved June 19, 2015, from http://www.economist.com/news/international/21646200-thailands-fishing-industry-rife-trafficking-and-abuse-here-be-monsters

Turner, B. (1978). *Man-made disasters.* London: Wykeham.

Wachtendorf, T. (2009). Trans-system social ruptures: Exploring issues of vulnerability and resiliency. *Review of Public Research, 26*(4), 379–393.

Walt, V. (2016, May 30). Stubborn frictions could undermine Europe's fight against Terror. *Time*, 187(20), 9-10.

Wernick, D., & Von Glinow, M. (2012). Reflections on the evolving terrorist threat to luxury hotels: A case study on Marriott International. *Thunderbird International Business Review, 54*(5), 729-746.

York, B. (2005, November 23). Panic in a small town. *National Review* (online). Retrieved December 27, 2016, from http://www.nationalreview.com/article/216070/panic-small-town-byron-york

Zsidisin, G., Meinyk, S. & Ragatz, G. (2005). An institutional theory perspective of business continuity planning for purchasing and supply management. *International Journal of Production Research, 43*(16), 3401–3420.

Zsidisin, G., Ragatz, G., & Meinyk, S. (2005, March). The dark side of supply chain management. *Supply Chain Management Review,* 46–52.

Chapter 3: Sources of Organizational Crises

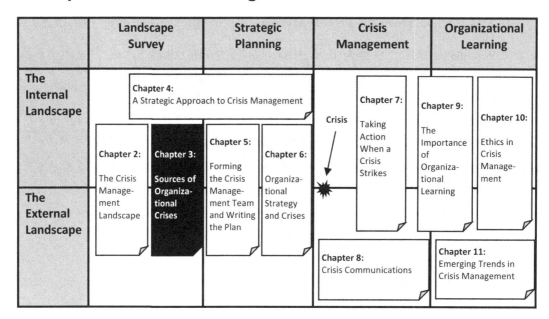

Learning Objectives

After reading this chapter, each student should be able to:

1. Explain how political-legal forces in the macroenvironment can facilitate organizational crises.
2. Explain how economic forces in the macroenvironment can facilitate organizational crises.
3. Explain how social forces in the macroenvironment can facilitate organizational crises.
4. Explain how the various technological forces in the macroenvironment can facilitate organizational crises.
5. Discuss how the five stages of the industry life cycle can influence different types of organizational crises.
6. Discuss how the five stages of the organizational life cycle can breed various types of crises.

Opening Chapter Case: Volkswagen - Polluting the Air with Clean Emission Cars – Part 1

On September 18, 2015, the United States Environmental Protection Agency (EPA) announced that Volkswagen (VW) had violated air standards by installing software on certain diesel engine cars that would deceive emissions testing (Terry-Armstrong, 2016). The crisis that followed illustrates that efforts to mislead the public often unravel over time. As Hartley (1993) noted in his analysis of business ethics violations – "unethical and illegal actions do not go undetected forever" (p. 65). The case is extraordinary because the Volkswagen strategy appears to have been based in part on its ability to "fool" vehicle emissions testing equipment and sell cars that exceeded the required emissions standards by 10 to 40 times (Patra, 2016; Shepardson, 2015). The remainder of this section provides a contextual discussion and analysis of the crisis.

Volkswagen's Market Strategy

The Volkswagen Group is the largest carmaker in Europe and consists of the following brands:

- Audi - premium cars (Germany)
- Bentley – luxury cars (United Kingdom)
- Bugatti – sports cars (France)
- Ducati - sport motorcycles (Italy)
- Lamborghini – sports cars (Italy)
- MAN – trucks and busses (Germany)
- Porsche – sports cars (Germany)
- Scania – trucks and busses (Sweden)
- SEAT – cars (Spain)
- SKODA – cars (Czech Republic)
- Volkswagen – cars (Germany)
- Volkswagen Commercial Vehicles – vans and small trucks (Germany)

Penetrating the US market has always been challenging for Volkswagen because of the wide range of customer tastes and stringent governmental emissions requirements. In addition, Volkswagen was known for diesel-powered vehicles, while the US was dominated by gasoline-powered automobiles. Volkswagen addressed this challenge by emphasizing the environmental appeal of its clean diesel engines.

The seeds of the crisis can be traced to 2007 when then CEO Martin Winterkorn pushed for aggressive growth to outpace General Motors and Toyota as the world's leading automaker by 2018 (Rothfeder, 2017). VW would accomplish this in part by selling clean-diesel automobiles that polluted less and achieved 30% better fuel economy (Tuttle, 2015). The strategy seemed to be working until an EPA official decided to test the emissions standards of the clean diesel cars. The EPA had not uncovered any problems with Volkswagen's clean diesel cars in seven years of testing, but a group of researchers working at West Virginia University discovered something quite different (Jung & Park, 2016).

A Noxious Discovery

John German, a senior fellow with the International Council on Clean Transportation, was testing so-called clean diesel cars to demonstrate that they are indeed clean (Krishner & Jordans, 2015). German had arranged to use West Virginia University equipment because it enabled testing on a vehicle as driven under normal driving conditions. Dynameters—used at many government inspection stations—only test vehicles on a set of rollers that simulate different speeds while the vehicle is stationary.

In May 2014, German and his colleagues tested three vehicles, a 2012 VW Jetta, a 2013 VW Passat, and a BMW X5. All three vehicles used diesel fuel, so German assumed they would perform well. The BMW met his expectations, but the levels of nitrogen oxide emissions from the VW models exceeded EPA limits. He repeated the two procedures twice with identical outcomes (Shepardson, 2015). The results were profound; German and his colleagues had just discovered that the typical driving of two VW clean-diesel vehicles not only exceeded government regulations but did so on a grand scale (Krishner & Jordans, 2015).

John German submitted his report to the EPA in May 2014. He also sent a copy to Volkswagen, thinking that the company might be able to identify the technical problem that explained the results. He did not suggest deception as a possibility. Ironically, neither the EPA nor VW responded to German about the report (Patra, 2016). However, in December 2014, an EPA report revealed that VW had decided to recall 500,000 cars in the US to reinstall software that would correct the problem, although the cause was not mentioned. VW entered crisis mode in 2014, and the situation worsened in 2015.

Case Discussion Questions

1. What *political factors* in both the United States and Europe influenced the Volkswagen crisis?
2. What *economic factors* impacted this case?
3. What *social factors* affected the automotive industry during the early 2010s? Consider how consumers in different countries view vehicles as a means of transportation, status symbols, or both.

4. What *technological factors* surfaced in this case?

Introduction

Crises such as the one at Volkswagen emanate from various sources; they are not merely random events. Understanding how these sources impact an organization can help its managers minimize the effects of subsequent crises or avoid them altogether. Strategists often view the firm's external environment regarding political-legal, economic, social, and technological forces. This inquiry is often called a **PEST analysis**. These four categories not only help managers craft strategies for their organizations, but they also lay the groundwork for examining the external landscape from a crisis perspective. In this chapter, we discuss how these forces are linked to crises in organizations. We also review the industry and organizational life cycles and their applicability to effective crisis management.

Crises and the External Environment

Organizations exist within a complex network of political-legal, economic, social, and technological forces, as depicted in Figure 3.1. Together, these elements make up the organization's external environment, also called the **macroenvironment**. Changes in any of these areas can increase the likelihood of a crisis.

Some crises are difficult to categorize because they are rooted in more than one area of the macroenvironment. The COVID-19 pandemic is a prime example. It has political-legal (e.g., workplace and product liability), economic (e.g., widespread unemployment), social (e.g., the use of facemasks and social distancing to slow the spread), and technological (e.g., the development of treatments and vaccines) dimensions. However, we address each force individually to underscore how different environmental influences can contribute to crisis development in different ways.

Political-Legal Forces

Political-legal forces include the outcomes of government officials' decisions, the impacts of existing and new legislation, and judicial court decisions, as well as the decisions rendered by various regulatory commissions and agencies at all levels of government. As with the other forces, political-legal factors can affect different firms in the same industry in different ways.

Politically Motivated Events

The September 11, 2001, terrorist attacks sparked political decisions in the United States that created both crises and opportunities. Following the sharp decline in domestic air travel, airlines on the verge of bankruptcy campaigned for and received $15 billion in government support in 2002 and an additional $2.9 billion in 2003 (Sevastopulo, 2003). The subsequent war in Iraq created crises for organizations as well, especially those with strong global ties. For example, during the early part of the military conflict, when Allied forces were marching toward Baghdad, many firms modified their advertising campaigns, fearing that their television promotions might be considered insensitive if aired alongside breaking coverage of the war. This move was intended to avoid a potential public relations crisis. At the same time, other firms viewed the war as an opportunity for revenue growth. They began planning for Iraq's future needs in the areas of cell phones, refrigerators, and automobiles. After Saddam Hussein's regime was ousted in mid-2003, American firms competed vigorously for lucrative reconstruction contracts. Overall, the war created crises for some firms but opportunities for others (Cummins, 2003; King, 2003; Trachtenberg & Steinberg, 2003).

Figure 3.1 Crises and the External Landscape

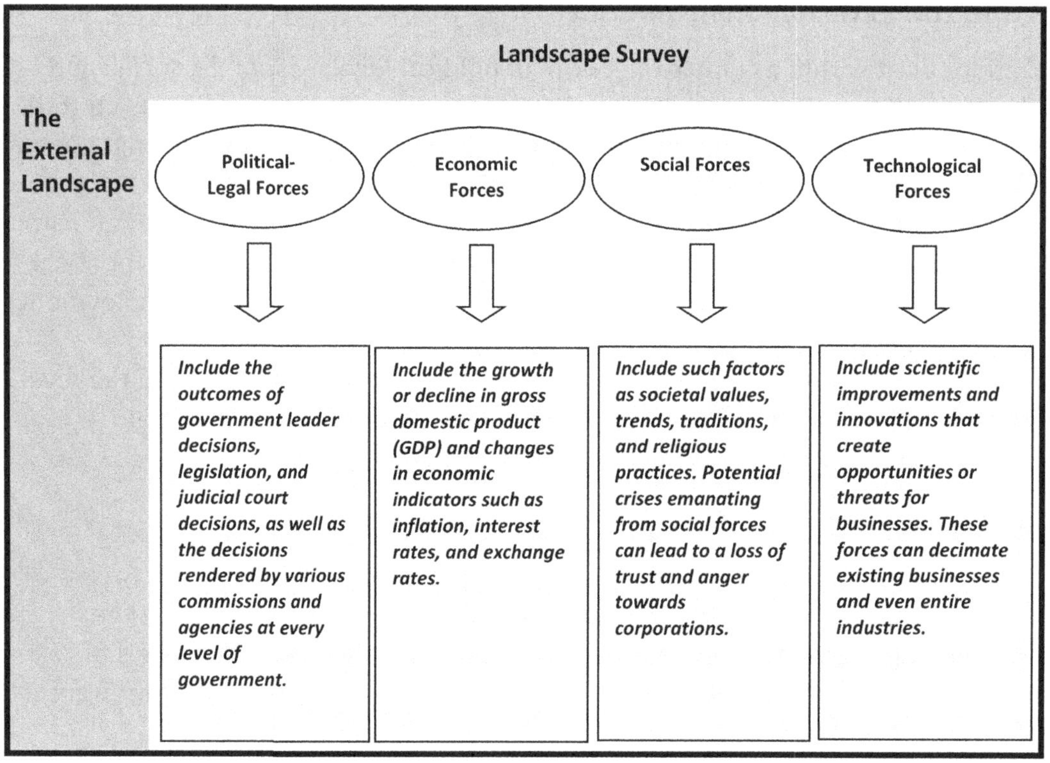

More recently, the wave of refugees to the European Union, the United States, and Canada has provoked an assortment of responses ranging from those welcoming the newcomers to those seeking immediate deportation. These debates undoubtedly influenced Britain's decision to leave the European Union (EU). Additionally, Donald Trump's election as US president and countless other political battles in Europe and North America have influenced their respective political environments. All sides raise legitimate concerns, making it difficult for organizations to respond accordingly. For some, the refugees are key customers and a source of labor (Damoc, 2016).

Laws and Regulations

Most societies have regulations that affect business operations. Table 3.1 summarizes some of the significant legislation in the United States over the past century. Although the details surrounding major legislation are always complicated, most of these laws can be viewed as responses to an industry or organizational crisis that already existed (Hartley, 1993). For example, the **Foreign Corrupt Practices Act** (FCPA) prohibits US firms from paying bribes to foreign officials to advance their business interests. The FCPA was passed in response to the infamous Lockheed bribery case. In this incident, Lockheed paid $12.5 million in bribes and other commissions to secure a sale of $430 million in commercial aircraft to All-Nippon Airways in Japan (Carroll & Buchholtz, 2003). At the time, Lockheed argued that paying bribes was an accepted way of doing business in Japan.

Organizations are often affected by legislation and other political events specific to their lines of business. For example, changing legislation that concerns food safety and health can lead to organizational crises. Consider the appearance of variant Creutzfeldt-Jakob disease (vCJD), better known as **Mad Cow Disease**, a rare disorder of the brain transmitted through tainted meat. When it began to surface in the United Kingdom in 1996, most European nations responded by banning British beef. Firms could not ensure safety, and financial losses were staggering (Higgins, 2001). Although measures were implemented to stop the spread of the disease, collateral damage affected other stakeholders in the beef and food-related industries. For example, the economic impact in Canada was around $10 billion in lost trade and compensation (Fortier, 2008). As an example, a single diseased cow in northern Alberta in 2003 led to a widespread closing of the borders, with thousands of cattle slaughtered and sales of Canadian beef falling to crisis levels, from $1.10 per pound to 30 cents (Fortier, 2008). While the disease can be considered a crisis, the reaction to it created a secondary crisis.

More recently, the employment of slavery has been detected in some supply chains globally, particularly in less developed countries. Recent legislation in both the US and the UK addresses this problem. The California Transparency in Supply Chains Act (2010) requires companies conducting business in California with revenues of $100 million or more to explain on their websites their actions to keep slavery out of their supply chains. (Ma, Lee, & Goerlitz, 2015).

Table 3.1 Examples of US Legislation and Preceding Crises

Legislation	Purpose	Crises Preceding the Law
Title VII of the Civil Rights Acts (1964)	Prohibits discrimination against protected employment groups based on age, religion, race, and gender.	Numerous cases involving discrimination against specific groups.
Occupational Safety & Health Act (1970)	Requires employers to provide a hazard-free working environment.	A response to various workplace safety issues that had occurred in the previous decades.
Federal Mine Safety & Health Act (1977)	Seeks to ensure a safe working environment for miners.	Accidents emanating from the hazardous working environment that miners face.
Foreign Corrupt Practices Act (1978)	Outlaws direct payoffs and bribes to foreign governments or business officials.	A response to the early 1970s Lockheed bribery incident, in which the company paid bribes to secure contracts to sell aircraft to All-Nippon Airways, a Japanese airline.
Oil Pollution Act (1990)	Mandates that oil storage facilities and vessels provide a detailed plan of how they will respond to a massive oil spill.	A response to the 1989 *Exxon Valdez* oil spill in Prince William Sound, off the coast of Alaska.
Aviation & Transportation Security Act (2001)	Created the Transportation Security Administration to help ensure the safety of the nation's air travel system.	A response to the terrorist attacks on the World Trade Center in New York City on September 11, 2001.
Sarbanes-Oxley Act (2002)	Makes businesses more accountable by requiring them to adhere to higher standards of financial disclosure.	A response to numerous corporate scandals involving inappropriate bookkeeping practices, including the most famous one, the Enron Corporation.
CAN SPAM Act (2003)	The Controlling the Assault of Non-Solicited Pornography and Marketing Act prescribes regulations for email spammers.	A response to the proliferation of unwanted email that has glutted cyberspace.
Food Allergen Labeling & Consumer Protection Act of 2004 (FALCPA)	Requires the labeling of known allergens on food labels.	Various cases concerning illness or death from ingesting a food substance.
Patient Protection & Affordable Care Act (2010)	Increases regulation of health care providers and insurance companies to lower costs and expand coverage; requires employers with 50 or more full-time equivalent (FTE) employees to provide health insurance or pay a tax penalty.	Firms with more than 50 FTE employees that were not already providing insurance experienced a significant increase in costs.

Similarly, the UK's Modern Slavery Act of 2015 requires companies to produce a slavery and human trafficking statement detailing their efforts to keep these activities out of their supply chains and other parts of the business (Whincup, Garbett, & McNicholas, 2016). Both laws require companies to state if they are NOT doing anything to curtail slavery in their supply chains. This legislation requires disclosure, not any anti-

slavery action per se. Hence, the motivation for companies to act against slavery is based on public perception.

In the US, the election of President Donald Trump sparked momentum to repeal the controversial **Affordable Care Act**. This legislation required smaller businesses to assume more costs for employee healthcare and included an individual mandate requiring US adults to obtain insurance or pay a tax penalty. The individual mandate was revoked in 2018, but the employer mandate requiring employers with 50 or more full-time equivalent (FTE) employees to provide health insurance was not.

Economic Forces

Economic forces can also be a source of organizational crises. Growth or decline in gross domestic product (GDP) and shifts in economic indicators such as inflation, interest rates, and exchange rates can be problematic for many companies. Other factors, such as overexpansion of credit and surges in energy prices and health care costs, can also create challenges for firms in many industries.

The Overexpansion of Credit

Overexpansion of credit, particularly in the subprime mortgage industry, created an economic crisis in the United States that had a ripple effect worldwide. Extending credit can have its advantages when the debt is paid back promptly. However, when excessive debt causes business and consumer spending to decrease, the economy slows. To offset this problem, the Federal Reserve and other central banks often extend additional credit, initiating a continuous cycle of debt and spending. Hence, expanding credit can create what appears to be economic growth in the short term, as well as a "bubble" and economic stagnation in the long term (Kline, 2010). In other words, when artificially stimulated "demand" is met, an economic slowdown follows. Economists define a **recession** as two consecutive quarters of declines in GDP. Recessions can create crises for many organizations because spending decreases, and budget cuts typically follow. The ripple effect produced by recessions can create even more crises. Sometimes these cutbacks occur in vulnerable areas, such as safety and equipment overhaul. When safety is compromised, or equipment is not repaired or replaced promptly, accidents will be the result.

Much can be gleaned about personal consumption from observing the link between consumerism and credit. When consumers do not have the financial means to purchase what they desire, they often attempt to buy it on credit. Consumers with poor or marginal credit histories represent substantial payback risks, especially during economic declines. Before the financial crisis of 2008, such consumers were granted mortgages for relatively expensive homes, often with escalating interest rates, balloon payments, and other features that built the groundwork for the crisis.

An interesting side note on the credit discussion is the positive thinking industry's relationship to the economic crisis. The industry includes motivational speakers, self-help books, and an endless array of online materials that compel individuals to view themselves and their abilities more confidently. This increased sense of self may have contributed to an increased desire for material goods, amplifying a cycle of consumerism that is not based on adequate financial resources. Instead, individuals spend today and hope to pay later. Ehrenreich (2009) surmised this type of irrational exuberance contributed to the 2008 economic crisis.

Hence, the positive thinking movement offers some insight into the consumer end of the mortgage problem during the 2007 recession. Many consumers believed they were entitled to own homes beyond their economic means. The Federal Reserve, government policy promoting homeownership, and entities like Fannie Mae and Freddie Mac flooded the market with excessive funds at artificially low interest rates. Likewise, the mortgage companies that promoted these loans were overly optimistic as well. The result was not only a crisis for the mortgage companies and the recipients of their loans but a worldwide recession that jolted service and manufacturing industries alike.

The Volatility of Oil Prices

Rising oil prices can drain anticipated profits by raising operating costs. During the recovery from the worldwide recession in 2008, oil prices declined from $145 per barrel in 2008 to only $27 in early 2016 (Hartmann & Sam, 2016). During the COVID-19 pandemic in 2020, oil prices were even negative for a brief period due to plummeting demand and limited storage capabilities. Low oil prices help companies and consumers by reducing factories' operating costs and reducing the price of fuel. This combination often spurs growth, but not in all industries (Milmo, 2016). "A good economy usually benefits most, but not all firms and consumers.

For strategists and crisis managers, two scenarios exist regarding ongoing lower oil prices. Some economists maintain the oil industry naturally cycles, and when prices are low, they will eventually rise, and vice versa. Some argue that the cycle moves about every 8 to 10 years (Hardy, 2015). Others view prices between $50 and $60 per barrel as a "new normal" supported by recent advances in technology (Hartmann & Sam, 2016), although prices remained well below this range during the COVID-19 pandemic. This debate can be informed by a real-time check of global oil prices (https://oilprice.com/).

The lower per-barrel prices can potentially raise environmental costs. Specifically, declines in oil prices are linked to increases in shale oil production; US oil production increased from 4.7 million barrels in 2008 to 9.0 million barrels in 2015 (Kim, 2015). Firms employ recent technology known as hydraulic fracturing ("fracking") to access oil hidden in shale layers. Some environmentalists are concerned about groundwater integrity around fracking sites and have lobbied successfully to prohibit fracking in France, the state of New York, and parts of Canada (Stephen, 2015).

Fracking has contributed to lower oil prices because it enables greater production in the US and Canada, thereby reducing dependence on oil from other parts of the world. Organization of Petroleum Exporting Countries (OPEC) members have been hurt by fracking and have sought to increase revenues by increasing output, leading to further price declines (Kehoe, 2016).

Some analysts fear that lower oil prices may reduce research on alternative energy. This explanation is plausible, but investments into solar, electric, wind, and other energy sources are likely to continue because their long-term payouts could be sizeable. The development of electric vehicles by Tesla and other manufacturers and more fuel-efficient aircraft such as the Boeing 787 Dreamliner continues (Kehoe, 2016). Moreover, global climate change initiatives and government subsidies also reward firms whose products do not rely on fossil fuels. This turbulence in the economy has challenged managers to remain focused on how these issues will affect their firms. Having strategic plans ready to address any negative effect is imperative.

Social Forces

Social forces can trigger crises and include such factors as societal values, trends, traditions, and religious practices. Societal values are beliefs that most citizens hold in high esteem. In the United States, prominent values include individual freedom, fairness, concern for the environment, diversity, consumer rights, and opportunity (Parnell, 2020). Potential crises emanating from social forces can lead to a loss of trust and anger toward corporations, and various forms of social disapproval, including boycotts, harmful websites, and bad publicity. When these negative feelings are expressed through social media, the message can spread in a matter of hours. Such feelings can become the breeding ground for crises in organizations, as was experienced in the 2020 racial unrest following the death of George Floyd in Minneapolis.

Distrust of Corporate America

One social force of keen interest is the anti-corporate sentiment shared by many consumers. Early manifestations of corporate distrust occurred when ordinary people believe unfounded rumors. An interesting example involved Procter & Gamble in the early 1980s. The rumor concerned the widespread belief that its corporate logo was a satanic symbol, and its chief executive officer (CEO) was a devil worshiper, a claim the CEO allegedly made on the *Merv Griffin* television program (Cato, 1982). What followed was the distribution of literature urging consumers to boycott Procter & Gamble. Although the rumor was not true, the company spent heavily to stop those who were spreading the literature, mostly photocopied flyers. In the early 1990s, another dark rumor surfaced, claiming that the popular Cabbage Patch Dolls were possessed by the devil (Steele, Smith, & McBroom, 1999). This case shows how unsubstantiated and even bizarre communications can create mistrust among stakeholders.

While most positive actions of firms are largely unreported, executives do not always live up to society's ethical standards. Consider the US coal mining industry's ongoing reputation for management-labor strife. While the safety record for coal mining is historically abysmal, fatalities have declined markedly during the past century; the US Department of Labor provides current statistics (US Department of Labor, 2015). Nonetheless, 2010 was not a good year for the industry. In one notable case, an April 5 methane explosion at the then, Massey Energy Upper Big Branch coal mine near Beckley, West Virginia, killed 29 miners. An independent investigation found that the explosion was preventable had Massey Energy followed basic safety standards of the mining industry ("WV Governor's report," 2011).

This accident demonstrates that even in hazardous industries like coal mining, some firms are more effective at crisis prevention and management than others. Indeed, safety problems and public distrust of Massey Energy is not a recent occurrence. From 2005 to May 2010, the Mine Safety and Health Administration (MSHA) issued Massey 1,342 safety violations totaling $1.89 million in fines. Rather than addressing the safety violations, Massey chose to contest these citations in court by challenging the regulations (Barrett, 2011; Ceniceros, 2011; Smith, 2010).

Massey's former CEO, Don Blankenship, was widely criticized for his role in promoting production at the expense of worker safety. A *Rolling Stone* feature article on Blankenship labeled him "The Dark Lord of Coal Country" (Goodell, 2010). However, it was the explosion at the Upper Big Branch mine that sealed his fate. Blankenship was found guilty of conspiracy to violate federal mine safety violations and served a year in prison. During the trial, evidence convinced the jury that Blankenship had led his company to use safety violations strategically to reduce costs. Practices included communicating with miners underground when safety inspectors were nearby, falsifying coal dust samples, and not following safety regulations for ventilation procedures (Jensen, 2015). Although Blankenship never explicitly told his managers to violate mine safety standards, his micromanaging style and strong influence encouraged managers to interpret policy and meet production goals, regardless of the costs. Indeed, at Upper Big Branch, three other managers also served time in prison:

- David Hughart, the former president of the Green Valley Coal Group, a Massey subsidiary, received a 42-month sentence for conspiring to violate mine health and safety laws and impeding mine safety inspectors. Specifically, Hughart was part of a conspiracy to pre-notify lower-level supervisors working in the mines when mine safety inspectors were on the premises (Lannom, 2013).
- Hughie Stover, the former security director at the Upper Big Branch mine received a three-year sentence for lying to federal prosecutors and destroying thousands of pages of documents related to the accident (Murphy, 2015).
- Gary May, a former Upper Big Branch mine superintendent, was sentenced to 21 months in prison for violating mine safety regulations (Jensen, 2015).

The *Occupy Wall Street* movement launched in 2011, is another example of corporate distrust. This movement, which involved the takeover of Manhattan's Zuccotti Park by live-in protestors, was unique because it was framed as a battle between the middle class and the super-rich. On the political left, the movement was seen more deeply as a reaction to income inequality in the US (Penny, 2016) and that 1% of the richest Americans are to blame. Labor activist Amy Dean (2012) saw it as an opportunity for union expansion. Critics on the political right noted that the wealthiest 1% pay substantial taxes and create millions of jobs through entrepreneurial ventures (Easton, 2012) and should not be vilified. Many Americans had mixed views or were uncertain how to interpret the movement as they watched protestors occupy Zuccotti Park for several months before being evicted by police.

Preoccupation with "the Bargain"

The distrust of corporate America also extends to other industries like discount retail, where a hefty premium is placed on low prices. Some Americans believe workers in this industry are underpaid and treated unfairly (Ehrenreich, 2001). To sell goods at low prices, big-box retailers must control costs. Keeping labor costs low is a necessity, and employees are offered limited benefits (Shell, 2009).

Americans' preoccupation with the bargain extends beyond price, as consumer pressures can prompt retailers to sacrifice quality. Many appliances and electronics are built at rock-bottom costs, and consumers often discard them after a short time and purchase a low-price replacement. The craftsmanship and quality once valued in the United States—when consumers were willing to pay more for higher-quality goods— seems to have been replaced with a broad preference for lower quality products at lower prices (Crawford, 2009).

The societal emphasis on bargains has contributed to a loss of dignity of rank-and-file workers in retail establishments, as well as a decline in the quality of finished goods. However, this consumer shift is also linked to another broad crisis-related trend—the movement of manufacturing jobs overseas. While "corporate greed" is often blamed for the displacement of jobs, consumer preferences for low prices ultimately drive corporate behavior (Fishman, 2006; Shell, 2009). Large firms like Amazon and Walmart are often blamed for the problem as well. The reduction in wages at retailers like Walmart is linked to both automation and lower wages in other nations and creates an ongoing challenge for displaced workers.

Racial Equality

from the United States has made substantial progress in recent decades in the battle against racial discrimination. Organizations have contributed by ensuring access to customers and employees, regardless of race or ethnicity. The Denny's restaurant discrimination case is an example of how an incident of racism involving a large company can create a strong public backlash. The event began in 1993 when a waitress at an Annapolis, Maryland, restaurant purportedly refused to serve six African American Secret Service agents (Chin et al., 1993). The result was a significant media frenzy that eventually became a prominent story on the *CBS Evening News.* Because of the crisis, Denny's changed many of its human resource practices.

The appearance of racism, even if not intended, can result in serious public scrutiny. Cracker Barrel, a family-oriented restaurant chain based in Lebanon, Tennessee, found itself in a crisis when Rose Rock, mother of comedian Chris Rock, visited the Murrells Inlet Cracker Barrel (near Myrtle Beach, South Carolina) on May 16, 2006. Ms. Rock and her daughter waited for 30 minutes without service, while white customers were served (Fuller, 2006). The incident eventually led to a news conference, held in the restaurant's parking lot, which included activist Al Sharpton and officials from the restaurant's headquarters. The official statement made by Cracker Barrel was that the incident was a service issue, not a racial issue. Rock and her daughter had been seated but not assigned a server (Fuller, 2006).

On April 12, 2018, Starbucks found itself amidst racial accusations when a manager called the police to remove two black males from its Rittenhouse Square store in Philadelphia. The men were waiting for a friend and had not ordered any merchandise. When they requested to use the restroom, they were denied and asked to leave. Police arrived and arrested the two men, which created a social media frenzy that was critical towards Starbucks and the police. Starbucks CEO Kevin Johnson apologized in public and met with the two men (Barker, 2018). Starbucks later held racial bias training at company stores on May 29, 2018.

Concerns about racial discrimination were reignited in 2020 following the May 25 death of George Floyd in Minneapolis. The ensuing protests and social unrest in many large US cities initially focused on policing, but quickly expanded to include job opportunities for racial minorities and other grievances. Pressed by consumers, many companies like Amazon, Target, and Starbucks responded by making large financial contributions to Black Lives Matter—the political organization underpinning the movement—and other affiliated groups. The violence that accompanied many of the protests created a more urgent crisis for retailers and small businesses whose facilities were looted or destroyed.

Supply Chain Integrity

There is a growing concern over the integrity of supply chains for large multinational corporations (MNCs) that source products to developing nations. One of the first companies to feel the criticism over their supply chain was Nike, when, in the 1990s, sourced its athletic shoes to Asia. Nike quickly became the scapegoat for everything that is wrong with sourcing overseas, namely sweatshops.

The concerns about Nike, Walmart, and other firms can be attributed to national differences in culture, regulations, and economic development. The definition cited in chapter 2—a *hazardous* work environment with *exploitative* business practices—is highly subjective., Paying less than the US minimum wage, or using child labor, does not necessarily mean that a workplace is a sweatshop that exploits workers. Prospective workers in many developing nations line up to apply for jobs in facilities considered by many Westerners to be sweatshops. Without these employment opportunities, some turn to the illicit drug trade or prostitution to survive (Kennel, 1996). It is paramount that Westerners understand this dilemma. The sweatshop debate highlights differing work standards that exist between developed and undeveloped countries.

The modern slavery chronicled in chapter 2 threatens the integrity of the supply chain. A firm purchases food, clothing, or electronics from the Global South becomes part of a larger supply chain. Indeed, when slavery taints one part of the supply chain, it taints the entire chain, and the purchasing firm can quickly become part of the problem.

Most stakeholders, particularly those external to the company, demand that global supply chains be free of exploitative labor. Furthermore, the more a company sources to the Global South, and the deeper the supply chain tiers extend into those developing countries, the more the firm is exposed to risk from exploitative practices. Firms must fundamentally address two key questions: (1) How do we keep production costs low so that consumers will still buy our products? (2) How do we balance that goal by sourcing deep into supply chains in the Global South while maintaining the integrity of our supply chain?

Concern for the Environment and Sustainable Development

Sustainable development, "the development that meets the need of the present world without compromising the ability of future generations to meet their own needs" (Brundtland Commission, 1987, p. 54), has become a prominent concern, particularly in the US and the EU. Pursuing sustainability has both short- and long-term implications. Sustainability efforts can involve an investment of resources, an opportunity cost dilemma that balances profits with funds to protect and sustain resources. Nonetheless, consumers expect firms to engage in sustainable practice; those that are not perceived to do so risk a public relations crisis.

Corporate stakeholders do not always agree on how firms should address environmental issues. A prominent ecological concern for many industries—particularly those involved in heavy manufacturing—is the ongoing debate over **anthropogenic** (human-induced) **climate** change. Proponents contend that carbon dioxide produced by human activity is a primary cause of climate change. If unchecked, these changes will influence life in dramatic ways. Critics of the anthropogenic climate change hypothesis question the causal link between carbon dioxide in the atmosphere and global temperatures. While the two appear to be positively correlated (to the extent that average global temperatures can be measured and computed accurately), shifts in temperature seem to precede changes in carbon dioxide levels, not the other way around. In other words, critics acknowledge that there is climate change, but question whether industry activities are significant drivers. The scientific and political dimensions of this debate are complex and beyond the scope of this book. Nonetheless, firms must evaluate and consider stakeholder expectations.

Some question whether businesses, in general, should be leading the agenda in addressing environmental concerns and the need for sustainable development. Perhaps the government, not business, should be leading these efforts. This viewpoint holds that businesses generally exist to satisfy their stakeholders' needs and are ill-equipped to lead initiatives in climate change (Oreskes & Schendler, 2015). Many companies have taken an active role in the effort. Consider Interface, Inc., a modular carpet manufacturer based in Atlanta, Georgia. Manufacturing carpet creates vast amounts of waste, including carbon dioxide and wastewater filled with chemical dyes. In 1995, Interface's founder, Ray Anderson, set out on a mission to lead the company and the carpet industry in sustainable development and waste reduction. The industry generates a high amount of old carpet that ends up in landfills (Perman, 2014). Interface has used a life cycle assessment process to eliminate waste in its production process. The result has been a smaller environmental footprint, not only for Interface, but the entire carpet manufacturing industry because of competitors that are benchmarking Interface's practices (Hensler, 2014; Perman, 2014). Interface (2019) achieved a net zero footprint in 2019.

Technological Forces

Technological forces include scientific improvements and innovations that create both opportunities and threats for businesses. The rate of technological change varies considerably across industries and can affect a firm's operations, products, and services. In the following discussion, we look at two important technological forces, disruptive innovation, and problems with cyber crises.

Disruptive Innovation

The impact of technology on products and markets can be examined through the lens of **disruptive innovation**, a framework developed by Clayton Christensen (1997). Disruptive innovations cause at least two changes in the marketplace. First, non-consumers—people who did not buy the product previously—begin to purchase the product because it is usually simpler and less expensive. Second, consumers purchase more of the product over time, and eventually, sales of the cheaper version overtake those of more sophisticated rivals (Christensen, 2003). Hence, the market becomes disrupted from its original state. Christensen maintains that the new players in the industry gain market share by enticing non-consumers to try a cheaper, simpler alternative. Hence, the new product is not technologically superior, but it is *good enough* for a new buyer in the market (Markides, 2013).

   Disruptive innovations can create crises on two fronts: (1) incumbent firms may risk going out of business or, at a minimum, ceding a product line, and (2) new products that represent disruptive innovations may shift rapidly to mass production, thus leading to supply chain problems. In the first type of crisis, disruptive innovations can decimate existing businesses and even entire industries by shifting demand from one product to another. Early examples of such changes include the shifts from vacuum tubes to transistors, from steam locomotives to diesel and electric engines, from fountain pens to ballpoints, propeller airplanes to jets, and typewriters to computers (Wright, Kroll, &

Parnell, 1998).

New battery technology has also caused problems in the development of commercial aircraft. In January 2013, about a year after the introduction of the new Boeing 787 Dreamliner, all aircraft were grounded because of two incidents involving the new lithium batteries. On January 7, 2013, a parked Japan Airlines Dreamliner experienced a battery fire at Logan International Airport in Boston. Nine days later, a battery failed on an All Nippon Airways flight, prompting an emergency landing in Kagawa, Japan. As a result, the FAA grounded all Dreamliners until the problem was fixed (Williard, et al., 2013).

One of the biggest disruptors in recent years has been the Apple iPhone. Various versions of the device and its' imitators have revolutionized how messaging, photography, and small computing occur. Apple commonly begins to promote forthcoming products before they are available. Ironically, the introduction of the iPhone 5 demonstrated how forced labor could enter its supply chain (Simpson, 2013). Large numbers of employees were needed to staff its assembly plants in China and Malaysia, where cameras are made. Many of these workers come from other countries, such as Nepal, where employment is scarce. An informal network of recruiters was charging fees, unbeknownst to Apple, for workers to come to plants in Malaysia. Workers were hired but then saddled with high debts that took years to repay. To keep workers from straying too far, plant managers would keep their passports; hence, bonded labor had entered the supply chain, even though Apple does not condone the practice. To Apple's credit, it investigated similar incidents and reimbursed $16.4 million in excessive recruitment fees between 2008 and 2013 (Simpson, 2013).

Problems with Cyber Crises

The effects of the information technology (IT) revolution and the Internet have not always been positive. Information theft through hacking, pirating, and unauthorized entry into company information systems has created cyber crises for companies and organizations across many industries. When company websites are hacked, the credibility of the organization is questioned. Concerned stakeholders want to know why a system was hacked, what information has been compromised, and what can be done to prevent future breaches.

A hacking event can lead to (1) a confidentiality crisis, (2) an integrity crisis, or (3) an availability crisis (Williams, 2016). A **confidentiality crisis** involves the "breach" of a large amount of confidential data. For a hospital, this could involve patient records or financial records of clients. An **integrity crisis** involves the unauthorized alteration of large amounts of data. When data is breached, records can be transferred to another party (e.g., credit card numbers) with an alteration of data. The actual records are changed (e.g., changing a student grade in a university system). In a hospital, this could involve making unauthorized changes to patient records or prescriptions (Williams, 2016). Finally, an **availability crisis** renders large portions of an IT system unavailable to provide service, disabling administrative services such as billing, payroll, or production management functions.

The impact of a hacking event can be massive. The WannaCry ransomware attack affected networks in over 150 countries and could cost up to $4 billion to remedy all the damage (Roberts & Lashinsky, 2017). Regarding data breaches, which result in the selling of customer information, a company can expect to ultimately pay well over $100 for each lost or stolen record (ICM, 2016).

Crises and the Industry Life Cycle

Industry structures and competitors evolve constantly. An industry's developmental stage influences rivalry and potential profitability among competitors (Hofer, 1975; Miles, Snow, & Sharfman, 1993). Likewise, the industry life cycle stage can serve as a breeding ground for certain types of crises. In theory, each industry passes through five distinct phases of an industry's life cycle: introduction, growth, shakeout, maturity, and decline.

Stage 1: Introduction

In a young industry, demand for the industry's outputs is low, while product and service awareness is still developing. Most purchasers are first-time buyers and tend to be relatively affluent, risk-tolerant, and innovative (Parnell, 2021). Process technology is crucial because firms seek to improve their production and distribution efficiencies to introduce new and innovative products. Crises can develop with a new firm whose success is linked to developing technology, or whose innovative product design is particularly vulnerable to imitation or intellectual property theft.

The untested domain of a new industry can also create a potential crisis, as seen in the realm of transportation. As commercial air travel grew during the 1940s and 1950s, a string of aviation accidents also occurred. The causes of these accidents included pilot error, weather conditions, and design flaws in the aircraft. The British-made de Havilland Comet and the US-built Lockheed Electra experienced multiple fatal crashes. Both aircraft suffered from structural defects in their earlier models. The de Havilland Comet was the world's first commercial jet, launching service in 1952. Multiple fatal crashes revealed a structural flaw in the aircraft that eventually led to significant design changes (Winchester, 2010).

Likewise, the Lockheed Electra was one of the first commercial turboprop aircraft. It also had two significant crashes involving the loss of a wing during the 1950s. Lockheed spent $25 million to modify and strengthen the plane's design, which became one of the most successful models in commercial aviation history (Magnuson, 1985). The de Havilland Comet also enjoyed success. Unlike the Electra, which had existing aircraft retrofitted with safety and structural improvements, the Comet was improved by developing later versions from the first-generation aircraft.

Stage 2: Growth

Growth occurs when demand rises. Technological issues are addressed so that production can increase to meet the demand. The industry grows rapidly until market demand approaches saturation. Fewer first-time buyers remain, and most purchases tend to be upgrades or replacements. Many competitors are profitable, but they may be cash poor because available funds are heavily invested in new facilities or technologies (Parnell, 2021).

Some industries have been around for decades but are currently enjoying a new wave of growth. One example is the cruise ship industry, which entered a surge of growth during the 2000s and 2010s as baby boomers and their families seek vacation retreats. However, the industry suffered through several high-profile cruise ship fires, including the 2006 Carnival Cruise incident involving the *Star Princess,* a ship carrying 3,813 passengers and crew when it caught fire while bound for Jamaica. Two people suffered significant smoke inhalation, and one person died of a heart attack (Hayhurst, 2006).

In 2009, Princess Cruises experienced a fire in the engine room on its MS *Royal Princess,* a small ship that was cruising off Port Said, Egypt. Fortunately, there were no fatalities, but the ship had to cancel its remaining cruise time as it was assisted back to port. In this fire, a unique carbon dioxide flooding system was used to extinguish the blaze. Ship firefighting is different in that every gallon of water used to fight a fire must be pumped off the ship lest the vessel sink. Using carbon dioxide has been successful with smaller fires in confined spaces, a situation that exists on ships (Rielage, 2010).

While a fire can bring an immediate threat to passenger and crew safety, the ship must return to port after the fire is extinguished, often in a compromised position. The February 2013 fire and subsequent power loss on the Carnival Triumph illustrates the ordeal passengers must endure. The ship stalled in the Gulf of Mexico and limped back to Mobile, Alabama. During the five-day ordeal, passengers had to use plastic bags in place of bathrooms, and many had to sleep on deck due to the foul smell of sewage (Griffin & Bronstein, 2013). Despite the negative experience of many passengers and the outrage of lawmakers, Carnival responded by upgrading its ships, hiring a new CEO, and adding key personnel to oversee passenger safety and health. Carnival also began a public relations program to upgrade its image and promote the attractiveness of cruising the seas. Carnival refunded 110% of fares to dissatisfied customers and committed to investing $300 million to upgrade fire suppression systems and add generator power. Micky Arison remained as chairman of the board but stepped down as CEO. The crisis management efforts paid off, as Carnival received recognition from YouGov's Brand Index as "the most-improved US brand in consumer perception" (Ruggeri, 2015: 33).

Another incident common to the entire industry is that of passengers who (presumably) fall overboard. According to one report, someone disappears overboard every few weeks on a cruise ship. Analysts assume that most of these incidents are suicides or are associated with alcohol, but murder cannot be ruled out in all instances (Thompson, 2014).

Although rare, a cruise ship accident can constitute a major crisis. A high-profile accident occurred on January 13, 2012, when the cruise ship *Costa Concordia* hit a rock close to shore off Giglio Island, Italy. The accident caused the vessel to take on water and become partially submerged. Eleven of the ship's 4,200 passengers were confirmed dead, and another 24 were missing (Mouawad, 2012). The *Costa Concordia* is owned by Costa Cruises, a part of Carnival Corporation. The accident occurred when the ship deviated from its ordinary course and sailed close to the shore. The reason for the change was unclear, but the captain of the ship, Francesco Schettino, claimed that he was ordered to do so by company officials (Pianigiani, 2012).

The cruise industry encountered a more severe crisis in 2020 when the COVID-19 pandemic prompted a precipitous decline in demand and halted excursions for months while governments struggled to contain the spread of the virus. We do not view this example as movement through the subsequent stages, but rather as a temporary, but serious hiatus.

Stage 3: Shakeout

As growth slows, the industry may enter a shakeout stage. At this point, industry growth is no longer strong enough to support the increasing number of rivals. Competitive crises become common, as firms take advantage of economies of scale. As a result, some of the industry's weaker competitors may not survive (Parnell, 2021).

A shakeout may occur if a marginally performing firm encounters a crisis. Such was the case when the Mexican restaurant chain Chi-Chi's experienced an outbreak of hepatitis A in September 2003. The crisis sickened more than 660 people and caused three deaths. Unfortunately, the chain was already in Chapter 11 bankruptcy at the time (Veil, Liu, Erickson, & Sellnow, 2005). Unfortunately, the impact of the crisis was enough to put the company out of business permanently.

Stage 4: Maturity

Industry maturity occurs when the market demand for the industry's outputs is entirely saturated. Virtually all purchases are upgrades or replacements, and industry growth may be slow if it is growing at all. Industry standards for quality and service have been established, and customer expectations tend to be more consistent than in previous stages (Parnell, 2021). When an industry reaches maturity, its remaining firms tend to be large and are more likely to become targets of interest groups, trade unions, and the like.

Because industry leaders tend to be larger, high-profile companies, they can also be targets for criticism from various stakeholders. A large company may be singled out for questionable practices, while smaller companies in the same industry may go unnoticed. Nestlé was targeted for a massive boycott in the 1970s for marketing infant formula to third world countries. However, smaller companies followed the same marketing strategy but were not attacked. The newly created Environmental Protection Agency targeted Union Carbide in 1970 because of its size and because it polluted the Ohio Valley area in West Virginia (Hartley, 1993).

Stage 5: Decline

Sales decrease when an industry approaches the final stage, decline. This trend often begins when consumers turn to more convenient, safer, or higher-quality offerings from firms in substitute industries. Some firms may divest their business units in this stage, whereas others may pursue a new wave of growth associated with a similar product or service (Parnell, 2021). As companies in these industries weaken, they become more prone to financial crises.

The tobacco industry has experienced its share of crises, including product sales declines in the United States and Europe, as well as aggressive antismoking campaigns and lawsuits. Indeed, this is an industry in decline, at least in the United States. A more recent example is the regional shopping mall industry, which has been declining in the US for two decades. Early indoor mall closings began in Chicago, Dallas, Los Angeles, San Francisco, Milwaukee, and other major cities (Kilborn, 2003). Regional mall shopping has been replaced by one-stop shopping at supercenters and power center retailers that offer one-stop shopping for food and other items (Ryan, 2008). Prices at these outlets are often lower because of reduced overhead costs. The contribution of Amazon and other online retailers to this decline is also difficult to understate. Like tobacco, the reduction in shopping malls seen in the US has not occurred everywhere.

Although retail sites have always been prone to some threat of robbery, some shopping malls have attracted a criminal element. Consider the once-famous Mall of Memphis in Tennessee. The two-level mall featured a larger than the average food court, a five-screen movie theater, an indoor ice-skating rink, and a safe atmosphere. However, the mall became a target for robberies and violent crime in the late 1990s and early 2000s. In one high-profile example, a 71-year-old shop manager was shot in the parking lot during a robbery (Kilborn, 2003). As crime engulfed the mall and the surrounding neighborhood, anchor stores Dillard's and JC Penney departed, triggering an exodus of smaller retailers. The Mall of Memphis closed in December 2003 after 22 years of operation. The facility was a victim of crime, declining neighborhoods, and changing customer shopping habits (Maki, 2006). This mall, along with hundreds of others, closed after many years of successful service. The last years of many of these malls were full of crises, however, culminating in severe security and crime problems.

Crises and the Organizational Life Cycle

While the sources of crisis events can be associated with industry factors, many others are unique. Organization-specific factors may be linked to a firm's stage in the organizational life cycle, the most common description of which is a five-stage model based on previous scholarship (Lester, Parnell, & Carraher, 2003; Miller & Friesen, 1984). The following discussion examines the organizational life cycle as a source for different crisis events.

Stage 1: Existence

Stage 1, also known as the existence or entrepreneurial stage (Quinn & Cameron, 1983), marks the beginning of an organization's development (Churchill & Lewis, 1983). The firm seeks to identify enough customers. Decision-making and ownership are in the hands of one or a few individuals.

Most firms in this stage are small; however, many young organizations are launched with a significant amount of venture capital and may be quite large (Starbuck, 2003). The existence stage is characterized by long hours and diverse responsibilities on the part of the owners and employees. Because enough resources are not yet available to hire staff specialists, employees may have to share responsibilities and even perform duties with which they might lack familiarity.

Sources of crises for organizations in the existence stage are often associated with resources and specialization. A new firm may lack the resources to protect itself from acts such as copyright infringement and may not be able to hire the specialists necessary to perform critical functions. Many organizations seek partnerships with other firms to address this problem. Because employees often perform multiple roles, the potential for mental errors or physical accidents may also be greater during this stage.

When companies are young, the emphasis on formalized employee safety may be lacking. The inexperience and lack of maturity in making decisions can affect the approach to operating a business. For example, Film Recovery Systems, Inc., experienced a crisis early in its history. The company was formed to extract silver from used film. Most of the employees were illegal immigrants of Mexican and Polish heritage who did not speak English well. During the company's first two years, an employee died from what was later determined to be acute cyanide poisoning. The subsequent investigations identified multiple conflicting causes. Although the company provided safety equipment for the employees to wear, many employees refused to wear it. In some instances, employees were fired for not taking these safety precautions. However, the medical examiner ruled that the victim's cause of death was from breathing cyanide fumes at the facility. After several court cases, three company officials were sentenced for involuntary manslaughter. Eventually, the firm went bankrupt (Sethi & Steidlmeier, 1997).

Stage 2: Survival

The survival stage is characterized by growth (Adizes, 1979). During this stage, the organization seeks to formalize structure (Quinn & Cameron, 1983) and establish distinctive competencies, special abilities that distinguish a firm from its competitors (Miller & Friesen, 1984. Firms in this stage typically focus on generating enough cash flow to survive (Churchill & Lewis, 1983).

The company's is often due to a unique differentiating feature that makes it attractive to consumers. Odwalla, Inc., is an example of a firm that was in the growth stage when it experienced a crisis. The company had enjoyed success based on marketing its juices as fresh, with as little processing as possible. In October 1996, an *E. coli* outbreak in its unpasteurized apple juice product contributed to the death of a 16-month-old girl and caused 61 other children to become ill (Lawrence, 1999). Before the crisis, Odwalla made its juices without preservatives or any artificial ingredients. Also, the juices were not pasteurized because the process changed the flavor and depleted essential vitamins and enzymes. This differentiating factor led to the company's success and, ultimately, to a crisis as well. Odwalla survived, but in the process switched to the flash pasteurization of its juice to prevent another *E. coli* outbreak (Lawrence, 1999).

The Best Western case, presented in chapter 1, illustrates how processes that are important to customer safety and welfare may be overlooked in the growth stage. As the delegation of core processes increases, oversight is diluted, thus setting the stage for a crisis. At Best Western, safety standards for venting the swimming pool heater were overlooked, causing the deaths of three guests.

Stage 3: Success

Organizations in the success stage have passed the survival test, growing to a point when top management focuses on planning and strategy and leaves daily operations to middle and unit managers. Formalization and bureaucracy are the norms in the success stage, as can be seen through written job descriptions, the adoption of official policies and procedures, standardization of work, a clear division of labor, and hierarchical reporting relationships (Quinn & Cameron, 1983). However, the owners, managers, and employees must be vigilant because overconfidence and complacency resulting from their confidence are dangerous and represent a source of vulnerability.

When an organization succeeds, it may become the target of various forms of extortion. Cracker Barrel, the Lebanon, Tennessee-based restaurant chain, was a victim in 2004. In this plot, a mother and son planted a mouse in a soup bowl at the Newport News, Virginia store. The two family members, Carla and Ricky Patterson, were later convicted of attempted extortion (Lockyer, 2007). Likewise, hamburger chain Wendy's faced an unusual crisis in March 2005 when a San Jose, California, customer, Ann Ayala, allegedly found a human finger in her chili. Law enforcement officials quickly got involved and attempted to identify the fingerprint. The finger was also autopsied and was determined to have been inserted after the chili was cooked. This clue led investigators to suspect product tampering. Mrs. Ayala and her husband planted the finger in the chili to collect monetary damages from the company. Nonetheless, Wendy's lost millions of dollars in sales in the Northern California market during the ordeal (Coombs, 2006).

Sometimes, accepting responsibility at the outset of a potential crisis can prove costly. In June 2014, reports surfaced that a KFC employee in Jackson, Mississippi asked a 3-year-old girl with scars from a pit bull attack to leave the restaurant because her injuries disturbed other patrons. Photos of the girl surfaced on the Internet. KFC called the alleged incident reprehensive, committed $30,000 to help her family pay for medical bills, and promised a thorough investigation, ultimately hiring a private investigator when it could not verify the claims. Surveillance videos never showed the family in the restaurant on the day in the question, and none of the store's employees had any knowledge of the incident, leading many to conclude that the charge was a hoax. The family had been raising funds online through GoFundMe for medical expenses; the total raised grew from $578 to over $135,000 in the days following the initial claims. KFC did not retract its $30,000 pledge (Watkins, 2014).

With the advent of social media, any organization, but especially large ones, are vulnerable to attacks. BP and the Gulf of Mexico oil spill back in 2010 received a massive wave of public criticism. In 2017, United Airlines was the subject of a social media onslaught over its forceful removal of Dr. David Dao, a passenger who was already seated on a flight (Parnell & Crandall, 2017).

Stage 4: Renewal

The renewing organization seeks to recreate a leaner firm that can respond more quickly and effectively to environmental changes (Miller & Friesen, 1984). In effect, the renewal stage can be viewed as one in which a firm seeks to regain control over how it responds to crisis-creating shifts in its environment. Firms in the renewal stage are trying to recapture a spirit of collaboration and teamwork that fosters innovation and creativity.

To renew itself, an organization may take radical steps to boost market share. Consider the sports entertainment genre of professional wrestling and the demand for new, more elaborate stunts, many of which are dangerous to perform. Unfortunately, in 1999, pro wrestler Owen Hart fell 78 feet to his death when one went awry (Gegax & Adler, 1999). The resulting lawsuits and negative publicity were setbacks for World Wrestling Entertainment (WWE), the event's promoters.

Despite the popularity and resurgence of professional wrestling, it has also encountered another crisis, a high death rate of wrestlers under 45. One study found that wrestlers had a death rate seven times higher than the general population and were 12 times more likely to die of heart disease (Applebome, 2010). At the core of the problem is the use of steroids to enhance bodybuilding and the abuse of prescription drugs to treat painful injuries. The unusual circumstances surrounding the death of wrestler Chris Benoit in 2007 raised national attention. Benoit hung himself after choking his wife and son to death in their Atlanta home. There were conflicting reports on what might have contributed to Benoit's destructive behavior. An autopsy report found he had significant levels of steroids and the painkiller hydrocodone in his system (Walton & Williams, 2011). The implication is that the incident could have been a form of "roid rage." However, an autopsy Benoit brain conducted at West Virginia University indicated he had severe dementia and brain damage due to repeated concussions, most likely, from his wrestling career (Nelson & Sherwood, 2010). The physical toll and subsequent drug use that professional wrestling takes on its stars prompted the WWE to implement a Talent Wellness Program in 2006 to address health concerns involving substance abuse (Herman et al., 2014).

The Volkswagen case discussed at the beginning and end of this chapter also illustrates challenges with the renewal stage. Recall that Volkswagen was attempting to penetrate the diesel market in the United States. The diesel market is part of a larger carmaking niche that touts clean energy with extended mileage. Volkswagen's strategy was misaligned, as most other carmakers were pursuing hybrid and electric car models to attack the same market. Of course, as is now known, the strategy proved disastrous.

Stage 5: Decline

Firms may exit the life cycle at any stage by going out of business, but those that progress through the stages and are unable to achieve renewal eventually reach the decline stage. When this occurs, the internal environment is typically characterized by politics and power (Mintzberg, 1984) as organization members become more concerned with personal rather than organizational goals. Decline ensues, followed by decreased profits and market share. Control and decision-making tend to return to a handful of people as a desire for the power and influence of earlier stages erodes the organization's viability. During this stage, management cannot sustain the momentum or the competitive edge that is critical to success. Lack of energy or interest causes the company to make too many mistakes, become complacent, and in some cases, simply give up.

Sometimes, a single crisis can put an organization out of business permanently. Such was the case with Chalk's Ocean Airways, a niche-oriented carrier that flew flights from the port of Miami, Florida, to the Bahamas in vintage seaplanes. The company had been going through some rough financial times when, on December 19, 2005, one of its planes crashed, killing all 18 passengers and both pilots. The accident, flight 101 from Miami to Bimini, occurred about a minute after takeoff from the waterway. The right wing separated from the plane's fuselage, causing it to crash in the shallow waters below. The age of the aircraft—a Grumman Turbo Mallard (G-73T) manufactured in 1947—and structural cracks in the wing contributed to the accident (National Transportation Safety Board [NTSB], 2007).

A. B. "Pappy" Chalk founded the airline in 1917. Its beginnings were humble, operating on Miami's Flagler Street under a beach umbrella with a desk and a phone number nailed to a nearby utility pole (Stieghorst, 2007). After World War I, when Chalk returned after flying for the military, he renamed the airline Chalk's Flying Service in 1919 to fly tourists and fishermen to the Bahamas. Over the years, many different owners operated the airline, including the late television talk show host Merv Griffin (Stieghorst, 2007). In 1980, a hotel and casino development company bought the airline. This company sold it to several South Florida investors, who used the operating name Pan Am Air Bridge (NTSB, 2007). James Confalone, owner of the company at the time of the accident, bought the airline in 1999 in bankruptcy court (Goodnough, Wald, & Lehren, 2005).

The airline was headquartered in Watson Island, a small island adjacent to the Port of

Miami, where the planes would take off from the waterway, the same channel where the ships also arrive and depart. At the time of the accident, Chalk's operated three G-73T aircraft offering six to eight flights daily to the Bahamas. On the day after the crash, Chalk's operated one more flight, after which it ceased operations (NTSB, 2007). Unlike most airline crashes, the Chalk's Flight 101 accident proved to be fatal to the company.

Many firms in the decline stage function amidst severe challenges. Whether it is a struggle against stiff competition, a problem with cash flow, or an internal battle for control of the organization, the resolution of a crisis inevitably determines the organization's survival or failure. Figure 3.2 summarizes the organizational life cycle.

Figure 3.2 – Crises and the Organizational Lifecycle

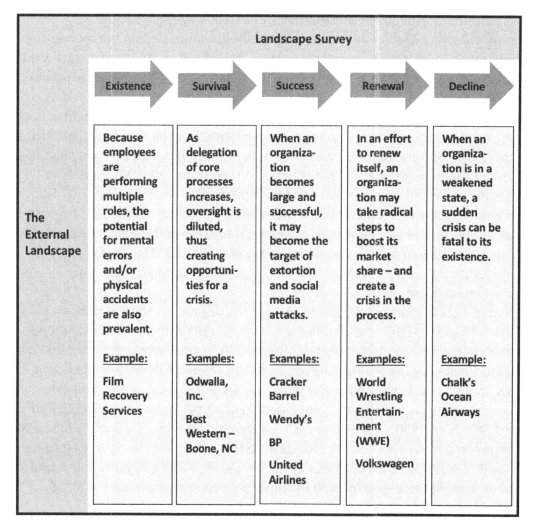

Summary

Crises can originate from multiple sources external to the organization. These forces can be analyzed by examining the firm's macroenvironment, including political-legal, economic, social, and technological forces. Political-legal forces include politically motivated events such as terrorism, the outcomes of elections and legislation, and the decisions rendered by various commissions and governmental agencies. Economic forces include growth or decline in gross domestic product and an increase or decrease in economic indicators such as inflation, interest rates, and exchange rates. The overexpansion of credit and the volatility of oil prices have sparked many organizational crises.

Social forces include societal values, trends, traditions, and religious practices. Social forces specific to crises include a general distrust of corporate America, the preoccupation of consumers with low prices, racial equality, supply chain integrity and concern for the environment and sustainable development. Technological forces include scientific improvements and innovations that create opportunities or threats for businesses. Disruptive innovation and problems with cyber crises are two forces that can create problems for organizations.

Organizational crises can also be examined in terms of the industry life cycle. This life cycle affects many firms that offer similar products or services. With each stage of this cycle—introduction, growth, shakeout, maturity, and decline—specific crisis vulnerabilities are more prominent. Likewise, the organizational life cycle and its corresponding stages of existence—survival, success, renewal, and decline—can breed specific types of crises.

Discussion Questions

1. Identify political trends that have contributed to or could contribute to a crisis.
2. How can political-legal and economic events interact to create a crisis?
3. What crisis events are discussed the most on the social media and Internet sites that you visit?
4. What examples of resistance to technology have you seen where you work? Have you experienced resistance at your college or university? If so, do you think this resistance constitutes a crisis?
5. Identify the organizational life cycle stage in which your company functions. What specific crises are associated with this stage of the life cycle?
6. How can the stage in the industry life cycle affect crises in organizations?
7. Which industries are most vulnerable to crises? Why?

Chapter Exercise

The class should form four groups, each representing one of the four factors discussed in the chapter: political-legal, economic, social, and technological. Each group creates a list of crises that originate from the factor. Display these lists in the classroom and identify the ones that seem to transcend multiple categories, such as crises that have both political and economic dimensions. Conclude the session by addressing trends in the four categories that could spawn fcrises.

Closing Chapter Case: Volkswagen - Polluting the Air with Clean Emission Cars – Part 2

In the European market, diesel engines sell well, and it is not difficult to meet government emissions standards. However, in the US, emission standards are more stringent. In 2007, the Environmental Protection Agency (EPA) set stricter emission standards for diesel engines. After Barak Obama was elected president in 2008, higher gas mileage rules were also imposed (Rothfeder, 2016). For Volkswagen (VW), trying to penetrate the US market with clean diesel cars presented a challenge.

VW did not have the diesel engines ready to meet the new standards. Arguably, VW was not even close, placing pressure on its engineers to devise a quick solution. Volkswagen's culture is top-down, autocratic arrangement (Jung & Park, 2017), and management did not want to hear about problems engineers were having meeting the new standards (Rothfeder, 2016).

But enter the market they did, and with clean diesel engines that appeared to meet the strict standards after all. However, some in the auto industry sensed that deception might be involved (Sorokanich, 2016). Not only did the cars circumvent the testing procedure, but they were also emitting 10 to 40 times more than the allowable pollution levels (Patra, 2016; Shepardson, 2015). Although they did not immediately claim a defeat device was the cause, VW eventually admitted in September 2015 that one was behind the crisis.

A **defeat device** is a software program that caused the engine emissions to become lower and within EPA limits when the car is being tested. The software can detect when the vehicle is being tested for emissions by monitoring the speed, engine operation, air pressure, and steering wheel position (Patra, 2016). When the software utilized by VW recognized the test mode, it caused the emission levels to decrease. Once the vehicle was out of the inspection station and driven under normal conditions, the software shifted the car into a different mode, marked by more engine power and higher emissions.

John German and his colleagues at West Virginia University discovered the deception because the test cars were driven with Portable Emissions Measurement Systems (PEMS) equipment. This equipment measured the exhaust as the vehicle was being used under normal driving conditions, something the defeat device software could not discern. Ironically, the EPA conducted testing of emissions, but it used a dynamometer; the defeat device software could detect this driving scenario, and hence, evaded the EPA's monitoring. The EPA was embarrassed; critics noted it seemed unable to detect the violation of the standards it set (Jung & Park, 2017).

Worldwide, there were approximately 11 million cars that had the defeat device software installed. In the US, about 500,000 vehicles were affected, comprising the following VW diesel models with the 2.0-liter engine (Jung & Park, 2017):

- Jetta: 2009-2015
- Beetle: 2012-2015
- Passat: 2012-2015
- Jetta Sport Wagon: 2009-2014
- Golf: 2010-2015
- Golf Sport Wagon: 2015
- Audi A3: 2010-2015.

Diesels accounted for only 3% of the US automobile market at the time (Tuttle, 2015), compared to about 41% in the European Union (EU). EU incentives promote diesel fuel over gasoline, making it the fuel of choice because it is less expensive. Germany, the United Kingdom, France, and Belgium had 2.8 million, 1.2 million, 984,000, and 500,000 vehicles affected (Jung & Park, 2017; McHugh, 2015).

Why did Volkswagen resort to deception?

Some analysts speculate that VW's deceit was bred in the autocratic, top-down management culture that pervades the company (Jung & Park, 2017; Rothfeder, 2016). In such an environment, top management dictates the goals, and lower-level managers and engineers deliver. There is no room for challenging senior management in this kind of culture. As one insider put it, the VW culture was "fueled by intimidation at every level, which creates a borderline, or sometimes, over the borderline, unethical culture" (Rothfeder, 2016). VW did not possess the technology to meet the new stringent emission codes set by the EPA, yet the launch date for clean diesel was not changed. Top management insisted the cars be introduced to the market and that they meet the rigid standards. There was no wiggle room for discussions or alternate launch dates.

To meet this unattainable goal, engineers resorted to software that would pass the inspection and pollute the environment beyond government standards. Similar technology had been used in the diesel community in Europe, which allowed emergency vehicles to exceed pollution controls for short periods when the car required extra engine performance (Rothfeder, 2016). VW effectively made this approach more mainstream so that it could fool the dynameter based testing equipment.

The Aftermath

In 2015, Volkswagen revealed rogue engineers in the company programmed software that allowed 2.8 million vehicles sold since 2008 to outwit emissions tests. Michael Horn, head of Volkswagen Group of America, said he was unaware of the cheating until a few days before a September 3, 2015 meeting where VW officials revealed the problem to regulators. A month into the scandal, the company had already set aside over $7 billion to resolve the issue through recalls. By 2018, the crisis had cost VW more than $32 billion in penalties, fines, and compensation for consumers. As with many ethical breaches, the crisis that ensues can severely damage the firm (Bernhard, 2008; Harder & Spector, 2015).

The financial impact of the scandal was devastating. VW reported its first quarterly loss in 15 years during the 2015 third quarter, $3.9 billion (Jung & Park, 2016). VW's stock value plunged 35%, losing $33 billion in market value (Tuttle, 2015). CEO Martin Winterkorn resigned and accepted responsibility, although he denied any wrongdoing. However, in May 2018, he was charged with conspiracy and wire fraud for his role in the defeat device deception (Muller, 2018).

External stakeholders were angry, especially customers who had purchased VW clean diesel vehicles. Indeed, clean diesel had been marketed as a green alternative to traditional gasoline models, and customers paid a premium price to purchase these vehicles (Jung & Park, 2017).

As a major automobile manufacturer, VW has amassed many models and has a long history of regular and premium-priced cars that have been well received in the global marketplace. Many were surprised to learn that the firm—or at least some of VW's leadership—had contrived to enter the diesel market with small cars that would fool emission testing equipment. Such a move did not seem necessary for a company that was already enjoying a long history of outstanding success.

But software crises in the automotive industry are not limited to Volkswagen. In 2017, the US Justice Department sued Fiat Chrysler Automobiles NV, accusing the automaker of using illegal software on over 100,000 diesel-powered Jeep Grand Cherokees and Ram pickups to cheat on emissions tests. In 2018, Nissan announced that staff at some of its Japan plans falsified auto-emissions and fuel-economy data for 913 cars tested as far back to 2013. Some analysts blamed corporate pressure to cut costs and keep production lines moving. In contrast, an internal Nissan report blamed management for setting unrealistic targets and relying on factory workers to figure out the details (Gale, 2018).

Moreover, product-related crises in the automobile industry may be traced to suppliers and can simultaneously affect multiple manufacturers. For example, defects in Takata airbags supplied to various auto manufacturers have been linked to numerous deaths and injuries. When deployed, the airbags can explode and spray shrapnel throughout the vehicle. In 2015, Takata was fined $70 million by the US National Highway Traffic Safety Administration (NHTSA) for delays in reporting the defects. Internal reports suggest that members of Takata's US staff raised concerns about misleading testing reports between 2000 and 2010. However, Takata argued that rushed production to meet deadlines, not test discrepancies, were responsible for the deaths (Riley, 2017; Spector, 2015).

Some crisis events can only be managed, while others can be avoided altogether. The VW emission crisis is in the latter category. It not only involved deceiving almost every stakeholder, but it also cost the company billions. Including recalls, buybacks, software fixes, and fines, the total cost of the scandal hit the $33 billion mark by 2020. This estimate does not reflect long term losses related to company goodwill and reputation and lost customers who may never consider purchasing a VW vehicle again.

The diesel gate scandal haunted Volkswagen for several years. German courts were sympathetic to consumer claims, constantly increasing financial liability for the firm. In 2018, VW launched a marketing campaign focused on environmental responsibility, but many consumers remain resentful. The extent to which VW drivers should be compensated for the scandal remains an open question. In the interim, many VW drivers who wish to sell their vehicles must endure unacceptable losses. Volkswagen looks forward to the day when it can completely turn the corner, but it is unclear when that will occur.

Case Discussion Questions

1. Describe the relationship between goal setting and unethical behavior.
2. Discuss examples of how aggressive goal-setting led to unethical behavior, and ultimately, a crisis.

References

Adizes, I. (1979). Organizational passages: Diagnosing and treating life cycle problems. *Organizational Dynamics, 8*(1), 3–24.

Applebome, P. (2010, August 26). Politics, wrestling and death. *New York Times,* p. 19.

Barker, C. (2018, April 19). Waiting while Black: Racial incident at Starbucks sparks outrage. *Amsterdam News*, p. 4.

Barrett, P. (2011, August 29). Cleaning America's dirtiest coal company. *Bloomberg Businessweek,* 48–55.

Bernhard, M. (2018, August 2). Volkswagen is dogged by emissions scandal. *Wall Street Journal,* p. B3.
Brundtland Commission. (1987). Development and International Economic Co-operation: Environment, Report of the World Commission on Environment and Development, p. 54.

Carroll, A., & Buchholtz, A. (2003). *Business and society: Ethics and stakeholder management.* Mason, OH: Thomson South-Western.

Cato, F. (1982). Proctor & Gamble and the devil. *Public Relations Quarterly*, 27(3), 16–21.

Ceniceros, R. (2011). Game changer for mine safety? *Business Insurance*, 45(48), 1–2.

Chin, T., Naidu, S., Ringel, J., Snipes, W., Bienvenu, S., & DeSilva, J. (1993). Denny's: Communicating amidst a discrimination case. *Business Communication Quarterly, 61*(1), 180–197.

Christensen, C. (2003). *The innovator's dilemma: The revolutionary book that will change the way you do business.* New York: Harper Paperbacks.

Christensen, C. M. (1997). *The innovator's dilemma: When new technologies cause great firms to fail.* Boston: Harvard Business School Press.

Churchill, N., & Lewis, V. (1983). The five stages of small business growth. *Harvard Business Review, 61*(3), 30–50.

Coombs, W. (2006). *Code red in the boardroom: Crisis management as organizational DNA.* Westport, CT: Praeger.

Crawford, M. (2009). *Shop class as soulcraft: An inquiry into the value of work.* New York: The Penguin Press.

Cummins, C. (2003, March 24). Business mobilizes for Iraq. *Wall Street Journal,* pp. B1, B3.

Damoc, A. (2016). Fortress Europe breached: Political and economic impact of the recent refugee crisis on European states. *Annals of the University of Oradea, Economic Science Series, 25*(1), 20-29.

Dean, A. (2012). Occupy Wall Street. *Harvard International Review, 33*(4), 12-15.

Easton, N. (2012, September 24). Stop beating up the rich. *Fortune, 166*(5), 114-119.

Ehrenreich, B. (2001). *Nickel and dimed: On (not) getting by in America.* New York: Henry Holt and Company.

Ehrenreich, B. (2009). *Bright-Sided: How the relentless promotion of positive thinking has undermined America.* New York: Henry Holt and Company.

Fishman, C. (2006). *The Walmart effect: How the world's most powerful company really works—and how it's transforming the American economy.* New York: Penguin.

Fortier, J. (2008). U of O research examines risks of mad cow disease. *Ottawa Business Journal, 13*(33), 14.

Fuller, K. (2006, October 19). Restaurant: Poor service wasn't bias: Rock speaks to media on Cracker Barrel incident. *The Sun News* (Myrtle Beach, SC). Retrieved October 28, 2006, from Ebscohost database.

Gale, A., & McLain, S. (2018, February 4). Companies everywhere copied Japanese manufacturing. Now the model is cracking. *Wall Street Journal.* Retrieved July 28, 2019, from https://www.wsj.com/articles/companies-everywhere-copied-japanese-manufacturing-now-the-model-is-cracking-1517771142

Gegax, T., & Adler, J. (1999, June 7). Death in the ring. *Newsweek,* 64–65.

Goodell, J. (2010, November 29). The Dark Lord of Coal Country. *Rolling Stone.* Retrieved February 17, 2017, from http://www.rollingstone.com/politics/news/the-dark-lord-of-coal-country-20101129

Goodnough, A., Wald, M., & Lehren, A. (2005, December 22). Airline grounds fleet after seaplane crash. *New York Times,* p. 27.

Griffin, D., & Bronstein, S. (2013, December 18). Carnival knew of fire danger before cruise, documents show. *CNN*. Retrieved July 25, 2019, from https://www.cnn.com/2013/12/17/travel/carnival-cruise-triumph-problems/index.html

Harder, A., & Spector, M. (2015, September 18). EPA Accuses Volkswagen of Dodging Emissions Rules. *Wall Street Journal*. Retrieved July 28, 2019, from https://www.wsj.com/articles/epa-accuses-volkswagen-of-dodging-emissions-rules-1442595129

Hardy, J. (2015). Just the facts. *Business in Calgary, 25*(6), 60-63.

Hartley, R. (1993). *Business ethics: Violations of the public trust.* New York: John Wiley.

Hartmann, B., & Sam, S. (2016, March 28). What low oil prices really mean. *Harvard Business Review Digital Articles*, 1-6.

Hayhurst, L. (2006, March 31). Princess offers full refunds. *Travel Weekly*, 10.

Hensler, C. (2014). Shrinking footprint: A result of design influenced by life cycle assessment. *Journal of Industrial Ecology, 18*(5), 663-669.

Herman, C., Conion, A., Rubenfire, M., Burghardt, A., & McGregor, S. (2014). The very high premature mortality rate among active professional wrestlers is primarily due to cardiovascular disease. *PLOS One, 9*(11), 1-11.

Higgins, A. (2001, March 12). It's a mad, mad, mad-cow world. *Wall Street Journal,* pp. A13–A14.

Hofer, C. (1975). Toward a contingency theory of business strategy. *Academy of Management Journal, 18*(4), 784–810.

ICM (Institute for Crisis Management), (2016). *Annual ICM crisis report: News coverage of business crises during 2015.* Retrieved October 20, 2018, from https://crisisconsultant.com/icm-annual-crisis-report/

Interface, Inc. (2019, November 4). Interface announces mission zero success, commits to climate take back. https://www.prnewswire.com/news-releases/interface-announces-mission-zero-success-commits-to-climate-take-back-300949740.html

Jensen, J. (2015). Blankenship found guilty of conspiracy. *Coal Age, 120*(12), 56-61.

Jung, J., & Park, S. (2016). Case study: Volkswagen's diesel emissions scandal. *Thunderbird International Business Review, 59*(1), 127-137.

Kehoe, J. (2016, February 15). What's at stake in an economy with low oil prices. *Harvard Business Review Digital Articles,* 1-5.

Kennel, P. (1996, August 21). The sweatshop dilemma. *The Christian Science Monitor, 88*(187). Retrieved July 25, 2019, from https://www.csmonitor.com/1996/0821/082196.opin.opin.2.html

Kilborn, P. (2003, January 24). An enormous landmark joins the graveyard of malls. *New York Times*, p. 12.

Kim, M. (2015, January 19-25). Enjoy our low oil prices: Here's why they tumbled. *Indianapolis Business Journal, 35*(48), 24.

King, N., Jr. (2003, April 11). The race to rebuild Iraq. *Wall Street Journal*, pp. B1, B3.

Kline, S. (2010). Not your father's recession. *Production Machining, 10*(10), 56.

Krishner, T., & Jordans, F. (2015, September 21). Faced with overwhelming evidence, VW admits thwarting pollution controls. *Associated Press*. Retrieved July 28, 2019, from https://www.680news.com/2015/09/21/faced-with-overwhelming-evidence-vw-admits-thwarting-pollution-controls-for-years/

Lannom, A. (2013, September 13). David Hughart sentenced to nearly 4 years in prison. *State Journal (WV), 29*(36), 13.

Lawrence, A. (1999). Odwalla, Inc., and the E. coli outbreak (A), (B), (C). *Case Research Journal, 19*(1).

Lester, D., Parnell, J., & Carraher, S. (2003). Organizational life cycle: A five-stage empirical scale. *International Journal of Organizational Analysis, 11*, 339–354.

Lockyer, S. (2007). Scams: Communication and crisis plans guard restaurants against cons and crooked insiders. *Nation's Restaurant News, 41*(21), 78–80.

Ma, J., Lee, H., & Goerlitz, K. (2015). Transparency of global apparel supply chains: Quantitative analysis of corporate disclosures. *Corporate Social Responsibility and Environmental Management, 23*, 308-318.

Magnuson, E. (1985, February 4). Crash of a troubled bird. *Time, 125,* 19.

Maki, A. (2006, September 20). Walmart may put store at once-proud Memphis, Tenn., shopping location. *Commercial Appeal*. Retrieved April 21, 2012, from EBSCOhost Newspaper Source Plus Database.

Markides, C. (2013). Disruptive reality. *Business Strategy Review, 24*(3), 36-43.

McHugh, J. (2015). Volkswagen diesel scandal update 2015: Affected countries are largely in North America, Europe, but Asia not immune. *International Business Times.* Retrieved October 15, 2018, from https://www.ibtimes.com/volkswagen-diesel-scandal-update-2015-affected-countries-are-largely-north-america-2137284

Miles, G., Snow, C., & Sharfman, M. (1993). Industry variety and performance. *Strategic Management Journal, 14*(3), 163–177.

Miller, D., & Friesen, P. H. (1984). *Organizations: A quantum view.* Englewood Cliffs, NJ: Prentice Hall.

Milmo, S. (2016). Oil dips, prospects rise? The Chemical Engineer, 897, 35-37.

Mintzberg, H. (1984). Power and organization life cycles. *Academy of Management Review, 9*(2), 207–224.

Mouawad, J. (2012, January 18). Industry weighs effect of ship accident. *New York Times,* p. 1.

Muller, J. (2018, May 3). WV's former CEO Martin Winterkorn charged with fraud and conspiracy in diesel-cheating case. *Forbes.* Retrieved October 15, 2018, from https://www.forbes.com/sites/joannmuller/2018/05/03/vws-former-ceo-martin-winterkorn-charged-with-fraud-and-conspiracy-in-diesel-cheating-case/#5f7919724e90

Murphy, T. (2015). The fall of king coal. *Mother Jones, 40*(6), 30-61.

National Transportation Safety Board. (2007). In-flight separation of right wing, Flying Boat, Inc. (doing business as Chalk's Ocean Airways) Flight 101, Grumman Turbo Mallard (G-73T), N2969, Port of Miami, Florida, December 19, 2005. *Aircraft Accident Report NTSB/AAR-07/04.* Washington, DC.

Nelson, E., & Sherwood, R. (2010, August 26). Chris Benoit's murder, suicide: Was brain damage to blame? *ABC News.* Retrieved July 28, 2019, from https://abcnews.go.com/Nightline/chris-benoits-dad-son-suffered-severe-brain-damage/story?id=11471875

Oreskes, N., & Schendler, A. (2015, December 4). Corporations will never solve climate change. *Harvard Business Review Digital Articles, 2-5.*

Parnell, J.A. (2020). *Strategic Management: Theory and Practice (6th edition)*. Solon, OH: Academic Media Solutions.

Parnell, J., & Crandall, W. (2017A). The contribution of behavioral economics to crisis management decision-making. *Journal of Management & Organization.*

Patra, B. (2016). The deliberate deception: Case study on Volkswagen emission scandal. *Vilakshn, XIMB Journal of Management, 13*(1), 139-148.

Penny, L. (2016). The ghosts of Zuccotti Park. *New Statesman, 145*(5333), 18-19.

Perman, S. (2014, September 8). Using fishing nets to make carpets cleaner. *Bloomberg Businessweek, 4393,* 44-46.

Pianigiani, G. (2012, January 26). Captain of doomed cruise ship says course change was an order. *New York Times,* p. 12.

Quinn, R., & Cameron, K. (1983). Organizational life cycles and shifting criteria of effectiveness: Some preliminary evidence. *Management Science, 29*(1), 33–41.

Rielage, R. (2010, July). Shipboard firefighting is a different animal. *Fire Chief,* 19–20.

Riley, C. (2017, September 29). Volkswagen's diesel scandal cost hit $30 billion. *CNN Money*. Retrieved October 16, 2018, from https://money.cnn.com/2017/09/29/investing/volkswagen-diesel-cost-30-billion/index.html

Roberts, J. & Lashinsky, A. (2017, July 1). Hacked: Business under cyberassault. *Fortune*, 52-59.

Rothfeder, J. (2016, July 1). The Volkswagen settlement: How bad management leads to big punishment. *The New Yorker*. Retrieved, October 9, 2018, from https://www.newyorker.com/business/currency/the-volkswagen-settlement-how-bad-management-leads-to-big-punishment

Rothfeder, J. (2017, January 17). At Volkswagen, a scandal where executives could pay the price. *The New Yorker*. Retrieved July 29, 2019, from https://www.newyorker.com/business/currency/at-volkswagen-a-scandal-where-executives-could-pay-the-price.

Ruggeri, R. (2015). Cruising to comeback. *The Strategist, 21*(2), 32-33.

Ryan, T. (2008). The future of the regional mall. *SGB, 41*(10), 22.

Sethi, S., & Steidlmeier, P. (1997). *Up against the corporate wall: Case in business and society (6th ed.).* Upper Saddle River, NJ: Prentice Hall.

Sevastopulo, D. (2003, October 2). US airlines are on life support. *Financial Times,* p. 15.

Shell, E. (2009). *Cheap: The high cost of discount culture.* New York: Penguin Group.

Shepardson, D. (2015, September 24). How VW got caught cheating emissions test. *Detroit News*. Retrieved July 9, 2017, from http://www.detroitnews.com/story/business/autos/foreign/2015/09/24/vw-caught/72715074/

Simpson, C. (2013, November 7). An iPhone tester caught in Apple's supply chain. *Bloomberg Business*. Retrieved February 22, 2017, from http://www.bloomberg.com/bw/articles/2013-11-07/an-iphone-tester-caught-in-apples-supply-chain

Smith, S. (2010). A "Massey"ive catastrophe. *EHS Today, 3*(5), 8.

Sorokanich, B. (2016, June 28). VW emissions cheat was an "open secret" for seven years, says Volvo exec. *Road and Track*. Retrieved July 9, 2017, from http://www.roadandtrack.com/new-cars/car-technology/news/a29753/vw-tdi-diesel-emissions-cheat-open-secret-volvo/

Spector, M. (2015, November 25). Takata US staff saw problems in airbag tests. *Wall Street Journal,* pp. B1, B6.

Starbuck, W. H. (2003). The origins of organization theory. In H. Tsoukas & C. Knudsen (Eds.), *The handbook of organization theory: Meta-theoretical perspectives* (pp. 143–182). Oxford, UK: Oxford University Press.

Steele, T., Smith, S., & McBroom, W. (1999). Consumer rumors and corporate communications: Rumor etiology, background, and potential devastating consequences. *Journal of Marketing Management, 9*(2), 95–106.

Stephen, M. (2015). Much ado about fracking. *Canada Plastics, 73*(6), 16-19.

Stieghorst, T. (2007, October 23). Chalk's Airlines loses flight license; its airport lease could be cancelled. Retrieved February 6, 2017, from http://www.aviationpros.com/news/10384737/chalks-airlines-loses-flight-license-its-airport-lease-could-be-canceled

Terlep, S. (2011, November 29). GM scrambles to defend Volt. *Wall Street Journal,* pp. B1, B2.

Terry-Armstrong, N. (2016). The Volkswagen scandal - The high cost of corporate deceit. *Busidate, 24*(1), 9-13.

Thompson, K. (2014). Troubled waters. *Popular Mechanics, 191*(2), 58-61.

Trachtenberg, J., & Steinberg, B. (2003, March 20). Plan B for marketers. *Wall Street Journal,* pp. B1, B3.

Tuttle, H. (2015). Volkswagen rocked by emissions fraud scandal. *Risk Management Magazine.* Retrieved October 9, 2018, from http://www.rmmagazine.com/2015/12/01/volkswagen-rocked-by-emissions-fraud-scandal/

US Department of Labor (2015). Retrieved October 29, 2018, from https://arlweb.msha.gov/MSHAINFO/FactSheets/MSHAFCT10.asp

Veil, S., Liu, M., Erickson, S., & Sellnow, T. (2005). Too hot to handle: Competency constrains character in Chi-Chi's green onion crisis. *Public Relations Quarterly, 50*(4), 19–22.

Walton, L., & Williams, K. (2011). World Wrestling Entertainment responds to the Chris Benoit tragedy: A case study. *International Journal of Sport Communication, 4,* 99–114.

Watkins, B. (2014 June 24). KFC: No proof employee asked scarred girl to leave. *USA Today.* Retrieved May 6, 2019, from www.usatoday.com/story/news/nation/2014/06/24/kfc-disfigured-child-update/11322523/

Whincup, D., Garbett, S., & McNicholas, C. (2016). The Modern Slavery Act 2015: 10 key points for business. *Employee Relations Law Journal, 41*(4), 64-68.

Williams, C. (2016, November). Five action lists for a cyber crisis. *Hospitals & Health Networks, 90*(11), 36-40.

Williard, N., He, W., Hendricks, C., & Pecht, M. (2013). Lessons learned from the 787 Dreamliner issue on lithium-ion battery reliability. *Energies, 6,* 4682-4695.

Winchester, J. (2010). *Civil aircraft—Passenger and utility aircraft: A century of innovation.* London: Amber Books.

Wright, P., Kroll, M., & Parnell, J. (1998). *Strategic management: Concepts.* Upper Saddle River, NJ: Prentice Hall.

WV Governor's report places blame for Upper Big Branch explosion on Massey, agencies. (2011, June). *Coal Age, 116*(6), 10.

Zart, N. (2018). Breaking news: VW scandal problems continue with German courts siding against the carmaker. *Clean Technica.* Retrieved October 20, 2018, from https://cleantechnica.com/2018/03/14/breaking-news-vw-scandal-problems-continue-german-courts-siding-car-maker/

Chapter 4: A Strategic Approach to Crisis Management

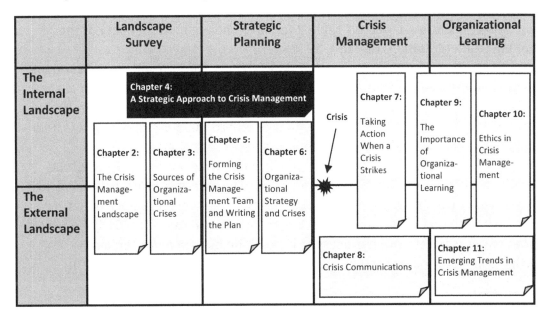

Learning Objectives

After reading this chapter, each student should be able to:

1. Identify and describe the four key distinctions of a strategic orientation perspective.
2. Identify and describe the five steps in the strategic management process.
3. Describe the two dimensions that contribute to environmental uncertainty.
4. Explain how environmental uncertainty affects the crisis planning process.
5. Explain how environmental scanning can help or hinder the crisis planning process.
6. Describe how a SWOT analysis can help identify potential crisis events in the future of an organization.
7. Discuss how organizational culture affects the crisis planning process.

Opening Chapter Case: Duck Boat Tragedy - Part 1

Duck boats (often called "ducks") are amphibious vehicles that were initially used in World War II to ferry supplies and troops from sea to land. They were employed in France during the Normandy Invasion and many other missions requiring amphibious movement of resources. Today's ducks have been refurbished from the original military vessels and are most commonly used at tourist attractions. They are popular in Branson, Missouri, where visitors can ride on Table Rock Lake and enjoy the scenery of the surrounding Ozark Mountains (Barrett, 2018).

On July 19, 2018, a duck boat encountered high winds, took on water, and suddenly sank in Table Rock Lake near Branson, killing 17, nine from one family (Barrett & Lazo, 2018). Cell phone video captured the boat in distress as it was heading back to land moments before it capsized. The company that operated the duck boat business, Ride the Ducks Branson, closed after the accident and never reopened.

Ducks were built for wartime missions and were not designed to last beyond the military theater (Bonvento, 2018). However, many ducks were later used afterWorld War II for military training and in tourist attractions. There were 118 duck boats registered with the US Coast Guard at the beginning of 2018 (Barrett, 2018). Reusing a duck boat requires a restoration process to rebuild the hull so that it remains seaworthy. The restoration cost was around $80,000 in 2000 (Hoffmann, 2000).

The Accident

On July 19, 2018, at Table Rock Lake outside of Branson, Missouri, the weather was calm early in the day. But conditions in the Ozark Mountains can change quickly. Two duck boats were out on the lake when a severe thunderstorm warning was issued at 6:30 p.m. One boat returned to land successfully, but at 7:09 p.m., but a 911 call indicated that the other boat was in distress. It had encountered severe wind and choppy waves and was taking on water. Cell phone video showed the boat being tossed around as waves overtook the front of the vessel.

There were 31 people on board, including two crew members. By the end of the day, the boat was submerged in 70 feet of water, and 17 people had drowned. Ironically, the vessel initially capsized in 15 feet of water but drifted into deeper waters due to the lake currents (Bonvento, 2018).

Life jackets were on board the boat. None were utilized on July 19, but it is unclear whether they would have saved lives anyway. A duck boat canopy can trap passengers onboard as the vessel takes on water, thus, creating a fatal condition (Bonvento, 2018; Maher, 2018).

The captain was widely criticized for launching the boat when severe thunderstorms were forecast (Bauer, Cummings, Adler, & McKinley, 2018; Bonvento, 2018). The camera and recording data salvaged from the sunken boat revealed the following approximate sequence of events (*NTSB News Release*, 2018):

- 6:27 p.m. - The captain and driver boarded the vehicle.
- 6:28 p.m. - An individual informs the captain and driver to take the water portion of the tour first (this seems to indicate some acknowledgment of the pending storm, although the official weather bulletin was not issued until 6:32 pm).
- 6:29 p.m.)- While the passengers board, the captain mentions looking at the weather map before the trip.
- 6:33 p.m. - The duck boat departs from the terminal on land.
- 6:50 p.m. - The captain provides safety information on life jackets and emergency exits. He then moves to the driver's seat to prepare the vessel for entry into the water. The driver takes a seat behind the captain's chair.
- 6:55 pm. - The boat enters calm water.
- 7:00 p.m. - Whitecap waves and high winds suddenly appear.
- 7:04 p.m. - The bilge alarm activates, indicating that water is entering the duck boat.
- 7:08 p.m. - The recording data ended.

The sequence of events confirms a sudden storm hit Table Rock Lake as forecasted. Although other boats were on the water, they were substantially more extensive and buoyant. Some passengers on these boats took cellphone video of the duck boat attempting to return to land; they are readily available on YouTube.

History of Accidents

Although some critics have suggested that the ducks are inherently unsafe and should be banned, there have been only a few recorded accidents. Three other duck boat accidents are noteworthy:

May 1, 1999: The duck boat, Miss Majestic, sank on Lake Hamilton in Hot Springs, Arkansas. Thirteen people died in an accident that occurred only 300 feet from shore. The boat sank 30 seconds after taking on water (Beddingfield, 1999), and a design flaw in the boot system, which covers the drive axles, was identified as the cause (Gordon, 2007).

July 7, 2010: A stalled duck boat on the Delaware River was hit by a barge being pushed by a tugboat, resulting in two fatalities. The captain of the tugboat was preoccupied with calls from his cellphone involving a family emergency. He had moved to a part of the boat where his view of the river was blocked. The captain was later sentenced to one year in prison for the maritime equivalent of involuntary manslaughter. The captain of the duck boat suspected an engine fire and anchored the vessel in the river. However, the smoke he saw from the engine was steam from the radiator because the radiator cap had not been adequately placed (Todt, 2012). Unfortunately, this area of the river was also a busy shipping lane, and the need to anchor in that area contributed to the accident.

September 25, 2015: A duck boat driven on land crashed into a bus full of international students, killing five students and injuring 69. The crash occurred on the Aurora Bridge in Seattle after the duck boat axle broke, causing it to cross the center line and collide into the side of the bus. All five of the fatalities were passengers on the bus. Meanwhile, 11 people were ejected from the duck boat and sustained injuries, seven of which were severe. The National Transportation Safety Board later ruled that improper maintenance was a factor in the crash (Bellisle, 2016).

Are Duck Boats Unsafe?

From a crisis management perspective, the answer is yes. These four accidents are related to boat design and improper maintenance. During a violent storm, the boats can be deadly, as evidenced by the 2018 accident in Branson. On calm water, they are safe, assuming there are no leaks of the boot, which seals the drive axle of the vessel, as that is what caused the 1999 disaster in Arkansas. Both of those accidents can be attributed to boat design.

The 2010 accident was not attributable directly to the duck boat, but to the barge that hit it. However, the duck boat was in the center of the shipping lane because of a mechanical failure. This accident was caused by a maintenance issue that should have been corrected before the boat departed. The 2015 accident on the road was not a boat problem, but a traffic accident. However, the axle failure was due to improper maintenance. These four accidents have resulted in 37 fatalities, including five victims on the bus the duck boat hit in Seattle. Given this information, how can tour operators that use duck boats ensure the safety of their guests?

Case Discussion Questions

1. Suppose you are a crisis consultant to a tourist company that uses duck boats to take tourists on a lake to enjoy the scenery and learn about the history of the area. They are also used on the highway for special events and on side roads before entering the water. Would you recommend that the company continue to use the duck boats? Why or why not?
2. If the ducks are used, what safety guidelines would you propose?

Introduction

Effective crisis management requires that managers understand both the sources of crisis events and the strategies needed to identify and prepare for them. A crisis event rarely occurs *out of the blue*. Instead, it usually follows one or more warning signs. Typically, a series of precondition events occur before a crisis can commence. These events eventually lead to a trigger event that ultimately causes the crisis (Shrivastava, 1995; Smith, 1990). One of the critical events that launched crisis management occurred in 1984, when deadly methyl isocyanate gas leaked from a storage tank at a Union Carbide plant in Bhopal, India. The accident initially killed more than 2,500 people and injured another 300,000. The trigger event for this crisis was water entry into a storage tank that subsequently caused the unit's temperature and tank pressure to rise. Numerous preconditions contributed to the origin of this accident. These included shutting down a refrigeration system designed to keep the gas cool, failing to reset the tank temperature alarm, neglecting to fix a nonfunctioning gas scrubber, and not performing the maintenance and repair on an inoperative flame tower designed to burn off toxic gases (Hartley, 1993). Each of these four systems was designed to help alert plant workers of a gas leak and contain the toxic effects of that leak. Each of them was inoperable on the day of the accident.

The warning signs of an evolving crisis may not be identified until it is too late, either because decision-makers are not aware of them or because they do not recognize them as serious threats. Sometimes managers are merely in denial. They may exhibit a mindset known as optimism bias, a tendency to overestimate the probability of a positive occurrence and underestimate the possibility of an adverse event (Parnell & Crandall, 2017). Some assert that a crisis cannot happen to their organization or that the probability of it occurring is so low that it does not warrant spending the time and resources required to prevent it (Nathan, 2000; Pearson & Mitroff, 1993). In some cases, the warning signs are ignored altogether, even though these preconditions are signaling an impending crisis. For example, Toyota's unintended acceleration problem with its Camry model was preceded by a year's worth of problems with stuck accelerators (Institute for Crisis Management, 2011). All of this underscores the importance of assessing crisis vulnerability, the practice of scanning the environment, and identifying those threats that could happen to the organization.

In this chapter, we examine crisis management from a strategic point of view. First, we overview the challenges managers face as they assess the external environment, particularly its uncertainty. We then proceed to the heart of identifying potential crises and employ the SWOT (Strengths, Weaknesses, Opportunities, and Threats) analysis, a widely used tool in strategic planning. We close this chapter with a short discussion on the link between organizational culture and crisis planning.

A Strategic Approach to Crisis Management

Crisis management requires a *strategic* mindset or perspective (Bouve, Steens, & Ruebens, 2018; Chong & Park, 2010; Kausar & Baghoor, 2017; Parnell, 2020). There are four critical distinctions of a **strategic orientation**.

1. A strategic orientation is based on a systematic, comprehensive analysis of internal attributes, also referred to as strengths and weaknesses, and factors external to the organization, commonly referred to as opportunities and threats.  Readers familiar with strategic management recognize this process as the SWOT analysis. A systematic approach helps keep managers from overlooking potential crises. Thus, we must look both inside and outside the organization to identify risk factors.

2. A strategic orientation is long-term and future-oriented—usually several years to a decade into the future—but also built on a knowledge of events from the past and present.

3. A strategic orientation is distinctively opportunistic, always seeking to take advantage of favorable situations and avoiding pitfalls that may occur either inside or outside the organization.

4. A strategic orientation involves important choices. Preparing for every conceivable crisis can be costly; priorities must be established. For example, resources must be spent to ensure safety in the workplace. Committing resources, however, takes money directly off the bottom line. With a strategic approach, the expenditure can contribute to the organization's long-term health. It should not be viewed solely as a cost, but as an investment in the company's longevity (and safety) and its employees.

Because of these distinctions, the overall crisis management program must include the top executive and members of the management team (Taneja, Pryor, Sewell, & Recuero, 2014). The chief executive is ultimately accountable for the organization's strategic management and any crises that emerge. In most organizations, CEOs rely on a *team* of top-level executives, all of whom play instrumental roles in the strategic management of the firm (Carpenter, 2002; Das & Teng, 1999).

Strategic decisions designed to head off crises are made within the context of the **strategic management process**, which can be summarized in five steps (Parnell, 2020):

1. *External analysis.* Analyze the opportunities and threats or constraints in the organization's macroenvironment, including industry and external forces.
2. *Internal analysis.* Analyze the organization's strengths and weaknesses in its internal environment; reassess its mission and goals as necessary.
3. *Strategy formulation.* Formulate strategies that build and sustain competitive advantage by matching the organization's strengths and weaknesses with the environment's opportunities and threats.
4. *Strategy execution.* Implement the strategies developed in the previous step.
5. *Strategic control.* Engage in strategic control activities when the strategies are not producing the desired outcomes.

Crisis impact can vary markedly across firms and industries because of strategic and external factors. The COVID-19 pandemic illustrates this reality. Estimates suggest that more than twice as many US retailers closed in 2020 than in 2019. Apparel, furniture, and department stores reported the most casualties. For JCPenney, Kmart, Gap, GNC, and others, the pandemic accelerated an ongoing transition from storefront to online shopping. Others were hit on different fronts as well. For example, Brooks Brothers' store closures and bankruptcy filing was also triggered by a decline in demand for dress clothes as more people worked from home. Some discount stores such as Family Dollar, Dollar Tree, Dollar General, and Ross Stores opened more stores as consumers sought to purchase necessities at reduced prices (Kapner & Santiago, 2020).

External analysis

Crisis management is an important consideration in each step but in different ways. In the first step, managers identify the sources of crises in the firm's external environment. Typically, the organization's external opportunities and threats are identified to determine specific vulnerabilities of concern. The threat of online viruses and other denial-of-service (DoS) attacks, for example, may suggest that firms invest in upgrading firewall and virus protection measures so that its website is not taken offline by hackers (Robb, 2005; Williams, 2016). Also related to technology is the opportunity to use social media outlets in addition to the company's regular Web page. Twitter is a vital tool for fast communication with external stakeholders. Social media helps organizations connect with stakeholders more effectively. A strong social media presence can be important during a crisis because a company can use more personalized media outlets to communicate its side of the story to stakeholders (Jacques, 2009).

Government regulations, often formed in response to a previous crisis, are part of the external environment. Following a salmonella outbreak and subsequent recalls of tomatoes in 2008, the US Food and Drug Administration strengthened inspection and other measures to reduce the likelihood of a recurrence. Initially, the agency focused on tomatoes as the culprit. Later, various types of peppers were also part of the investigation (O'Rourke, 2008). Food-related firms, from growers to producers to restaurants, should consider how this crisis evolved and what strategic changes might be appropriate (Zhang, 2008). Ultimately, those in the food manufacturing industry must be knowledgeable concerning what is now labeled as *food traceability*. This term requires all food processors to to track inputs through the entire supply chain (Schrader, 2010).

African swine fever virus decimated Chinese hog herds in 2019, resulting in the culling of at least 200 million pigs and reducing Chinese production of about 30% from 2018 levels. Buyers in China and elsewhere turned to other suppliers, namely those in the US. Pork prices increased substantially (Haddon & Bunge, 2019; Maltais & Bunge, 2019).

Internal analysis

The second step focuses on vulnerabilities within the organization that may result during a crisis. Typically, the organization's internal strengths and weaknesses are identified to identify vulnerabilities. For example, a poorly trained workforce could contribute to a workplace accident or dubious advertising claims about one's competitors could lead to litigation. Equipment that is aging or poorly maintained is another common weakness.

The Chalk's Ocean Airways crash, mentioned in Chapter 3, is an example of a company whose uniqueness contributed to its popularity over many decades. In 2003, the airline had been cited in the *Guinness Book of World Records* as the world's oldest continuously operating airline (Scammell, 2003). The company was a novelty in South Florida because it flew vintage seaplanes to the Bahamas, which made it popular with local Bahamians who found the arrangement convenient when returning home. Indeed, flying in seaplanes in modern aviation was a strength that the airline possessed because it was a visit back to nostalgic times. Unfortunately, the vintage seaplanes also embodied a weakness that was not apparent to its mechanics: structural fatigue cracks caused by years of use and exposure to saltwater. "This accident tragically illustrates a gap in the safety net with regard to older airplanes," said Mark Rosenker, National Transportation Safety Board (NTSB) chairman. "The signs of structural problems were there—but not addressed. And to ignore continuing problems is to court disaster" (Vines, 2007, p. 14).

Strategy formulation and implementation

The third and fourth steps concern developing and executing the firm's strategies at the various functional levels. Indeed, some strategies are more prone to crisis events than others. For example, a strategy that emphasizes global expansion into less stable emerging nations engenders a greater risk of crisis than a robust domestic market orientation. Some crisis-laden strategies are unavoidable, but a strategic perspective helps managers evaluate them properly (Kaplan & Mikes, 2012).

Strategic control

Outcomes are assessed in the strategic control stage. Once completed, the organization must counter undesirable or unanticipated consequences that emanate from the strategy. When a strategy is executed as planned, control may be minimal. When execution difficulties exist, or unforeseen problems arise, the nature of strategic control may need to change to crisis prevention or even crisis response. Monitoring mechanisms must be established so that corrective action can be taken when necessary. **Strategic control** is useful in crisis management because it often signals a future problem. For example, accounting controls can indicate embezzlement. Figure 4.1 depicts how these five strategic steps fit within the crisis management framework. Chapter 3 provided the foundation for the second step in the process—examining the external landscape. This chapter builds on that discussion and focuses on steps 2 and 3, internal analysis, and strategy formulation. In the next section, we examine environmental uncertainty pertaining to the strategic and crisis management process.

Figure 4.1 – A Strategic Approach to Crisis Management

	Landscape Survey	Strategic Planning	Crisis Management	Organizational Learning
The Internal Landscape	2. Internal Analysis		Crisis	
The External Landscape	1. External Analysis	3. Strategy Formulation	4. Strategy Execution	5. Strategic Control

Understanding Environmental Uncertainty

Chapter 3 discussed many external sources of crises: political-legal, economic, social, and technological forces. Preventing crises would be easier if managers always had perfect information, but they do not. An essential step in the strategic management process—analyzing the external environment—presents one of the most critical challenges for preventing crises: understanding and managing **environmental uncertainty**.

Managers must develop a systematic process to obtain information about the organization's environment (Bowers, Hall, & Srinivasan, 2017). Ideally, top managers should be aware of the multitude of external forces that influence an organization's activities. Uncertainty occurs when decision-makers lack enough current, reliable information and cannot accurately forecast future changes. In practice, decision-makers in any organization must render decisions even when environmental conditions are uncertain.

Forecasting amidst uncertainty can be difficult. On the morning of December 24, 2013, the United Parcel Service (UPS) hub in Louisville, Kentucky was flooded with a volume of packages far exceeding its forecast of 7.75. A shortage of planes stranded many packages, forcing UPS to inform many Americans that the gifts they ordered would not arrive in time for Christmas as promised. Online Christmas sales increased 63% over the previous year, and retailers like Toys-R-Us and Dick's Sporting Goods were making December 24 delivery available for orders submitted as late as 11:00 p.m. on December 23, 24 hours later than was permitted in 2012. UPS handled about 50-60% of e-commerce orders at the time (Stevens, Ng & Bando, 2013).

Environmental uncertainty consists of two dimensions, the environment's rate of change and its overall complexity. Based on the work of Robert Duncan (1972), figure 4.2 depicts environmental uncertainty as a 2x2 matrix with the two dimensions of environmental change on the y-axis and environmental complexity on the x-axis, shown at the top. Although created over 40 years ago, this framework remains one of the best known and researched models of environmental uncertainty (Silveira-Martins & Rosseto, 2018).

Duncan's framework references environmental factors, which are a wide assortment of activities and functions related to both the internal and external workings of the company. Internal factors consist of three groups, what Duncan called components: personnel, functional units, and the integration of goals. External factors included five components: customers, suppliers, competitors, socio/political groups, and technology issues. Duncan's (1972) premise was that this array of environmental factors could be arranged by looking at their rate of change and their overall complexity. Slow-changing environments were labeled stable, while fast-changing environments were termed unstable. Complexity was either simple or complex. The resulting 2x2 matrix creates four cells, each depicting a different environment based on the two dimensions.

Figure 4.2 - Environmental Uncertainty and Crisis Management

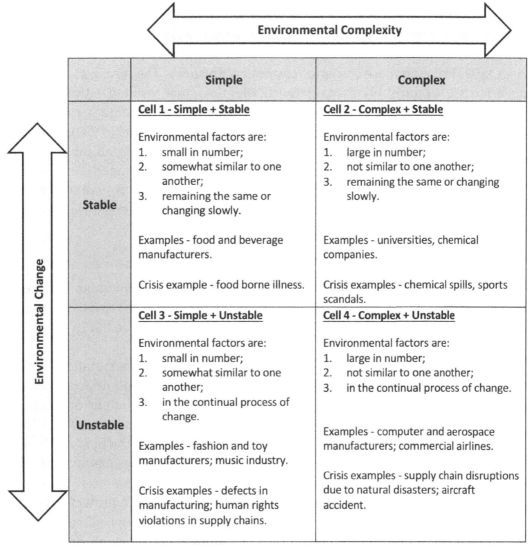

Adapted from Duncan (1972).

Crisis events can occur in all four environments, so one environment is not necessarily preferable. However, highly unstable and complex environments (Cell 4) are prone to more uncertainty than the other three cells. Organizations in environments marked by low uncertainty should be managed differently from those characterized by high uncertainty. When uncertainty is low, it is easier to identify risk and create standard operating procedures or heuristics to mitigate it. However, when uncertainty is high, systems are difficult to develop because processes tend to change more frequently. In this situation, decision-makers are often granted more freedom and flexibility to adapt to its environment as it changes or as better information on the environment becomes available. Discussions, scenario planning, and using outside experts can help address risks in these types of environments (Kaplan & Mikes, 2012).

Sometimes, decision-makers enter unknown territory during a crisis. Scholar Karl Weick (1993) labeled these scenarios **cosmology episodes**. The term was initially applied to a 1949 forest fire at Mann Gulch, Montana, that resulted in the deaths of 13 smokejumpers. The event consisted of a unique interaction of weather, fire, and geography that trapped the smokejumpers fighting the fire (Weick, 1993). Even though the smokejumpers were experienced and the fire was not considered substantial, the events that unfolded were new to those involved and ended in tragedy. Indeed, there is a sense where crisis events can become cosmology episodes because of the task of confronting the unknown. Such incidents require a rethinking of cognitive paradigms so that new sensemaking can occur (O'Grady & Orton, 2016).

Managing Environmental Uncertainty

Many techniques are available for managing uncertainty in the environment. The first consideration, however, is whether the organization should adapt to its environment or attempt to influence or change it. Sometimes firms have no choice but to adapt, as was the case for most during the COVID-19 pandemic.

Urban hospitals represent a classic example of environmental adaptation when the surrounding neighborhoods where they are located become crime-ridden, a common problem for many urban facilities. Moving the hospital is usually not an option because it is located to serve a specific community. Separating it from local crime is challenging, so measures are taken to ensure the safety of the buildings and the patients. Employing extra security guards, installing perimeter lighting, using security cameras, and utilizing metal detectors are all methods of adapting to the environment.

Occasionally, a business may seek to change its environment to protect it from a crisis. Farmers have used special cannons to ward off approaching hail that might damage crops. For example, in central California, fruit growers have recently started using cannons to combat hail from early spring storms (Curlee, 2016). These anti-hail cannons send a loud popping noise into the air, directed squarely at the storm at hand. Although the practice stems back to the 1890s—and is scientifically debatable—a resurgence of this practice has occurred in both Europe and the United States (Griffith, 2008). Automaker Nissan has used this unusual method for dealing with hail. The company has a production facility in Canton, Mississippi, with a storage area of 140 acres. Hail is a significant concern because of the body damage it can cause to an automobile. To respond to this threat, Nissan installed its anti-hail system using sound-producing hail cannons. Using weather-sensing equipment, when conditions are right for hail, a sonic wave is fired into the air every five and a half seconds to prevent the hail from forming (Foust & Beucke, 2005). However, the cannons created a secondary crisis when neighbors complained about the noise and petitioned the government to require Nissan to stop the practice. Yet, county officials have not found Nissan in violation of existing laws, although they did ask the company to explain to the board how the cannons are supposed to work (Chappell, 2005).

There are other techniques for managing uncertainty. One is buffering, a common approach whereby organizations establish departments to absorb uncertainty from the environment and buffer its effects (Thompson, 1967). For example, purchasing departments perform a buffering role by stockpiling resources for the organization, so a crisis will not occur if they become scarce. Likewise, even companies that follow lean management practices are learning that some buffering is necessary to avoid an interruption within their supply chains (Ganguly & Guin, 2007; Giuntini, 2012).

Another technique is imitation, an approach whereby an organization mimics a successful key competitor. Presumably, organizations that imitate their competitors reduce uncertainty by pursuing "safety in numbers." The concept of imitation is paramount in crisis management as companies seek to learn what other organizations are doing to avoid crises. The literature on high-reliability organizations (HROs) has helped to achieve this goal by extolling how those companies in high-risk environments manage to stay incident-free (Bourrier, 2011; Roberts & Bea, 2001). High-risk environments occur when high amounts of risk and complexity are present in the environment. Examples include aircraft carriers, submarines, electric power grids, nuclear power plants, and air traffic control networks (Bierly, Gallagher & Spender, 2014).

Imitating the successful crisis management techniques of other organizations can be advantageous as well. The crisis management plans for many universities and government agencies are publicly available online. Much can be learned by studying rivals, but managers should understand the differences between organizations before attempting to imitate a rival. Hence, assessing crisis risks must begin with an examination of the organization's internal and external environments.

Environmental Scanning

Keeping abreast of changes in the external environment that can lead to crises presents a key challenge. **Environmental scanning** refers to collecting and analyzing information about relevant trends in the external environment. A systematic environmental scanning process reduces uncertainty and organizes the flow of current information related to organizational decisions. Also, scanning provides decision-makers with an early warning system about changes in the environment. This process is also an essential element in risk identification. Because organization members often lack critical knowledge and information, they may scan the environment by interacting with outsiders, a process known as **boundary spanning.**

Environmental scanning is future-oriented in that it provides a basis for making strategic decisions. It must not be too general (Kumar, Subramanian, & Strandholm, 2001), but specific to organization. Hence, the goal is to provide *adequate* environmental scanning to produce information relevant to the firm (Groom & David, 2001). Although managers may possess knowledge that could mitigate a crisis or prevent it from occurring, they still need to act on that information and make the appropriate decisions.

The infamous crisis that erupted between Royal Dutch/Shell and the environmental activist group Greenpeace illustrates that important cues can still be ignored by management. This incident has been labeled a "predictable surprise," one with plenty of warning indicators, yet caught the company off guard (Watkins & Bazerman, 2003). The incident involved Shell's plan to sink an obsolete oil platform, the *Brent Spar,* in the North Sea. On April 29, 1995, Greenpeace activists boarded the platform and announced they would block its sinking because of radioactive contaminants stored on the structure. Shell responded by blasting the protestors and their boats with water cannons, a move that turned out to cause a significant public relations crisis for the company. After the water cannon incident, opposition to Shell's plans grew in Europe, leading to a boycott of Shell service stations in Germany. Protestors damaged 50 German gas stations, firebombing two of them, and riddling one with bullets (Zyglidopoulos, 2002). Less than two months after the initial Greenpeace protest, Shell gave in and abandoned its plan to sink the *Brent Spar.*

Watkins and Bazerman (2003) note that Royal Dutch/Shell was surprised by the turn of public opinion against them. However, the company had an abundance of information indicating that protests by Greenpeace would likely involve the physical occupation of the platform by activists. Even other oil companies protested Shell's plans. The case illustrates that misreading external signals can still occur even when those signals prove to be reliable.

Environmental scanning should be viewed as a continuous process. Top managers must plan for and identify the information needed to support strategic decision-making and develop a system to secure it. Information is collected, analyzed, and disseminated to the appropriate decision-makers, usually within the firm's functional areas. This information must be acted on and not ignored, as the A. H. Robins case illustrates.

In the early 1970s, A. H. Robins manufactured the Dalkon Shield, a plastic intrauterine contraceptive device (IUD). More than 4 million IUDs were implanted in women by doctors swayed by the company's optimistic research reports (Hartley, 1993). However, warnings from the external environment began to surface almost immediately after the product was introduced. Women were afflicted with pelvic infections, sterility, septic abortions, and in a few cases, death (Barton, 2001; Hartley, 1993). An analysis of information coming in from the external environment would have prompted most companies to halt IUD production, but A. H. Robins persisted in marketing the product. It continued to promote the device as safe, even though management knew there were problems. In the end, thousands of victims sued the company. Eventually, the firm's poor financial standings resulting from lawsuit payoffs led to the sale of the company to American Home Products in 1989 (Barton, 2001).

Large organizations may engage in environmental scanning activities by employing one or more individuals whose sole responsibility is to obtain, process, and distribute important environmental information to their organization's decision-makers. These individuals continually review articles in trade journals and other periodicals and watch for changes in competitor activities. They also monitor what is being said about the company on the Internet, including blogs and other social media outlets. Alternatively, organizations may contract with a research organization that offers environmental scanning services and provides them with real-time searches of published material associated with their organizations, key competitors, and industries. In contrast, decision-makers at many smaller organizations must rely on trade publications or periodicals such as The *Wall Street Journal* to remain abreast of changes that may affect their organizations.

Managers often lack objectivity when evaluating the external environment because they perceive selectively through the lens of their own experiences, professional expertise, and operating departments. This scenario can result in a silo mentality when employees do not look beyond their positions or departments. Ignoring the big picture can pose future crisis risks. For example, cutting the budget of a human resource (HR) department to trim overall costs may sound tempting to the vice president of finance. Still, lapses in HR can lead to inadequate training and loosely enforced safety rules, both of which can contribute to industrial accidents (Sheaffer & Mano-Negrin, 2003).

In an example of functional bias based on CEO background, the now-defunct Massey Energy has long suffered from a tarnished reputation based on its disregard for safety regulations outlined in the coal mining industry (Barrett, 2011). Under the direction of its former CEO, Don Blankenship, the company performed well financially, but at the expense of miner safety (Fisk, Sullivan, & Freifeld, 2010). The result was a decade of mining accidents involving 54 fatalities. According to David McAteer, a governor-appointed investigator of the company's mining accidents between 2000 and 2010, "No United States coal company had a worse fatality record than Massey Energy" (Barrett,

2011, p. 51). The company did not respond adequately to the external cues to prevent a crisis. Instead, Massey alerted staff when inspectors were about to arrive at the mine (Fiscor, 2011) and maintained separate books to cover up safety violations from in-mine safety reports required by federal law (Ward, 2011).

A fundamental problem associated with environmental scanning is determining which available information warrants attention, so it is important to develop sensitive indicators that trigger responses. The December 2004 Asian tsunami detailed later in this chapter illustrates the point. Although an earthquake had been detected, scientists were unsure of the exact size of the resulting tsunami. They were unable to share their observations with countries that would soon be affected because their governments lacked environmental scanning systems (Coombs, 2006).

Identifying Potential Crises Using the SWOT Analysis

The first step in assessing the likelihood of a crisis specific to an organization is to survey the internal and external environments. This process involves the collection of data and perspectives from various stakeholders. The data are integrated into an overall assessment of specific crisis threats that appear to be most prominent. Typically, each threat is ranked in terms of its likelihood and potential impact on the organization. Those crisis threats at the top of the list become the focus of prevention and mitigation efforts.

For example, in 2003, the Pacific Area Travel Association (PATA) provided a framework for its members to identify crisis threats to their organizations, most of which are involved with destination tourism. Using a **SWOT analysis** to identify such threats can also help assess crisis vulnerability (Parnell, 2020; Pennington-Gray, Thapa, Kaplanidou, Cahyanto, & McLaughlin, 2011).

Strengths

Most crises are not driven by organizational strengths. However, as Veil (2011) notes, however, a track record of success can blind management to perceiving warning signals from potential crises.

Location is a crucial strength in some organizations, particularly those in the tourism industry. Lodging establishments can be worthy retreats for tourists in exotic places, such as on islands and beaches. However, a coastal location can become a vulnerability when a hurricane, typhoon, or tsunami emerges. Such was the case for many tourist hotels in Southern Asia when an earthquake occurred off the coast of the island of Sumatra in Indonesia in December 2004. This event triggered a devastating tsunami that caused widespread damage and up to 250,000 fatalities throughout the region. Many of the victims were staying at resorts hotels that were unprepared for such an event

(Cheung & Law, 2006).

Table 4.1 Examples of Strengths and Potential Crisis Events

Internal Strengths	Corresponding Potential Crises
Extremely fast company growth	• Loss of managerial control over operations can occur, particularly when the company has multiple locations over a wide geographic area. This condition can eventually result in defective products and poor service quality. Franchises are especially prone to this type of crisis. • Rapid growth can also lead to high debt and cash flow problems.
Unique differentiating product or service characteristic	• If the product or service offering is new, its uniqueness could later result in a product or service defect. For example, certain elective surgeries and dietary supplements can lead to physical problems.
Charismatic organizational leader	• Some charismatic leaders have led their organizations into financial ruin because their boards did not question their judgment. • Some leaders become so influential that they take on a godlike status and are not challenged by stakeholders. Some successful athletic coaches exemplify this behavior.
The company is both large and successful	• Employees may feel they are not compensated enough, particularly if the company is earning "record profits." • Environmental activists search for any evidence that suggests the company is harming the natural environment. Large companies make good targets because they are more visible to the public. • Social-minded stakeholders claim the company does not "share its wealth" with those in need. • The government watch a company more closely and look for ways to hide income, polluting the environment, harming natural resources, or hiring or firing employees illegally. • Politicians look for *any* wrongdoing on the part of the company, so they can establish a reputation among their constituents as being "tough on greedy corporations."

Management researchers Gilbert Probst and Sebastian Raisch (2005) identified organizational strengths that can eventually lead to problems. For example, excessive growth, what many would deem a desirable performance outcome, can be offset by problems with high debt and an overemphasis on expanding through company acquisitions. In this respect, a strength can lead to a crisis. Likewise, a strong leader in the organization can result in a top-down culture. The followers put blind faith in the leader and fail to approach the leader's strategies with critical questioning (Probst & Raisch, 2005). This situation is further exasperated when boards of directors rubber-stamp the CEO's agenda, often exhibiting groupthink instead of challenging executives with tough questions, further shifting the balance of power dangerously in favor of the CEO (Zweig, 2010). Table 4.1 provides examples of organizational strengths that could result in organizational crises.

Weaknesses

While the link between crises and strengths may not be evident initially, it is both intuitive and well established in the literature. Weaknesses identified in the SWOT analysis should be reviewed considering their potential for breeding crises in the organization. For example, when an organization ignores sound HR practices, a crisis is more likely (Lockwood, 2005). For example, Rent-A-Center eliminated its HR department when its new CEO, J. Ernest Talley, took over in August 1998. The company also changed to a less female-friendly workplace, according to depositions from more than 300 company officials over a 47-state region. Talley's anti-female policy became well known within the company, including several quotes indicating that women should not be working there. Without an HR department, women had no internal recourse for discrimination. Charges of discrimination increased, and many of its female employees filed a class-action lawsuit, eventually resulting in a $47 million verdict against the company (Grossman, 2002).

There are potential crises associated with this strategy. The same employees are on the front lines every day and offer the first contact a customer has with the company's products and services. In general, organizations are better off when they are well trained, loyal, and satisfied with their jobs. Also, large and successful companies are more likely to be criticized for their wages and benefits, as complaints at Amazon and Walmart so often illustrate (Ehrenreich, 2001; Fishman, 2006; Institute for Crisis Management, 2011). Table 4.2 summarizes examples of internal weaknesses that could lead to organizational crises.

Opportunities

A SWOT analysis also examines the organization's opportunities existing in the external environment. Opportunities can generate strategic alternatives a company may pursue to expand its market share. However, vulnerabilities can surface and escalate into a crisis, particularly as the firm considers globalization options.

Table 4.2 Examples of Weaknesses and Potential Crisis Events

Internal Weaknesses	Corresponding Potential Crises
Poorly trained employees	• Industrial accidents in the workplace may occur. • Poor service to the customer can result in lost sales and negative publicity. • In manufacturing settings, defective products may trigger product recalls and negative publicity.
Poor relationship with a labor union	• Labor strikes during contract negotiations can halt production. • More grievances resulting from day-to-day operations can result in production slowdowns and negative ill-will towards management. • Negative publicity in the media can result as labor strife is visible to the community and other stakeholders.
Poor ethical orientation of top management	• White-collar crime due to ethical and legal breeches of the law. • Cash-flow problems due to negative publicity and perhaps, boycotts.
Aging production facilities and equipment	• More machine breakdowns can occur, resulting in lost productivity, higher operating costs, and product defects. • When neglected to compromise safety, industrial accidents can occur, resulting in severe injuries and loss of life.
Understaffed Human Resource Department	• Discrimination against legally protected groups and sexual harassment charges can occur. • Higher operating costs can lead to budget cuts in training and, ultimately, industrial accidents, employee absenteeism, and turnover.
Lack of competitive employee benefits	• Negative publicity from both internal and external stakeholders can occur. • Lack of employee loyalty could lead to hiring only marginal employees and a cycle of continuous employee turnover.
Haphazard safety inspections	• Industrial accidents coupled with increased workplace injuries are likely. • The larger the organization, the more likely it will endure negative publicity.
Employee substance abuse	• Increased industrial accidents, workplace injuries, and product quality problems may result.
Lack of a crisis management team and plan	• Slow and ineffective response to crisis events can occur. • A negative public perception of the organization results because the firm is seen as unprepared.

Many firms have responded to Internet opportunities by shifting some or all their sales offerings online. Indeed, this practice was a means of survival for many organizations during the COVID-19 pandemic. Nonetheless, the learning curve associated with this transition can be quite steep. However, companies that generate online sales are open to crises related to cybersecurity, including theft of personal records of consumers and denial-of-service attacks (DOS) by hackers.

Table 4.3 outlines three possible scenarios in which a strategic response to opportunities may breed a crisis.

Table 4.3 Examples of Opportunities and Potential Crisis Events

External Opportunities	Corresponding Potential Crises
Expand product availability by moving from a retail storefront to an omnichannel arrangement (i.e., physical and online distribution)	• Offering products online can lead to denial-of-service cyberattacks by hackers. • While hackers are usually external to the organization, a disgruntled employee could also become one.
Expand company manufacturing facilities to another part of the world via a greenfield venture strategy	• In this option, the company builds and owns its manufacturing facility in a different host country. While the quality and process can be controlled more effectively than through a licensing approach (see the next option), there is also the risk of outside interference from the host country. • In some instances, companies have been taken over by the host country's government and become state-owned.
Outsource to another company outside the home country	• Because jobs in the home country are usually lost, the company could incur negative publicity from external stakeholders, particularly former employees, labor unions, politicians, and municipalities that once hosted the business. • If the outsourcing is through a licensing agreement, there is the possibility that parties in the host country may pirate proprietary information. • The outsourced company's product may be defective due to a lack of control over the production process. This situation creates a two-pronged crisis. First, the defective product itself creates problems received by the final consumer. Second, a public image problem occurs because the firm decided to outsource overseas in the first place.

Threats

Threats reside outside of the organization and are a familiar source of crises. Ironically, an opportunity in one organization can be a threat in another. For example, in the southeastern United States, weather concerns such as hurricanes are included in the risk assessment (Kruse, 1993). Other regions of the United States, such as California, are vulnerable to earthquakes and wildfires. In the destination tourism industry, international hotels, particularly those with Western brands, are at risk for terrorist attacks because they represent Western interests (Neumayer & Plumper, 2016). Urban and rural locations can also engender different types of crises. Events such as riots, power outages, and severe weather can be especially treacherous in densely populated regions.

Some external threats are common to an industry. For example, evidence supports various health risks associated with indoor tanning (Banerjee, Hay & Greene, 2015; Petit, Karila, Chalmin, & Lejoyeux, 2014). Tanning patrons are mostly female, and unfortunately, melanoma is one of the two most common cancers for young women ages 20-29. When adjusting for outdoor tanning dangers, indoor tanners are about two times more likely to be diagnosed with melanoma or some other type of skin cancer compared with non-indoor tanners (Geller, 2015). Some states have enacted restrictions on teens using indoor tanning beds, but overall, the rate at which adolescents use these devices has not been reduced (Driscoll & Darcy, 2015; Hession et al., 2013). Similarly, cigarette manufacturers denied a link between smoking and health problems until the evidence became overwhelming. Table 4.4 overviews various external threats that can evolve into a crisis.

Organizational Culture and Crisis Planning

Culture refers to the commonly held values and beliefs of a group of people (Weitz & Shenhav, 2000). **Organizational culture** refers to the shared values and patterns of belief and behavior accepted and practiced by the members of an organization (Duncan, 1989). An organization's culture is the basis for many day-to-day decisions in the organization. Long-term members understand it well, and newcomers usually learn it quickly. For example, members of an organization whose culture values innovation are more likely to invest the time necessary to develop creative solutions to complex problems (Deal & Kennedy, 1982). An innovative organization is more likely to "do its homework" and take the steps necessary to prevent crises from occurring. This homework includes setting up crisis management teams, developing plans, and practicing mock disasters to learn how to manage a crisis more effectively.

Table 4.4 Examples of Threats and Potential Crisis Events

External Threats	Corresponding Potential Crises
Changing demographics of the surrounding neighborhood	• The organization may become a target for crime, such as vandalism or robbery. • Sales revenue may decline.
Severe weather	• The building and facilities may be damaged by wind, snow, or flooding. • Sales revenue may be interrupted while the building undergoes repair.
Dysfunctional customers or employees	• There could be an incident of workplace violence.
Poor-quality products from a supplier	• The components assembled into the final product cause product defects. • If the component was outsourced, negative publicity might follow.
Consumer activism due to inferior products or some other activity of the company	• Consumer lawsuits may develop in the case of poor-quality products. • Boycotts of the company's products and services can result.
Extortionists	• Product tampering may occur. • Online extortionists may threaten the company's website with a denial-of-service or piracy of confidential data.
Earthquake, wildfire, or another natural disaster	• Structural damage to the building and information technology systems can occur. • Injuries and fatalities could occur to employees and customers. • Interruptions in the supply chain may occur.
Rumors/Negative publicity	• Loss of revenue due to boycotts and negative publicity may result. • Negative attention could appear on the Internet through hate sites, blogs, and other social media outlets such as Facebook and Twitter.
Terrorism	• Direct physical attacks on buildings can result in damage, injuries, and fatalities. • Attacks outside the organization may disrupt the supply chain.

Organizational culture exists at two levels. At the *surface level,* one can observe specific behaviors and artifacts of the organization, such as accepted forms of dress, company logos, office rituals, and ceremonies, such as awards banquets. These outward behaviors reflect the second level of organizational culture—a more profound, *underlying level* that includes shared values, belief patterns, and thought processes common to the organization (Schein, 1990).

The underlying level of culture is the most critical to understand because it influences how organizational members think and interpret their work. Embracing a culture of crisis planning must occur at the underlying level first before it is evident at the surface level. Indeed, as crisis communications expert Timothy Coombs (2006) put it, crisis management must become the organization's DNA.

Organizational culture also contributes to the firm's crisis management response (Bowers, Hall, & Srinivasan, 2017). As Marra (2004) points out, organizational culture helps determine the success of crisis communications, a primary facet of the overall crisis management process. In the realm of crisis management, there appear to be *crisis-prepared* cultures that support crisis planning and those that do not, appropriately labeled *crisis-prone* (Pearson & Mitroff, 1993). Managers should seek to develop and support crisis-prepared cultures in their organizations.

Even though crisis planning is an integral part of the strategic management process, not all managers view it as essential. Nonetheless, an organization's crisis vulnerability is linked to its cultural norms and assumptions (Smith & Elliott, 2007). In other words, being diligent about crisis planning involves a cultural shift for some organizations that have not been active in crisis management planning. As a result, organizations often do not have effective crisis management plans because their managers have not cultivated a mindset that values this process (Weick & Sutcliffe, 2001). Many managers are engrossed with "putting out today's fires" and do not think they have time to plan for tomorrow's contingencies. Therefore, they have not developed the critical tools needed for a comprehensive crisis management plan (Simbo, 2003).

Many organizations fail to engender a culture of crisis preparedness. At one end of the scale, many managers carry an "it can't happen to us" mentality (Nathan, 2000; Pearson & Mitroff, 1993) and argue that "nobody gets credit for fixing problems that never happened" (Repenning & Sterman, 2001). Other managers are reactive concerning crises by contemporaneously managing events as they unfold. Because of their cultures, some organizations seem to develop blind spots and completely miss the cues that signal a crisis (Smallman & Weir, 1999).

Other managers are more proactive and plan for future potential crises by evaluating worst-case scenarios. Managers who have become experienced organizational crises tend to engage more vigorously in crisis planning (Carmeli & Schaubroeck, 2008).

Summary

The crisis management process should be viewed from a strategic perspective and should be part of its overall strategic planning agenda. This process should include (1) an external analysis of its opportunities and threats, (2) an internal analysis of the firm's strengths and weakness, (3) a strategy formulation stage, (4) a strategy execution stage, and finally, (5) a strategic control emphasis.

Analyzing the external environment can help prevent a crisis because it involves assessing environmental uncertainty. Uncertainty occurs when decision-makers lack enough current, reliable information about their organizations and cannot accurately forecast. Uncertainty is lowest in organizations where environments are simple and stable. Organizational crises can occur at any level of environmental uncertainty but is especially vulnerable in highly complex and unstable environments.

Environmental scanning refers to collecting and analyzing information about relevant trends in the external environment. A systematic environmental scanning process reduces uncertainty and organizes the flow of current information related to organizational decisions while providing decisionmakers with an early warning system for changes in the environment.

The SWOT analysis enables management to identify the crisis threats that are specific to their organization. Ironically, it is not just organizational weaknesses and external threats that can lead to crises. The firm's internal strengths and external opportunities, under the right circumstances, can breed crises as well.

Finally, the organization's culture influences the enthusiasm that exists for crisis management. Developing a crisis management plan may involve changes in the company's culture, including changing how management and staff view crises in general.

Discussion Questions

1. Why should crisis management be integrated with an organization's strategic planning process?
2. What are the four types of environmental uncertainty that exist in the external environment? How is each one linked to a potential set of crises?
3. What is environmental scanning? What tools are available to help management scan the environment so that it would yield information useful to identify potential crises?
4. How can an organization's strengths be a source of crises?
5. How can organizational opportunities facilitate crises?

6. How can a company change its organizational culture to become more responsive to crisis planning?

Chapter Exercise

1. Identifying potential threats to an organization is an effective method to prepare for future crises. Perform a crisis vulnerability assessment of your college, university, or organization.
2. Identify potential crises in each realm of the SWOT analysis (i.e., strengths, weaknesses, opportunities, and threats). Assess each crisis threat in terms of its likelihood and potential impact.

Closing Chapter Case: Duck Boat Tragedy - Part 2

In part one of this case, we examined the events surrounding the 2018 duck boat disaster on Table Rock Lake near Branson, Missouri. In part 2, we explore the findings of the National Transportation Safety Board (NTSB) and probe the question of profits over safety. We do not seek to place blame, but to identify solutions appropriate for all stakeholders.

Findings and Recommendations of the NTSB

The NTSB issued the following recommendations to improve the seaworthiness of duck boats after the 1999 accident on Lake Hamilton in Hot Springs, Arkansas (*NTSB News Release*, 2002):

- Reserve buoyancy should be provided by constructing watertight compartmentalization within the vessel. Doing so will provide additional buoyancy if the boat takes on water. However, this is also a time-consuming and expensive upgrade.
- In the intermittent period before reserve buoyancy can be achieved, the canopies should be removed. This will facilitate escape from the boat in the event of a potential sinking.
- If the canopy has been removed, and additional buoyancy has not been provided, passengers should wear life vests. (Interestingly, the board specifically recommended not wearing life vests if the canopy is still intact).
- In the absence of reserved buoyancy, close unnecessary access plugs, reduce the size of through-hull penetrations and install independently powered electric bilge pumps.

NTSB recommendations are not legally enforceable, so duck boat operators are free to implement any or all of them. Furthermore, operators of duck boats function independently, so they are free to follow their safety protocols. Unfortunately, the recommendations by the NTSB do not appear to have been implemented in Branson. The reserve buoyancy that would have kept the boat afloat was not evident, and the canopy was still intact (Maher, 2018).

Land Operations of Ducks and the Problem of Following Through

The 2015 accident on the Aurora Bridge in Seattle, Washington, occurred on land. It resulted in five fatalities and was attributed to a faulty axle that had not been appropriately maintained (Bellisle, 2016). Ironically, the protective boot covering the drive axle led to the 1999 accident in Arkansas. The defective boot allowed water to enter the boat rapidly and caused it to sink within 30 seconds (Beddingfield, 1999). Herein lies a critical factor that shows how these two accidents were related. The drive axle makes a boat amphibious; without it, a boat is not a land vessel.

The NTSB (2015) investigation revealed that improper maintenance was the main factor in the failure of the drive axle. Other findings included:

- Stretch vehicles, like the one that crashed, need to have their axle housings repaired or replaced. Stretch vehicles are duck boats that are modified from the original vessel, so they are longer than the original boat. As such, stretch vehicles using the original axle must be modified as well. Modifications to the axle to account for the longer length of the vessel were not done correctly, creating the potential for axle failure, which occurred.
- The Seattle-based company that modified the duck boats into stretch boats was called Ride the Ducks International (RTDI). RTDI never registered with the National Highway Transportation Safety Administration (NHTSA) as a motor vehicle manufacturer. As a result, it avoided NHTSA oversight.

Profits before Safety?

Critics often charge that crises such as these illustrate that companies value profits over safety. From a cost perspective, operating managers know that money spent on maintenance could bolster short-term profits, explaining why some firms continue to use outdated equipment and why some accidents eventually occur. Labor devoted to maintenance increases expenses but is required to repair or replace a faulty part. Delaying an expenditure can improve the income statement in the short run but can also create long-term vulnerabilities. The duck boat is a unique, almost one-of-a-kind vessel that makes maintenance and standardized procedures more complicated because there is little vehicle/vessel history with which to work.

According to an attorney representing the families of the Table Rock Lake victims, "Despite countless explicit warnings, (the) defendants repeatedly chose to value profits over the safety of their passengers" (Maher, 2018, p. A3). In addition to ignoring the NTSB recommendations, a 2017 inspection indicated the boats might fail in bad weather because of the placement of the bilge pumps and exhaust systems. Bilge pumps are necessary to pump out water that enters the boat. If these do not function properly, the vessel could sink.

Nonetheless, one could argue that there have been millions of duck boat passengers who have never been involved in an accident. Therefore, the Table Rock Lake accident could be viewed as a **black swan**, a rare, unpredictable, and highly impactful event with little or no precedence. Indeed, the weather was calm when the boat left. However, while the weather conditions may have been unique, the warnings and recommendations made to protect a duck boat against those rare weather events had been made clear before the accident. Those recommendations were not followed.

Case Discussion Questions

1. The 2018 accident at Table Rock Lake could be viewed as (1) an error on the part of the captain, (2) a matter of profits over passenger safety, or (3) a combination of the two. Discuss the merits of each perspective and outline a strategy for addressing them that reduces the likelihood of a similar crisis in the future.
2. What examples from the transportation industry suggest that pilot (or driver/captain) error caused the accident?
3. What examples from the transportation industry suggest that management might have focused on profits at the expense of safety?

References

Banerjee, S., Hay, J., & Greene, K. (2015). Indoor tanning addiction tendencies: Role of positive tanning beliefs, perceived vulnerability, and tanning risk knowledge. *Addiction Research & Theory, 23*(2), 156-162.

Barrett, J. (2018, September 4). Wary tourists chill duck-boat business. *Wall Street Journal,* p. A3.

Barrett, J., & Lazo, A. (2018, July 21). Death toll rises to 17 in boat incident. *Wall Street Journal,* p. A3.

Barrett, P. (2011, August 29). Cleaning America's dirtiest coal company. *Bloomberg Businessweek,* 48–55.

Barton, L. (2001). *Crisis in organizations II.* Cincinnati, OH: Southwestern.

Bauer, L., Cummings, I., Adler, E., & McKinley, E. (2018, July 20). Weather Service issued warnings of excessive winds before duck boat sank, killing 17. *The Kansas City Star.* Retrieved November 26, 2018, from https://www.kansascity.com/news/state/missouri/article215222260.html

Beddingfield, K. (1999, May 17). The aftermath of a fatal sinking. *US News & World Report, 126*(99), 66.

Bellisle, M. (2016, November 16). Improper maintenance, broken axle led to Ride the Ducks crash, NTSB rules. *The Seattle Times*. Retrieved November 23, 2018, from https://www.seattletimes.com/seattle-news/ntsb-ruling-expected-today-on-cause-of-ride-the-ducks-crash/

Bierly, P., Gallagher, S., & Spender, J. (2014). Innovation decision making in high-risk organizations: A comparison of the US and Soviet attack submarine programs. *Industrial and Corporate Change*, *23*(3), 759-795.

Bonvento, M. (2018). Avoiding the next tragedy. *Marine Log, 123*(9), 29-30.

Bourrier, M. (2011). The legacy of the high reliability organization project. *Journal of Contingencies and Crisis Management, 19*(1), 9–13.

Bouve, J., Steens, H., & Ruebens, M. (2018). Business continuity and risk management at a strategic level: Case study of the Flemish government. *Journal of Business Continuity & Emergency Planning, 11*(3), 223-231.

Bowers, M., Hall, J., & Srinivasan, M. (2017). Organizational culture and leadership style: The missing combination for selecting the right leader for effective crisis management. *Business Horizons, 60*(4), 551-563.

Carmeli, A., & Schaubroeck, J. (2008). Organisational crisis preparedness: The importance of learning from failures. *Long Range Planning, 4,* 177–196.

Carpenter, M. A. (2002). The implications of strategy and social context for the relationship between top management heterogeneity and firm performance. *Strategic Management Journal, 23,* 275–284.

Chappell, L. (2005, August 22). Nissan's booming, neighbors fuming. *Automotive News, 4,* 36.

Cheung, C., & Law, R. (2006). How can hotel guests be protected during the occurrence of a tsunami? *Asia Pacific Journal of Tourism Research, 11*(3), 289–295.

Chong, J., & Park, J. (2010). A conceptual framework and research propositions for integrating TQM into crisis planning. *Review of Business Research, 10*(2), 69–74.

Coombs, W. (2006). *Code red in the boardroom: Crisis management as organizational DNA.* Westport, CT: Praeger.

Curlee, D. (2016). Noisy cannons discourage hail damage in fruit. *Western Farm Press*, *38*(10), 8.

Das, T., & Teng, B. (1999). Cognitive biases and strategic decision processes: An integrative perspective. *Journal of Management Studies, 36,* 757–778.

Deal, T., & Kennedy, A. (1982). *Corporate cultures: The rites and rituals of corporate life.* Reading, MA: Addison-Wesley.

Driscoll, D., & Darcy, J. (2015). Indoor tanning legislation: Shaping policy and nursing practice. *Pediatric Nursing*, *41*(2), 59-88.

Duncan, R. (1972). Characteristics of perceived environments and perceived environmental uncertainty. *Administrative Science Quarterly, 17,* 313–327.

Duncan, W. (1989). Organizational culture: "Getting a fix" on an elusive concept. *Academy of Management Executive, 3,* 229–236.

Ehrenreich, B. (2001). *Nickel and dimed: On (not) getting by in America.* New York: Henry Holt and Company.

Fiscor, S. (2011). MSHA provides update on UBB explosion. *Coal Age, 116*(7), 30–34.

Fishman, C. (2006). *The Walmart effect: How the world's most powerful company really works—and how it's transforming the American economy.* New York: Penguin.

Fisk, M., Sullivan, B., & Freifeld, K. (2010, April 25). The accountant of coal. *Business Week,* 48–51.

Foust, D., & Beucke, D. (2005, October 5). Heading off storms. *Business Week,* 16.

Ganguly, K., & Guin, K. (2007). A framework for assessment of supply-related risk in supply chain. *Journal of Supply Chain Management, 4*(4), 86–98.

Geller, A. (2015). Indoor tanning dangers. *Pediatrics for parents, 30*(7/8), 18.

Giuntini, R. (2012). Contingency planning: Ten good ways to keep a supply chain from going bad. *Material Handling & Logistics, 67*(1), 44-47.

Gordon, J. (2007). Family-owned duck boat tour business recovers. *Arkansas Business, 24*(14), 2.

Griffith, M. (2008). The return of the anti-hail cannons. *Weatherwise, 61*(4), 14–18.

Groom, J., & David, F. (2001). Competitive intelligence activity among small firms. *SAM Advanced Management Journal, 66*(1), 12–29.

Grossman, R. (2002). Paying the price. Events at Rent-A-Center prove that when employers don't respect HR today, they'll pay tomorrow. *HR Magazine, 47*(8), 28–37.

Haddon, H., & Bunge, J. (2019, May 20). Swine fever to lift meat prices in US. *Wall Street Journal*, pp. B1, B2.

Hartley, R. (1993). *Business ethics: Violations of the public trust.* New York: Wiley.

Hession, M., Campbell, S., Balk, S., & Cummins, D. (2013). Pediatricians' perspectives on indoor tanning. *Pediatric Dermatology, 30*(5), 626-627.

Hoffman, M. (2000). If it drives, but floats like a duck, it's hard to insure. *Business Insurance, 34*(18), 10.

Institute for Crisis Management. (2011). *Annual ICM crisis report: News coverage of business crises during 2010.* Retrieved November 16, 2018, from http://crisisconsultant.com/images/2010CrisisReportICM.pdf

Jacques, A. (2009). Domino's delivers during crisis. *Public Relations Strategist, 15*(3), 6–10.

Kaplan, R., & Mikes, A. (2012). Managing risks: A new framework. *Harvard Business Review, 90*(6), 48-60.

Kapner, S., & Santiago, L. (2020, July 17). Store closings on track to double this year as virus hits retailers hard. *Wall Street Journal*, p. B1.

Kausar, S., & Baghoor, G. (2017, October). Challenging the multilayered crises within organizations through application of effective human resource strategies. *Pakistan Business Review*, 529-544.

Kruse, C. (1993). Disaster plan stands the test of hurricane. *Personnel Journal, 72*(6), 36–43.

Kumar, K., Subramanian, R., & Strandholm, K. (2001). Competitive strategy, environmental scanning, and performance: A context specific analysis of their relationship. *International Journal of Commerce and Management, 11,* 1–33.

Lockwood, N. (2005). Crisis management in today's business environment: HR's strategic role. *SHRM Research Quarterly, 4*(4), 1–9.

Maher, K. (2018, July 31). Missouri boat operator is accused of ignoring warnings. *Wall Street Journal*, p. A3.

Maltais, K., & Bunge, J. (2019, March 29). China pork virus shifts business to US. *Wall Street Journal*, pp. B1, B2.

Marra, F. (2004). Excellent crisis communication: Beyond crisis plans. In D. P. Millar & R. L. Heaths (Eds.), *Responding to crisis: A rhetorical approach to crisis communication* (pp. 311–325). Mahwah, NJ: Erlbaum.

Nathan, M. (2000). The paradoxical nature of crisis. *Review of Business, 21*(3), 12–16.

Neumayer, E., & Plümper, T. (2016). Spatial spill-overs from terrorism on tourism: Western victims in Islamic destination countries. *Public Choice, 169,* 195-206.

NTSB (2015). *Amphibious Passenger Vehicle DUCK 6 Lane Crossover Collision with Motorcoach on State Route 99, Aurora Bridge Seattle, Washington September 24, 2015.* Retrieved November 26, 2018, from https://www.ntsb.gov/investigations/AccidentReports/Reports/HAR1602.pdf

NTSB News Release (2018, July 27). Initial Review of Duck Boat Digital Video Recorder System Completed. Retrieved November 26, 2018, from https://www.ntsb.gov/news/press-releases/Pages/nr20180727

NTSB News Release, (2002, April 2). NTSB determines cause of 1999 "Duck" boat sinking. Retrieved November 23, 2018, from https://www.ntsb.gov/news/press-releases/Pages/NTSB_Determines_Cause_of_1999_Duck_Boat_Sinking.aspx

O'Grady, K., & Orton, J. (2016). Resilience processes during cosmology episodes: Lessons learned from the Haiti earthquake. *Journal of Psychology & Theology, 44*(2), 109-123.

O'Rourke, M. (2008). Some say tomato, some say jalapeno. *Risk Management, 55*(9), 14–16.

Parnell, J. (2020). *Strategic management: Theory and practice* (6th ed.). Solon, OH: Academic Media Solutions.

Parnell, J., & Crandall, W. (2017). The contribution of behavioral economics to crisis management decision-making. *Journal of Management & Organization.*

Pearson, C., & Mitroff, A. (1993). From crisis prone to crisis prepared: A framework for crisis management. *Academy of Management Executive, 71,* 48–59.

Pennington-Gray, L., Thapa, B., Kaplanidou, K., Cahyanto, I., & McLaughlin, E. (2011). Crisis planning and preparedness in the United States Tourism Industry. *Cornell Hospitality Quarterly, 52*(3), 312–320.

Petit, A., Karila, L., Chalmin, F., & Lejoyeux, M. (2014). Phenomenology and psychopathology of excessive indoor tanning. *International Journal of Dermatology, 53,* 664-672.

Probst, G., & Raisch, S. (2005). Organizational crisis: The logic of failure. *Academy of Management Executive, 19*(1), 90–105.

Repenning, N., & Sterman, J. (2001). Nobody ever gets credit for fixing problems that never happened. *California Management Review, 43*(Summer), 64–88.

Robb, D. (2005). Defending against viruses, worms and DoS attacks. *Business Communications Review, 35*(12), 24–27.

Roberts, K., & Bea, R. (2001). Must accidents happen? Lessons from high-reliability organizations. *Academy of Management Executive, 15*(3), 70–78.

Scammell, H. (2003). Chalk's Ocean Airways. *Air and Space Magazine.* Retrieved August 9, 2019, from http://www.airspacemag.com/history-of-flight/cit-scammell.html

Schein, E. (1990). Organizational culture. *American Psychologist, 45,* 109–119.

Schrader, R. (2010). Six actions to enable efficient traceability. *Food Logistics, 121,* 34–35.

Sheaffer, Z., & Mano-Negrin, R. (2003). Executives' orientations as indicators of crisis management policies and practices. *Journal of Management Studies, 40*(2), 573–606.

Shrivastava, P. (1995). Industrial/environmental crises and corporate social responsibility. *Journal of Socio-Economics, 24(*1), 211–217.

Silveira-Martins, E., & Rosseto, C. (2018). Mapping of scientific production on uncertainty in international environmental basis. *Brazilian Journal of Management, 11*(1), 78-101.

Simbo, A. (2003). Catastrophe planning and crisis management. *Risk Management, 40*(2), 64–66.

Smallman, C., & Weir, D. (1999). Communication and cultural distortion during crises. *Disaster Prevention and Management, 8*(1), 33–41.

Smith, D. (1990). Beyond contingency planning: Towards a model of crisis management. *Industrial Crisis Quarterly, 4*(4), 263–275.

Smith, D., & Elliott, D. (2007). Exploring the barriers to learning from crisis: Organizational learning and crisis. *Management Learning, 38*(5), 519–538.

Stevens, L., Ng, S., & Banjo, S. (2013, December 27). Behind UPS's Christmas eve snafu. *Wall Street Journal*, pp. B1-B2.

Taneja, S., Pryor, M., Sewell, S., & Recuero, A. (2014). Strategic crisis management: A basis for renewal and crisis prevention. *Journal of Management Policy and Practice, 15*(1), 78-85.

Thompson, J. (1967). *Organizations in action.* New York: McGraw-Hill.

Todt, R. (2012, May 2). New video shows fatal 2010 Philly duck boat crash. US News Online. *The Associated Press*. Retrieved on November 23, 2018 from https://login.proxy181.nclive.org/login?url=http://search.ebscohost.com/login.aspx?direct=true&db=n 5h&AN=848fca0f3f2144829646d8e2cfbd0e07&site=ehost-live

Veil, S. (2011). Mindful learning in crisis management. *Journal of Business Communications, 48*(2), 116–147.

Vines, M. (2007). Intelligence. *Business and Commercial Aviation, 101*(1), 13–26.

Ward, K. (2011, June 29). MSHA: Massey covered up Upper Big Branch safety hazards. *Charleston Gazette*. Retrieved August 9, 2019, from http://wvgazette.com/News/201106290959

Watkins, M., & Bazerman, M. (2003). Predictable surprises: The disasters you should have seen coming. *Harvard Business Review, 81*(3), 72–80.

Weick, K. (1993). The collapse of sensemaking in organizations: The Mann Gulch disaster. *Administrative Science Quarterly, 38,* 628–652.

Weick, K., & Sutcliffe, K. (2001). *Managing the unexpected.* San Francisco: Jossey-Bass.

Weitz, E., & Shenhav, Y. (2000). A longitudinal analysis of technical and organizational uncertainty in management theory. *Organization Studies, 21,* 243–265.

Williams, C. (2016). Five action lists for a cyber crisis. *Hospitals & Health Networks*, *90*(11), 36-40.

Zhang, J. (2008, June 12). Food-safety measures faulted. *Wall Street Journal,* p. A4.

Zweig, D. (2010). The board that couldn't think straight. *Conference Board Review, 47*(2), 40–47.

Zyglidopoulos, S. (2002). The social and environmental responsibilities of multinationals: Evidence from the Brent Spar case. *Journal of Business Ethics, 36,* 141–151.

Chapter 5: Forming the Crisis Management Team and Writing the Plan

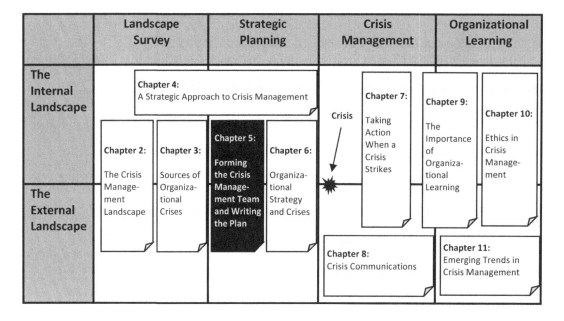

Learning Objectives

After reading this chapter, each student should be able to:

1. Identify and describe the five goals of the crisis management team.
2. Describe the ideal characteristics of members on the crisis management team.
3. Identify the key individuals who should be on the crisis management team.
4. Describe the opportunities and challenges involved with virtual crisis management teams.
5. Identify and describe the various problems that can occur within crisis management teams.
6. Identify and describe the various components of the crisis management plan.
7. Identify and discuss the different forms of crisis management training.
8. Describe the purposes of a mock disaster.
9. Describe the process of setting up a mock disaster.

Opening Chapter Case: The University of North Carolina at Pembroke Braces for Hurricane Florence – Part 1

On September 11, 2018, Hurricane Florence was heading for the North Carolina coast. For several days, the University of North Carolina at Pembroke (UNCP) had actively monitored the storm's position and its potential impact on the university and its internal and external stakeholders. North Carolina Governor Roy Cooper issued mandatory evacuations on the coast and warned citizens – "Don't bet your life on a monster" (Barrett, 2018). Florence was about to devastate the Carolinas.

Just two years earlier, in 2016, Hurricane Matthew brought torrential rains and flooding to the area (Gronberg, 2016). Many UNCP employees suffered damage to their homes, and some were destroyed. The university closed for five class days while buildings and facilities dried out, and crews restored power.

Hurricane damage can emanate from wind, rain, or both. Rain was the culprit with Hurricane Matthew, resulting in substantial flooding in Pembroke and nearby Lumberton, 12 miles east. Many professors and students—stakeholders of the university—lived in Lumberton and experienced Matthew's wrath. Their memories added to the anxiety and fear of another approaching storm. Matthew's flooding was less widespread north of Pembroke, but high winds caused pine trees (which have relatively weak root systems) to topple on power lines, causing widespread outages.

UNCP was well acquainted with crisis management procedures. It had an active crisis management team and plan, practiced mock disasters and drills, and met regularly to learn from past crises. The university had even completed three annual active shooter drills involving extensive participation from local emergency providers (Scott Billingsley, personal communication, October 5, 2018). But on September 11, 2018, UNCP found itself facing a new crisis, Hurricane Florence. The university was able to mitigate the impact of the storm, but it could not prevent the coming onslaught.

Case Discussion Questions

1. Does your university or organization have a plan for hurricanes or other weather-related emergencies? If so, what are the details of the plan? If you are not sure, you might locate it online.
2. A hurricane is an example of a crisis that must be mitigated because it cannot be prevented. What mitigation strategies are required for weather-related events in your area?

Introduction

A crisis management team (CMT) and a crisis management plan (CMP) can help an organization prepare for crises. The CMT and the CMP represent the core of an organization's crisis planning efforts. The team meets first, develops the plan, and tests it through mock disaster drills. This chapter explores each of these processes in detail.

Forming the Crisis Management Team (CMT)

The CMT is the most effective and appropriate starting point for crisis planning.

Goals of the CMT

The primary mission of the CMT is to plan for potential crises and manage those that occur. Developing this mission involves five specific goals, as illustrated in Figure 5.1.

Figure 5.1 Goals of the Crisis Management Team (CMT)

	Landscape Survey	Strategic Planning	Crisis Management	Organizational Learning
The Internal Landscape	1. The CMT identifies the crisis threats the organization is facing.	2. The CMT develops the crisis management plan (CMP).	Crisis	5. The CMT leads the post-crisis evaluation so that learning can occur.
The External Landscape		3. The CMT leads training in the area of crisis management.	4. The CMT actively manages a crisis when one occurs.	

1. *The CMT identifies the crisis threats the organization is facing.* Every organization faces threats that are unique to its industry and in some cases, to its location. The CMT considers these factors as it evaluates the specific risks that could instigate a crisis. The team cannot formulate a response for every potential crisis, so it must be flexible (Clark & Harman, 2004). Most threats cluster into crisis families or groups for which preparations can usually be made (Coombs & Holladay, 2001; Pearson & Mitroff 1993). Viewing threats as clusters simplifies the threat assessment phase because managers can plan responses to potential families (categories) of crises rather than to each potential crisis.

2. *The CMT develops the crisis management plan (CMP).* The CMT develops a crisis management plan (CMP) that addresses the potential crisis threats identified in the first step. The plan also contains key contact information for vendors and other important stakeholders. The plan is often posted on the organization's website or another area that is conspicuous to a broad cross-section of employees and other significant stakeholders.

3. *The CMT facilitates training in crisis management.* The CMT oversees the crisis training efforts in the organization. Two training levels are recommended, one for the CMT, and one for the organization members at large. Team training should occur at regularly scheduled intervals. The training content usually revolves around reviewing the crisis management plan and conducting simulated drills (Coombs, 2007). These mock drills are necessary because the CMT does not know how well it can function during a crisis unless the team and crisis plan are tested periodically (Clark & Harman, 2004). Training activities should coordinate with internal and external constituencies. For example, when setting up a mock disaster drill, it is necessary to contact external stakeholders such as fire departments and emergency medical service (EMS) organizations.

4. *The CMT actively manages a crisis.* When a crisis occurs, the CMT is activated and manages the event. This phase of the team's experience is most crucial because it exposes performance levels in two areas: (1) How well was the crisis handled, and (2) how well did members of the team work together?

5. *The CMT leads the post-crisis evaluation to facilitate organizational learning.* The post-crisis assessment determines how well the crisis was managed and addresses the following questions:
   - What did we learn, and what can we do to prevent a similar one in the future?
   - What can be done to mitigate the impact of a similar crisis in the future?
   - Which aspects of the crisis response were performed effectively?
   - Which aspects of the crisis response need improvement?

Scheduling the evaluation sessions is the most important factor in the post-crisis evaluation phase. These sessions should occur soon after the event, while the crisis details are still familiar to everyone. Waiting too long can lead to forgetfulness (Kovoor-Misra & Nathan, 2000), hampering the organization's ability to make necessary improvements.

Team Member Characteristics

The CMT has been referred to as the "nerve center of the crisis management process"

(Gilpin & Murphy, 2008, p. 134). As a result, CMT members must have a specific and complementary set of individual characteristics that allow them to work well in a group setting. A diverse team that includes members from various functional areas is ideal (Uitdewilligen & Waller, 2018; Waller, Lei, & Pratten, 2014). Effective CMT members typically share seven characteristics.

Critical Thinking Skills

Critical thinking includes analyzing problems, challenging assumptions, and evaluating alternatives (Coombs, 2007; Gilpin & Murphy, 2008). Critical thinkers can read between the lines and discern intentions. Each team member must also learn and evaluate as the crisis unfolds (Antonacopoulou & Sheaffer, 2014). Understanding the accumulation of details to an event and how they lead to a crisis is essential (Roux-Dufort, 2009).

Ability to Work in a Team Environment

CMT members must like people and enjoy working in team settings. A CMT assignment is not appropriate for an employee who prefers to work independently. Above all, CMT members must be willing to work toward shared goals (Coombs, 2007).

Ability to Think Under Pressure

CMT members should be able to think and work under pressure (Clark & Harman, 2004). Employees react to stress in different ways, and some do not manage it effectively. For CMT members, stress should be a motivator, a shot of adrenaline that makes them want to lead during a crisis (Chandler, 2001).

Ambiguity Tolerance

Perfect information is always preferred, but managers typically make crisis decisions under uncertainty. Ambiguity tolerance enables a decision-maker to be effective, even when the desired information is not available (Chandler, 2001). Improvisation skills can help when a crisis develops quickly (Drabek & McEntire, 2003; Rankin, Dahlbäck, & Lundberg, 2013).

Effective Listening Skills

Team members need to be able to listen effectively to stakeholders and victims. Listening skills also include the ability to hear the untold story.

Speaking & Writing Competence

Effective speaking skills are a must. Team members who are assigned to communicate with the media require excellent verbal skills. Writing skills are also necessary, particularly for team members responsible for social media communication.

Team Composition

CMTs are typically cross-functional (James & Wooten, 2010) and include top managers with a breadth of strategic vision and the authority to make decisions and render resources when a crisis strikes (Pearson & Sommer, 2011). Team members should include managers in marketing, production, finance, and other functional areas (Coombs, 2007). Representatives from the following areas are recommended:

Company Chief Executive Officer or President

The chief executive officer (CEO) or president should always have an active interest in the CMT. However, the size of the organization will dictate the capacity in which the top executive should serve. In smaller organizations, including the CEO on the CMT is ideal. In large organizations, a vice president for administration or operations may represent top management (Barton, 2001). A top manager does not always lead the CMT or serve as the company spokesperson during a crisis. This role is often assigned to a member of the public relations department or someone else with specialized training in corporate communications. However, a strong CEO presence is essential when a crisis impacts the public.

Human Resources

The capability, resilience, and commitment of employees can help or hinder an organization in its effort to survive a crisis (Simms, 2014). As such, it is always advisable to include a representative from human resources (HR) on the CMT for several reasons. First, HR serves as a liaison between management and employees. Individual employees can be affected by a crisis in many ways, and HR represents their interests in the crisis management process (Lockwood, 2005). Second, HR has knowledge that can be useful during a crisis, including next-of-kin details, the number of employees in each facility, and language/cultural barrier knowledge that is especially important if the company operates globally (Millar, 2003). Finally, HR should have a network of trauma counselors on contract when a crisis involved severe injuries or a loss of life.

Accounting and Finance

A crisis can affect business continuity, directly impacting cash flow, stock valuation, and cash disbursement. For example, Bayer AG acquired Monsanto and its Roundup weed killer for $63 billion in 2018. In the following year, plaintiffs claiming Roundup caused their cancer won three high-profile jury trials and were awarded damages over $2 billion. In the first major case, a California man was awarded $280 million in damages (later reduced to $78 million on appeal). In another case, a San Francisco jury identified exposure to Monsanto's Roundup as a "substantial factor" contributing to a man's non-

Hodgkin lymphoma. Bayer AG suffered a single-day decline in the stock price of 9.6% (Bender, 2019b). With over 11,000 cases filed against Bayer at the time, many investors worried about future liabilities and abandoned the stock altogether. By mid-2019, Bayer's stock price had dropped from over $30 to about $15 per share, shrinking its market capitalization by more than 40% to below $59 billion, less than what the company paid for Monsanto (Bender, 2019a).

Accurate and timely accounting practice is critical to business continuity. A representative with accounting and financial expertise is appropriate for the CMT to plan for financial stability. There may also be a need to secure funds quickly for relief operations. Accountability is particularly critical if funds are being disbursed abroad.

Security

The head of the organization's security or police force should be a member of the CMT. Many crises will involve this department's services, such as in the case of a workplace violence incident. This department also serves as a liaison with law enforcement departments outside the company whose help may be needed.

Public Relations

This functional area goes by various names in different organizations, such as public information, public affairs, or community outreach. During a crisis, this department sends the information and viewpoints of the organization to its public stakeholders. Hence, the official company spokesperson to the general media usually resides in this department. The public relations department also helps predict the public perception of the organization and issues related to the specific crisis at hand. Usually, these departments have established ties with various media and social media outlets. A crisis event is not the first time the spokesperson and the media will have had contact.

Legal Counsel

An attorney should be a CMT member to provide legal expertise, particularly when deciding how much information should be disclosed to outside stakeholders during a crisis. The legal counsel and public relations director must work together and should agree on the appropriate amount of disclosure.

Operations

Representation from the core operations of the organization should be part of the team. In a manufacturing facility, the plant manager would be the logical choice. At a major university, core areas such as food service, student housing, records, the director of plant and facilities, and the academic departments should be represented. For a public-school system, school psychologists should be part of the team to assess threats and manage student mental health issues when they arise (Heslip, 2015).

Table 5.1 Understanding the Challenges of Virtual Teams

Trends That Encourage the Use of Virtual Teams	Challenges Confronting Virtual Teams
• Company strategies moving toward outsourcing and strategic alliances • Widespread use of Internet technologies • Shorter project and product cycle times • Need for faster, high-quality decisions • Restrictions on corporate travel accounts • Threat of terrorism	**Loss of nonverbal cues**: Communicating with Zoom, Webex, or other means reduces the richness of communication. Cues gained in face-to-face communication can be more difficult to interpret in virtual environments, especially when participants do not provide video. **Reduced opportunities to establish working relationships**: With a reduction of face-to-face time with colleagues, building effective working relationships can be difficult. **Time zone differences**: Team members have different schedules. Time zones can affect appropriate deadlines as well. **Complicated and unreliable technology**: The quality of Internet and intranet systems can vary widely across organizations. **Difficulty in building consensus**: The lack of communication richness, the distance between organizational members, and the asynchronous nature of email and other virtual communication can cause delays. **Different cultures**: Cultural differences are always a challenge in global firms, even in face-to-face communications. The virtual environment can reduce some of these challenges when written language is emphasized. However, differences in the meanings of words and colloquial expressions must be considered.

Source - Adapted from Nunamaker et al. (2009), p. 114.

Outside Consultants

Many organizations employ an outside consultant when forming a CMT and developing an initial CMP to help navigate the learning curve. Consultants also offer advice concerning certain types of crises. For example, in cases involving workplace violence, a psychologist with appropriate experience can advise the CMT on both mitigating and preventing such a crisis (Simola, 2005).

Given the growth of virtual teams and the expansion of organizations' boundaries in general, CMTs must also be prepared to operate virtually. One of the first challenges that must be addressed is the location of the command center. Will it be at company headquarters or close to the crisis? Organizations should designate a backup command center in case the main command center becomes inoperative. This situation occurred during the September 11, 2001, terrorist attack when the New York City Office of Emergency Management lost its state-of-the-art center. After the first tower caught fire and collapsed, the emergency operations center was unusable because of its location across the street from the building (Davis, 2002).

Virtual Crisis Management Teams

Virtual teams exist when members are geographically dispersed. They are common in many organizations, especially following the COVID-19 pandemic. They present many challenges, however, as overviewed in Table 5.1.

Trust can enhance the effectiveness of virtual teams (Jelavic & Salter, 2017; Kimble, 2011). Trust building must occur before a major crisis develops. Hence, virtual teams of any type should engage in regularly scheduled activities that help team members work together and establish their expected roles (Nunamaker, Reinig, & Briggs, 2009; Sadri & Condia, 2012).

The appropriate communication tool must also be utilized, depending on the task at hand. Routine information sharing can be shared via email, whereas complex problem-solving discussions require a richer communication format that utilizes web conferencing platforms such as Skype (Hill & Bartol, 2018). Richer forms of communication also provide participants a chance to observe verbal and visual cues (Chandler & Wallace, 2009; Dhawan & Chamorro-Premuzic, 2018), a feature that can be especially useful in cross-cultural discussions.

Potential Problems Within CMTs

As with any team, problems can arise. As previously mentioned, interpersonal skills and a team orientation are essential. Groups that are dysfunctional when planning for a crisis will remain dysfunctional when a crisis strikes (Barton, 2001). Many problems can occur within the CMT (Bertrand & Lajtha, 2002):

Not Understanding the Symbolic and Sacred Aspects of a Crisis

A crisis is more than just an event; it is an attack on a specific stakeholder or institution, whether inside or outside the organization. Crises are often interpreted as "symptoms of underlying problems" and, as such, can be viewed as "policy fiascos" (Bovens & 't Hart, 1996). Crises "challenge the foundation of organizations, governmental practice, and even societal cohesion" (Lagadec, 2004, p. 167). As a result, individual stakeholders may feel threatened by these events and perceive a more profound significance. For example, when a large company is involved in an environmental accident, the event is not just "an accident." It may be viewed as a corporate behemoth exploiting the natural environment for financial gain. When media and community stakeholders appear to act irrationally or against the organization, the CMT should seek to understand the reasons why (Bertrand & Lajtha, 2002). In other words, most stakeholders do not try to act irrationally. From their point of view, their behavior is reasonable.

Inability to Make Decisions When Information is Incomplete or Inaccurate

Managers are trained to make decisions after they obtain enough information to identify the best course of action. When a crisis strikes, the CMT must make difficult decisions when information is incomplete or even inaccurate.

Lack of Top Management Interest and Involvement

Promoting a crisis preparedness atmosphere without senior managers on board is very difficult. The potential loss from a crisis can be immense. Top managers should recognize this reality and support the crisis management process.

Lack of Psychological Preparation Provided to CMT Members

Crisis team members often bring emotional baggage to the meetings. Some are more adept than others at handling the stresses and fears of working on the team. Fatigue can also play a role, earlier for some members, later for others. In most cases, the CMT must address a rapidly changing set of challenges. Training for the emotional or psychological aspects of these assignments should be included.

In summary, "crises are characterized by the absence of obvious solutions, the scarcity of reliable information when it is needed, the lack of adequate time to reflect on and debate alternative courses of action" (Bertrand & Lajtha, 2002, p. 185). While it is easy to list the functional departments that should be represented on the CMT, it is much more sobering to realize the intensity of the challenges team members must face.

Several other challenges can surface with the CMT, including groupthink, operating in different time zones, verbal aggressiveness, and the presence of a Machiavellian personality.

Groupthink

Janis (1982) identified **groupthink** as a problem in the decision-making process of groups and teams. Groupthink occurs when the team does not consider all the alternatives and potential outcomes associated with an issue. The rationale is that group members, unwilling to speak up and question the status quo, leader or the conventional wisdom, remain passive to not upset the equilibrium of the group. Groupthink frequently occurs in times of crisis (Chandler & Wallace, 2009).

Groupthink can produce negative consequences, so combatting it on the CMT is important (Simola, 2005). Training that promotes critical thinking helps because it improves situational assessment abilities and promotes better contingency planning (Wright-Reid, 2018). Crisis teams can benefit from an outside consultant who can offer expertise and challenge the group on erroneous assumptions. The team leader should be impartial and open to new ideas before a decision is made (Cho, 2005). Above all, different points of view should be fostered as a means of combating poor decision making. "The presence of team members who view the problem differently may stimulate others in the team to discover novel approaches that they would not have considered, thereby leading to better decisions" (Gomez-Mejia & Balkin, 2012, p. 323).

Practicing in Different Time Zones

When a crisis spans time zones, coordination problems can surface. For the multinational corporation with locations worldwide, it is necessary to negotiate different time zones and languages. Perhaps a key manufacturing facility has been hit by a typhoon, tsunami, or earthquake or a factory on the other side of the world has caught fire. Coordinating relief efforts to get the facility back online is more difficult because of logistic and time complications. A virtual CMT can help address this challenge.

Verbal Aggressiveness

Different personalities can affect CMT operations. Some team members can become overbearing or even hostile under pressure. They should be screened out as CMT candidates early in the team selection process because they can obstruct group decision making and hamper open communication (Chandler, 2001). Specific criteria should be established for membership on a CMT.

Machiavellian Personality

Machiavellians are cunning, constantly scheming, and typically follow an "ends justifies the means" approach. Machiavellian managers focus on personal agendas, not the organization. (Chandler, 2001). Such individuals should be avoided. If others on the CMT are compliant, a Machiavellian type could lead to groupthink.

The Crisis Management Plan (CMP)

Once the CMT is in place, efforts can be made to construct the crisis management plan (CMP). The CMP does not merely exist on a company website or in a notebook on a shelf; it is a systematic way of thinking about organizational crises. Top management support is essential when developing the CMP (Pennington-Gray, Thapa, Kaplanidou, Cahyanto, & McLaughlin, 2011).

In managing a crisis, flexibility is preferable to a rigid step-by-step procedure. In technical operations, such an approach is necessary for the diagnosis and remedy of specific problems. In a crisis, however, when human, technical, and other unknown elements are integrated, some degree of flexibility is required to discern and act on the situation. A standard operating procedure (SOP) manual is essential.

Plans compiled merely to address compliance concerns do not set a proper tone (Bertrand & Lajtha, 2002). Ultimately, a CMP should encourage the CMT to think critically about what could happen and plan to mitigate the effects. We suggest a proactive approach. An outline of what should be included in a CMP is provided in the Appendix at the end of this book.

Essential Components of the Plan

The CMP is often posted online. The degree of detail can vary, but a concise plan is usually preferable to promote flexibility during a crisis response (Barton, 2001; Coombs, 2007). The following components are recommended to help organize the CMP and make it accessible to the entire organization.

Cover Page

The cover page includes the organization's name, general contact information, date of distribution, and the company logo. The page also labels the document as the crisis management plan. It may be appropriate to add a disclaimer stating that the document is confidential and unauthorized use is prohibited.

Table of Contents

Although the document should not be too long, a table of contents is helpful. CMPs posted online should include appropriate links to sections within the document and appropriate websites for emergency providers and other crisis websites that could be useful. Links should be checked periodically to ensure that they are still active.

Crisis Management Team Members

Team members should be listed along with their respective departments and contact information, including email addresses, office phones, home phones, and cell phone numbers.

Team Member Responsibilities

This section can vary in its degree of detail. Additional depth and details are required in larger, more complex organizations. CMT members are often selected to represent functional areas, so they are expected to operate within their areas of expertise during a crisis. Before a crisis occurs, it should be clear who oversees the CMT and represents the company with outside stakeholders. It is also important to maintain flexibility so the team can adapt to the crisis at hand.

Activation of the CMT

The CMP should include the procedures for activating the CMT. Usually, the team will be activated by a team member or at the request of a key internal stakeholder. It is also essential that employees in the organization know who is on the team. In some cases, employees may contact a team member instead of law enforcement if they are unsure if an event constitutes a crisis. When this occurs, the CMT determines if law enforcement should be involved.

Command Center Locations

The command center is a prearranged meeting location where the CMT gathers during a crisis. The CMP should clearly label both this location (the primary command center) and the alternate command center if the primary one is damaged in the crisis The alternative command center should not be so close to the primary center that an event such as a flood or a fire could render both unusable.

Suppose the crisis involves a crime or physical damage to a building. In that case, an incident command center may be set up nearby when emergency response providers are working an event while the CMT is meeting at the command center. With this arrangement, clear communication links between the incident command center and the CMT at the primary command center are required. Such a scenario could occur if there is a hostage situation in one location of the complex while the CMT meets in another part. These types of separate command centers are common on college and university campuses because of the sprawling complex of buildings.

Response Plans for Specific Crisis Situations

The CMP should prepare a list of prospective crises that are most likely. This section is the longest in the CMP because specific crises are identified, and a response plan is provided for each one. The plan should list the potential crisis at the top of the page and then follow a series of bullet points on how to manage that event. For example, most CMPs have a response page for a bomb threat. Hotels are required to have an evacuation plan for their guests and employees. A fire is typically the most severe hotel crisis because mass casualties are possible (Gonzalez, 2008). In the mining industry, the Mine Safety and Health Administration (MSHA) should be notified within fifteen minutes of a mining accident (Yanik, 2016).

The length of the response plan varies according to the crisis. Individuals who write response plans should be thorough yet concise, remembering that too many steps in the response plan can create confusion and limit flexibility. Table 5.2 lists common crisis events that colleges and universities have faced, and hence, should be considered potential crises to address in their plans.

Distribution of the CMP

In the past, many organizations did not distribute the CMP to individuals who were not CMT members. This has changed, however. Unless the plan discusses proprietary information, distribution across the organization is recommended, including posting the plan on the company intranet and providing copies to stakeholders (Matchen & Hawkins, 2015).

Crisis Management Training

The CMT is charged with the oversight of training in crisis management. Training can range from simple meetings that review the CMP to classroom instruction on crisis management aspects. It can also include conducting smaller disaster drills that test a segment of the crisis response or elaborate mock disasters so the team can practice its response. If the organization is large, the HR department may be better equipped to lead training exercises in crisis management (Moats, Chermack, & Dooley, 2008; Simms, 2014).

Regular CMT Meetings

The CMT should hold scheduled meetings several times a year. Such meetings provide training opportunities as well as opportunities for team members to interact and bond. Some crises might warrant more frequent sessions. Potential training activities that can be held during meetings include reviewing the CMP, conducting tabletop exercises, planning for larger-scale disaster exercises or **mock disasters**, and presenting new material on crisis management.

Reviewing the CMP

Continuous improvement is a critical part of CMTs responsibility. The CMT should review the CMP frequently to maintain familiarity. Hard copies of the CMP should be updated if electronic access to the plan is temporarily unavailable during a crisis.

Table 5.2 Potential Crises for American Colleges and Universities

Type of Crises	Examples
Alcohol-related deaths	A major problem at many colleges and universities is alcohol abuse among students, sometimes resulting in binge-related deaths. Frequently, the abuse occurs at fraternity parties. In February 2017, Timothy Piazza, a Beta Theta Pi pledge at Penn State University, died after he fell several times while drinking large amounts of alcohol with fraternity members (Jacobs, 2018). Charles Terreni, Jr., a University of South Carolina student, died in March 2015, at the Pi Kappa Alpha house after a night of heavy drinking. A toxicology report found his blood alcohol level at 0.375, more than four times the legal driving limit (Ellis, 2015).
Fires	The US Fire Administration's study of campus fire fatalities in residential buildings found that 94% of fatal campus fires occurred in off-campus housing. Also, 76% of all deadly campus fires had alcohol as a factor (US Fire Administration, n.d.). In October 2007, an off-campus fire at an Ocean Isle, North Carolina, beach condominium killed seven university students during fall break.
Athletic scandals	The University of Louisville's basketball program is tainted with stories of prostitutes being hired to entertain recruits. As a result, the NCAA orders the university to forfeit 123 victories, including the 2013 national championship (Tracy, 2018). Former Penn State football coach, Jerry Sandusky, is found guilty in July 2012, for sexually molesting young boys within the campus athletic facilities.
On-campus shootings	Chris Harper Mercer killed ten people in October 2015, at Umpqua Community College in Oregon. A former student, One L. Goh, went on a shooting rampage in April 2012 at his previous school, Oikos University, killing seven people. In February 2010, **a** disgruntled biology professor, Amy Bishop, killed three of her colleagues in a department meeting at the University of Alabama at Huntsville.
Floods	Hurricanes Matthew in 2016 and Florence in 2018 cause power outages, wind damage, and flood university campuses in North and South Carolina. A threatening flood in April 2009 closed the campus of Valley City State University in North Dakota. With three weeks left in the semester, the university had to deliver all remaining face-to-face courses online.
Contagious diseases	College and university students are typically at a higher risk for influenza and meningitis because of the close living conditions associated with residence halls. COVID-19 became a pandemic in early 2020. Most colleges and universities finished their spring semesters and conducted summer classes online. Some returned to face-to-face instruction in the fall semester with safety protocols, while others remained online.
Building mold	During the fall 2018 semester, mold was found in residence halls at the University of Maryland and the University of Tennessee. Students had to be relocated to other residence halls and local hotels until the mold is cleaned in both cases. The university where the authors reside had a mold outbreak in an academic building in 2003. The result was the complete evacuation of the building for an entire semester while the building was cleaned and the source problem resolved.

Tabletop Exercises

A **tabletop exercise** occurs in a meeting room and discusses how the team would respond to a specific crisis. It is a form of a disaster drill, but without the realistic scenarios that are characteristic of a mock disaster. A tabletop exercise can be an

inexpensive way to rehearse for a real disaster (Careless, 2007). The term *tabletop* is essential because the training never leaves the physical or virtual meeting room; hence, tabletop exercises have some limitations.

Tabletop exercises can be facilitated by an outside consultant (Beckage & Jaworski, 2017). A one- or multi-day training workshop can be held in conjunction with a tabletop exercise. For example, workshops combined with tabletop exercises have been used for training against coastal terrorism (Richter et al., 2005) and a blowout of an underwater oil well (Bitto, 2017). Cognitive mapping has also been used as a tabletop exercise, with participants asked to draw spatial maps of a developing crisis and then develop scenarios for managing the event

(Alexander, 2004). This type of exercise is useful for those involved in disaster response activities.

Updating Crisis Management Capabilities

This training approach can be flexible. An outside consultant or guest speaker might join a face-to-face conversation, or the team can participate online. The objective is to learn new material that will assist the team in its response to a crisis.

Disaster Drills

While a mock disaster is more comprehensive and tests the overall team response, a **disaster drill** is a smaller exercise that addresses one aspect of the crisis response (Coombs, 2007). Drills test a part of the crisis response. Examples of training drills include the following:

- *Sending an emergency phone message and email to all the employees in the organization.* This drill is practical because an alert of a crisis may be required at a moment's notice. Perhaps a tornado i sin the area, or an individual garnering a weapon is on company grounds. The drill should also include sending text or voice messages.
- *Conducting a building evacuation drill.* This drill is similar to a standard fire drill. Building evacuations frequently occur in schools as part of their regularly

scheduled training. Provisions for removing people with disabilities must also be addressed. For example, evacuating a university library would necessitate that specific individuals be assigned to assist students or staff with mobility disabilities (Matchen & Hawkins, 2015). While evacuations are relatively straightforward in schools and universities, they can be more complicated in other settings, such as in a nursing home. Residents of nursing homes may also need to leave the area after a building evacuation, especially if there is threatening weather, such as a hurricane or a flood. An inadequate evacuation of a nursing home can result in patient deaths. Indeed, after Hurricane Katrina, two nursing homes in Louisiana were charged with negligent homicide in the deaths of 34 residents (Dewan & Baker, 2005). Two items essential to an effective nursing home evacuation include clear travel routes and adequate hydration provisions for the patients (Castle, 2008).

- *Testing a procedure that is unique to the facility.* Libraries have unique crisis scenarios because they house collections of materials at risk for roof leaks, pest infestations, fire, theft, mold, security problems, and dust and dirt (Yeh, McMullen, & Kane, 2010). A typical crisis scenario for a library is the loss of documents and books due to water damage. Considering this possibility, some libraries practice unique water drills. The Stetson University Law Library held a drill scenario in which a water sprinkler head malfunctioned and was spraying water onto shelves of books. The personnel practiced draping the shelves with plastic tarps as quickly as possible (Rentschler & Burdett, 2006).

- *Conducting an **active shooter exercise**.* These drills involve the simulation of an armed individual on the premises of the facility. They need to coordinate with local law enforcement agencies and other emergency providers to assist in the drill. Shopping malls are often utilized for this type of exercise for good reasons. On October 21, 2010, a man claiming to have a gun barricaded himself in a store at the Roseville Galleria in California, later resulting in a fire that caused substantial damage to the mall. On January 8, 2011, a gunman killed six people at a strip shopping center in Tucson, Arizona (Bell, 2011).
One shopping mall operator, the Cafaro Company of Youngstown, Ohio, has conducted six active shooter exercises at its facilities. In Bridgeport, West Virginia, a January 2001 exercise at the Meadowbrook Mall involved two "recently fired employees" who demanded to see the mall manager. The role-playing involved shots being fired. Participants included nearly 200 volunteer shoppers, the West Virginia State Police, the county sheriff's department, a local hospital, and teams from the US Federal Bureau of Investigations (FBI) (Bell, 2011).

- *Accessing and using firefighting equipment.* Such equipment is required in all buildings, but training employees to properly use the equipment may be inconsistent. Local fire departments are usually willing to provide such training onsite. In addition, the fire department can also learn more about the unique features of the building, helping it compile a prearranged response to a fire
- *Conducting a **lockdown drill.*** Rather than exiting the building, classrooms (or buildings) are secured by locking the doors and requiring students (or employees) to stay inside. A lockdown seeks to protect the occupants of the structure in a shooting or related incident. Lockdown drills became more frequent after deadline shootings in Columbine, Colorado, and on the Virginia Tech campus (Kass & Marek, 2005). Such exercises are not limited to schools, however. Incidents of workplace violence also require that employees be in a secure place in the event of a shooting.
- ***Sheltering in place.*** A variation of the lockdown drill involves securing the building and moving occupants to a more central location for additional security. This type of drill, called "sheltering in place," has been practiced in school systems near US ports because they have been identified as potential terrorist targets (Jacobson, 2003). Sheltering-in-place drills can include shutting down heating and air conditioning systems and sealing air inflow openings near windows. Such a move would be likely in response to a chemical or biological terrorist attack.
- *Conduct shower drills.* In a very specialized drill, companies that use hazardous chemicals are encouraged to conduct **shower drills** (Hayes, 2011). However, a worker may be exposed to a dangerous chemical. If so, it might be necessary to flush the chemical off the skin as quickly as possible. Shower units that offer privacy can be positioned in work areas and should provide adequate water pressure at comfortable temperatures for 15 minutes, the required Occupational Safety and Health Administration (OSHA) standard.

Simulation-based Training

Simulation-based training creates scenarios that CMTs may encounter. It is interactive, immersive, and useful for skill development (Waller, Lee & Pratten, 2014). A mock disaster is a scenario that is recreated so that crisis management participant-stakeholders can practice their responses. It operates in real-time and in as realistic a setting as possible. Mock disasters are more comprehensive than disaster drills and are essential in testing the CMP (Perry, 2004).

Purpose of a Mock Disaster

A mock disaster can serve multiple purposes. Its practicality is enhanced by the number of people who can participate, the media attention received, and the usefulness of testing the organization's crisis response. A mock disaster serves several fundamental purposes:

A mock disaster activates and tests the CMT. This type of exercise involves the full activation of the CMT and the appropriate emergency providers in the community, such as law enforcement, fire departments, and emergency medical services. One of the most important goals is to ensure that the CMT is alerted to a crisis promptly. The working dynamics of the team can also be evaluated. Do team members work effectively as a unit? Are there any interpersonal problems that need to be addressed? Is there anyone who is not a good fit to serve on the team?

A mock disaster tests the communication systems and networks that will be used during an actual crisis. Telephone systems, mobile radios, the intranet, social media messaging, and the Internet should all be activated and used during the drill. Also, local fire and police departments may have special equipment they need to test. For example, robots are used in certain firefighting situations and bomb removal and detonation. A mock disaster is an excellent opportunity for testing this type of specialized equipment.

Banks should test their crisis readiness regularly. In 2009, the Farmington Savings Bank (FSB) staged a mock disaster to examine the components of its backup information systems arrangement. The bank had 13 branches in central Connecticut at the time. The scenario involved working with its disaster recovery provider, which supplied a trailer, a power generator, and 20 computers (Arnfield, 2009). After conducting the training exercise, bank executives learned that if more than ten phone lines were in use, the satellite link did not function properly. Also, slow bandwidth affected the printing of documents stored on the disaster recovery server. Remedying these problems was relatively easy.

A mock disaster tests the effectiveness of the command center. If the command center has never been used for an actual crisis, it should be activated during the mock disaster. When Concord University in Athens, West Virginia, held its first mock disaster, a significant shortcoming was discovered with its primary command center. All radio communications were funneled into a large room, the same general area where the media members were also assembling. When mock reporters heard the reports coming in from the incident command center, they demanded an explanation from the college president, who just happened to be listening to the same reports in the command center (Crandall, 1997). After the drill, a new command center in a different building was designated with a separate room for media briefings.

A mock disaster helps foster relationships with local police and fire departments. In a real emergency, the local fire and police departments will be the first responders to the incident. Developing relationships with these agencies before a crisis occurs is recommended. The mock disaster helps accomplish this goal.

The CMT may function quite well in a non-crisis setting because regularly scheduled meetings and training sessions are low-stress contact points. A mock disaster, however, adds a sense of urgency and purpose to the working relationships of the CMT. After

working together on a large-scale exercise, which can be physically and emotionally challenging, the team might become more cohesive.

A well-designed mock disaster can test the key areas of crisis response and expose areas that need improvement. At the Stetson University Law Library, the mock disaster discussed previously revealed that response times to a water leak emergency needed to be improved (Rentschler & Burdett, 2006). A mock disaster at the Arco Chemical plant in South Charleston, West Virginia, revealed that media briefings were being rushed, which was problematic because the drill involved a sinking barge full of chemicals spilling its contents into the Kanawha River (Swift, 2004).

Another common area of weakness during a crisis is message overload; too much information going through the system can be difficult for employees to interpret. "A common failure is basic system overloads . . . Are too many messages being sent? Are people not understanding all the messages? Are they not coming in chronological order?" (Morton, 2011, p. 26). Are the messages accurate? These are serious concerns.

A mock disaster can also alert the CMT where additional training is needed. For example, all mock disasters should include holding a staged press conference and answering hypothetical questions from reporters. Training other employees in this function, in addition to the official spokesperson is helpful. The company spokesperson may not be available during a crisis that requires a response to the media. Mock disasters can be useful in evaluating the performance of company spokespersons.

Organizing a Mock Disaster

A mock disaster requires extensive planning. There should be a person in charge, a set of goals and objectives, a delegated list of duties, and a timeline for scheduling the drill. Several additional guidelines should be considered.

Determine the objectives of the drill. A mock disaster tests some response systems, but not the organization's entire crisis response capability. The CMT should determine several vital areas that need to be tested and include those in the plan. All mock disasters should test communication capabilities and interviews with the media.

If specific equipment is part of the crisis response, then it should be tested as well. The *Exxon Valdez* oil spill in Alaskan waters is known for the massive amounts of oil that damaged the environment. What is less well known is that Exxon had a response plan for an oil spill in that area. Unfortunately, the boat designated to set up perimeter booms around the spill was being repaired at the time of the spill (Hartley, 1993). Hence, the role of equipment is paramount, so testing that equipment should be part of the mock drill.

Develop a scenario that represents a realistic, potential crisis in the organization. Crisis assessment activities reveal possible crisis events that could occur in the organization. Some of these crises have geographic considerations, such as earthquakes along the whole west coast of the United States, volcano activity at Mount St. Helens and Mount Rainier, hurricanes in the southeastern United States, terrorism at various targets throughout the world, and wildfires in drier locations in the western US. Some potential crises are industry-specific: chemical spills (production industries), *E. coli* outbreaks (food industries), school violence (education), and computer hacking and viruses (any industry that depends on online sales). Thus, the mock disaster should involve a scenario that represents a potential crisis.

Ensure that top management is supportive and involved in the drill. Support and participation in the mock disaster demonstrate that management takes these activities seriously. One of the authors of this book was a member of the CMT at Concord University. The president of the university was also a member of the CMT and active in the mock disasters and training held at the school. His enthusiasm helped carry the drills through to successful implementation and completion. It also demonstrated that he cared about instilling a culture in the organization that supported crisis planning.

Include as many stakeholders as feasible when planning the mock disaster. Despite their seriousness and intensity, mock disasters are also social undertakings. While such drills are not meant to be festive or partylike, they need not be overly stressful. Including as many individuals as possible who have a link to the drill is advisable. Enthusiasm for the training can be high because participants are taking part in a social exercise while engaging in activities outside of their everyday routines. Coalescing around a common goal is also a satisfying experience.

Include local police, fire, and other emergency services in the planning and execution of the mock disaster. Police and fire departments invest heavily in training. Most will be receptive to taking part in a mock disaster because it serves as a training opportunity for their departments. It also helps CMT members become acquainted with some of the key personnel in the emergency services departments.

Use mock reporters and victims. The realistic scenario of being interviewed by the media can be unexpected and intimidating. Local university journalism students make a good source of mock reporters and are usually readily available. The drama or theater department can supply "victims" who can be made up to look injured (Crandall, 1997; Kennedy, 2015).

Invite members of the media to observe and report on the drill. The training event can be featured in newspapers, on television, and online. The publicity generated is usually beneficial because it portrays the organization as proactive in its crisis management efforts. Local reporters can offer advice from their perspectives, some of which may be quite useful to the CMT.

Ensure that all employees and stakeholders—especially those who will experience the drill firsthand—are fully aware of the exercise in advance. The mock disaster should be well publicized to all employees and the local community so that local citizens do not mistake the drill for a real crisis. One of the authors lives near a large military base that occasionally conducts mock exercises in the community. One such drill involved the use of a military team descending on an abandoned motel. Helicopters were flying overhead, and soldiers were maneuvering around the facility. The exercise was so extensive that spectators gathered across the street to watch. Fortunately, the community received advanced notice, and some members even found the event entertaining. Several years later, the local fire department set fire to the entire facility in a dramatic blaze as a training exercise. Again, the community knew to expect a spectacular fire that night.

Unfortunately, not communicating a mock disaster adequately can have devastating results. In December 2015, a simulated terrorist attack was held at Strathmore University in Nairobi, Kenya. The drill included gunshots (with rubber bullets). Students and staff at the university were not adequately informed that this was only a drill. When the gunshots commenced, many thought it was an actual terrorist attack, remembering that several months earlier, the terrorist group al-Shabab killed 148 people in an attack on Garissa University in Kenya. Students and staff at Strathmore tried to escape, some by climbing out windows and wading through the Mbagathi River. One female staff member jumped from the third floor of a building and later died (Wang, 2015).

During the Mock Disaster

Planning a mock disaster requires a detailed orientation. The actual drill should proceed well if the appropriate guidelines are followed. It is also important not to create a real crisis during the drill. Such events do occur and can result in injuries. If the fire department is involved, it will likely have a safety officer who helps ensure that nobody is seriously injured.

Nonetheless, anyone planning an exercise should be aware of potential problems. In 2002, journalism faculty at Syracuse University were preparing to conduct a mock disaster to test their students' skills when the simulated chemical spill that was planned became a real spill. Two hours before the mock disaster, a real crisis developed when brown puddles of unknown origin formed inside the university's biological research center. The building was evacuated, and a hazardous material team arrived along with police and fire personnel (Strupp, 2002).

Consider another example. In 2007, an elaborate search-and-rescue drill involving about 400 people was held off the coast of Newfoundland. The objective of the drill was to respond to a scenario in which a ferry was on fire. The drill involved evacuating passengers from the ferry into lifeboats but took a realistic turn when several passengers on one of the lifeboats were overcome by exhaust fumes and had to be airlifted by helicopter to a hospital (Brautigam, 2007).

Mistakes occur during drills, but this is not a problem unless damage or injuries are extensive. Indeed, one of the purposes of a drill is to identify crisis response weaknesses. Those involved should record any shortcomings and discuss them when the mock disaster is debriefed. One animal shelter staged a mock disaster involving the evacuation of all animals from the facility. Such an incident would be required if a natural disaster such as a hurricane was threatening. Several minor problems developed during the drill, including a fight between two dogs held by volunteers in the waiting queue and a cat that escaped from its cage. Moreover, the volunteers who helped with the mock drill were plentiful but untrained in carrying out their required roles, complicating the process considerably (Irvine, 2007). Hence, formal training for the volunteers was warranted.

Finally, mock drills should be recorded. When Concord University staged its first mock disaster, two photographers made video recordings. One cameraperson was located at the incident command center, where the disaster scenario took place. The other recorded the meetings in the central command center, where most of the CMT was meeting. This arrangement was later useful for evaluation because CMT members at the command center could view what was happening at the incident area, and vice versa (Crandall, 1997).

After the Mock Disaster

Immediately after the drill, food and refreshments should be provided for all of those who participated. This step might seem trivial but is highly recommended because a drill can be exhausting. This social gathering also gives individuals time to reflect, relax, and build camaraderie.

Within one week of the drill, a meeting should be held to debrief and discuss what was learned. Some teams may choose to debrief immediately after the mock disaster, especially if the drill was short, and participants were not exhausted. Otherwise, it is preferable to debrief later when CMT members are more relaxed. The debriefing should occur soon after the event, preferably within a week, lest team members forget some of their experiences. The lessons learned from the mock disaster may result in changes to the crisis management plan. These changes should be made soon in the master document and any additional associated locations such as the organization's website.

Summary

This chapter emphasized forming the crisis management team (CMT) and writing the crisis management plan (CMP). The CMT develops a list of threats the organization may encounter and oversees the writing of the CMP. The CMP revolves around addressing these threats and providing other guidelines for how the organization should respond to a crisis.

The CMT also leads the training needed for crisis response. Regular meetings should be held to keep team members familiar with the crisis plan and provide training for specific crisis events. Testing the crisis response of the organization is also essential. Tabletop drills are short and confined to usually one room. A disaster drill is broader in scope and involves testing a single component of its crisis response. A mock disaster is more extensive in its inclusion of stakeholders and the number of tested crisis components. All these exercises fine-tune the CMT so that it is ready when a crisis occurs.

Discussion Questions

1. Discuss how groupthink can be a problem for a crisis management team. How can groupthink be prevented?
2. How do problems associated with a crisis management team differ from those related to other teams?
3. If you are a CMT leader, how would you ensure that team members regularly review the crisis management plan?
4. Why is it a good idea to require your suppliers to have a crisis management plan?
5. What types of disaster drills are practiced regularly at your place of employment? If none, what would you propose for a disaster drill exercise?

6. What scenarios would comprise a useful mock disaster where you work or study?

Chapter Exercise

All students and practitioners of crisis management should be able to write a crisis management plan. Also, the ability to organize a training program and a mock disaster is desirable. This course exercise is designed to be a comprehensive project that accomplishes each of these goals.

General Guidelines

1. Assign students in the class to teams of four to six members. Each team should work with the management team of a local organization to compile a crisis management plan. For this first step, the instructor should serve as the liaison between the organization and the student team.
2. Employed students already have an entry into their organizations. These are potential companies for the project and can be pursued with the approval of the instructor.
3. Each team should design a mock disaster for that organization. Keep in mind that the purpose of this drill is to test the organization's CMP and its crisis response capabilities.
4. Each team should formulate a crisis training program schedule for the organization.
    *   Indicate how often meetings should be held and what training modules should be provided.
    *   Designate which training is for the CMT only and which should include all employees.
5. Each team should present its CMP, mock disaster plan, and training program schedule to the class. If possible, a representative from the respective organization should also be present.

Specific Guidelines

1. In organizing the CMP, remember that many such plans are already posted on the Internet. College and university plans are readily available for review and can provide useful insights into organizing your team's plan. Also, the Appendix at

the end of this book provides an outline of areas that should be addressed in your CMP.

2. Recall that a landscape survey of the internal and external environment is necessary to assess that organization's crisis vulnerability. A SWOT analysis is also helpful (see Chapter 4). Include this information in the plan as well.
3. Be sure the CMP is realistic for the organization you have selected. Do not address crisis scenarios that are not relevant to the organization.
4. Designate a backup command center in your plan and explain how a virtual command center would be organized.
5. Prepare a timeline for the mock disaster. Identify what should occur two months before the drill, one month before, two weeks, two days, and so on. Use a timeline that is feasible for your mock disaster.

Closing Chapter Case: The University of North Carolina at Pembroke Goes into Crisis Management Mode Against Hurricane Florence – Part 2

Hurricane Florence was approaching the University of North Carolina at Pembroke, and the campus CMT was preparing for the worst. On Monday, September 10, 2018, five crisis management team members met to plan for the specific event. The team was designated as the core group to manage preparations for the hurricane. It consisted of the director of human resources, the associate academic provost, the head of university communications and marketing, the interim chief of staff, and the head of campus safety and emergency operations.

The team began preparations to evacuate the campus of *all* students. Before the arrival of Hurricane Matthew in 2016, 800 students had remained on campus (Scott Billingsley, personal communication, October 5, 2018). Only minimal campus damage from Matthew was anticipated, but the storm took an unexpected turn and made a direct hit on UNCP. The result was a campus-wide power outage and significant flooding. The students who had remained on campus required evacuation, a considerable undertaking. For Hurricane Florence, the crisis management team determined that all students would have to leave to avoid a similar problem.

Although the storm was not expected to make landfall until Friday, September 14, the team decided on Monday to close the campus on Tuesday afternoon—three days earlier—and direct all students to leave. Special provisions were made to accommodate international students. A sister campus within the UNC system, the University of North Carolina at Charlotte, housed some of them.

The crisis management team met twice a day throughout the week as Hurricane Florence approached. They discussed various scenarios that could occur and talked through the options. Preparations were ordered to secure the campus, including the removal of all flags, banners, and other objects that could become dangerous projectiles in high winds. Several buildings were protected with perimeters of sandbags to keep potential floodwaters from intruding. Generators were fueled to provide essential electrical services, one of which would maintain the computer information systems during and after the storm. Because some of the parking lots were prone to flooding, campus and staff vehicles were moved to higher ground.

The CMT also ensured that stakeholders received accurate and timely information before, during, and after the hurricane. Emails, text alerts, and the university website

were all utilized for communicating with stakeholders.

Hurricane Florence arrived on Friday, September 14, and brought high winds and heavy rain. The university experienced a power outage and some flooding, as anticipated. During the storm and its immediate aftermath, over 200 emergency personnel from various agencies remained on the campus. They assisted in campus overhaul efforts as well as working in the local community.

The preparations and efforts of the crisis management team and UNCP staff mitigated the storm's impact, which caused only minor damage to the campus. Unfortunately, the surrounding areas did not fare as well. Widespread flooding caused some faculty and staff to lose their homes. Many in the UNCP community have volunteered time and resources to help those who experienced substantial losses rebuild their lives.

Case Discussion Questions

1. Suppose that, due to unforeseen circumstances, 100 students could not be evacuated from the campus. Given that there is no power and flooding is occurring devise a plan to house and feed the students.

2. One of the most challenging decisions for a university under these circumstances is determining a day to reopen the campus for classes. Colleges and universities serve students that live both on and off campus. Also, during a hurricane, many students return home. How would you determine when your college or university should reopen after a storm?

This case is based on the authors' experiences, all three of whom worked at UNCP at that time. Dr. Scott Billingsley, the Associate Provost and member of the crisis management team also provided insight.

References

Alexander, D. (2004). Cognitive mapping as an emergency management training exercise. *Journal of Contingencies and Crisis Management, 12*(4), 150–159.

Antonacopoulou, E., & Sheaffer, Z. (2014). Learning in crisis: Rethinking the relationship between organizational learning and crisis management. *Journal of Management Inquiry, 23*(1), 5-21.

Arnfield, R. (2009). Dress rehearsals reveal holes. *Bank Technology News, 22*(5), 26.

Barrett, M. (2018, September 11). Hurricane Florence will be 'a monster,' Cooper says; mandatory evacuation for coast. *Asheville Citizen Times*. Retrieved October 6, 2018, from https://www.citizen-times.com/story/news/local/2018/09-11/hurricane-florence-monster-nc-gov-roy-cooper-says/1267840002/

Barton, L. (2001). *Crisis in organizations II*. Cincinnati, OH: South-Western.

Beckage, J., & Jaworski, M. (2017). The value of tabletop exercises to crisis response. *Buffalo Law Journal, 89*(9), 3.

Bell, J. (2011). Mayhem at the mall: Cafaro training exercises prepare teams for crisis. *Chain Store Age, 87*(4), 72.

Bender, R. (2019a, May 20). Bayer's Roundup Problem Slashes Its Market Value. *Wall Street Journal*, pp. B1, B2.

Bender, R. (2019b, March 21). Cancer verdict pummels Bayer. *Wall Street Journal*, pp. A1, A7.

Bertrand, R., & Lajtha, C. (2002). A new approach to crisis management. *Journal of Contingencies and Crisis Management, 10*(4), 181–191.

Bitto, R. (2017). Two-day drill prepares operators to respond to blowouts. *World Oil, 238*(7), 23.

Bovens, M., & 't Hart, P. (1996). *Understanding policy fiascos*. New Brunswick, NJ: Transaction.

Brautigam, T. (2007, September 28). Mock disaster turns real. *Toronto Star*, p. A03.

Careless, J. (2007). Practice, practice, practice. *Mobile Radio Technology, 25*(3), 46–49.

Castle, N. (2008). Nursing home evacuation plans. *American Journal of Public Health, 98*(7), 1235–1240.

Chandler, R. (2001). Crisis management: Does your team have the right members? *Safety Management, 458*, 1–3.

Chandler, R., & Wallace, J. (2009). The role of videoconferencing in crisis and emergency management. *Journal of Business Continuity and Emergency Planning, 3*(2), 161–177.

Cho, C. (2005). Information failures and organizational disasters. *MIT Sloan Management Review, 46*(3), 8–10.

Clark, J., & Harman, M. (2004). On crisis management and rehearsing a plan. *Risk Management, 51*(5), 40–43.

Coombs, W. (2007). *Ongoing crisis communication: Planning, managing, and responding* (2nd ed.). Thousand Oaks, CA: Sage.

Coombs, W., & Holladay, S. (2001). An extended examination of the crisis situation: A fusion of the relational management and symbolic approaches. *Journal of Public Relations Research, 13*, 321–340.

Crandall, W. (1997, April). How to choreograph a disaster. *Security Management*, 40–43.

Davis, S. (2002). Virtual emergency operations centers. *Risk Management, 49*(7), 46–52.

Dewan, S., & Baker, A. (2005, September 14). Owners of nursing home charged in deaths of 34. *New York Times.* Retrieved October 3, 2018, from http://www.nytimes.com/2005/09/14/national/nationalspecial/14storm.html?pagewanted=all

Dhawan, E., & Chamorro-Premuzic, T. (2018, February 27). How to collaborate effectively if your team is remote. *Harvard Business Review*, 2-5. Retrieved, October 4, 2018, from https://hbr.org/2018/02/how-to-collaborate-effectively-if-your-team-is-remote

Drabek, T., & McEntire, D. (2002). Emergent phenomena and the sociology of disaster: Lessons, trends, and opportunities from the research literature. *Disaster Prevention Management, 12,* 97-112.

Ellis, S. (2015, April 8). Coroner: USC student Terreni died of 'toxic' blood alcohol level. *The State.* Retrieved October 8, 2018, from https://www.thestate.com/news/local/article17854100.html

Gilpin, D., & Murphy, P. (2008). *Crisis management in a complex world.* New York: Oxford University Press.

Gomez-Mejia, L., & Balkin, D. (2012). *Management: People, performance, change.* Upper Saddle River, NJ: Prentice Hall.

Gonzalez, G. (2008). Hotel disaster plans must consider an array of exposures. *Business Insurance, 42*(24), 12–13.

Gronberg, R. (2016, October 12). UNC system deals with Hurricane Matthew's aftermath. *The Herald Sun* (Durham, NC).

Hartley, R. (1993). *Business ethics: Violations of the public trust.* New York: Wiley.

Hayes, C. (2011). Be proactive: Conduct emergency shower drills. *Facility Safety, 46*(1), 60.

Heslip, V. (2015). Communication matters: A place at the table with the threat management and crisis response teams. *Communiqué, 44*(4), 16.

Hill, S., & Bartol, K. (2018). Virtual virtues: Three steps for improving team performance. *BizEd, 17*(1), 56-57.

Irvine, L. (2007). Ready or not: Evacuating an animal shelter during a mock emergency. *Anthrozoos, 20*(4), 355–364.

Jacobs, J. (2018, June 13). Ex-fraternity member at Penn State is first to plead guilty in hazing death of Timothy Piazza. *The New York Times.* Retrieved October 7, 2018, from https://www.nytimes.com/2018/06/13/us/fraternity-death-penn-state.html

Jacobson, L. (2003, April 30). Disaster drills emphasize plans to "shelter" pupils at school. *Education Week, 22*(33), 6–7.

James, E., & Wooten, L. (2010). *Leading under pressure: From surviving to thriving before, during, and after a crisis.* New York: Taylor & Francis.

Janis, I. (1982). *Groupthink: Psychological studies of policy decisions and fiascoes* (2nd ed.). Boston: Houghton Mifflin.

Jelavic, M., & Salter, D. (2017). Managing transnational virtual teams: Cultural and technological considerations. *Canadian Institute of Management, 42*(1), 12-15.

Kass, J., & Marek, A. (2005, April 4). What happened after Columbine. *US News & World Report,* 28–29.

Kennedy, K. (2015, August 27). It's only a drill: Pittsburgh Technical Institute students put on mock disaster. *The Beaver County Times (PA).*

Kimble, C. (2011). Building effective virtual teams: How to overcome the problems of trust and identity in virtual teams. *Global Business and Organizational Excellence, 30*(2), 6–15.

Kovoor-Misra, S., & Nathan, M. (2000, Fall). Timing is everything: The optimal time to learn from crises. *Review of Business,* 31–36.

Lagadec, P. (2004). Understanding the French 2003 heat wave experience: Beyond the heat, a multi-layered challenge. *Journal of Contingencies and Crisis Management, 12*(4), 160–169.

Lockwood, N. (2005). Crisis management in today's business environment: HR's strategic role. *SHRM Research Quarterly, 4*, 1–10.

Matchen, Jr., D., & Hawkins, J. (2015). Faced with crisis. *AALL Spectrum, 20*(2), 19-23.

Millar, M. (2003, October 28). HR must be at forefront of crisis management plans. *Personnel Today,* 7.

Moats, J., Chermack, T., & Dooley, L. (2008). Using scenarios to develop crisis managers: Applications of scenario planning and scenario-based training. *Advances in Developing Human Resources, 10*(3), 397–424.

Morton, J. (2011). Practice makes perfect. *Buildings, 105*(2), 26.

Nunamaker Jr., J., Reinig, B., & Briggs, R. (2009). Principles for effective virtual teamwork. *Communications of the ACM, 52*(4), 113–117.

Pearson, C., & Mitroff, A. (1993). From crisis prone to crisis prepared: A framework for crisis management. *Academy of Management Executive, 71,* 48–59.

Pearson, C., & Sommer, S. (2011). Infusing creativity into crisis management: An essential approach today. *Organizational Dynamics, 40,* 27-33.

Pennington-Gray, L., Thapa, B., Kaplanidou, K., Cahyanto, I., & McLaughlin, E. (2011). Crisis planning and preparedness in the United States tourism industry. *Cornell Hospitality Quarterly, 52*(3), 312–320.

Perry, R. (2004). Disaster exercise outcomes for professional emergency personnel citizen volunteers. *Journal of Contingencies and Crisis Management, 12*(2), 64–75.

Ranking, A., Dahlbäck, N., Lundberg, J. (2013). A case study of factor influencing role improvisation in crisis response teams. *Cognition, Technology & Work, 15,* 79-93.

Rentschler, C., & Burdett, P. (2006, Spring). Mock disaster at Stetson Law Library prepares staff for a real one. *Florida Libraries,* 13–15.

Richter, J., Livet, M., Stewart, J., Feigley, C., Scott, G., & Richter, D. (2005, November). Coastal terrorism: Using tabletop discussions to enhance coastal community infrastructure through relationship building. *Journal of Public Health Management Practice,* S45–S49.

Roux-Dufort, C. (2009). The devil lies in details! How crises build up within organizations. *Journal of Contingencies and Crisis Management, 17*(1), 4–11.

Sadri, G., & Condia, J. (2012). Managing the virtual world. *Industrial Management, 54*(1), 21–25.

Simms, J. (2014, June). Don't panic! People Management, 22-28.

Simola, S. (2005). Organizational crisis management: Overview and opportunities. *Consulting Psychology Journal: Practice and Research, 57*(3), 180–192.

Strupp, J. (2002, September 2). Chemical scare tests reactions. *Editor and Publisher,* 4.

Swift, K. (2004). Crisis stage. *ABA Journal, 90*(1), 75.

Tracy, M. (2018, February 20). Louisville must forfeit basket championship over sex scandal. *The New York Times*. Retrieved October 7, 2018, from https://www.nytimes.com/2018/02/20/sports/ncaabasketball/louisville-ncaa-title.html

US Fire Administration (n.d.). Campus fire fatalities in residential buildings (2000-2015). FEMA. Retrieved October 5, 2018, from https://www.usfa.fema.gov/downloads/pdf/publications/campus_fire_fatalities_report.pdf

Uitdewilligen, S., & Waller, M. (2018). Information sharing and decision-making in multidisciplinary crisis management teams. *Journal of Organizational Behavior, 39,* 731-748.

Waller, M., Lei, Z., & Pratten, R. (2014). Focusing on teams in crisis management education: An integration and simulation-based approach. *Academy of Management Learning & Education, 13*(2), 208-221.

Wang, Y. (2015, December 1). Kenyan university fails to warn of realistic terrorism drill, causing panic and death. *The Washington Post.* Retrieved October 3, 2018, from

166

https://www.washingtonpost.com/news/morning-mix/wp/2015/12/01/kenyan-university-fails-to-warn-of-realistic-terrorism-drill-causing-panic-and-death/?utm_term=.7ac345c4ed1a

Wright-Reid, A. (2018). Managing stress in a crisis. *Journal of Business Continuity & Emergency Planning, 11*(3), 267-278.

Yanik, K. (2016, August). Crisis management. *Pit and Quarry, 109*(2), 70-75.

Yeh, F., McMullen, K., & Kane, L. (2010). Disaster planning in a health sciences library: A grant-funded approach. *Journal of the Medical Library Association, 98*(3), 259–261.

Chapter 6: Organizational Strategy and Crises

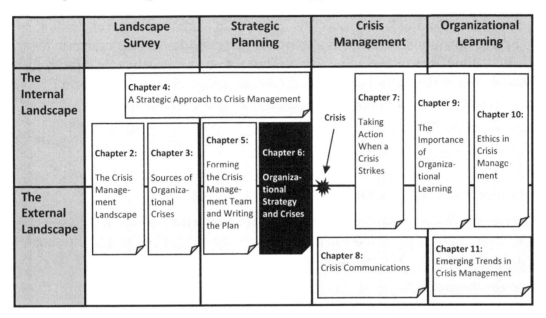

Learning Objectives

After reading this chapter, each student should be able to:

1. Discuss crisis vulnerabilities when a company competes in a single industry, multiple related industries, or multiple unrelated industries.
2. Identify crisis vulnerabilities associated with a corporate growth strategy.
3. Identify crisis vulnerabilities associated with a stability strategy.
4. Identify crisis vulnerabilities associated with a retrenchment strategy.
5. Discuss crisis vulnerabilities linked to a cost leadership strategy.
6. Discuss crisis vulnerabilities linked to a differentiation strategy.
7. Discuss crisis vulnerabilities that exist when a company seeks to combine cost leadership and differentiation strategies.
8. Identify and discuss the strategic control process and its relationship to crisis forecasting, prevention, and management.

Contemporary Crisis Case: Rana Plaza - Part 1

The 2013 collapse of Rana Plaza in Dhaka, Bangladesh exemplifies widespread human and financial costs that can emanate from a crisis. The crumbling of Rana Plaza resulted in the 1,138 deaths, mostly low-skilled female workers. The accident was linked to clothing brands worldwide, some unaware that their garments were being produced at Rana Plaza.

In our assessment of the Rana Plaza crisis, we refer to a brand as a line of clothing offered by a company and a retailer as a company that provides various brands in the same store. A brand may or may not utilize a retail outlet, as it may be sold directly to consumers online or through a factory store. Our discussion focuses on the term "brand" more often because brands, not retailers, are more closely linked to outsourcing in less developed countries with low labor costs. There are exceptions, however. For example, clothing intended for Walmart and JC Penny's, both retailers, were found in Rana Plaza after the collapse.

What Makes Rana Plaza a Contemporary Organizational Crisis?

We refer to Rana Plaza as a **contemporary organizational crisis** because it (1) is a collective crisis, (2) is transboundary in geographic scope, (3) goes deep into the supply chain, and (4) is driven by a cost-leadership strategy.

It is a collective crisis

Rana Plaza is a **collective crisis** because it involves multiple companies (Comyns & Franklin-Johnson, 2018). At Rana Plaza, 28 fashion brands were manufactured in the collapsed building. Numerous retailers that offered these brands were also linked to the crisis. Such crises occur because of a transition from vertical integration to supplier-based manufacturing, with suppliers often located in less developed countries. The Rana Plaza crisis is a by-product of globalization.

It is transboundary in geographical scope

The Rana Plaza case is an example of a **transboundary crisis** because it affected stakeholders across the world. From a retail perspective, brands from the European Union (EU) and North America were affected the most. From a country perspective, Bangladesh was the primary stakeholder because it provided a low-cost source of clothing. Other countries such as Cambodia, Vietnam, Burma, and Ethiopia offer similar sourcing arrangements as well (Vara, 2016).

It goes deep into the supply chain

The Rana Plaza crisis goes deep into the supply chain at tiers beyond the brand companies' audits. A brand may audit its first-tier manufacturers but is unwilling or unable to audit its second- and third-tier suppliers. Moreover, sub-contracting by first-tier suppliers without the brand's knowledge is common in the readymade garment (RMG) industry (Jacobs & Singhal, 2017). For example, a large retailer like Walmart may place a large order, but the manufacturer may not be able to fulfill it as promised. The supplier subcontracts part of the order to another manufacturer without Walmart's knowledge to meet the required completion date. Because fashions change abruptly, brands typically offer little price or completion date flexibility once the purchase orders are set. Subcontracting occurs because the manufacturer in Bangladesh does not want to lose a large business account like Walmart.

It is driven by a cost leadership strategy

A **cost leadership** strategy seeks cost reductions in manufacturing a product, typically to sell a product or service at a low price. As a result, suppliers and subcontractors are sought anywhere labor is the cheapest and a low per-unit cost can be achieved. The RMG industry is not a high-technology endeavor; a manufacturer typically contains just a building and many sewing machines. Required employee skills are minimal, and the barriers to entry are few, making it easy for prospective entrepreneurs to join the fray.

Brands seek to offer their products at the lowest prices to facilitate frequent style changes, producing garments that need not be durable but must be offered at low prices. Brands often seek low-cost producers in less developed countries with modest regard to quality. Manufacturers are reluctant to raise prices to fund improvements in working conditions or safety, lest they lose contracts to rivals with lower costs (Shell, 2009).

Consumers consistently maintain that they do not want their clothing made in sweatshops, but many base their purchase decisions on price with little concern or knowledge about production (Cooper, 2014). This raises an interesting dilemma: which entities drive the purchase cycle of the RMG industry, the brands, or the consumers? If brands raise their prices, consumers will shop elsewhere. Many consumers say they do not want to wear clothing made in sweatshops, but their good intentions do not always translate into purchase decisions.

The Collapse of the Rana Plaza Building

The Rana Plaza building was in the Savar district of Dhaka, Bangladesh. It was an eight-story building that was initially certified for only five floors, but three were added (without a permit) to house five separate garment factories (Cooper, 2014). Rana Plaza was built on swampland, an unstable setting for such a building. Ironically, crews were adding a ninth floor at the time of the collapse (Harvey, 2014).

Herein lies a critical problem. Buildings in Bangladesh are generally constructed quickly, without proper approval, and then rarely inspected because so few inspectors exist. Building safety laws exist in Bangladesh, but enforcement is sporadic (Cooper, 2014).

Prior to the Rana Plaza incident, there were two other manufacturing accidents in Dhaka related to building quality. In December 2010, 29 workers died in a fire at a sportwear factory. In November 2012, 112 workers died at the Tazreen Fashions factory. What made the Tazreen fire even more deadly was that managers had locked the gates that would have allowed workers to use the stairs to escape the fire (Harvey, 2014).

Two days before Rana Plaza collapsed, cracks were identified on load-bearing walls in the building. The retail shops on the lower floors were closed, but the five garment factories on the upper floors remained open. Their managers allegedly told workers that if they did not report to work, they would lose one month's salary. Many workers complied, albeit fearfully, to be crushed to death when the building collapsed (Cooper, 2014).

Case Discussion Questions

1. Many consumers claim to be willing to pay more for products manufactured in safe environments. In the RMG industry, however, they tend to base purchases primarily on price. How can you explain this ostensible contradiction?
2. What drives the purchase patterns in the RMG industry, the consumers, or the brands and retailers? Put differently, do consumers *force* brands and retailers to offer low prices, or do companies seek to lure consumers with low prices? Consider only the RMG industry in your response.

Introduction

Effective crisis management requires a **strategic mindset**; top managers must be alert to the crisis vulnerabilities that can occur. This chapter examines the reciprocal relationship between organizational strategy and crisis planning. Crisis management should be part of the strategic management process, but the strategy selected can influence the frequency and types of crises that emerge. This chapter begins by examining the strategy-crisis nexus. We then explore the intricate relationships between corporate-level strategies and crises and between businesses-level strategies and crises. The chapter concludes with a discussion on strategic control and how it helps managers forecast and prevent future crises.

Strategy and Crises

Strategy refers to top management's plans to develop and sustain competitive advantage to fulfill the organization's mission. **Strategic management** is a broader term and involves top management's analysis of the environment in which the organization operates and the plan for implementation and control of the strategy (Parnell, 2020).

Much of this analysis resembles what must be done to heighten crisis preparedness in an organization. Hence, there is a vital and robust link between the strategic management process and crisis management (Parnell, 2016; Pauchant & Mitroff, 1992; Preble, 1997).

The prevalence of organizational crises can be related to a firm's strategy. Some strategies are more crisis-prone than others. For instance, a company following a corporate strategy of external growth may facilitate certain types of calamities associated with the businesses they acquire (Probst & Raisch, 2005). In this sense, a firm's strategy can foreshadow the kind of crisis that may occur.

Corporate Level Strategies

The concept of organizational strategy can be examined from the corporate and business levels. The corporate strategy (also called the firm strategy) reflects the broad strategic approach top management formulates for the organization. Specifically, the corporate strategy delineates the industry, or industries, in which the firm operates and its overall plan for success. The business strategy (also called the competitive strategy) outlines each business unit's competitive pattern—an organizational entity with its mission, set of competitors, and industry. Business strategies are crafted so that each business unit can attain and sustain competitive advantage, a state whereby successful strategies cannot be easily duplicated by rivals (Cockburn, Henderson, & Stern, 2000; Parnell, 2020). As we will see, the choice of strategies at both corporate and firm levels can influence the types of crises the organization may face.

There are two steps involved in strategy development at the corporate (firm) level. The first is to identify the corporate profile by assessing the markets or industries in which the firm operates. The second is to identify a strategy to manage the firm's size, an approach that often—but not always—incorporates growth. Both dimensions and their links to crisis planning are discussed next.

The Corporate Profile

At the corporate level, top management defines the **corporate profile** by identifying the specific industry, or industries, in which the organization operates. Three basic profiles are possible: (1) operate within a single industry, (2) operate in multiple, related industries, or (3) operate in multiple, unrelated industries. Each profile has inherent advantages and disadvantages, creating the potential for different types of crises. Due to complexities with business units, identifying the most effective corporate profile can be challenging.

Single industry

An organization that operates in a single industry can benefit from specialized knowledge by concentrating its efforts in one business area. For instance, McDonald's operates exclusively in the restaurant industry and pursues internal growth by expanding outlets and increasing sales in each one. McDonald's success makes the firm an easy target for critics whose concerns include bulky packaging practices (Adams, 2005; Sethi & Steidlmeier, 1997), nutrition (Morrison, 2012), and pay practices (Swarns, 2015).

Operating in a single industry can be risky if there is a major crisis involving the company's main product. Such was the case with Texas-based ice cream maker Blue Bell Creameries, which almost shut down permanently after listeria was discovered in its products in 2015. Three fatalities were linked to Blue Bell's ice cream, and the company was forced to close all four of its manufacturing plants to isolate the cause and sanitize the factories (Elkind, 2015). In addition to the temporary closure, ice cream in 23 states was recalled, eliminating revenue for several months. With no sales and expenses mounting because of the recall and plant cleanings, Blue Bell had to lay off 1450 of its 3900 employees, further deepening the crisis. Fortunately, the company stayed afloat after receiving a $125 million loan from Texas billionaire, Sid Bass (Elkind, 2015; Newman & Gasparro, 2015).

In 2020, Blue Bell agreed to pay $19.35 million and plead guilty to two misdemeanors related to shipping contaminated ice cream. The US Justice Department alleged Blue Bell's former CEO, Paul Kruse, tried to know what he knew about the contamination. Kruse was charged with seven felonies, including conspiracy and wire fraud (Newman, 2020).

Blue Bell eventually recovered, but not all single industry companies hit with a crisis have been as fortunate. Frozen beef processor Topps Meat Company had to shut its doors permanently after it was hit with a 21.7-million-pound recall of ground beef in 2007. E. coli was found in its ground beef, which caused illnesses in Florida, Maine, Ohio, New York, and Pennsylvania. Topps was a single-plant operation and had been in business since 1940. John Nalivaka, a consultant to the meat and livestock industry, noted: "It's one of the problems for a single plant, small or large. If you have a recall and that plant is down, your whole financial well-being suffers" (Belson & Fahim, 2007).

Food crises are not limited to illness. IKEA sells food products like it does furniture—a few staples in large quantities. IKEA has gained success with salmon, roast beef, smoked reindeer steak, and meatballs. But the company encountered problems in February 2013 when samples showed that meat heading for IKEA restaurants contained horse meat. Food sales account for about 5% of IKEA's €27 billion revenue, including sales of about 150 million meatballs annually. An investigation launched by Sweden-based supplier Dafgard traced the horse meat to two Polish slaughterhouses no longer in use.

IKEA discarded the tainted meat and pulled 3.5 million additional portions of meatballs from the shelves (none containing horse), donating them to the European Federation of Food Banks. The company appeared to recover by December of the same year. According to IKEA spokeswoman Ylva Magnusson, "We now well more meatballs than we did before" (*Wall Street Journal*, 2013, B1).

Multiple related industries

Firms operating in a single industry are more susceptible to sharp downturns in business cycles; hence, they can be prone to economic crises. As such, an organization may operate in more than one industry to reduce uncertainty and risk. It may diversify by developing a new business line or acquiring other businesses with complementary product or service lines, a process known as related diversification. The key to successful related diversification is the development of synergy among the related business units. Synergy occurs when the two previously separate organizations join to generate higher effectiveness and efficiency than each would have generated separately. Synergy is not always easy to achieve, particularly if one of the firms has experienced a major crisis. This scenario occurred when Dow Chemical acquired Union Carbide in 1999. Union Carbide's Bhopal (India) gas leak disaster in 1984 created a "guilt by association" crisis for Dow, which immediately became the target of protests from groups that wanted the old Bhopal facility cleaned up because of groundwater contamination (Baldauf, 2004).

Some analysts suggest that Walmart operates in a single industry—retail—but it is probably more accurate to identify two closely related industries, discount retail for Walmart stores and wholesale clubs for its Sam's Club business. Walmart seeks synergy by driving down costs in both companies. Walmart stores and Sam's Clubs share distribution facilities as well. The firm's impressive growth has created a love-hate relationship with its external stakeholders.

Walmart is a large, retail-focused firm whose high visibility makes it vulnerable to crises, particularly those associated with public relations. In January 2018, Walmart announced that it would raise wages and benefits for many of its more than one million hourly workers due to the passage of the Tax Cuts and Jobs Act of 2017. Not surprisingly, the reaction was positive. But within hours, it was also revealed that 63 Sam's Club stores would also be closing as well, engendering adverse reactions from external stakeholders (Corkery, Scheiber, & Cohen, 2018).

Atlanta-based ValuJet, one of the first budget airlines in the United States experienced a crash on May 11, 1996, when Flight 592 plunged into the Florida Everglades, killing all passengers and crew. Safety violations in the cargo area mistakenly allowed the introduction of oxygen containers, which exploded in flight. The airline blamed its Miami subcontractor, SabreTech, for loading full oxygen containers that should have been empty (Englehardt, Sallot, & Springston, 2004). Not surprisingly, SabreTech blamed ValuJet for the mistake, while the FAA and the National Safety Transportation Board (NTSB) put the scrutiny on ValuJet. The airline was already under an FAA safety review before the crash.

The NTSB investigation revealed safety deficiencies, particularly in terms of subcontracting maintenance to SabreTech. Immediately after the crash, the FAA forced the airline to ground half of its flights while it investigated the airline's day-to-day operations. The agency found deficiencies in maintenance and ordered the airline to stop flying on June 17, just over a month after the crash of Flight 592. In August 1997, the NTSB found ValuJet at fault for poor oversight of its subcontractor SabreTech. The final NTSB report produced four years later blamed ValuJet, SabreTech, and even the FAA for lax oversight (Englehardt, Sallot, & Springston, 2004).

ValuJet, seeking survival, growth, and a sorely needed image change, merged with AirTran and adopted the AirTran name as part of its rebuilding effort (Beirne & Jensen, 1999). Changing the name of a company can help distinguish bad memories. In the instance of ValuJet, the crisis was further removed when Southwest Airlines acquired AirTran in 2010. Such transformations have also been carried out by Philip Morris (now Altria) and Anderson Consulting (now Accenture) (Keating, 2012).

Another example is Alpha Natural Resources, a coal company based in Abingdon, Virginia. On June 1, 2011, Altria acquired Massey Energy, a company with a less-than-stellar reputation (see Chapter 3). Massey Energy was notorious for safety violations and incorporating a culture where wrongdoing was overlooked (Barrett, 2011). The challenge for Alpha was to remain profitable, protect miner safety, and assimilate the two companies' cultures. The decision to acquire Massey was a strategic one, and industry watchers hoped that Alpha's oversight would end the string of mining accidents experienced under Massey. As part of the deal, Alpha also acquired the liability associated with Massey's negligence associated with the disaster at Upper Big Branch that killed 29 miners in 2005. In the largest settlement ever for a mine accident, Alpha accepted the obligation to pay a total of $209 million. This figure included $1.5 million for each of the 29 victims who died and for two other miners who were injured (Tavernise & Krauss, 2011). This acquisition was expensive for Alpha and, ultimately, initiated a string of events that led the company in and out of bankruptcy before being merged into Contura Energy in 2016 (*Engineering & Mining Journal*, 2016).

Multiple, unrelated industries

A business may choose to operate multiple businesses in unrelated industries, usually because its managers wish to reduce company risk by spreading resources across several markets, an approach known as **diversification**. These firms pursue an unrelated diversification strategy by acquiring businesses not related to the core domain. In terms of potential crises, this strategy also has its challenges. By attempting to expand their core competencies, firms may find themselves in unfamiliar territory, thereby heightening crisis potential. This scenario happened to the once-respected A. H. Robins Company when it departed from its core product line to pursue the marketing of the ill-fated Dalkon Shield, an intrauterine contraceptive device known as an IUD. The product was later associated with health problems and was ultimately withdrawn from the market. The legal fallout was so devastating that A. H. Robins had to enter bankruptcy and was acquired later by another company (D'Zurilla, 1998).

Problems can arise when firms are diversified solely to achieve rapid increases in share values. A host of abuses can result, but most notably, ethical issues whereby managers seek to artificially inflate the value of the firm (Hosmer, 2011). Table 6.1 summarizes the link between the corporate profile and crisis risk.

Johnson & Johnson (J&J) operates in the broad healthcare industry, but its business ventures are so varied that one could argue they compete in multiple industries. The company offers a wide range of consumer products in the baby/beauty products line as well as healthcare products. It also produces pharmaceutical and nonpharmaceutical drugs and a wide array of medical devices. While the common thread is healthcare, the industries in which J&J operates are diverse. However, competing in complex environments can be risky.

J&J provided one of the first examples of excellent crisis response when it faced instances of tainted Tylenol in 1982 and 1986. It used its corporate credo as a basis for guiding the company through this ordeal. J&J's response created a standard against which other firms would be judged, but the company's stellar reputation for corporate responsibility has been drawn into question several times in the past decade. On April 14, 2009, the company learned that some of the raw materials used to make children's and infant Tylenol formulas were tainted with Burkholderia cepacia bacteria. Although J&J denied using these materials, the company used others that were part of the same batch. Nonetheless, the company continued shipping the medicines until June 4, the day that US Food and Drug Administration (FDA) investigators cited the firm for violating acceptable manufacturing practices. However, J&J did not launch a recall of the bottles until August 21 and did not make the recall public until September. Its internal testing revealed no contamination, and the FDA did not link side effects to the products. J&J did not notify the FDA of its actions, as encouraged by regulators (Rockoff, 2010a).

In September 2010, US officials charged J&J with failing to swiftly and adequately inform regulators about a nationwide withdrawal of Motrin. Rather than issuing a product recall, J&J instigated a "phantom recall" by commissioning a contractor to secretly purchase all stocks of the product (Brewster, 2011). FDA deputy commissioner

Joshua Sharfstein acknowledged that pharmaceutical companies have no legal obligation to inform the FDA when recalls are initiated, nor does the FDA have any legal authority to dictate the procedure utilized by the company. Nonetheless, J&J Chairman Bill Weldon (now retired) acknowledged that the company "let the public down" and "should have handled things differently" (Jack, 2010). In the end, the recall cost J&J hundreds of millions of dollars in lost sales (Rockoff, 2010b, B3).

Table 6.1 – The Corporate Profile and Risk Factors

	Risk Factors	Examples
Operate in a single industry	High visibility of the company makes it a "target" for criticism from external stakeholders.	McDonalds Wal-Mart
	Vulnerability exists if the company offers a limited product line.	Blue Bell Topps Meat
Operates multiple businesses in related industries (related diversification)	The parent company must be careful when it acquires a company previously damaged by a crisis.	Union Carbide/Dow Chemical ValuJet/AirTran Massey Energy/Alpha Natural Resources/Contura Energy
Operate multiple businesses in unrelated industries (unrelated diversification)	Potential exists to operate outside of its original core, thus opening it up to a crisis.	A. H. Robins
	A business may be viewed as a portfolio, creating an incentive to falsify income statements and balance sheets to look attractive to investors while driving up stock prices and bringing in bonuses for top executives.	Tyco Enron

Johnson & Johnson: Crises in multiple, unrelated industries

The first children's Tylenol products returned to the shelves in mid-November 2010, but J&J had to address a decline in consumer confidence, the encroachment of rival brands, and even cheaper private-label brands that had thrived during the recent economic recession. According to an annual survey administered by Brand Keys, consumer loyalty to Tylenol declined 7% during the year. Perrigo, a leading manufacturer of store-brand nonprescription drugs, gained nearly 20% in market share during the crisis (Rockoff, 2010b). The damage had been significant to J&J, which was once held in the highest esteem.

In 2018, a new crisis emerged. In July, a jury awarded $4.14 billion in punitive damages and $550 million in compensatory damages to 22 women who claimed asbestos in J&J baby talcum powder caused their ovarian cancer (Hsu, 2018). J&J has vowed to appeal the verdict. In December, *Reuters* published a report saying J&J had known for decades that it had asbestos in its baby powder (Girion, 2018). If proven, J&J could face a massive wave of lawsuits covering almost 50 years of potential liabilities (Duggan, 2018). However, J&J Chairman and CEO Alex Gorsky firmly refuted the report and released a video promoting the safety of its talcum powder. The facts surrounding the alleged coverup are undoubtedly relevant, but even if the company is eventually vindicated of any wrongdoing, the crisis has been severe and costly. Moreover, J&J's history underscores that competing in multiple industries carries unique challenges, particularly when healthcare is involved.

Corporate Strategies

After an organization's corporate profile is determined, its corporate strategy is established. Three possibilities exist: An organization may attempt to increase its size significantly (i.e., growth), remain about the same size (i.e., stability), or become smaller (i.e., retrenchment).

Growth

Most firms seek to grow, and this strategy can be realized in several ways. **Internal growth** occurs when a firm increases revenues, production capacity, and its workforce. This type of growth can occur by expanding the business or creating new ones. **External growth** is accomplished when an organization merges with or acquires another firm. Mergers seek to improve competitiveness by sharing or combining resources.

When a company grows, it becomes more noticeable to the public. A surge in popularity means the public generally likes the product or service being offered. However, it also means the company is more vulnerable. Growth strategies include the potential for becoming a target of social media or even extortion because the firm is larger and more visible. The Wendy's severed finger incident (see Chapter 3) illustrates such an extortion attempt. Although Wendy's made no payments, the fast-food chain still suffered a 2.5% decline in sales for the quarter (Langston, 2006).

Another type of crisis can occur when a company enters a strategic alliance as part of its growth strategy. **Strategic alliances**—often called partnerships—occur when two or more firms agree to share the costs, risks, and benefits of pursuing new business opportunities. Such arrangements include joint ventures, franchise/license agreements, joint operations, cooperative long-term supplier agreements, marketing agreements, and consortiums. Strategic alliances can be temporary, disbanding after the project is finished, or can involve multiple projects over an extended time (Parnell, 2020). Many strategic alliances fall under the category of global outsourcing, thereby creating unique crisis vulnerabilities.

The late 1990s and early 2000s witnessed a sharp increase in strategic alliances (Reuer, Zollo, & Singh, 2002). There are many examples of partnerships, especially where technology and global access are vital considerations. IBM and Apple Computer have exchanged technology to develop more effective computer operating systems. General Motors (GM), Ford, and Chrysler are jointly researching to enhance battery technology for electric and alternative fuel cars powered by electricity, hydrogen, and other alternative energy sources. Perhaps the most dramatic example of strategic alliances is occurring in China, where every major automobile manufacturer in the world is working with firms in the Chinese auto market to build vehicles (Casey, Zamiska, & Pasztor, 2007; Chu, 2011).

Strategic alliances enable a firm to expand its reach into new markets while utilizing a partner firm's expertise. Strategic alliances can also be vulnerable to crises, especially if the partner firms do not agree explicitly on their contribution to the alliance or if they do not have a common agreed-upon approach to identify vulnerabilities and an action plan to address crisis management.

Stability

There are times when a company may seek to retain its current size, at least temporarily. A **stability** strategy may be pursued for a short time when there is significant political and economic uncertainty. Many US firms adopted a wait-and-see approach in the early 2010s when the economy struggled to recover from the mortgage crisis, and the regulatory environment became more cumbersome. Stability may also be pursued after a period of excessive growth. Early in its history, computer maker Dell sought a period of stability strategy after achieving a 285% growth over two years so the company could address needs for new facilities and managers (Burrows & Anderson, 1993). Indeed, rapid growth can create crises, including a potential for the company's premature demise (Probst & Raisch, 2005).

A stability strategy may also be advisable in other instances. If a firm's industry is not growing, then internal growth must come at the expense of rivals, a tricky proposition. The costs associated with growth may not justify the benefits. Moreover, a small firm known for quality and excellent service may choose to remain small to provide a high level of personal customer attention. While growth is usually desirable, stability may be pursued temporarily or even over the long term in certain instances (Parnell, 2020).

Retrenchment

A **retrenchment** strategy seeks to decrease the size of the organization and often follows a downturn. Indeed, an economic crisis—a significant decline in sales—represents one such scenario. However, a retrenchment strategy usually follows an acute organizational crisis. A major fire, negative publicity, product recall, or a breach of ethics by management can all be factors that lead to a decrease in revenue and, therefore, instigate the need to retrench.

Retrenchment can take one of three forms: turnaround, divestment, or liquidation. A turnaround is the most conservative approach, whereas liquidation is the harshest. A **turnaround** seeks to transform the corporation into a leaner, more efficient firm. It includes such actions as eliminating unprofitable outputs, pruning assets, reducing the size of the workforce, cutting costs of distribution, and reassessing the firm's product lines and customer groups (Parnell, 2020). From a crisis management perspective, a turnaround strategy also includes any strategic initiative that management deems necessary to improve the company's performance in a specific area.

Denny's restaurants needed a turnaround—particularly in its human resource management practices—after agreeing to pay $54 million to resolve several racial discrimination lawsuits stemming from incidents in the early 1990s. Although social media outlets were not yet widespread, the late-night television comedians at the time were poking fun at the chain regularly. Show hosts Arsenio Hall and Jay Leno attacked the company as an example of Southern bigotry and intolerance. The crisis that gathered the most news coverage involved the poor service that six black Secret Service officers received at an Annapolis, Maryland, Denny's in 1993. The agents claimed to experience humiliating and discriminatory service while their white colleagues enjoyed a hearty breakfast (Adamson, 2000). However, these setbacks illustrate how a company can not only withstand a crisis but can benefit from it in the long run. According to Ray Hood-Phillips, Chief Diversity Officer at Denny's, "A decade ago, the restaurant chain Denny's was nearly synonymous with racism." After the devastating lawsuit, the company viewed its turnaround as requiring "a holistic approach to diversity" (Brathwaite, 2002, p. 28). This move involved changing the company's culture through intensive diversity training, increasingly effective recruiting practices, and a more valid performance appraisal system.

Some turnaround strategies may reduce the size of the workforce. If there are layoffs, management should be prepared to justify them to departing employees and survivors. Employees may be given opportunities to leave voluntarily—generally with an incentive—to make the process as harmonious as possible. When this occurs, those departing may be the top performers who are most marketable, leaving the firm with a less competitive workforce. When layoffs are just "announced," morale is likely to suffer considerably. Hence, turnarounds involving layoffs are often more challenging to implement than anticipated (Murray, 2001). Furthermore, layoffs should be averted when possible because of the devastating consequences on employees, their families, and the local community (Macky, 2004). Instead, the decision to reduce the workforce should be based on the long-term cost adjustments that are needed at the firm (Gandolfi, 2008).

If layoffs occur, several actions can mitigate some of the adverse effects. Top management is encouraged to communicate honestly with all employees, explaining why the downsizing is necessary and how terminated employees were selected. Everyone, including those employees who remain in the organization (i.e., the survivors), should be made aware of how departing employees will be supported. Employees should also be encouraged to use available services, including educational retraining funds through the government and company outsourcing services. Although these measures will not eliminate all the harsh feelings associated with layoffs, they can help keep the process under control.

Some executives are widely recognized as turnaround specialists and may be brought in as temporary CEOs to lead the process and orchestrate such unpopular strategic moves as layoffs, budget cuts, and reorganizations. Also, crisis management consulting firms are abundant and can advise on the specifics of crisis management planning and communicating with the media. Robert "Steve" Miller, a major player in the Chrysler turnaround, has served as CEO of Waste Management and the automobile parts supplier Federal-Mogul, as well as a consultant on turnaround issues to such companies as Aetna. According to Miller, the CEO of a company seeking turnaround should be honest with employees from the outset and seek their input. He or she should also spend time with customers. As Miller put it, "Listen to your customers. [They] are usually more perceptive than you are about what you need to do with your company" (Lublin, 2000, p. B1).

Divestment—selling one or more business units to another firm—often occurs when firm leaders believe the organization is facing a crisis. Divestment may be necessary when the industry is in decline or when a business unit drains resources from more profitable units, is not performing well, or is not synergistic with other corporate holdings. During Denny's turnaround discussed previously, the firm also pursued a degree of divestment by selling its Coco's and Carrows restaurants (Kruger, 2004).

Liquidation terminates the business unit by selling its assets. Liquidation is, by definition, a last-resort response to a severe crisis. In effect, it can be viewed as divestment of *all* the firm's business units and should be adopted only under extreme conditions, as adverse outcomes will result. Shareholders and creditors will experience financial losses, managers and hourly employees will lose their jobs, suppliers will lose a customer, and the local community will suffer an increase in unemployment and a decrease in tax revenues. Hence, liquidation should be considered only when other forms of retrenchment are not feasible.

Business Strategies

Whereas the corporate-level strategy addresses industries in which a firm competes, the business-level strategy focuses on customers, their needs, and core competencies. The challenging task of formulating and implementing a strategy for each business unit is based on many factors (Parnell, 2020).

The first step in formulating a business strategy is to select a broad, generic strategy to compete with rivals and then fine-tune it to accentuate the organization's unique set of resource strengths (Campbell-Hunt, 2000; Parnell, 2020). Porter's (1980) generic strategy framework serves as a good starting point for assessing business strategies. According to Porter, a business unit must address two primary competitive concerns. First, managers must determine whether the business unit should **focus** on an identifiable subset of the industry in which it operates or seek to serve an entire industry. For example, many specialty clothing stores in shopping malls adopt the focus concept and concentrate their efforts on limited product lines intended primarily for a small market niche. In contrast, most chain grocery stores seek to serve the "mass market"—or at least most of it—by selecting an array of products and services with broad appeal.

Second, managers must determine whether the business unit should compete primarily by minimizing its costs relative to its rivals (what Porter calls low-cost or cost leadership) or through differentiation by offering unique and unusual products and services (Parnell, 2020). Decisions regarding these two competitive concerns create four generic strategies: cost leadership, cost leadership with focus, differentiation, and differentiation with focus. The crisis vulnerabilities associated with each of these strategies is discussed in kind.

Cost Leadership (Low-Cost)

Businesses that utilize a **cost leadership or low-cost** strategy produce basic, no-frills products and services. They provide their products and services to an entire market and appeal primarily to price-sensitive consumers (Parnell, 2020). Walmart's discount retail business is a quintessential example of such a cost leader. Businesses using a low-cost strategy are susceptible to price competition from other firms, particularly large rivals that enjoy economies of scale. This constant pressure to reduce costs may cause a firm to cut corners, ultimately leading to a crisis.

Companies often seek to reduce costs by contracting some or all of its production to other firms in developing countries where labor costs are lower. The Rana Plaza case that begins this chapter illustrates the dilemma that can occur. As companies cut costs, they can become engulfed in a "race to the bottom," a practice described in Chapter 2. The problem with this approach is that foreign contractors may sacrifice worker safety to cut costs. Companies that source to developing nations need to be aware of these tradeoffs, as their brand reputations can suffer when accidents occur at these factories.

While the supply chain example illustrates how the low-cost strategy can translate into low prices, it also reminds the customer that there can be a "high cost to low prices," an adage that author Charles Fishman (2006) made famous in his book on Walmart. Fishman's critique of the big box was intense:

> *Walmart's brilliant, obsessive focus on a single core value – delivering low prices – created what became the largest and most influential company in history. And yet the drive for low prices is also the cause of the troubling elements of the Walmart effect: low wages, unrelenting pressure on suppliers, products cheap in quality as well as price, offshoring of jobs. (Fishman, 2006, p. 14)*

Indeed, Walmart's obsession with cost containment has resulted in lower prices, but with lower wages and fewer employee benefits. Walmart pressures its suppliers to drive down costs but promises them volume if they meet specific targets. Many suppliers struggle to meet the cost targets, and some have opted not to sell to Walmart as a result (Fishman, 2006). The Walmart example underscores that cost leadership—like all business strategies—contains specific crisis vulnerabilities.

Many organizations seek to reduce the number of permanent full-time employees through lean staffing as part of a cost leadership strategy. Doing so can improve firm performance but can also create challenges when a crisis strikes. For example, the largest cost category in many industries, including hospitals, is labor. In the late 2010s, many US hospitals cut back on personnel. When the pandemic hit in 2020, most struggled to provide Covid-19 patients with the needed one-on-one help from critical-care nurses. Many hospitals instituted on-the-fly training and relied heavily on expensive traveling nurses. In Arizona, hourly pay for short-term, contract-based intensive care nurses rose from $85 to $145 an hour, a cost many small, rural hospitals could not afford (Gold & Evans, 2020).

Focus-Low-Cost

The previous section addressed a low-cost strategy designed to serve an entire industry, but some cost leaders *focus* their efforts on a specific market niche. The focus-low-cost strategy seeks low overall costs while meeting the needs of consumers in a narrow segment of the market (Parnell, 2020).

Businesses following a focus-low-cost strategy tend to be smaller than those adhering to a low-cost strategy. A business usually requires more resources to reach an entire industry successfully. Smaller companies are often ill-equipped for such an endeavor but can succeed by concentrating on one or a few market niches.

Like the low-cost strategy, the focus-low-cost can also result in customer complaints concerning the quality of products and services. If a company is suspected of cutting corners, the backlash can be severe, especially if customer service is involved. Consider the case of Spirit Airlines, a budget carrier based in Miramar, Florida. This company operates in the airline industry's ultra-low-cost niche, minimizing costs and targeting low- to moderate-income consumers that might not afford to fly on traditional carriers. In 2012, the airline found itself in a crisis when it refused to refund a $197 ticket to a passenger with cancer. The incident received national attention when his doctor told the passenger Jerry Meekins, he could not fly because he had esophageal cancer. Meekins had booked a ticket from St. Petersburg, Florida, to Atlantic City, New Jersey, but had not bought insurance, thinking he would make the flight (Watson, 2012). When the airline refused to refund the ticket, the story went viral and painted the company as ruthless and uncaring. A "Boycott Spirit Airlines" page appeared on Facebook with more than 21,000 "likes" (Miller, 2012). Public perception was not in favor of the airline and even resulted in two Atlantic County assemblymembers asking Spirit Airlines to change its refund policy (Watson, 2012). After considerable negative publicity, then CEO Ben Baldanza reversed his decision and allowed the refund (Nicas, 2012), but by then, the damage had already been done to the airline's reputation.

While Spirit's refund policy resembles those of other airlines, the crisis is noteworthy for three reasons. First, the victim was a veteran of the US Marine Corps, so denying the refund seemed antipatriotic to many. Second, Spirit had many customer complaints about service in general, so the refund request was viewed as just another problem. Indeed, Kate Hanni, the Executive Director of Flyers Rights, once commented on Spirit's approach to customer service: "They're the worst airline in the US. They put no money back into customer service, which is a black hole at Spirit. Spirit Airlines has a history of cruelty toward their passengers, but they continue to treat them like meat in a seat because their fares are so low, they are confident people will continue to fly with them" (Miller, 2012).

Third, Baldanza tried to justify his decision not to issue a refund, maintaining that it would not be fair to the other passengers. His argument has some logic but poor optics. Public relations consultant and author Fraser Seitel commented that the airline could have simply transferred the ticket to Mr. Meekins' daughter, who he was flying to see, a move that actually might have generated positive publicity for the airline (Miller, 2012). All three of these factors created a recipe for disaster and helped explain why a common customer complaint became an organizational crisis.

Spirit Airlines may have more at risk from a crisis perspective than some of its rivals because the company, like most focus-low-cost businesses, is relatively small. As one analyst noted, "Spirit is still small – carrying just one percent of the nation's fliers—and one public relations fiasco, such as a plane crash or lengthy labor strike, could damage its profitability and growth, according to industry analysts" (Nicas, 2012, p. A1).

Another airline that follows a focus-low-cost strategy, Allegiant Air, found itself at the center of an investigative report on its safety practices by *60 Minutes* in April 2018. The report stated that malfunctions increase with the age of the aircraft. Indeed, Allegiant has used a business model of acquiring older planes to reduce costs. As a result, the number of aborted takeoffs, in-flight mechanical problems, and emergency landings are higher than the industry norm, due in part to its aging MD-80 fleet, the average age of which is 28 years (Koenig, 2018). Allegiant has not had an accident involving fatalities, but the concern over using older aircraft creates an uneasy perception in the minds of many consumers.

Differentiation

Businesses that utilize a **differentiation** strategy tend to be larger firms seeking to meet the demands of an entire industry. Differentiators produce products and services that can be readily distinguished from those of competitors (Parnell, 2020). While all businesses are concerned with costs, differentiators place a greater emphasis on quality than do cost leaders.

As discussed in Chapter 3, Chi-Chi's suffered a major crisis when its Beaver Valley Mall location near Pittsburgh, Pennsylvania, was identified as the source of a Hepatitis A outbreak. Chi-Chi's was a differentiator focused on Mexican food, a difficult niche to serve effectively (Lockyer, 2004). The crisis erupted rather innocently and was unnoticed. Employees were chopping green onions for the salsa, not knowing that the ice packed with the product had melted and soaked into the onions for hours. Unfortunately, the ice was laden with the Hepatitis A virus (Veil, Liu, Erickson, & Sellnow, 2005). What resulted was the sickness of over 660 people and three fatalities. This crisis, along with severe competition and bankruptcy, sealed the fate for the 27-

year-old chain (Lockyer, 2004). Another focus-oriented business had become a victim of a crisis.

Other Mexican restaurants have experienced similar crises. Chipotle temporarily closed 40 stores in 2015 after an outbreak of serious illnesses linked to *E. coli* bacteria that ultimately sickened more than 1,000 people. In early 2020, Chipotle agreed to pay $25 million to resolve criminal charges stemming from the mishap (Newman, 2020). The company recovered, however, and navigated the early stages of COVID-19 well. By investing in digital operations and building more drive-thrus, Chipotle tripled its online sales in 2020. A small number of stores—mostly in shopping malls—remained closed in 2020, and sales declined from the previous year, but the chain survived by expanding dining options that do not require customers to enter the store (Haddon, 2020).

Businesses emphasizing differentiation may be more threatened by abrupt shifts in consumer tastes, particularly when the economy shifts. When oil prices spiked in 2008, consumer preferences moved away from sport utility vehicles (SUVs), large cars, and trucks to smaller, more fuel-efficient alternatives. Carmakers like Ford and GM developed vehicles that were stylish and fun to drive, but not necessarily fuel efficient. When the average price of gasoline in the US hit four dollars a gallon in 2008, they faced a crisis. Venture capital was also beginning to pour into startup firms worldwide racing to develop vehicles that consumed less gas or utilized alternative, cleaner, and cheaper fuels (Stewart, 2008; Taylor, 2008).

When gasoline prices spiked to four dollars a gallon again in 2012, carmakers had begun to develop plug-in hybrids and fully electric vehicles (EVs). With the introduction of EVs, however, a new array of crises ensued. EV maker Tesla experienced two fires in its Model S cars caused by road debris hitting the battery pack. To address the situation, Tesla installed an underbody shield to protect the battery pack from impacts it may receive from road debris (Nishimoto, 2014). The Chevy Volt had problems with battery fires after accident testing, forcing General Motors to offer loaner cars to Volt owners while the company worked to fix the problem (Terlep, 2011). Interestingly, GM abandoned the Volt in late 2018 amid lower oil prices and concerns that the US federal EV subsidy of $7500 might not be renewed. GM is joining Tesla and other rivals in the race to develop self-driving vehicles, a promising technology, but one fraught with crisis potential.

Focus-Differentiation

Differentiators may seek to satisfy all customers' needs in an industry or may *focus* their efforts on a market niche. Whether differentiators or cost leaders, businesses pursuing a focus strategy tend to be comparably small, so a crisis can be devastating. Indeed, larger companies like Walmart have relatively more resources to buffer the effects of a crisis.

The Chalk's Ocean Airways case addressed in Chapter 4 illustrates how one major crisis can decimate a business following a focus-differentiation strategy. Chalk's offered vintage seaplane flights between the Bahamas and South Florida. Its strategy's selective nature made it vulnerable to a crisis when in 2005, Flight 101 went down just minutes after takeoff, ending the life of what was once the nation's oldest airline.

Odwalla follows a focus-differentiation strategy (see Chapter 3). In 1996, a non-pasteurized fruit juice it marketed caused an infant's death and made dozens of people violently ill (Levick & Slack, 2011). Fortunately, the company overcame the crisis by offering an immediate apology and promised to compensate all the families affected fairly. It also changed its juice processing to include flash pasteurization, which kills any bacteria present in the juice. Even Bill Marler, the attorney representing the victims and their families, had good things to say about Odwalla: "If you look at what people remember (from the case), everyone remembers the positive stuff about what Odwalla did" (Levick & Slack, 2011, p. 15). Odwalla not only survived but has performed well since the crisis.

Crises can threaten restaurants operating in a market niche. Established in 1951, Bullock's Bar-B-Q is a popular eatery and the longest-operating restaurant in Durham, North Carolina. Famous patrons include Dolly Parton, Garth Brooks, Kris Kristofferson, and Joe Biden. On April 20, 2010, more than a dozen patrons reported ill effects later determined to be salmonella. Business declined 80% shortly after the outbreak. Sam Poley, Durham Convention and Visitors Bureau's marketing director and a former chef himself, recruited an overflow crowd of chefs and restaurant owners for lunch at Bullock's on May 7 to show their support. Steps can be taken to reduce the likelihood of salmonella poisoning, but it is virtually impossible to eliminate the possibility. As Poley put it, "...every chef knows, there but for the grace of God go I" (Wise, 2010, p. 3B).

After investigating the incident, the Durham County Health Department said the likely cause of the salmonella bacteria was a commercial product, pasteurized egg whites, and not improper food handling by employees. However, the North Carolina Department of Agriculture and Consumer services tests could not confirm that the egg product was contaminated with salmonella. According to several blog comments, the customers who got sick used takeout rather than eating in the restaurant (WRAL.com, 2010). In cases like this, the product might have been held at improper temperatures before consumption, creating an environment for bacteria growth. Restaurants that offer takeout options must consider this reality as one of their crisis vulnerabilities. The Bullocks example illustrates how a small niche-oriented business can be affected by a crisis outside its control. Fortunately, Bullocks recovered and is doing well.

Combining Low-Cost and Differentiation

Michael Porter (1980) warned against combining low-cost and differentiation strategies. Doing so can leave a business **stuck in the middle** because actions designed to support one strategy could work against the other. Indeed, differentiating a product can increase costs, ultimately eroding a firm's basis for cost leadership. Moreover, some cost-cutting measures may be directly related to quality and other bases of differentiation. Following this logic, a business should choose *either* low-cost *or* differentiation, but not both. Combining the two approaches can be challenging. Some businesses do so successfully, but they tend to be the exception.

Consider two examples. McDonald's was initially known for consistency in food across locations, friendly service, and cleanliness. These bases for differentiation catapulted McDonald's to market share leader, allowing the firm to negotiate for beef, potatoes, and other vital materials at the lowest possible cost. JetBlue Airways was launched in 2000 to provide economical air service among a limited number of cities. JetBlue has minimized costs by squeezing more seats into its planes, selling its tickets directly to customers, and shortening ground delays. Although commonly viewed as a discount airline, JetBlue has also distinguished itself by providing new planes, satellite television on board, and leather seating (Parnell, 2020).

Businesses that pursue a combination strategy also share the crisis vulnerabilities associated with pursuing cost leadership or differentiation. Put another way, companies like McDonald's and JetBlue are susceptible to crises related to attempts to lower costs and provide distinctive service. Hence, the combination strategy is more difficult to execute and can also place greater strains on crisis managers.

Strategic Control

Just as strategic control is a part of the overall strategic management process, it can also be a tool in the crisis management process. The goal of strategic control is to determine how the organization's strategies are successful in attaining its goals and objectives. Managers track the implementation and adjust the strategy as necessary (Picken & Dess, 1997). Gaps between the intended and realized strategies (i.e., what was planned and what happened) are identified and addressed during this stage. The process of strategic control can be likened to that of steering a vehicle. After the accelerator is pressed (executing the strategy), the control function ensures that the organization moves in the right direction. When a simple steering adjustment (i.e., a managerial decision) is not enough to modify the vehicle's trajectory, the driver can resort to other means, such as applying the brake or shifting gears (other managerial decisions). Similarly, strategic managers can steer the organization by instituting minor modifications to prevent crises or resort to more drastic changes in response to an ongoing crisis, such as altering the strategic direction altogether (Parnell, 2020).

The need for strategic control is brought about by two key factors. First, it is essential to know how well the firm is performing. Without strategic control, there are no clear benchmarks and, ultimately no reliable measurements that indicate how well the company is performing. Second, organizations must negotiate uncertainty in their environments. For example, one of the authors of this book found himself in a crisis when a major weather event shut down the facility he was managing. The result was a significant loss of revenue for about a week. The strategic control system in place was able to identify the financial extent of the crisis and its impact on the firm. Although revenue declined, the control mechanism was able to show that the poor performance was not the fault of the manager, but the weather. The extent of that crisis was easily measured by comparing the results to those of the previous year's revenues for the same period. Because the manager was accountable for sales and profits based on a projected budget, provisions were made to not penalize him because of the inclement weather. Indeed, some environments exist where managers are told to "suck it up" and work that much harder so the original forecast can be reached. This practice is unreasonable and penalizes managers for forces beyond their control.

The Strategic Control Process

Strategic control is a five-step process (Parnell, 2020).

1. Top management determines the focus of strategic control by identifying the internal factors that can serve as effective measures for the chosen strategy's success or failure. The external factors that could trigger responses from the organization are also identified.
2. Benchmarks established for the internal factors can be compared to actual performance after the strategy is implemented.
3. Management measures and evaluates the company's actual performance, both quantitatively and qualitatively.
4. Performance evaluations are compared with the established standards.
5. If performance meets or exceeds the standards, corrective action is usually unnecessary. If performance falls below the standard, then management typically takes remedial action.

Step 1 – Identify Factors to Track

Strategic control encompasses external and internal dimensions. Although individual firms usually exert little or no influence over the external and industry forces (see

Chapters 2 and 3), they must be monitored continuously because their shifts can have strategic ramifications. Specifically, strategic control consists of modifying the company's operations to defend it more effectively when a crisis emerges. Recall the six broad trends in the crisis management landscape identified in Chapter 2:

1. Crises have become more transboundary.
2. Terrorism remains a threat.
3. Social media and the Internet intensify the effects of a crisis.
4. Human-induced missteps are at the core of most crises.
5. Environmental damage and the sustainability of resources can trigger a global impact.
6. Globalization increases the risk of organizational, supply chain, and societal crises.

A shift in one or more of these factors can alter the strategy and, therefore, its crisis management preparedness. In Chapter 3, we reviewed the PEST analysis concept, a strategy tool that evaluates the political, economic, social, and technological trends in the external environment. Understanding these external factors is necessary for devising a firm's corporate and business strategies.

Step 2 – Develop Standards or Benchmarks

Once broad factors are identified to track company performance, management must identify specific indicators that serve as surrogates of company performance. These indicators often include factors related to revenue, expenses, and profitability. Still, they may also include machine breakdowns (if applicable), quality scores, and indicators involving employee well-being such as accident rates, tardiness, absenteeism, amount of sick days taken, and workplace injuries. Pre-designated goals or benchmarking against other companies should be established for each of these items. Assessing these performance indicators can help identify early warning signs that a crisis may be looming.

Step 3 – Measure Performance Both Quantitatively and Qualitatively

Firm performance may be evaluated in many ways. Management can compare current operating results with those from the preceding quarter or year. A fundamental problem with performance measurement is that one measure can be pursued to the detriment of another. The common goals of growth and profitability versus safety concerns come to mind. Accidents cause many crises in organizations due to inadequate training and faulty equipment. Expenditures in these areas decrease short-term profits, yet a single accident can severely hurt the firm's long-term viability or even close it down.

Many companies have begun using a balanced scorecard approach to measuring performance. A balanced scorecard considers an array of quantitative and qualitative factors, such as return on assets (ROA), market share, customer loyalty and satisfaction, speed, and innovation (Kaplan & Norton, 1996, 2000). Managers assign a weight and specific means of measurement to each indicator. For example, they might customer satisfaction a 10% weight and measure it with customer survey scores. The key to employing a balanced scorecard is selecting an array of performance indicators explicitly tailored to the firm and its strategic position. Indicators that can predict potential crises such as customer satisfaction, accident rates, or product quality measures should be considered. Table 6.2 provides a list of possible indicators.

Table 6.2 Balanced Scorecard Indicators and Potential Crises

Indicator to Include on the Balanced Scorecard	Potential Crises (or root causes) that it Represents
Number of accidents in a work section or unit	Accident and safety issues; potential employee lawsuits
Absenteeism by employees in a work section or unit	Motivational problems; substance abuse; poor supervision
Number of grievances (union setting) or employee complaints in a non-union work environment	Morale problems; abusive supervision; potential for workplace violence
Employee satisfaction survey	Problems with morale, supervision
Machine or work section downtime	Major production interruption due to accidents, fire, or significant machine breakdown
Percentage of defective product(s)	Potential for recalls; negative publicity; poor production processes
Negative media reports on the Internet and social media outlets	Adverse publicity; consumer boycotts
Customer complaints	Negative media attention; future loss of revenue
Returned or defective product rates	Negative media attention; injured customers; poor production processes

Step 4 – Compare Measurements to Goals or Benchmarks

The process of comparing actual results with pre-designated goals or benchmarks can help identify an impending crisis. For example, the presence of dust is often monitored in industrial settings. Under ideal conditions, dust can cause an explosion that can level a building. West Pharmaceuticals in Kinston, North Carolina, experienced a dust-related blast that killed six people and injured many others in 2003. The irony of this explosion was that the company had a regular cleanup program for dust in the processing area. However, a suspended ceiling installed several years before had accumulated a large amount of dust that was not accessible during a routine cleanup. This dust fueled the fatal explosion (Dawson, 2003).

Because of the threat of dust explosions, industrial and pharmaceutical companies are always aware of the dangers that can occur. Dust levels are regularly monitored to prevent an explosion. At chemical plants, temperature and pressure are monitored continuously against established norms. An increase in temperature can cause a gas to expand, ultimately increasing the gas's pressure in its holding tank. Hence, a pressure gauge on a tank holding a lethal chemical is a mechanism for control. When the pressure exceeds the normal range, the operator must decide how to prevent the release of the chemical in the tank. The temperature of the tank can be lowered, or the chemical can be moved to another tank.

In a well-maintained chemical plant, control mechanisms such as pressure and temperature indicators can alert employees to take measures that prevent the release of dangerous chemicals. Suppose that the same scenario exists, except that the temperature of the chemical starts to rise, and there is no way to move it or alter the temperature of the tank. After some time, the tank pressure release valve opens, and the dangerous chemical spews into the atmosphere as a lethal gas. Strategic control enters a more acute phase where the factory must now contain the leak, protect the employees, and warn members of the community that a gas leak has occurred. Unfortunately, the scenario just described is precisely what happened at the Union Carbide plant in Bhopal, India, where methyl isocyanate spewed out of its holding tank after reaching a pressure that the container could not contain. This incident, discussed in Chapter 3, is an example of control mechanisms that had gone awry. It remains the worst industrial accident on record (Carroll, & Buchholtz, 2012).

While specific industrial measures must be made to help prevent accidents, financial controls must be taken seriously to prevent managerial fraud. Tyco offers one of the most vivid examples of fraud by a CEO. Although the company had controls in place, they did not stop the theft of $600 million from within the company in 2002. Tyco CEO Dennis Kozlowski abused his power, and managerial controls failed to stop his "spider spinning a web of deceit" (Coombs, 2006, p. 56) in the following areas:

- Kozlowski hid transactions from the Board of Directors, but then told lower-level managers that the Board had approved those same actions.
- He gave a $1 million party for his wife. The party was held in Sardinia and featured an ice sculpture of David (the statue) urinating high-priced vodka. The party was charged to Tyco.
- He misused the Tyco compensation program by exploiting relocation, bonuses, and automobile expenses (Coombs, 2006).

Having controls is not enough. Controls must be taken seriously, as this now infamous case illustrates.

Step 5: Take Corrective Action

Strategic control emphasizes continuous improvement whereby managers seek to improve the long-term efficiency and effectiveness of the organization. In other words, control is not viewed as an action necessary only when a firm is in crisis. Instead, managers should think consider which strategic controls to enact and look for opportunities to enhance performance even when operations seem to be going well. In this regard, crisis management can be viewed as an outgrowth of strategic control. In Chapter 9 we will discuss an outgrowth of this type of strategic control: organizational learning.

The notion of strategic control highlights the link between a firm's strategy and the subsequent crisis events. When a crisis occurs, top management should address the situation and implement strategic changes to decrease the likelihood of similar crises in the future.

Identifying crisis events in the early stages is not always easy. Acknowledging the  sales declines brought about by a product boycott is not challenging to realize but sensing the early warning signals so that action can be taken to mitigate their effects can be. Some warning signs are universal, such as product return rates. Others are more organization-specific, such as high absenteeism levels and excessive employee grievances. Exercising strategic control requires that performance is measured, compared with previously established standards, and followed by corrective action, if necessary. Not meeting a performance indicator is often an early warning sign that a potential crisis may exist. Corrective action should be taken at all levels if actual performance is below the standard unless extraordinary causes of the discrepancy can be identified, such as a halt in production when a fire shuts down a critical supplier. Whenever possible, managers should anticipate reasonable corrective measures *before* a strategy is implemented. Doing so lowers the likelihood that threats and problems turn into crises.

Summary

A strategy is a top management plan to develop and sustain competitive advantage to fulfill the organization's mission. Organizational crises can be related to a firm's strategy. The firm's corporate strategy seeks to define the industries in which the company should compete and the growth trajectory that should be pursued. The decisions it makes in these areas will influence the types of crises it may face in the future.

The business strategy defines how the firm will operate, given its chosen industry. The generic strategy framework is a useful starting point for crafting a competitive strategy. Cost leadership and differentiation—without or in conjunction with a focus orientation—embody unique crisis vulnerabilities.

The strategic control process is necessary to signal when a crisis may be imminent. By design, controls communicate to management when something is wrong. However, management must be willing to take controls seriously and abide by the rules of control parameters. This chapter illustrates how failure to comply with controls can lead to industrial accidents and fraud.

Discussion Questions

1. What crisis vulnerabilities exist when a company competes in:
   - a single industry?
   - multiple, but related industries?
   - multiple, and unrelated industries?
2. What types of crises can occur when a company is following a growth strategy?
3. How can a retrenchment strategy drive a crisis?
4. What types of crises might a company encounter when it is:
   - a low-cost strategy?
   - a focus-low-cost strategy?
   - a differentiation strategy?
   - a focus-differentiation strategy?
5. How can ineffective strategic control result in an organizational crisis?
6. What would a balanced scorecard look like where you work?

Chapter Exercise

The low-cost strategy contains crisis vulnerabilities. Several examples have been provided in this chapter. In this exercise, you will form teams of three to four students and propose a balanced scorecard for a company following a low-cost strategy.

To begin, select one of the following companies:

- Walmart
- Spirit Airlines
- Motel 6
- IKEA
- Taco Bell
- Aldi

Each of these companies pursues a form of cost leadership. Conduct an Internet search and determine the types of crises these companies have faced in the past. Identify the crises that appear to have been linked to cost leadership.

From your research, prepare a balanced scorecard for your company. In addition, list the types of crises the company might face.

Contemporary Crisis Case: Rana Plaza - Part 2

The 2013 collapse of Rana Plaza introduced at the beginning of this chapter ultimately killed 1,138 workers and injured many more. Clothing brand labels found in ruins were linked to 28 major companies. Some, such as Walmart, were unaware that their products were being made in Rana Plaza. Still, such manufacturing often occurs via covert outsourcing when an approved manufacturer outsources part of an order to another factory without informing the primary client (e.g., Walmart). A web of undisclosed relationships linked the factories of Rana Plaza with brands that were unaware that a "Rana Plaza factory" even existed.

Why does covert outsourcing occur? Because manufacturers cannot fulfill the large orders and short deadlines often mandated by the brands. Herein lies one of the dilemmas of operating in the readymade garment (RMG) industry in Bangladesh. No manufacturer wants to turn away business because of limited capacity. Instead, they tend to accept orders, no matter how large, without discussing the maze of subcontracting that might be needed to meet the time and cost requirements.

The Readymade Garment (RMG) Industry in Bangladesh

The RMG industry has promoted economic development in Bangladesh because firms typically require limited capital and technology, and low-skilled labor is readily available, mostly women with few job alternatives (Kabir, Maple, & Fatema, 2018). Indeed, low-skilled women make up 80% of the workforce in the RMG industry in Bangladesh (Ahmed & Raihan, 2014). There are over 5,000 factories in the RMG industry, most of them in Dhaka, which represented 13% of the country's gross domestic product (GDP) at the time of the crisis (Meiers, 2014).

Fast fashion is one of the most recent trends in the RMG industry. Before the fast-fashion era, apparel supply chains operated with *high* fashion designs and long (*slow*) response times as designers and retailers forecasted demand a year in advance, tailoring their design releases by season—spring, summer, fall, and winter. However, over time, customer demand for *low* prices and *fast* response times have changed the nature of supply chains dramatically (Crandall, 2017). The concept of fast fashion helps explain the firm deadlines brands stipulate in their orders to their manufacturers. Clothing must reach the store quickly, as the next fashion cycle is just around the corner.

Low technology is common in the RMG industry. Typical factories require a sewing machine and a human operator, but it is difficult to automate the manufacturing process. Low-skilled workers are needed, which is why Bangladesh has become the world's number two producer of clothing, behind China (Jacobs & Singhal, 2017).

The RMG industry offers enormous benefits for Bangladesh. The industry boosts the country's GDP, it employs a high number of low-skilled women, and the startup costs are low. But external pressure to keep costs extremely low and production on time results in factories that are not well constructed, poor working conditions, and a maze of subcontracting. The owners of the factories are reluctant to raise wages and improve working conditions because doing so increases production costs. Despite what they often report in surveys, many consumers are unwiling to pay more to provide improved working conditions or are just uninformed about their choices.

The Brands Inside Rana Plaza

Amidst the ruins of Rana Plaza were labels associated with 28 brands, some sold at moderate and high-end retailers. Eight troubled companies and their crisis responses were analyzed by Comyns & Franklin-Johnson (2018) and included Auchan (France), Benetton (Italy), Carrefour (France), El Corte Inglés (Spain), JC Penny (United States), Loblaw (Canada), Mango (Spain), and Primark (Ireland).

Primark and Loblaw acknowledged they had sourced with a manufacturer in Rana Plaza and expressed condolences to the victims. Auchan and Carrefour initially denied they had sourced from Rana Plaza but later acknowledged their brand names were in the ruins, probably due to subcontracting. Mango, Benetton, and El Corte Inglés admitted they had used the factories in Rana Plaza but said their involvement with those contractors had been minimal. JC Penny neither acknowledged nor denied its involvement with any contractor at Rana Plaza (Comyns & Franklin-Johnson, 2018).

Case Discussion Question

Suppose you are a purchaser for a major brand in the RMG industry and some of your products were discovered at Rana Plaza. Your company has no records authorizing production orders with any of the apparel factories operating in Rana Plaza. Social media is abuzz with the news that your labels were in the rubble and have accused your company of partnering with sweatshops. Devise a crisis management response to address this situation, including communication strategies with internal and external stakeholders and message content.

References

Adams, R. (2005). Fast food, obesity, and tort reform: An examination of industry responsibility for public health. *Business and Society Review, 110*(3), 297–320.

Adamson, J. (2000). How Denny's went from icon of racism to diversity award winner. *Journal of Organizational Excellence, 20*(1), 55-68.

Ahmed, S., & Raihan, M. (2014). Health status of the female workers in the garment sector of Bangladesh. *Journal of the Faculty of Economics and Administrative Sciences, 4*(1), 43-58.

Baldauf, S. (2004). Bhopal gas tragedy lives on, 20 years later. *Christian Science Monitor, 96*(111), 7.

Barrett, P. (2011, August 29). Cleaning America's dirtiest coal company. *Bloomberg Businessweek, 4243*, 48-55.

Beirne, M., & Jensen, T. (1999). AirTran continues its comeback. *Adweek, 40*(30), 4.

Belson, K., & Fahim, K. (2007, October 6). After extensive beef recall, Topps goes out of business. *The New York Times*. Retrieved 12/04/2018, from https://www.nytimes.com/2007/10/06/us/06topps.html

Brathwaite, S. (2002). Denny's: A diversity success story. *Franchising World, 34*(5), 28–29.

Brewster, P. (2011). Johnson & Johnson and the "phantom" recall: Practical advice to prevent risk management and quality systems from failing to identify and address sentinel events. *Health Lawyer, 23*(6), 1-12.

Burrows, P., & Anderson, S. (1993, July 12). Dell Computer goes into the shop. *Business Week*, 138-140.

Campbell-Hunt, C. (2000). What have we learned about generic competitive strategy? A meta-analysis. *Strategic Management Journal, 21,* 127–154.

Carroll, A., & Buchholtz, A. (2012). *Business & society: Ethics, sustainability, and stakeholder management.* Mason, Ohio: South-Western Cengage Learning.

Casey, N., Zamiska, N., & Pasztor, A. (2007, September 22). Mattel seeks to placate China with apology. *Wall Street Journal, 250*(70), A1–A7.

Chu, W. (2011). How the Chinese government promoted a global automobile industry. *Industrial and Corporate Change, 20*(5), 1235-1276.

Cockburn, I., Henderson, R., & Stern, S. (2000). Untangling the origins of competitive advantage. *Strategic Management Journal, 21,* 1123–1145.

Comyns, B., & Franklin-Johnson, E. (2018). Corporate reputation and collective crises: A theoretical development using the case of Rana Plaza. *Journal of Business Ethics, 150*, 159-183.

Coombs, W. T. (2006). *Code red in the board room: Crisis management as organizational DNA*. Westport, CT: Praeger.

Cooper, S. (2014). Improving worker safety in global supply chains: The case for a global safety & health management standard. *Professional Safety, 59*(10), 29-33.

Corkery, M., Scheiber, N., & Cohen, P. (2018, January 12). Good news (and bad) at Walmart. *The New York Times*, p. 1.

Crandall, R. (2017, September). Fast Fashion and the Supply Chain, *APICS Magazine, 27*(4), 28-29.

Dawson, B. (2003, June 30). Powder causes West explosion. *Rubber & Plastics News, 32*(24), 1.

Duggan, W. (2018, December 14). Johnson & Johnson falls following Baby Powder asbestos report. *Benzinga*. Retrieved 12/19/2018, from https://www.benzinga.com/news/18/12/12852851/johnson-johnson-falls-following-baby-powder-asbestos-report

D'Zurilla, W. (1998). Reflections of a Dalkon Shield arbitrator. *Dispute Resolution Journal, 53*(1), 13–15.

Elkind, P. (2015, October 1). How Blue Bell blew it. *Fortune, 172*(5), 122-126.

Engineering & Mining Journal, (2016, August). Contura acquires Alpha's core assets, 217(8), 20.

Englehardt, K., Sallot, L., & Springston, J. (2004). Compassion without blame: Testing the accident decision flow chart with the crash of ValuJet flight 592. *Journal of Public Relations Research, 16*(2), 127-156.

Fishman, C. (2006). *The Walmart effect: How the world's most powerful company really works—and how it's transforming the American economy*. New York: Penguin.

Gandolfi, F. (2008). Cost reductions, downsizing-related layoffs, and HR practices. *SAM Advanced Management Journal, 73*(3), 52-58.

Girion, L. (2018, December 14). Johnson & Johnson knew for decades that asbestos lurked in its Baby Powder. *Reuters*. Retrieved 12/19/2018, from https://www.reuters.com/investigates/special-report/johnsonandjohnson-cancer/.

Gold, R. & Evans, M. (2020, September 18). Yearslong Drive for Efficiency Left Hospitals Overwhelmed. *Wall Street Journal*, pp. A1, A11.

Haddon, H. (2020, July 23). Chipotle triples its online sales. *Wall Street Journal*, p. B3.

Harvey, B. (2014). Supply chain safety: Emerging initiatives in the aftermath of Rana Plaza in Bangladesh. *Professional Safety, 59*(5), 66-68.

Hosmer, L. (2011). *The ethics of management: A multidisciplinary approach (7th ed.)*. New York, NY: McGraw-Hill/Irwin.

Hsu, T. (2018, July 13). Jury awards $4.7 billion in talcum powder case. *The New York Times, 167*(58022), B6.

Jack, A. (2010, October 1). J&J criticized over cough remedy action. *Financial Times*, p. 19.

Jacobs, B., & Singhal, V. (2017). The effect of the Rana Plaza disaster on shareholder wealth of retailers: Implications for sourcing strategies and supply chain governance. *Journal of Operations Management, 49-51*, 52-66.

Kabir, H., Maple, M., & Fatema, S. (2018). Vulnerabilities of women workers in the readymade garment sector of Bangladesh: A case study of Rana Plaza. *Journal of International Women's Studies, 19*(6), 224-235.

Kaplan, R., & Norton, D. (1996). *The balanced scorecard: Translating strategy into action*. Boston: Harvard Business School Press.

Kaplan, R., & Norton, D. (2000). *The strategy-focused organization*. Boston: Harvard Business School Press.

Keating, C. (2012). Famous rebrandings. *Fortune, 165*(6), 15.

Koenig, D. (2018, April 16). Allegiant Air under fire after '60 minutes' safety report. *Associated Press.* Retrieved, 12/18/2018, from https://www.apnews.com/ace0e25aebc44d74b99dd646505a61eb

Kruger, D. (2004). Short-order chef. *Forbes, 173*(13), 106-108.

Langston, R. (2006). Just good business. *Communication World, 23*(5), 40–41.

Levick, R., & Slack, C., (2011). Owning up to error is a safeguard, not a liability. *Of Counsel, 30*(7), 15-17.

Lockyer, S. (2004). Chi-Chi's shuts all units; Outback buys site rights. *Nation's Restaurant News, 38*(40), 5, 170, 172.

Lublin, J. (2000, December 27). Tips from a turnaround specialist. *Wall Street Journal,* p. B1.

Macky, K. (2004). Organizational downsizing and redundancies: The New Zealand workers' experience. *New Zealand Journal of Employment Relations, 29*(1), 63-87.

Meiers, R. (2014, April 24). To prevent another Rana Plaza, build better societies, not just better factories. *Harvard Business Review Digital Articles*, 2-4.

Miller, J. (2012). Spirit Airlines boss calls complaints 'irrelevant', says dying veteran should've bought insurance. Retrieved 12/18/2018, from http://www.foxnews.com/us/2012/05/03/spirit-airlines-outpaces-competitors-regarding-passenger-complaints-statistics/

Morrison, M. (2012, May 24). McDonald's shareholders defeat proposal to weigh impact on obesity. *Advertising Age.* Retrieved 11/27/ 2018, from https://adage.com/article/news/mcdonald-s-shareholders-defeat-obesity-impact-proposal/234961/

Murray, M. (2001, March 13). Waiting for the ax to fall. *Wall Street Journal,* pp. B1, B10.

Newman, J. (2020, May 1). Justice Department Files Charges Against Former Blue Bell CEO. *Wall Street Journal,* https://www.wsj.com/articles/justice-department-files-charges-against-former-blue-bell-ceo-11588371497. Accessed May 3, 2020.

Newman, J., & Gasparro, A. (2015, September 1). Blue Bell ice cream returns to stores. *Wall Street Journal,* p. B1.

Nicas, J. (2012, May 12). A stingy spirit lifts airline's profit. *Wall Street Journal,* p. A1.

Nishimoto, A. (2014). Tesla develops underbody shield to better protect battery pack. *Motor Trend, 66*(7), 24.

Parnell, J. (2016). Crisis management and strategic orientation in small and medium sized enterprises (SMEs) in Peru, Mexico, and the United States. *Journal of Contingencies and Crisis Management, 23*(4), 221-233.

Parnell, J.A. (2020). *Strategic management: Theory and practice (6th ed.).* Solon, OH: Academic Media Solutions.

Pauchant, T., & Mitroff, I. (1992). *Transforming the crisis-prone organization.* San Francisco: Jossey-Bass.

Picken, J. C., & Dess, G. G. (1997). Out of (strategic) control. *Organizational Dynamics, 26*(1), 35–48.

Porter, M. (1980). *Competitive strategy.* New York: Free Press.

Preble, J. (1997). Integrating the crisis management perspective into the strategic management process. *Journal of Management Studies, 34*(5), 669–791.

Probst, G., & Raisch, S. (2005). Organizational crisis: The logic of failure. *Academy of Management Executive, 19*(1), 90-105.

Reuer, J., Zollo, M., & Singh, H. (2002). Post-formation dynamics in strategic alliances. *Strategic Management Journal, 23*, 135–152.

Rockoff, J. (2010a, September 29). J&J's quality control draws scrutiny. *Wall Street Journal,* pp. B1, B2.

Rockoff, J. (2010b, November 18). Tylenol for kids returns to shelves. *Wall Street Journal,* p. B3.

Sethi, S., & Steidlmeier, P. (1997). *Up against the corporate wall: Cases in business and society.* Upper Saddle River, NJ: Prentice Hall.

Shell, E. (2009). *Cheap: The High Cost of Discount Culture.* New York: Penguin Group.

Stewart, J. (2008, May 28). Auto makers can find opportunity in $4 gasoline. *Wall Street Journal,* p. D3.

Swarns, R. (2015, April 6). McDonalds workers, vowing a fight, say raises are too little for too few. *The New York Times*, p. 15

Tavernise, S., & Krauss, C. (2011, December 7). Mine owner will pay $209 million in blast that killed 29 workers. The New York Times, p. 16.

Taylor, E. (2008, May 6). Start-ups race to produce "green" cars. *Wall Street Journal,* pp. B1, B7.

Terlep, S. (2011, November 29). GM scrambles to defend Volt. *Wall Street Journal,* p. B1.

Vara, V. (2016, October 31). The toll of cheap clothing. *Bloomberg Business Week,* 10-11.

Veil, S., Liu, M., Erickson, S., & Sellnow, T. (2005). Too hot to handle: Competency constrains character in Chi-Chi's green onion crisis. *Public Relations Quarterly, 50*(4), 19–22.

Wall Street Journal (2013, December 27), "Whatever happened to...?" pp. B1, B4.

Watson, S. (2012, May 2). Atlantic County assemblymen call on Spirit Airlines to change refund policy. *The Press of Atlantic City*. Retrieved 12/18/2018, from http://www.pressofatlanticcity.com/news/press/atlantic/atlantic-county-assemblymen-call-on-spirit-airlines-to-change-refund/article_18d30f1a-948c-11e1-9211-0019bb2963f4.html

Wise, J. (2010, May 8). Chefs' eat-in bolsters Bullock's. *News and Observer*, p. 3B.

WRAL.com (2010, July 16). Officials: Eggs, not employees caused illnesses at Durham restaurant. Retrieved 12/19/2018, from http://www.wral.com/news/local/story/7975607/

Chapter 7: Taking Action When a Crisis Strikes

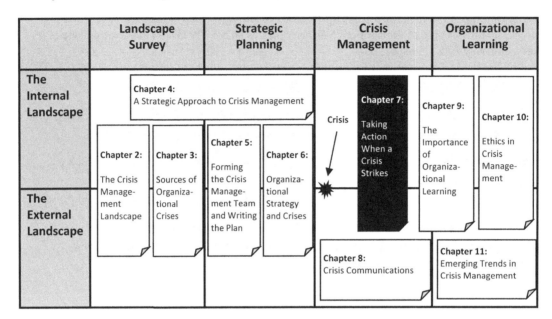

Learning Objectives

After reading this chapter, each student should be able to:

1. Discuss the strategies that can help address a crisis when it strikes.
2. Identify the leadership traits required of a crisis management team leader.
3. Describe the process of situational assessment.
4. Discuss the process of developing mitigation strategies to address a crisis.
5. Identify the initial communication strategies that should take place at the beginning of a crisis.
6. Identify the information required to manage a crisis effectively.
7. Discuss the importance of damage containment.
8. Describe the need to communicate with internal and external stakeholders.
9. Discuss the evaluation process of managing a crisis.
10. Discuss the strategies that should take place as a crisis unwinds.
11. Define and describe business continuity.
12. Discuss the importance of addressing employee needs after a crisis.

Opening Chapter Case: The Boeing 737 Max - Part 1

The Boeing 737 Max arrived on the market with much fanfare. It was designed to be a fuel-efficient, single-aisle, short-haul aircraft that would compete with the efficiency of its arch-rival, the Airbus A320neo. It has now become Boeing's best-selling aircraft. But crashes of the 737 Max in 2018 and 2019 have resulted in 346 fatalities. Both accidents have one factor in common, the inability of the pilots to shut down the maneuvering characteristics augmentation system (MCAS). This system controls the pitch of the aircraft to prevent a stall situation.

Background

The Boeing 737 was introduced in 1967 as the successor to the tri-engine 727. The 737 offered short-haul capabilities, fuel efficiency, and passenger comfort. It has become the best-selling model aircraft in history. The 737 Max is the fourth generation of aircraft since 1967. Competing with Boeing is its main rival, Airbus, a consortium of companies based in the European Union (EU). Airbus offers the A-320 as the primary competing model for the 737. Together, both planes comprise about 28,000 aircraft, or about 50% of the world's commercial airliners (Campbell, 2019).

Designing a new Generation as Opposed to Starting with a New Model

A new aircraft generation modifies an existing design, but a new model is an aircraft designed from scratch. The Boeing 787 Dreamliner is a new model, whereas the Boeing 737 Max is an example of a new generation. Building a new generation of an existing aircraft model is typically less costly than creating a new model, which can be fraught with uncertainty. Boeing learned this lesson well when it developed its 787 Dreamliner, which has been successful, but was costly to build, plagued with supply chain problems and way behind schedule when it was finally introduced (Denning, 2013).

Boeing was under pressure to develop a new short-haul airliner that would compete with the fuel efficiency of the new A-320neo, which was introduced in 2010, much to the surprise of the aviation community. The A-320 was developed with some degree of secrecy; its most prominent feature was the new engine option (neo), which would use 6% less fuel than the 737NG, the competing model at the time (Campbell, 2019). Fuel economy is a means of differentiating an aircraft.

With the A-320neo now on the market, Boeing was pressed to respond quickly with a more fuel-efficient aircraft that would serve the same market. Designing a new plane from scratch would take too much time, so it looked to develop a new generation of the 737. In 2011, Boeing announced it would introduce a new generation of the 737, the Max. The key technology that would have to change was the engines, the fuel guzzlers of the plane. The 737 Max was fitted with new LEAP engines that were 8% more fuel-efficient (Campbell, 2019). But the two LEAP engines could not safely fit under the wings of the 737 in its existing platform. Their clearance to the runway made them susceptible to scraping the runway. This problem required a solution.

To compensate, Boeing moved the LEAP engines up a bit on the wing and slightly more forward. If you view an airliner from the front, most have the engines attached below the wing. The Max appears to be attached into the wing, thus raising its height and giving it the necessary clearance from the runway. But this adjustment created another problem; the plane was now more susceptible to flying with its nose slightly upwards because of the aircraft's change of gravity (Gates, 2019). This flight attribute can lead to a stall, a condition whereby the nose of the plane pitches higher than it should be, which could cause the wings to lose their lift capabilities. To compensate for the improved likelihood of a stall and to make the 737 Max operate and feel like previous models of the 737, Boeing included software that would move the pitch of the nose down if it sensed the aircraft was entering a stall situation. This system was called the maneuvering characteristics augmentation system, or MCAS.

MCAS

The MCAS was designed to operate when the aircraft was in manual mode and with the flaps up. This means that it works after the plane has made its initial climb from takeoff, a point when the flaps are still in the down position. One only needs to look out the window while flying to see the flaps' movement during takeoff and landing. Of course, flaps are essential because they give the plane more lift on takeoff and provide additional lift capabilities when the aircraft is landing, a time when its airspeed is low, and the wings need more lift potential.

However, after the initial climb of an aircraft after takeoff, the flaps are pulled up into the wing so the plane can fly faster with less drag, a type of air friction that can increase fuel consumption. Reducing the drag by pulling the flaps up helps the aircraft fly more efficiently. However, the plane is still being operated in manual mode, not on autopilot. That is where the MCAS system is designed to be activated if needed. If the pilot is approaching a stall situation (i.e., the plane's pitch is too far up and the nose is up too high), then MCAS will push the nose back down to compensate, thus giving the wings the lift capabilities needed to sustain flight. An essential feature of MCAS is that it operates without the pilot's input; if the aircraft nose goes down because of a potential stall, MCAS does not issue a warning for the pilot to change the nose position; MCAS does it automatically. This feature of MCAS was later found to be part of the chain of events that led to the downing of the two aircraft. The MCAS also receives data from two angle-of-attack sensors mounted on the front fuselage of the plane. However, only one sensor at a time is used to input data to the MCAS, raising a severe risk scenario: What happens if the one sensor sending data to MCAS malfunctions?

The Angle-of-Attack (AoA) Sensors

Sensors operate by sending data to a control module. It is the control module that uses the system under examination. For example, various control modules in a car process data from sensors located throughout the vehicle. The engine control module (ECM) is constantly adjusting the amount of air and fuel going to the engine. These adjustments are made to improve fuel-efficiency while maintaining a reasonable amount of power. The driver is unaware of these adjustments, which are done through algorithms within the ECM with inputs from various sensors.

A commercial aircraft operates much the same way, with the flight control computer (FCC) making constant adjustments to make the flight smoother and safer. The AoA sensor tells the FCC the angle at which the plane is operating. If the angle is too steep and the aircraft is approaching a stall, the AoA sensor sends that data to the FCC. However, Boeing also developed the MCAS to compensate for flying when the plane is still in manual mode, and the flaps are up. This point is crucial because the MCAS adjusts the pitch of the aircraft if it stalls. Neither the pilot nor the automatic pilot is in control; it shuts down. An investigation revealed that a malfunctioning AoA sensor interfacing with MCAS contributed to both Boeing 737 Max crashed, the Lion Air Flight 610 crash in October 2018, and the Ethiopian Airlines Flight 302 in March 2019, killing 346 people.

Case Discussion Questions

1. How do automated systems assist vehicle drivers? What examples can you provide?
2. What systems in a passenger vehicle could malfunction and contribute to an accident?

Introduction

High-profile events such as the two crashes of the Boeing 737 Max highlight the importance of crisis preparation. Most crises do not receive as much attention as these examples, but they still constitute significant events for the firm. Indeed, anticipating and preparing for crises is much less traumatic and costly than experiencing an unexpected calamity without a plan for managing it. The COVID-19 pandemic reminds us that anticipating a crisis is crucial even if preparing is difficult. For some organizational leaders, this may involve confronting **paradigm blindness**. In this condition, people struggle to identify and process the information that threatens and disconfirms their worldview (Wheatley, 2006).

There are countless stories about the lack of a plan causing severe or even irreparable damage to a firm. There are also examples where proper planning and execution of a crisis plan kept the crisis under control and resulted in positive changes for the business (Borodzicz & van Haperen, 2002). Nonetheless, most crises are somewhat unexpected and difficult to predict.

This chapter focuses on the management practices and decision-making activities that should be implemented at the beginning, duration, and conclusion of a crisis event. The first part of this chapter addresses the initial response actions that help assess a crisis during its onset. The next section focused on response strategies and mitigation. The final part of the chapter discusses what happens after the crisis, including recovery, reentry, and business continuity. Ultimately, the organization must regroup and resume operations.

Strategies at the Beginning of a Crisis

The first step in the formal response to a crisis is to convene the crisis management team (CMT). Recall that the organization should have a pre-established team and a crisis management plan (CMP). Activating the team may be as simple as one member calling a meeting. Alternatively, an employee in the organization may alert a member of the CMT to the potential or developing crisis. Once convened, the team begins the process of assessing the situation.

The response to the onset of a crisis depends on the nature of the event. Some crises, such as an industrial accident, a senior executive's sudden death, the notification of a government investigation, or a chemical spill, can occur quickly and often with little or no warning. Others, such as a hostile takeover, union labor unrest, a consumer boycott, or corporate embezzlement, often take time to develop. The time available for managers to react to a crisis is related to its impact on the organization and its stakeholders. Having a CMP makes it possible to think and act expediently during the first few hours of a crisis. The CMP is a critical strategic, organizational tool responsible for initiating the crisis decision-making process by framing the problem, determining the parties responsible for implementing various actions, and justifying decisions.

Leadership of the CMT

Effective leadership from both the CMT leader and top management is essential (Wooten & James, 2008). This team is responsible for making and implementing decisions that help the organization resolve the crisis. An effective CMT needs (1) effective leadership, (2) the structure and resources necessary to respond to and contain a crisis, and (3) broad organizational support (Cavanaugh, 2003).

During a crisis response, CMT members should be knowledgeable about their roles on the team and willing to accept suggestions presented by members who are experts in other areas. The CMT leader must have an array of both leadership and management skills. Drawing from the experience of the military and the emergency services sector, Crichton, Lauche, and Flin (2005) identified the following skills needed for the CMT leader:

- *Situation assessment*: Identifying the problem accurately
- *Decision making*: Deciding what the CMT should do
- *Team coordination*: Getting the CMT and affiliated stakeholders to work together
- *Communicating*: Deciding how to receive and deliver relevant information
- *Monitoring*: Keeping abreast of key developments
- *Delegating*: Assigning tasks to individual CMT members
- *Prioritizing*: Determining the importance of incoming information and what should be done next
- *Planning*: Taking part in the planning process and encouraging task completion.

The CMT leader should utilize these competencies by taking charge of the situation, assessing the level of crisis seriousness, determining the level of resources needed, and then making the decisions that will resolve the crisis (Cavanaugh, 2003). Simultaneously, the leader should frequently communicate with team members to implement the crisis plan. Within the context of this role, the leader must recognize and execute these actions while remaining visible and available. Admiral Thad Allen of the US Coast Guard led the incident command efforts for the *Deepwater Horizon* oil spill in the Gulf of Mexico in 2010. To maintain visibility and availability during the crisis, he spent about half his time in Washington, DC, briefing representatives, government officials, and the media. He spent the rest of his time onboard Coast Guard vessels in the Gulf. He commented, "If you're not visible to your people out on the boats who are trying to pull a boon in Barataria Bay in 110-degree heat, then you're not a credible leader, because you don't understand what they're going through" (Berinato, 2010, p. 78).

The leader must remain calm and focused on the crisis management process while making decisions under significant pressure. The CMT leader may be required to make decisions without optimal information (Baran & Adelman, 2010). Moreover, those involved in the crisis face challenges to their assumptions about reality (Pearson & Clair, 1998). Recall that some crises create radically new experiences for the CMT, what management scholar Karl Weick (1993) called **cosmology episodes**. The Boeing 737 MAX case illustrates such an event as pilots were suddenly thrust into a situation whereby the flight control system (FCC) took away their ability to guide the plane.

Sherman & Harris, 2018 also note a cosmology episode when GM had trouble identifying the root cause of its ignition switch malfunction in its Chevrolet Cobalt. Engineers were perplexed as to why the defective ignition switch would stall until they discovered one of their engineers had modified the switch without documenting the changes. Once this was learned, GM could exit the cosmology episode as the root cause of the failure now made sense (Sherman & Harris, 2018).

All crises create tension and stress. **Acute stressors** for the CMT can include chaotic events, communication problems, time pressure, consequences, fear of failure, dealing with the media, and information problems, including overload, missing, or ambiguous information. Maintaining control allows the leader to sustain an objective perspective and see the way through complex and confusing scenarios. Hence, the leader must present an unbiased view quickly and methodically for all stakeholders (Rolston & McNerney, 2003).

A leader during one crisis might not lead during another crisis. Moreover, crisis leaders should also mentor less experienced team members. The leader is likely mentoring without even knowing it (Berinato, 2010; Schoenberg, 2005).

Situational Assessment

One of the CMT's first tasks is to assess the situation so that decisions can be made to mitigate the crisis (Wilson, 2004). **Situational assessment** refers to the information processing and knowledge creation aspects of crisis management (Coombs, 2007). It promotes situational awareness so that CMT members can predict how a crisis might evolve (Endsley & Garland, 2000). Three classic cases in the crisis management literature offer great insights on how the initial stages of situational assessment can be deceiving. They offer lessons learned for crisis managers today. We overview these three cases next.

The 1989 Hillsborough Soccer Tragedy

A tragic case involving errors in the situational assessment stage of a crisis occurred at the 1989 Hillsborough soccer match in Sheffield, England. In this incident, 97 fatalities occurred in a section of the stands that had become thronged with people. Most of the victims were crushed to death (Taylor, 1990). Police assumed it was a simple case of overcrowding, not a substantial safety concern (Crichton et al., 2005).

The tragedy was triggered by a police decision to open the gates at the Leppings Lane entrance to the stadium so that fans could enter the stands more quickly in advance of the 3:00 P.M. start. Officials were concerned that the situation outside of the stadium could result in a crush, where fans would be pinned against each other or trampled to death. The police decided to open the gates to the stadium at 2:52 P.M. to relieve the pressure. Unfortunately, supporters rushed into already crowded sections 3 and 4 (Elliott & Smith, 1993). The fans at the front of the stands suffocated because they were stuck between the wall and the fence with nowhere to go.

Numerous photographs and videos showed an odd display of behavior—fans reaching to be pulled up by other fans on the upper terrace, as well as spectators seeking to climb over the fence just near the pitch (i.e., field). Police mistakenly took this to be a sign of a "pitch invasion" by fans, but it was a desperate attempt to escape the deadly crush of the crowd. At 3:06 P.M., the police control room became aware of the situation's full extent and stopped the match. At 3:13 P.M., cutting equipment was requested to extract fans penned against the fence. Unfortunately, many of them had already died (Elliott & Smith, 1993). Ironically, a decision to save lives outside of the stadium resulted in mass casualties inside the stadium. The situation had not been appropriately assessed, and lives were lost.

The 1992 Los Angeles Riots

The Los Angeles riots in 1992 are another example of an erroneous assessment of the crisis, in this case, by the Los Angeles Police Department (LAPD). The riot was rooted in the police beating of Rodney King, an African American motorist who had been stopped by police on March 3, 1991. King had led police on a high-speed chase before being stopped and then continued to resist arrest once he was out of his vehicle. Police officers struck King 56 times with batons, in addition to kicking him and stomping on his head. The beating was recorded by an amateur photographer, who sold the tape to a Los Angeles television station (Miller, 2001).

The police officers making the arrest were tried for using excessive force. Before the trial, the video of the incident was played countless times on television, fueling contempt for the officers involved and the LAPD in general. The trigger event for the riots was not the video, but the officers' not guilty pleas. The verdict was announced on April 28, 1992, shortly after 3:15 P.M. By 5:30 P.M., the riots had begun.

The LAPD and the mayor's office were unprepared for what happened next. Mayor Thomas Bradley, fearing that a police presence during the verdict would provoke a negative response from the community, objected to police deployment during the verdict decision. Police Chief Daryl Gates was not available during the early stages of the riot but instead was attending a political rally in Brentwood. Hence, at the beginning of the riot, there was little police presence and no central control for managing the eventual deployment of police (Miller, 2001).

Unlike the public sector's response, private organizations were assessing the situation and quickly making their crisis preparations. Solomon (1992) examined how organizations responded to the rioting. Because of the danger of physical harm to employees, quick responses were required. Thrifty Corporation (later acquired by Rite Aid) operated about 1,000 pharmacies on the West Coast of the US, including 21 in the region Four of the stores were razed, and the other 17 stores were looted.

Company executives gave guidelines to managers. If a group of people approaching the stores looked threatening, if neighboring stores were having trouble, or if any fires were visible, they were to close (Solomon, 1992).

ARCO service stations responded quickly by closing stations, so underground gas tanks would not ignite. Employees were notified via a phone chain (email was not available yet) not to report to work because of the danger. ARCO quickly erected chain-linked fences around damaged stores. The company headquarters was located 25 miles southeast of the riot area, but executives at the home office were updated continuously on the riot (Solomon, 1992).

The Los Angeles riots were an example of misreading the actual situation. This case serves as an example of the importance of situational assessment. The Hillsborough stadium tragedy and the Los Angeles riots were unusual events. Still, the social unrest in many US cities following George Floyd's death is a reminder that similar events are possible. Can situational assessment be as tricky in less dramatic examples? Consider the problem that many companies faced when they attempted to assess the impact of the year 2000, known as Y2K.

The Y2K Crisis

We mentioned the Y2K crisis briefly in Chapter 2. The Y2K crisis was particularly interesting because it was difficult for leaders and CMTs to determine how it would affect their organizations. Conducting a situational assessment was also difficult. This crisis was different for three key reasons. First, it was associated with a specific date. At the turn of the century, computers could interpret a two-digit year as 1900 instead of 2000, triggering an array of potential problems. Second, there was an apocalyptic fervor associated with this event. A small number of Christians believed that this event would usher in the second coming of Christ, an event related to Biblical prophecy (Powell, Hickson, Self, & Bodon, 2001). Finally, many writers, church leaders, and other self-proclaimed experts—some with significant followings—offered their viewpoints on the issue.

Interestingly, many of these experts lacked any viable computer background. Nonetheless, they predicted that the Y2K computer bug would commence a series of events that would ultimately trigger a widespread meltdown of society, including but not limited to social upheaval, riots, food shortages, electric grid malfunctions, airplanes crashes, and even nuclear war. Misinformation was widespread, including the alleged story of a 104-year-old woman—presumably identified as four years old by a computer—who had received a note from the local school system reminding her to enroll in kindergarten. Florida-based televangelist James Kennedy shared this story in his booklet on the topic. Kennedy borrowed the story from another doomsday author, Michael Hyatt, who appeared on many Christian radio programs but neglected to tell his audience that it occurred in 1993, not 1999. The mistake was attributed to human error, not a computer malfunction. Various versions of the story were propagated, including different locations (Boston, 2000). Why and how this story spread so quickly is beyond the scope of this discussion. However, it reminds us that fake news existed before the proliferation of the Internet.

There are two reasons why crisis managers should understand how these thought processes developed and progressed. First, we must not presume that the cognitions exhibited during Y2K were entirely illogical. While some citizens naively believed what they heard without questioning it, those caught in the Y2K panic represented a variety of socioeconomic and educational backgrounds, including physicians, attorneys, and professors. Some of them even left their homes and set up remote communities in rural areas (McMinn, 2001). Second, the fact that many people believed a crisis was imminent runs counter to what we see in the crisis management literature; it is more common for the masses to be in denial.

Y2K was a unique crisis in that so many people both erred and were correct in their situational assessments. The concern over what the computer bug *might* do prompted most companies to fix the problem, which in the end, was not very difficult. And yet, the Y2K panic was spreading as if nothing could be done to stop the problem. All the while, computers by the thousands were being fixed every day, and well before year's end. When the new millennium arrived with no major snags, both sides on the Y2K issue claimed victory. The doomsayers claimed that their alarm raised the attention needed to remedy the bug, but others claimed that it would have been fixed anyway (Cowan, 2003).

Mitigation Strategies

Once managers complete the situational analysis, they can develop strategies for implementing a response to the crisis. Not all strategies will be effective at first, so the situation must be reevaluated regularly. Flexibility must be maintained because a crisis can evolve instantaneously. Care should be taken to address the crisis directly and restore confidence with the affected stakeholders.

The Sheetz convenience store chain experienced such a crisis in July 2004 when hundreds of customers in western Pennsylvania became sick from salmonella. The source was later found to be Roma tomatoes that Sheetz procured from one of its produce suppliers. Sheetz executives immediately called a press conference to alert their customers and the media that they would take full responsibility for the crisis. Shortly after that, the chain switched to a new type of tomato from a different supplier. Also, company chairman Steve Sheetz, president Stan Sheetz, and vice president Travis Sheetz personally visited stores to meet with customers. They offered to pay medical bills and lost wages to those who had become sick (Donahue, 2004). The company also posted a toll-free number on its website to field any questions that customers or other stakeholders might have. In this example, the mitigating strategies had to begin early and be sustained for several weeks until the crisis was brought under control.

At the beginning of a crisis, the primary goal is to minimize potential damage to the firm and its reputation. In some cases, the objective may even be to turn any potential negatives associated with the crisis into positives for the organization. For example, one of the first successful crisis management cases involved the 1990 cruise ship fire aboard the *Crystal Harmony,* a vessel owned by Crystal Cruises of Los Angeles, California. The company turned this crisis into a favorable situation by immediately convening its crisis management team and implementing its 61-page crisis management plan (Sklarewitz, 1991). The first task was to conduct the situational analysis, which involved assessing the damage to the ship and the extent of injuries. Fortunately, there were no injuries from the fire, which had started in an auxiliary engine room. However, because the ship had only minimal emergency power, it could not propel itself in the water. With 920 guests and 540 crew members, the CMT arranged to transport the vessel back safely to port as soon as possible.

Sometimes strategies need to be changed after implementation has already begun. In the *Crystal Harmony case,* the CMT later learned that the ship was able to regain 80% of its power, meaning the tugboats would no longer be needed. Once the vessel was safe, the CMT went to work preparing statements for the media. The director of public relations, Darlene Papalini, managed the media proactively by issuing press statements. Because of this forthcoming approach, media coverage of the event was minimal, which is what Papalini had desired (Sklarewitz, 1991).

Meanwhile, another part of the CMT was managing the refund process to the passengers. When guests disembarked from the ship, they received a full refund and were offered a $500 credit off any future cruise. The proactive crisis management had a positive spin: 280 passengers signed a letter expressing their appreciation for how the company managed the event (Sklarewitz, 1991).

The initial mitigation strategies also begin the long-range quest for managing and surviving the crisis. Decision-making during a crisis differs from other situations in various ways. During a crisis, the goal is to contain it and return the organization to normal operations quickly. Table 7.1 suggests seven decision-making functions that should take place during the management of a crisis (Wilson, 2003).

Table 7.1 Crisis Decision-Making

Decision-Making Step	Action Plan
Step 1: Alert and assemble the crisis management team.	As soon as the crisis is detected, the CMT should be activated.
Step 2: Collect all the relevant information.	Learn as much about the situation, including what happened, who was involved, where it took place and the current status of the crisis. This step not only occurs during the situational analysis but also throughout the crisis.
Step 3: Assign tasks and continue fact-finding.	The crisis management team should delegate duties as a project management team would.
Step 4: Develop solution alternatives.	Identify feasible solutions.
Step 5: Implement the chosen solution(s).	Implementation is often the most challenging part of the process. It requires competent and sufficient people, time, and money.
Step 6: Communicate with the media.	The organization should be proactive in meeting with the media and presenting its side of the story. If they do not, stakeholders will form opinions based on the facts they have.
Step 7: Review what happened.	Evaluate the decisions and the outcomes. What was learned, and how might a similar crisis be handled differently in the future?

Source - Wilson (2003), pp. 58-61.

Initial Communication

Chapter 5 stressed the importance of designating a spokesperson ahead of time to manage organizational communications with the media and keep stakeholders informed. In some instances, the organization must move quickly to make its first statements to the media. Exxon, a company that has been through many crises, experienced a refinery fire in Baton Rouge, Louisiana, on August 2, 1993. The company responded in less than 3 hours by issuing its first press release at 7:00 A.M. Follow-up statements were issued at 8:00 A.M., 9:00 A.M., 10:00 A.M., 12:15 P.M., 6:00 P.M., and

9:30 P.M. that same day (Duhe & Zoch, 1994). This crisis claimed the lives of three workers.

Many organizations use the Internet and social media as primary communication outlets during a crisis. Some have referred to social media outreach as "community management" and for a good reason (Deveney, 2018). The communications aspects of crisis management, including social media tools, are covered more extensively in Chapter 8.

Information Needs

Managers and affected staff from all company divisions must share a common and systematic approach to obtaining and utilizing information (Coombs, 2006). It is essential to monitor and evaluate the crisis and to adjust responses as needed. It can be challenging to know whether one is making the best decisions during an emergency, however. The CMT must recognize the importance of monitoring stakeholders' opinions and behaviors during a crisis and exercising its influence when possible. It may become necessary to reconsider the message and the communication strategy as the situation unfolds (Caponigro, 2000).

Two elements of information are essential in crisis management. First, details of the crisis should be made available to the CMT in a timely manner. An interesting comparison between the private and public sectors before Hurricane Katrina illustrates this point. Walmart's emergency operations center began tracking the storm six days before it hit New Orleans. Walmart reacted early to this timely information by sending bottled water, flashlights, batteries, tarps, canned tuna, and Pop-Tarts to stores that were likely to be in the path of the storm (Olasky, 2006). In contrast, government agency responses were hampered by late information, slow response, and a general inability to make decisions.

Second, information must be accurate. It must include the precise location, description, and status of the crisis. The 2016 Sago Mine disaster in West Virginia illustrates how muddled communications and tired emotions triggered a wave of inaccurate information messages concerning the fate of 12 trapped miners. They were later found dead, save for one, some 40 hours later by rescuers. The rescuers' original message was that "12 individuals" had been found, and one was alive. The radio message was transmitted through five underground relay stations and was conveyed through the rescuers' breathing masks, which they were wearing due to the carbon monoxide danger. Unfortunately, the message, muddied by all the communication noise, came out "12 alive" (Langfitt, 2006). The wave of misinformation morphed into a frenzied celebration outside the mine. The jubilance was silenced later by the news that 11 of the miners had perished.

Inaccurate information was also exemplified in the Hurricane Katrina disaster. The media displayed a vast amount of information, much of it accurate and dramatic, and some of it useful to those in crisis management capacities. But decision-makers seeking new information about the status of the damage or evacuations were often met with media reports of unfounded stories, some of which hindered crisis response. In one instance, a CNN report detailed how two patients had died because rescue helicopters were grounded due to false media reports of sniper fire (Olasky, 2006). Timely and accurate information is vital to managing a crisis. Crisis managers also need systems and resources that ensure a continuous flow of appropriate data. Structures, procedures, and processes for gathering and monitoring information must be established and continuously monitored throughout the crisis. It may be necessary to restructure or modify the information-gathering process as the situation evolves.

Strategies During the Crisis: Response and Mitigation

The mid-crisis stage represents a turning point for all affected stakeholders. Three potential scenarios may emerge at this stage. The first is the belief that the crisis is under control, and the damage can be contained. This scenario is a positive sign the organization may be able to continue operating in a close-to-normal capacity. In the second scenario, crisis managers must continue to assess the situation and bring it under control. The third scenario suggests that the outcome is hopeless, and managers should take steps to salvage whatever they can for the organization.

This third scenario was illustrated in 2012, when an unprecedented and costly crisis occurred within the beef processing industry. The main company affected by the event, AFA Foods, Inc., had to file for bankruptcy as a direct result of the crisis. Customers learned about a ground beef additive called "pink slime" in a blog post. Few were aware that pink slime is finely textured beef and was used as a filler for ground beef products for two decades (Gleason & Berry, 2012).

For AFA Foods, the crisis added a new dimension to its daily operations because it was already in financial straits. The company processed beef for several of the nation's fast-food chains. Pink slime, known in the industry as "boneless lean beef trimmings," was ground into its beef products. AFA Foods does not make the filler but purchases it from a supplier. One of them, Beef Products, Inc., experienced a sharp decline in demand and had to close three of its four plants just weeks after the crisis commenced (Gleason & Berry, 2012).

The pink slime case illustrates that during the crisis, unfolding events should be monitored to determine the following:

- Which of the three scenarios appears to be unfolding?
- What resources are available, and how long will it take to deploy them?
- How long will it take to execute a decision or solution?
- Who and what are the victims of the crisis? (Leskin et al., 2004)

All crises typically damage the organization in some way. Hence, the CMT must do what is feasible to contain the damage inflicted on people, the organization's reputation, and its assets. This task is the bottom-line goal for all crisis managers.

Damage Containment

Damage containment is the effort to keep the effects of a crisis from spreading and affecting other parts of the business (Mitroff & Anagnos, 2001). Management needs to gather resources such as capital, physical assets, and human resources to help contain the damage (Pearson & Rondinelli, 1998). The four-step crisis management process discussed in this book is both responsive and proactive. Figure 7.1 illustrates this tradeoff within the four steps of the framework.

Crisis communication should meet two goals. First, the organization should communicate with the media. This process requires the CMT to understand the issues, select the appropriate response, anticipate the need to communicate and prepare press releases (Barton, 2008). Second, organizational spokespersons should restore and maintain stakeholder confidence. This task may involve being at the scene of the crisis and working at a grassroots level to ensure that recovery efforts are being maintained. Former California Governor Arnold Schwarzenegger presided over a series of crises, from earthquakes and wildfires to urban crime and gang problems. During a string of fires, the governor was out in the field, both encouraging firefighters and consoling victims (Walsh, 2007). Schwarzenegger was widely praised during these crisis events for being responsive and available to his constituents.

As previously mentioned, communications must occur quickly from the affected firm. Conversations can be especially challenging when the crisis transcends several countries, however. In the following example, the trigger event for the crisis occurred at the Cannes Film Festival in France, while the backlash was felt primarily in China.

The Sharon Stone/Karma Comment Crisis

A major earthquake measuring 7.8 on the Richter scale jolted southwest China's Sichuan Province on May 12, 2008, resulting in almost 70,000 deaths. An outpouring of relief efforts worldwide followed to help the victims of this tragedy (Long, Crandall, & Parnell, 2010). However, the disaster took a strange twist on May 24, less than two weeks after the earthquake, when actress Sharon Stone was asked her feelings on the quake during the Cannes Film Festival:

> *"Well you know it was very interesting because at first, I'm you know, I'm not happy about the ways the Chinese were treating the Tibetans because I don't think anyone should be unkind to anyone else. And so, I have been very concerned about how to think and what to do about that because I don't like that. And then I've been this, you know, concerned about, oh how should we deal with the Olympics because they are not being nice to the Dalai Lama, who is a good friend of mine. And then all this earthquake and all this stuff happened, and I thought: Is that karma, when you are not nice that bad things happen to you . . ." (China Digital Times, 2008)*

Figure 7.1 – Proactiveness and Reactiveness in Crisis Management

	Landscape Survey	Strategic Planning	Crisis Management	Organizational Learning
The Internal Landscape	**Proactive** Seeks to determine the organization's internal strengths/ weaknesses and external opportunities/ threats that can lead to a crisis.	**Proactive** Seeks to formulate a crisis management team and a crisis plan that can be used to both prevent and mitigate potential crisis events.	Crisis **Reactive** Seeks to respond to the crisis events that do occur. Emphasis is on containing the damage and restoring normal operations.	**Proactive** Seeks to learn lessons from the crisis. Emphasis is on future prevention of a crisis and to function better as a crisis management team.
The External Landscape				

The karma comment created a wave of criticism on the Internet in China because the actress suggested that the country's earthquake was retribution for its policies on Tibet (Passariello & Meichtry, 2008). Chinese critics claimed she was ignorant of the Tibet issue and had no sympathy for those suffering from the earthquake.

The backlash in China was swift and decisive. Media reports described protestors tearing down billboards featuring the actress in advertisements (McLaughlin & Kaiser, 2008). Many cinemas on the Chinese mainland and in Hong Kong pledged not to show her films again. Ng See-Yuen, the founder of the UME Cineplex chain, said films featuring Stone would be banned from any UME cinema in Hong Kong and the Chinese mainland. Moreover, the Shanghai International Film Festival had also decided to permanently ban Stone and her films (Du, 2008).

Consider the impact this incident had on one company, Dior, a French firm that offers upscale clothing, cosmetics, and apparel for women. Stone was representing the company as a model. The karma comment erupted into a crisis for the firm's Chinese branch, Dior China. On May 27, 2008, three days after the Stone comment, Dior China issued the following statement through its Shanghai office: "We absolutely disagree with and cannot understand Sharon Stone's illogical remark" (Xiao & Li, 2012: 30).

On May 28, Dior China issued another statement, this time quoting the actress: "I am deeply sorry and sad about hurting Chinese people" (Horyn, 2008). On May 31, Stone issued a formal apology through CNN. However, a survey of 250,000 Chinese citizens found that 69% did not accept her apology and vowed never to forgive her (Xinhua, 2008). Many Chinese citizens wrote letters to Dior China to express their opinions, indicating they would never buy any Dior products if the company affiliated with Sharon Stone (Passariello & Meichtry, 2008). Under this pressure, Dior China began removing its advertisements with Stone's image nationwide (McLaughlin & Kaiser, 2008).

Assessing the Crisis

The evaluation process begins when the crisis commences and continues throughout its duration. The more the CMT can understand what is and what is not working in the crisis response, the more quickly the team can adjust its response. The following benchmark questions should be raised:

- How has the crisis affected both internal and external stakeholders' behaviors and opinions?
- To what extent have sales and share prices been affected?
- Which crisis response strategies and tactics were effective, and which were not?

Concerning the first benchmark, public opinion can work for or against the company. Human-induced crises are usually perceived more negatively by the general public than those resulting from natural disasters. Hence, human-induced crises such as corporate scandals or other ethical violations can harm the company's reputation. In the case of a natural disaster, however, the public's perception is often that the company is the victim of an outside threat that could not be controlled. Therefore, public opinion may generally still favor the organization, depending on how the crisis is managed.

The second benchmark is vital because revenues and shareholder values often decrease during a crisis (Coombs, 2006; Knight & Pretty, 1996). Ralph Erben, CEO of Luby's Cafeteria, Inc. (now defunct), knew immediately after a gunman killed 23 people in a Killeen, Texas, restaurant on October 16, 1991, that a massive selloff of Luby's stock would follow. On his flight to Killeen to address the crisis, he called the New York Stock Exchange and requested that stock sales be suspended (Barton, 2001).

Some crises can leave a lingering impact in an industry for years. Consider the travel and tourism industry; the crisis management effort is not just about keeping guests safe but also encouraging them to return to tourist destinations (Ali & Ali, 2010). The COVID-19 pandemic, the September 11, 2001, terrorist attacks, Hurricane Katrina in 2005, and the deadly 2004 tsunami that struck coastal communities along the Indian Ocean, created both primary crises, with their destruction and fatalities, and secondary crises, a loss of tourism in the affected areas (Kondraschow, 2006). Activities such as these have created a tourism crisis, including any unexpected events that affect traveler confidence in a destination and disrupt normal operations (World Tourism Organisation, 2010).

The third benchmark reminds us that not all crisis response strategies will be successful and that changes may be necessary. For Luby's, the company's crisis management plan called for the marketing manager to speak with the media. However, due to the severity of the massacre, CEO Erben decided that it would be better to serve as the spokesperson (Barton, 2001).

Evaluating the effectiveness of the crisis management effort requires critical information, including:

- Tracking sales and profits during and after the crisis
- Establishing a specialized communication avenue for stakeholders to call or email with questions and comments about the crisis and how it was managed
- Conducting focus groups to obtain information from key stakeholders
- Conducting surveys of external publics to determine their attitudes
- Documenting the information flow to and from the media
- Documenting those strategies that were and were not effective and investigating why (Caponigro, 2000).

The End of the Crisis: Getting the Organization Back on Its Feet

When a crisis subsides, an organization can begin to recover. Planning, perhaps from the CMP, can help accelerate the recovery and minimize the disaster's long-term adverse effects. During the restoration, the CMT needs to take stock, assess the damage, and determine what resources are readily available to the organization (Munneke & Davis, 2004).

Business Continuity

Business continuity refers to the organization's ability to resume or continue activities after a crisis occurs (Herbane, 2010). about it involves maintaining essential operating functions during and after a crisis. Meeting customer demand is vital, especially when a company is a critical player in a supply chain network (Zsidisin, Melnyk, & Ragatz, 2005). A crisis can affect the core functional areas of marketing, accounting, financial management, human resource management, and manufacturing. Two areas prone to interruption are the organization's management information system and its production operations capabilities.

MIS and Production Operations

Disaster recovery firms can provide backup software and computer equipment in an emergency. In preparation for a significant MIS disaster, some organizations have alternate worksites prearranged for possible use if a crisis takes down their primary operating facility. A **hot site** is a facility that has all the backup equipment and electronic connections required to operate the business. A **cold site** is a facility that lacks such material but is ready to be equipped when needed. **Warm sites** offer some but not all the equipment and connections necessary to operate the business (Bartlett, 2007).

When a crisis subsides, and the immediate threat has passed, the firm moves from a crisis response mode to a crisis recovery posture. The recovery effort depends on the extent of the damage that has taken place. For example, weather and natural disasters are common crises in the tourism industry (Pennington-Gray, Thapa, Kaplanidou, Cahyanto, & McLaughlin, 2011). As a result, some firms are closed for months because they either destroyed or suffered significant damage. Other firms that have experienced relatively minor damage may be able to open within a few hours or days. Some companies may remain open but have business units that are not operational because of localized damage, a common occurrence after a hurricane. Chain restaurants and retail stores may have geographically specific damage.

Assessing the state of business operations after the crisis helps determine the decisions that must be made next. Managers must determine whether the firm can meet stakeholder needs. If substantial rebuilding is necessary, facility upgrades may be in order.

Employee Needs After the Crisis

When employees are out of work because of a disaster, they may not be able to return once the company is functioning again. Employees need to support their families and might secure employment elsewhere if their economic needs are significant. As a result, some companies keep displaced employees on the payroll, but this move is feasible only if they have the resources to do so. Some US firms retained their employees during the COVID-19 pandemic even if there was little work for them to do. In this instance, the federal government provided funds to support the effort through the Coronavirus Aid, Recovery, and Economic Security (CARES) Act.

The Malden Mills Fire

A fire in Lawrence, Massachusetts, on December 11, 1995, commenced as an apparent boiler explosion at the Malden Mills complex. The plant manufactured fleece, a textile component in clothing and upholstery fabric, and about 700 employees. This single explosion led to a series of additional explosions, all of which were believed to be rupturing gas lines. These escalating events caused the fire to spread quickly. More than 200 firefighters from as far away as New Hampshire and Boston fought the blaze. Although there were no fatalities, 33 people were injured, eight critically ("December 11, 1995," 2005; McCurry, 1997).

CEO Aaron Feuerstein made two fateful decisions after the fire, (1) to rebuild the manufacturing facilities and (2) to pay the employees during the rebuilding process. Both decisions were expensive, especially considering that cash flow was compromised. Feuerstein received positive publicity for his decision to keep the employees on the payroll. His move was touted as a good model of employer–employee loyalty (Fisher, Schoenfeldt, & Shaw, 2003).

However, the decision to pay the employees came at a high cost to the company. While it generated waves of good press, it severely depleted cash reserves. In 2001, the company went through a bankruptcy, partly due to the $100 million debt after the fire in 1995. These tough financial times were also influenced by several unexpected factors, including warm weather the previous year (which hurt product sales), the loss of a critical customer, and an abundance of fleece knockoffs entering the market (Moreno, 2003). The resulting declines in sales and cash flow devastated the company while it was still reeling from the debt it had incurred after the fire.

In hindsight, Feuerstein may have contributed to a second crisis years later: bankruptcy. Many textile firms closed, outsourcing their production to companies in China and other countries during this time. Feuerstein not only paid his employees while they were not working but also operated the plant in the center of an expensive labor market. During this time, the company accumulated $100 million in additional debt, the seed of his subsequent undoing (Pacelle, 2003). However, markets such as the one in which Malden Mills operates can be tough and are subject to environmental jolts, as discussed in Chapter 3.

Feuerstein was eventually forced to retire in 2004 amid a turnaround strategy led by a new wave of management. In 2007, the company became part of Chrysalis Capital

Partners and later operated under Polartec's name (Clark, 2007). The complexity of the Malden Mills case and the unusual twists that took place after the fire reinforce the idea that paying for employees' wages during the reconstruction of a business devastated by a disaster must be taken cautiously.

Summary

A firm's response to a crisis can be viewed in three stages. Different tactics are appropriate during each stage. At the beginning of the crisis, the CMT should meet and begin the situational analysis. Managers should develop a strategy to manage the event as it unfolds. The CMP might need to be amended to address the specific situation. Others should address legacy and social media.

The mid-crisis stage focuses on response and mitigation. Managers should contain the damage and to respond to internal and external stakeholders' needs. Assessments should address which crisis response strategies are working, and which ones require modification. As the crisis wanes, the response seeks to assess the damage and get the organization up and running again.

Discussion Questions

1. What actions should be taken when a crisis ensues?
2. What are the desirable leadership traits of a CMT leader?
3. What is meant by situational assessment in crisis management? What problems can be created when mistakes are made in the situational assessment stage?
4. What significant decisions should be made during the management of the crisis event?
5. Why is it essential to establish and monitor an information-gathering system?
6. What is damage containment?
7. Why is consistent and continuous communication with the internal and external stakeholders important?
8. Why is it essential to evaluate what is going right and what is going wrong in managing the crisis?
9. What is business continuity, and why is it important?

Chapter Exercise

Divide the class into groups of three to five students. Each group should represent a crisis management team that is addressing the following scenario:

Suppose a significant snowstorm (or torrential rainstorm, depending on the climate) is about to hit your campus in the next 12 hours. Widespread power outages are likely, and travel will be nearly impossible once the event arrives. It is the first week of February, and most students have been back on campus for several weeks following the holiday break. Convene your team and discuss the following questions.

1. What actions should be taken immediately? In other words, within 4 to 6 hours before the arrival of the storm? As you discuss this question, consider the following:
   - Who will lead the crisis management effort on campus during this storm?
   - Which stakeholders should the communication spokesperson address, and what messages should be conveyed?
   - What type of information-monitoring requirements will your team need during the storm?
   - What possible crises could occur during the storm?
2. During the storm, what actions should be taken? Be sure to consider the following items:
   - How will you monitor the extent of the damage that occurs across the campus? Keep in mind that some communication networks may be compromised due to power outages.
   - What will be the main objectives of the CMT during the storm?
   - What social media tools and strategies can you use during the storm?
3. After the storm has passed, what actions should the CMT take? Consider the following:
   - What are the main priorities that must be addressed?
   - How will you assess the damage on campus?
   - What messages should be communicated to the students, parents, faculty, and staff?
   - What messages should be communicated to traditional and social media?

Closing Chapter Case: The Boeing 737 Max -   Part 2

The opening chapter case overviewed Boeing's crisis after cashes involving two of its 737 Max jets. In part 2, we consider how the causes and outcomes of the crashes are similar.

Examining the Two Crashes

On October 29, 2018, Lion Air Flight 610 took off from Jakarta, Indonesia, at 6:20 A.M. en route to Pangkal Pinang, Indonesia. After takeoff, but before the automatic pilot system had been activated, the aircraft's nose pitched down immediately after the flaps had been retracted. Over the next eight minutes, the pilots battled with the aircraft. They encountered 28 nose dives, each of which they would counteract by turning the MCAS system temporarily off, only to have it reactivate after a 5-second interlude. Each time the MCAS reactivated, it would send the plane into a 10-second nosedive, following the system's programming. Between the 10-second dives and the 5-second interludes, the aircraft lost cumulative altitude as the pilots could not recover the lost distance during the 5-second respites from MCAS. The pilots did not know that the MCAS was reading incorrect data from a damaged AoA sensor (Campbell, 2019). Twelve minutes after takeoff, the aircraft plunged into the Java Sea, killing all 189 passengers and crew.

The second Max crash took place on March 10, 2019, on Ethiopian Airlines Flight 302 from Addis Ababa Bole International Airport in Ethiopia to Jomo Kenyatta International Airport in Nairobi, Kenya. Ninety seconds into the flight, and just after the flaps had been retracted; the plane went into an unexpected nosedive. The pilots responded by pulling the nose back up, but after 5 seconds, the aircraft would—like the Lion Air Max—go into a 10-second nosedive, precisely like the Lion Air Max had done. The first officer correctly called out to the captain that the stabilizer trim controls should be disabled (Campbell, 2019). The call turned off the MCAS, even though the pilots did not know it existed in the flight control system. When it MCAS was disabled, the pilots had to resort to manually pulling the aircraft out of its nosedive through cables that extend from the flight deck to the tail of the plane. Due to the speed of the plane, the pilots could not manually pull up the nose. Out of desperation, they turned the electric stabilizer system back on, which reactivated the MCAS. The MCAS pushed the nose back down, and the plane eventually crashed into a field near Bishoftu, Ethiopia, killing all 157 passengers and crew.

Commonalities Between the Two Crashes

In both crashes, the MCAS was controlling the pitch of the plane without the pilot's consent. The pilots attempted to pull the aircraft's nose up, but the MCAS pushed it back down. They disabled the system for about five seconds, but the MCAS would reactivate and again, push the plane's nose back down for ten seconds. It was as if a sinister force was causing the plane to crash, and there was nothing the pilots could do to stop it.

There are three reasons why a system might behave in this manner. First, the MCAS might have been doing what it was designed to do by preventing the aircraft from going into a stall. This explanation assumes that the pilots were somehow erroneously flying the plane into a stall, which is not plausible.

A second scenario is that the MCAS system was flawed. This scenario is also unlikely as the software was written to correct a non-flying situation. If a software problem existed, then all 737 Max flights would have displayed the same erratic flying behaviors.

According to a third scenario, the AoA sensor might have been flawed and malfunctioned, which could occur if the sensor was damaged, perhaps due to weather or being struck by a foreign object such as a bird (Sider & Pasztor, 2019). This scenario is most likely as both crash reports indicate problems with the AoA sensor. A sensor that sends incorrect data to the MCAS could cause it to behave erratically. The pilots entered a cosmology episode, a flight situation they had never experienced before. No matter what assumptions, training, or flight experience they brought to the flight deck that day, it was not enough to resolve the problem. They did not know how to disable the MCAS so they could fly the aircraft properly. They did not even know the MCAS existed. A computer had mysteriously taken over the controls of the aircraft, and they could not stop it.

Complicating the crash stories is the problem of the sensor alert system, which is supposed to inform the pilots when the data readings from the two AoA sensors are out of sync. These were not working on all of the planes that Boeing had delivered, but they were working on the ones provided to American Airlines (Sider & Pasztor, 2019). A production problem was blamed for the alert system irregularities.

Fast-tracking and its Role in Certification

Boeing built the 737 Max quickly and did not inform the pilots in their training that the MCAS was even part of the system. Pilot training for the Max is minimal—150 minutes on an iPad. Additional certification is not required for pilots, a selling point of the plane (*Bloomberg News*, 2019; Campbell, 2019).

To certify an existing aircraft model, Boeing would only have limited authority to redesign the plane. However, when the new LEAP engines were added, two workarounds had to be arranged: (1) mount the engines higher and more forward on the wing, and (2) add the MCAS to adjust for the change in gravity this put on the aircraft. The MCAS was a workaround to make the engines work on the existing airframe (Campbell, 2019; Gates, 2019).

Certification of an existing aircraft platform also means the plane must feel the same as other aircraft in the same category to the pilots. Hence, the Boeing 737 Max must operate and behave similarly to other versions of the 737, such as the 737 NG. If the new plane design has a different feel, it is operating outside of the certification process; Boeing would have to apply for a new certification, a costly and time-consuming process. Hence, the MCAS was not designed to prevent a stall for safety reasons, but to behave like the previous versions of the 737 (Campbell, 2019).

Certification of an existing aircraft also means that training for the new generation is simple and to the point. The new aircraft must behave like the old one, which reduces training time and makes the plane more marketable. Training for pilots involved a self-administered computer course that takes about an hour to complete and no simulator training (Campbell, 2019, Gates, 2019). To simplify the process, Boeing did not include an extended discussion on MCAS or mentioned in the Max flight manual (Gates, 2019). This point later drew outrage from pilots who insisted they needed to know about the software, mainly since it could crash an aircraft (Gates, 2018).

The Problem of the Single-Sensor Input

There is no doubt that automated software has contributed to air travel safety, a point well documented in many venues. However, automation can also contribute to a crash (Frankel, 2019). Faulty sensors can send incorrect data to the flight control computer (FCC) and cause the aircraft to behave erratically. Pilots can overcome these situations with proper training, and the aircraft can remain safe (Fallows, 2019).

However, the 737 Max was designed to have one operating AoA sensor interact with the MCAS at a time. However, if the sensor was defective, it would send bad data to MCAS and cause the plane to fly erratically. Indeed, that appears to have happened, and the results were fatal. What is ironic about this design is that aircraft typically have multiple levels of redundancy to account for a sensor or system failure. Still, in the case of the MCAS, there was no redundancy. How and why the FAA approved this arrangement is unclear.

Sensors sometimes fail; there have been 216 recorded sensor failings since 2004 logged with the FAA (Devine & Griffin, 2019). But linking the functioning of a single sensor to MCAS is problematic in this case.

Implications

The two crashes of the 737 Max are major crises from a human loss perspective. The 346 victims and their families have experienced untold pain and suffering. Confidence in Boeing and the FAA declined considerably. Many have criticized the FAA for not taking more oversight in the rebuild of the Max (Gates, 2019).

The crisis also enabled Airbus to gain a deeper share in the A320neo market. In March 2019, Airbus secured a $35 billion deal with China for 290 A320 aircraft (*Crain's Chicago Business*, 2019). The US-China trade war did not help matters either, as it created incentives for China to seek aircraft orders outside of the US.

However, the crisis also incentivized China to develop a short-range aircraft. The C919 has been in development and had its first maiden flight in 2017. It is designed to compete with the Boeing 737 and A320 in the lucrative short-haul market. There were already 800 orders for the plane at the time of the crisis, but safety is a concern, as China does not have a strong history in commercial aircraft development (*Bloomberg News*, 2019).

Ironically, even after a crash, a model of aircraft can still be successful. The McDonnell Douglas DC-10, a large medium-range aircraft, was grounded in 1979 by the FAA when its cargo door design contributed to several high-fatality crashes. After design changes, the DC-10 became a best seller through the late 1980s (Doherty & Lindeman 2019).

The Boeing 737 has experienced problems. In the 1990s, two crashes occurred involving uncommanded movements of the rudder. In 1991, a United Airlines flight crashed in Colorado, killing 25 people. In 1994, a USAir flight near Pittsburgh crashed, resulting in 132 fatalities. Boeing redesigned a valve that US regulators suspected was a contributing factor in the crashes, and the 737 became a best-seller (Robison & Johnsson 2019).

As of 2020, the Boeing 787 Dreamliner has not experienced a crash, but one plane experienced a battery fire and another an in-flight battery malfunction. This crisis grounded all Dreamliners in 2013 from January to April (Williard et al., 2013). The battery system's design was enhanced to contain a fire should one occur, and the Dreamliner has become a successful, fuel-efficient, long-range aircraft.

Case Discussion Questions

1. Some in the aviation industry have suggested that commercial pilots today rely too heavily on automation to fly their aircraft. As a result, the skills needed to fly a plane manually are perishable if not maintained through practice of non-automated flying, also known as stick and rudder or hand flying. What examples of air crashes can you find in your research that support this finding?
2. The Boeing 737 Max case is ongoing. What are the latest developments?

References

Ali, S., & Ali, A. (2010). A conceptual framework for crisis planning and management in the Jordanian tourism industry. *Advances in Management, 3*(7), 59–65.

Baran, B., & Adelman, M. (2010). Preparing for the unthinkable: Leadership development for organizational crises. *Industrial and Organizational Psychology, 3,* 45–47.

Bartlett, N. (2007). Ready for trouble. *Credit Union, 73*(2), 38–42.

Barton, L. (2001). *Crisis in organizations II.* Cincinnati, OH: South-Western College Publishing.

Barton, L. (2008). *Crisis leadership now: A real-world guide to preparing for threat, disaster, sabotage, and scandal.* New York: McGraw-Hill.

Berinato, S. (2010). You have to lead from everywhere. *Harvard Business Review, 88*(11), 76–79.

Bloomberg News, (2019, March 18). The Chinese plane on Boeing's radar. *Bloomberg Businessweek*, 17-18.

Borodzicz, E., & van Haperen, K. (2002). Individual and group learning in crisis simulations. *Journal of Contingencies and Crisis Management, 10*(3), 139–147.

Boston, R. (2000, February). False prophets, real profits. *Church and State*, 13–15.

Campbell, D. (2019, May 2). The many human errors that brought down the Boeing 737 Max. *The Verge*. Retrieved 05/22/2019, from https://www.theverge.com/2019/5/2/18518176/boeing-737-max-crash-problems-human-error-mcas-faa

Caponigro, J. (2000). *The crisis counselor: A step-by-step guide to managing a business crisis*. Chicago: Contemporary Books.

Cavanaugh, J. (2003). Coolness under fire: A conversation with James Cavanaugh. *Leadership in Action, 23*(5), 7.

China Digital Times, (2008, May 30). Dior Drops Sharon Stone after Quake Comments. Retrieved May 27, 2019, from https://chinadigitaltimes.net/2008/05/dior-drops-sharon-stone-after-quake-comments/

Clark, D. (2007, March 20). Malden exits bankruptcy as Polartec. *Women's Wear Daily*, 10.

Coombs, W. (2006). *Code red in the board room: Crisis management as organizational DNA*. Westport, CT: Praeger.

Coombs, W. (2007). *Ongoing crisis communication: Planning, managing, and responding* (2nd ed.). Thousand Oaks, CA: Sage. Cowan, D. (2003). Confronting the failed failure: Y2K and evangelical eschatology in light of the passed millennium. *Nova Religio: The Journal of Alternative and Emergent Religions, 7*(2), 71–85.

Crain's Chicago Business, (2019, March 25). In new blow to Boeing, Airbus gets big China order. Retrieved 05/29/2019, from https://www.chicagobusiness.com/node/841241/printable/print

Crandall, W., & Menefee, M. (1996). Crisis management in the midst of labor strife: Preparing for the worst. *SAM Advanced Management Journal, 61*(1), 11–15.

Crichton, M., Lauche, K., & Flin, R. (2005). Incident command skills in the management of an oil industry drilling incident: A case study. *Journal of Contingencies and Crisis Management, 13*(3), 116–128.

December 11, 1995: Fire destroys Malden Mills. (2005, December 11). *Mass Moments*. Retrieved May 25, 2019, from http://massmoments.org/moment.cfm?mid=355

Denning, S. (2013, January 21). What went wrong at Boeing? *Forbes*. Retrieved August 23, 2019, from http://www.forbes.com/sites/stevedenning/2013/01/21/what-went-wrong-at-boeing/

Deveney, J. (2018). Crisis communications management on digital platforms. *Journal of Brand Strategy, 7*(2), 163-172.

Devine, C., & Griffin, D. (2019, April 30). Boeing relied on single sensor for 737 Max that had been flagged 216 times to FAA. *CNN Investigates*. Retrieved 05/25/2019, from https://www.cnn.com/2019/04/30/politics/boeing-sensor-737-max-faa/index.html

Doherty, T., & Lindeman, T. (2019, March 15). The problems that led to the Boeing 737 Max grounding. *Politico*. Retrieved 05/28/2019, from https://www.politico.com/story/2019/03/15/boeing-737-max-grounding-1223072

Donahue, B. (2004). True leadership in a crisis. *Convenience Store Decisions, 15*(9), 6.

Du, W. (2008, May 30). Netizens annoyed by Stone's ignorance. *China Daily Online*. Retrieved May 27, 2019, from http://www.chinadaily.com.cn/china/2008-05-30/content_6724266.htm

Duhe, S., & Zoch, L. (1994). A case study: Framing the media's agenda during a crisis. *Public Relations Quarterly, 39*(4), 42–45.

Elliott, D., & Smith, D. (1993). Football stadia disasters in the United Kingdom: Learning from tragedy? *Industrial and Environmental Crisis Quarterly, 7*(3), 205–229.

Endsley, M., & Garland, D. (2000). *Situation awareness, analysis, and measurement.* Mahwah, NJ: Lawrence Erlbaum.

Fallows, J. (2019, March 14). Reporter's notebook: 'Don't ground the airplanes. Ground the pilots.' *The Atlantic.* Retrieved, 05/28/2019, from https://www.theatlantic.com/notes/2019/03/dont-ground-the-airplanes-ground-the-pilots/584941/

Fisher, C., Schoenfeldt, L., & Shaw, J. (2003). *Human resource management (5th ed.).* Boston: Houghton Mifflin.

Frankel, T. (2019, March 18). Not just the 737: Angle-of-attack sensors have had problems. *The Washington Post.* Retrieved May 22, 2019, from https://www.heraldnet.com/nation-world/not-just-the-737-angle-of-attack-sensors-have-had-problems/

Gates, D. (2018, November 12). US pilots flying the 737 Max weren't told about new automatic systems change linked to Lion Air crash. *Seattle Times.* Retrieved May 28, 2019, from https://www.seattletimes.com/business/boeing-aerospace/u-s-pilots-flying-737-max-werent-told-about-new-automatic-systems-change-linked-to-lion-air-crash/

Gates, D. (2019, March 17). Flawed analysis, failed oversight: How Boeing, FAA certified the suspect 737 MAX flight control system. *Seattle Times.* Retrieved May 22, 2019, from https://www.seattletimes.com/business/boeing-aerospace/failed-certification-faa-missed-safety-issues-in-the-737-max-system-implicated-in-the-lion-air-crash/

Gleason, S., & Berry, I. (2012, April 3). Beef processor falters amid "slime." *Wall Street Journal,* p. B2.

Herbane, B. (2010). The evolution of business continuity management: A historical review of practices and drivers. *Business History, 52*(6), 978–1002.

Herman, M. (1995). When strikes turn violent. *Security Management, 39*(3), 32–35.

Horyn, C. (2008, June 1). Insensitive, Yes. But sorry? Well . . . *New York Times*, p. 2.

Knight, R., Pretty, D. (1996). The impact of catastrophes on shareholder value. Templeton College, University of Oxford. Retrieved October 10, 2018, from http://eternity.websurgeon.ca/papers/whitepapers/sedgwickreport.pdf

Kondraschow, R. (2006). The lessons of disaster. *Journal of Retail and Leisure Property, 5*(3), 204–211.

Langfitt, F. (2006). Covering the Sago Mine disaster: How a game of "whisper down the coal mine" ricocheted around the world. *Nieman Reports, 60*(2), 103–104.

Leskin, G. A., Morland, L., Whealin, J., Everly, G., Litz, B., & Keane, T. (2004). *Factsheet: Fostering resilience in response to terrorism for psychologists working with first responders.* Washington, DC: American Psychological Association.

Long, Z., Crandall, W., & Parnell, J. (2010). A trilogy of unfortunate events in China: Reflecting on the management of crises. *International Journal of Asian Business and Information Management, 1*(4), 21–30.

McCurry, J. (1997). Loyalty saves Malden Mills. *Textile World, 147*(2), 38–45.

McLaughlin, K., & Kaiser, A. (2008, May 30). Dior China drops Stone after quake comments. *Women's Wear Daily,* 24–25.

McMinn, L. (2001). Y2K, the apocalypse, and evangelical Christianity: The role of eschatological belief in church responses. *Sociology of Religion, 62*(2), 205–220.

Miller, A. (2001). The Los Angeles riots: A study of crisis paralysis. *Journal of Contingencies and Crisis Management, 9*(4), 189–199.

Mitroff, I., & Anagnos, G. (2001). *Managing crises before they happen.* New York: AMACOM.

Moreno, K. (2003, April 14). Trial by fire. *Forbes,* 92.

Munneke, G., & Davis, A. (2004). *Disaster recovery for law firms. In The essential formbook: Comprehensive management tools for lawyers: Vol. IV. Disaster planning and recovery (pp. 59–67).* Chicago: American Bar Association, Law Practice Management Section.

Olasky, M. (2006). *The politics of disaster: Katrina, Big Government, and a new strategy for future crisis.* Nashville: W Publishing Group.

Pacelle, M. (2003, May 9). Through the Mill: Can Mr. Feuerstein save his business one last time? *Wall Street Journal*, p. A1.

Passariello, C., & Meichtry, S. (2008, May 30). Dior pulls ads with Sharon Stone. *Wall Street Journal*, p. B.7.

Pearson, C., & Clair, J. (1998). Reframing crisis management. *Academy of Management Review, 23*(1), 59-76.

Pearson, C., & Mitroff, I. (1993). From crisis prone to crisis prepared: A framework for crisis management. *Academy of Management Executive, 7*(1), 48–59.

Pearson, C., & Rondinelli, D. (1998). Crisis management in Central European firms. *Business Horizons, 41*(3), 50–59.

Pennington-Gray, L., Thapa, B., Kaplanidou, K., Cahyanto, I., & McLaughlin, E. (2011). Crisis planning and preparedness in the United States Tourism Industry. *Cornell Hospitality Quarterly, 52*(3), 312–320.

Powell, L., Hickson, III, M., Self, W. R., & Bodon, J. (2001). The role of religion and responses to the Y2K macro-crisis. *North American Journal of Psychology, 3*(2), 295–302.

Robison, P., & Johnsson, J. (2019, March 18). The plight of the 737 Max 8. *Bloomberg Businessweek,* 15-17.

Rolston, L., & McNerney, D. (2003). Leading during times of crisis. *Innovative Leader, 12*(5), 1–2.

Schoenberg, A. (2005). Do crisis plans matter? A new perspective on leading during a crisis. *Public Relations Quarterly, 50*(1), 2–6.

Sherman, W., & Harris, R. (2018). Crisis? What crisis? Strategic crisis management, and the GM ignition switch crisis. *SAM Advanced Management Journal, 83*(1), 41-49.

Sider, A., & Pasztor, A. (2019, May 22). Boeing executive played down risks: Official suggest to pilots that sensor alerts were more of a nuisance than hazard. *Wall Street Journal,* p. B1.

Sklarewitz, N. (1991, May). Cruise company handles crisis by the book. *Public Relations Journal,* 34–36.

Solomon, C. (1992, July). The LA riots: An HR diary. *Personnel Journal,* 22–29.

Taylor, P. (1990). *The Hillsborough stadium disaster. Final Report.* London: Home Office.

Walsh, K. (2007, November 19). A film hero up to playing the real role. *US News & World Report,* 50–51.

Weick, K. (1993). The collapse of sensemaking in organizations: The Mann Gulch disaster. *Administrative Science Quarterly, 38,* 628–652.

Wheatley, M. (2006, Summer). Leadership lessons from the real world. *Leader to Leader, 41,* 16–20.

Williard, N., He, W., Hendricks, C., & Pecht, M. (2013). Lessons learned from the 787 Dreamliner issue on lithium-ion battery reliability. *Energies, 6,* 4682-4695.

Wilson, J. (2004, June 21–July 11). Now the disaster's happened, what am I supposed to do? *Accounting Today,* 24–25.

Wilson, S. (2003). Develop an effective crisis-management strategy. *Chemical Engineering Progress, 99*(9), 58–61.

Wooten, L., & James, E. (2008). Linking crisis management and leadership competencies: The role of human resource development. *Advances in Developing Human Resources, 10*(3), 352–379.

World Tourism Organisation. (2010). *Handbook on natural disaster reduction in tourist areas.* Madrid: World Tourism Organisation.

Xiao, J., & Li, H. (2012). Online discussion of Sharon Stone's karma comment on China earthquake: The intercultural communication of media events in the age of media convergence. *China Media Research, 8*(1), 25–39.

Zsidisin, G., Melnyk, S., & Ragatz, G. (2005). An institutional theory perspective of business continuity planning for purchasing and supply management. *Internal Journal of Production Research, 43*(16), 3401–3420.

Chapter 8: Crisis Communications

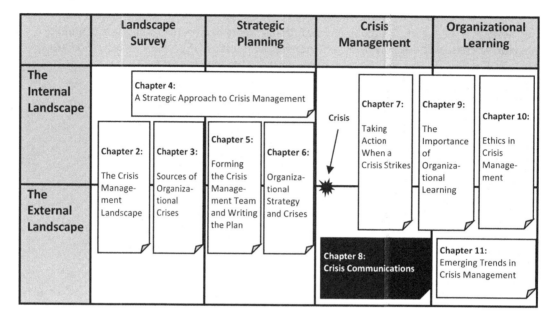

Learning Objectives

After reading this chapter, each student should be able to:

1. Discuss the importance of communicating with employees during a crisis.
2. Identify the traits required for the media spokesperson.
3. Identify and discuss the guidelines for holding a formal news conference.
4. Discuss the importance of communicating with customers and other external stakeholders.
5. Explain the strategies of situational crisis communication theory (SCCT) and when they should be employed.
6. Discuss why sensemaking is important given the presence of social media in the crisis management landscape.
7. Describe how crises can emanate from social media outlets.
8. Discuss how organizations can incorporate social media into their crisis communication plans.
9. Explain why communication effectiveness should be evaluated after a crisis ends.
10. Identify and discuss different types of media training.

Opening Chapter Case: United Airlines Wants you OFF the Plane! - Part 1

On April 9, 2017, Dr. David Dao was seated on United Express flight 3411, which was about to take off from Chicago for a short trip to Louisville, Kentucky. Shortly before the scheduled departure, an airline supervisor came on board the plane and announced: "We have United employees that need to fly to Louisville tonight … This flight's not leaving until four people get off" (Selk, 2017). The flight on which the United employees had been scheduled was delayed due to mechanical problems, so they boarded flight 3411 instead. Although passengers were offered vouchers to rebook their flights, nobody volunteered to leave the aircraft. United then selected four passengers to depart involuntarily, despite the fact they had already been seated.

Dr. David Dao, a pulmonologist, was one of the passengers selected. He refused to give up his seat, stating that he had patients to see the next morning. Then, United personnel made a fateful decision that would launch the airline into the public spotlight; they called Chicago Aviation Police to have Dr. Dao forcibly removed from the plane. The incident was recorded on a cellphone and widely circulated on social media. United Airlines, which once had promoted the motto, "fly the friendly skies," seemed much less friendly.

Overbooking Flights as a Strategy

According to United, the flight was not overbooked, but it appeared to have been from the standpoint of the passengers. Nonetheless, overbooking in the airline industry is a valid form of revenue enhancement (Carey, 2017). The business logic is that not all passengers who reserve a flight arrive on time. The no-show passengers create empty seats, which represent lost revenue, also known within the industry as "spoilage" (Klophaus & Pölt, 2006). Airlines use mathematical models to calculate how much a specific flight should be overbooked to fill aircraft without denying boarding to ticketed customers (Gerchick, 2013; Siddappa, Rosenberger, & Chen, 2007). When overbooking occurs, airlines offer financial incentives to passengers to take later flights. In most cases, enough volunteers are willing to accept the financial incentive and take a later flight.

The strategy of overbooking has been mostly successful, and the number of passengers affected by what the industry calls involuntary boarding denial has been relatively small. In 2016, approximately 660 million passengers boarded flights in the United States, of which only 434,425, or .07%, were "bumped" and *voluntarily* took a later flight. In total, 40,629 passengers, or .006%, were removed *involuntarily* (Hopper, 2017).

When four United crewmembers suddenly needed to travel to Louisville, the United flight was technically not overbooked but was full. Indeed, the airline had met its goal of filling every seat, but the need to transport crew members as passengers was not anticipated. United then offered $400 vouchers to incentivize four passengers to deplane. When nobody accepted, United offered $800, but there still were no takers, most likely because this was the last flight of the night to Louisville (Goldstein, 2017). United then resorted to its involuntary passenger removal policy and proceeded to remove four passengers. A young couple was told to leave the aircraft, which they did. However, when Dr. Dao was asked to depart, he refused.

The Removal of Dr. David Dao

Before the United incident, forcibly removing a ticketed passenger from an aircraft had only occurred when a person was disruptive or posed a security threat (Hopper, 2017). However, this situation was different. Dr. David Dao had firmly maintained that he was not leaving his seat. He had purchased a ticket, was already seated on his flight, and needed to see patients the next day (Selk, 2017).

Moreover, this was the last flight of the night going to Louisville. A United manager decided to call security personnel from the Chicago Department of Aviation, who boarded the aircraft and asked Dr. Dao, once again, to leave the plane. Cellphone video shot of the incident, which later appeared on *Inside Edition*, shows Dr. Dao on his cell phone talking to someone at United saying: "I'm a physician. I have to work tomorrow at 8:00...No, I am not going, I am not going." A few moments later, a security guard (not a police officer) pulled Dr. Dao from his seat and dragged him down the aisle. The resulting scream was heard "around the world," as cellphone video showed a bloody and dazed Dr. Dao being dragged away on his back. The video was soon posted on social media.

Case Discussion Questions

1. What other options could United Airlines have taken to avoid this crisis?
2. Some have called for airlines to stop the practice of overbooking altogether. Initiate a class discussion/debate between those who favor the practice and those who oppose it.
3. What changes could United make to prevent this type of crisis from recurring?

Introduction

Crisis communications have changed dramatically in the past decade and is often driven by social media. Over 80% of Americans are online each day, and Facebook alone touted almost 3 billion global users in 2020.

The Internet has changed the face of crisis management (Berinato, 2010). Much of what has been taught about crisis communications before the rise of the Internet remains true. Still, it is more important now than ever to monitor the Web for comments about and developments that affect your organization. A rapid response is expected. Before the Internet, it was acceptable to wait 24 hours before making a public statement to the media. Today, 24 hours is too long to wait.

Communication strategies help organizations manage a crisis successfully. The crisis management team (CMT) needs accurate information to communicate quickly to its stakeholders. Issues of fear, hostility, and anger can complicate an already complicated situation, and communications can become distorted and inaccurate. These complexities often result in rumors and imprecise information over the Internet that can make the situation worse. Hence, creating a communication structure that supports the flow of objective, truthful, and timely information is necessary to inform internal and external stakeholders about crisis management activities. When an organization communicates well, it is more likely to resolve a crisis. This chapter discusses crisis management communication practices, how they affect the respective stakeholders, and how the crisis communication function can be managed effectively.

Crisis management and crisis communication are intricately interlinked. As Scanlon (1975) recognized long ago, "Every crisis is also a crisis of information...Failure to control the crisis of information can ultimately fail to control the crisis" (p. 431). The study of organizational crisis communication has resulted in a greater understanding of the role communication plays in defining the origin of a crisis and launching the crisis recovery plan (Spillan, Rowles, & Mino, 2002/2003).

We begin this chapter by addressing the traditional fundamentals of crisis communication, focusing on legacy media—television, radio, and print media. We then consider a more recent form of communication, social media. We discuss its influence on the crisis communication function and suggest guidelines for employing it as part of the organization's crisis response. We evaluate the effectiveness of the crisis communication function and conclude with insights on the training needed for effective crisis communication.

Fundamentals of Crisis Communications

Communication strategies help explain the pre- and post-crisis plans to all affected stakeholders (Coombs, 2015; Seeger, Sellnow, & Ulmer, 1998). As the adage says, "perception is reality." Communication helps stakeholders understand what an organization is encountering and make sense of a crisis event (Seeger et al., 1998). The following sections overview the components of the crisis communication process.

Initiating the Crisis Communication Process

Activating the crisis management team (CMT) is the first step in managing a crisis. The CMT executes the crisis management plan (CMP), which includes a crisis communication plan to clarify procedures for communicating with internal and external stakeholders as the event unfolds. The primary goal of communications is to convey what has happened and how it plans to address the crisis. Communications with stakeholders must be carried out expediently to enhance the credibility of the organization and build trust. Messages should satisfy each audience's unique requirements and provide the tone, context, and consistency of all additional messages. Consistency is essential, while the detail and delivery methods may vary depending on the audience (Nelson, 2004).

Crisis Communication with Internal Stakeholders

When a crisis strikes, two communications functions must be addressed. First, managing the situation requires a command-and-control role that involves management, the owners, and selected employees. Second, the employee population needs to be updated on the status of the crisis, how it has affected the organization, and how it will be resolved.

The Command-and-Control Function

The location of the command center and its accompanying facilities is vital. The command center is the physical area where the company spokesperson and members of the media can communicate. The location should also be equipped to disseminate information to stakeholders who are not near the organization. Equipment such as telephones (landline and cellular), computer connections, Internet access, appropriate seating facilities, and other infrastructure items are required. Up-to-date, virtual meeting platforms are essential when the crisis involves coordination among multiple locations.

It is common for a large company with a designated corporate headquarters to experience a crisis in the field (i.e., at the unit level). Such would be the case if a restaurant or retail chain experienced a crisis at one of its stores. Under these conditions, the crisis and communication response are typically directed from the home office. The Chi-Chi's hepatitis A illness, Wendy's finger incident, and Luby's Cafeteria murders (addressed in previous chapters) were directed from locations above the unit level. This approach is common because crisis management and PR expertise often reside at the home office. Sometimes, however, the home office learns about a crisis well after it has commenced. This situation occurred with Bowater Incorporated during a weather event involving severe fog.

Bowater's Southern Division, a newsprint manufacturer in Calhoun, Tennessee, experienced a horrific crisis on December 11, 1990. At 9:05 a.m., a massive 99-vehicle accident occurred on Interstate 75, about 2 miles from the plant. For years, complaints about industrial fog produced by the mill's aeration ponds had been directed at the company (McLaren, 1994). Ironically, the multivehicle accident started when a speeding car collided with one of the company's tractor-trailers on the interstate. The resulting smoke and the already present fog created a whiteout condition that made visibility impossible for drivers near the accident scene. The accident became the worst in Tennessee's history, with 12 motorists perishing in the resulting collisions and fires. Surprisingly, the chairman of the board learned about the event on the evening news (Maggart, 1994). Internal communications within the company, which consisted of various mills throughout the southeastern United States, was haphazard to nonexistent. Some of the other mills received telephone calls shortly after the wreck, unaware that the accident had even taken place.

Communicating with Employees

Employees are critical to the success of any crisis management communication. They are continuously on the front line of the action and must also communicate with external stakeholders such as customers. In this role, they act as company ambassadors and should be up to date on how management is addressing the crisis (Weiner, 2006). It is also essential to communicate with employees who are not directly involved in managing the crisis or responding directly to outside stakeholders. Indeed, employees must even respond to questions from friends, neighbors, and clients (Valentine, 2007). Depending on the crisis, some employees may be apprehensive and fear job loss due to the crisis. Keeping them focused on day-to-day operations can offer reassurance and help maintain morale (Argenti, 2002; Reilly, 2008).

Setting up a discussion board on the company's intranet—which limits access to the organization's members—can be therapeutic and can promote socialization, especially if employees are separated geographically (Premeaux & Breaux, 2007). During Hurricane Katrina, McDonald's used toll-free numbers to communicate with employees and to account for any employees who might have been missing (Marquez, 2005).

One analogy that applies to employee communication during a crisis is the classic "mushroom" problem. Employees often complain that communication during a crisis is infrequent or nonexistent, and they feel like a mushroom — "They keep us in the dark and feed us garbage" (Reilly, 2008, p. 335). The remedy is to keep employees informed, even if the news is not always positive. Without reliable information, employees tend to speculate that the worst is happening. Most are generally concerned about their companies and want to be updated with frequent and candid updates (Barton, 2001).

Sometimes rapid communication is required, as in the case of a workplace violence incident. The Virginia Tech massacre was a seminal event that illustrates such a scenario. The April 2007 incident consisted of two attacks approximately three hours apart (Reilly, 2008). What is troublesome in communication is that students were still going to classes several hours after the first shooting (Madhani & Janega, 2007). Federal legislation was passed to require notification systems on university campuses and military bases to ensure that this problem would not recur (Magnuson & Parsons, 2014).

West Virginia University at Parkersburg was an early adopter when it installed an emergency paging system in all classrooms and critical administrative areas. The system consisted of paging phones and overhead broadcast speakers to provide quick messaging on the main campus in Parkersburg and at its rural Jackson County Center campus, 35 miles away (Gnage, Dziagwa, & White, 2009). it is standard practice to text faculty, staff, and students with emergency information.

Finally, employees should be advised *not* to respond to reporters' questions, but instead should refer all inquiries to the organization's designated spokesperson (Coombs, 2015; Wailes, 2003). Using a single designated spokesperson helps ensure the organization's message is consistent. Updating employees regularly on the progress and the crisis's status through internal reports can help maintain a sense of normalcy in day-to-day operations. It also has a significant effect on decreasing the flow of rumors and inaccuracies seeping out to the media (Wailes, 2003).

Crisis Communication with External Stakeholders

Communicating with external stakeholders requires designating a spokesperson skilled at interacting with various media outlets and public groups. Communication must also follow a strategy that fits the severity of the situation.

Designating a Spokesperson

Companies should designate a single spokesperson for press conferences and other traditional means of communication. There is no set rule on who this person should be, except that it should be consistent with the organization's hierarchy and culture. The appointed person may also vary according to the type of crisis encountered. A production crisis might be addressed more effectively by a member of the CMT with a production or manufacturing background. Likewise, a problem with information technology (IT) may be led by a crisis team member from another department.

When should the chief executive officer (CEO) be the spokesperson? In general, the more severe the crisis, the more likely the CEO should be in control and visible to the public. The classic case that supports this adage is the 1989 *Exxon Valdez* oil spill. CEO Lawrence Rawl chose to remain at Exxon headquarters rather than visit the oil-drenched

Alaskan coast. He sent other executives to manage the situation instead, creating the impression that he thought the crisis was trivial (Vernon, 1998). The United Airlines case addressed at the beginning of this chapter provides a contrast. United CEO Oscar Munoz made himself readily available to address the crisis and was quick to apologize for United's response once all the facts were known. In most cases, the designated spokesperson will not be the CEO, but an articulate top manager who can speak convincingly and with empathy. In many large organizations, this person has a background in public relations.

The spokesperson selected should be able to communicate effectively and professionally on behalf of the organization, not just because he or she is the most senior person available. Barton (2001) illustrates an example from the 1999 Columbine (Colorado) High School shootings. The initial spokesperson was selected because of seniority. Unfortunately, he lacked the relevant technical knowledge of the incident and was quickly replaced by a more knowledgeable spokesperson. A spokesperson's communication skills are critical because the role is a highly visible one.

Ideal Skills for the Spokesperson

The spokesperson should appear pleasant on camera, present crisis information clearly, and answer difficult questions effectively (Coombs, 2015). Appearing pleasant on camera means maximizing the delivery style elements of:

- *Maintaining eye contact.* The speaker should look at the audience at least 60% of the time.
- *Using hand gestures.* Hand movements emphasize a point.
- *Varying voice inflection.* Doing so helps avoid a monotone delivery style.
- *Changing facial expressions.* Avoid a blank stare, a "deer in the headlights" look.
- *Avoiding verbal disfluencies.* Avoid filler words and utterances like *um* and *uh* (Coombs, 2015).

Difficult questions should not be deflected. The spokesperson should communicate a sense of compassion and concern for the victims of a crisis. The restaurant chain Chi-Chi's stopped operating in the United States in 2004 due in part to a crisis it faced in September 2003. An outbreak of hepatitis A, stemming from a shipment of green onions used in salsa, resulted in three deaths and more than 600 illnesses (Veil, Liu, Erickson, & Sellnow, 2005). A divisional vice president made the first official public response by the company on November 4, 2003. In looking for the compassion and concern of the company's communication response, Veil and colleagues noted:

In this first public comment, the spokesperson did not express regret for the outbreak or compassion for the hundreds of victims. In effect, the message failed to characterize the company as caring or willing to serve the public need, and thus lacked character. (p. 20)

The spokesperson should present information clearly and avoid jargon. Some listeners misinterpret jargon as a means of avoidance or deliberate obfuscation (Reynolds & Earley, 2010). Hence, the spokesperson needs to explain the details of the crisis in a nontechnical manner that can be understood by a broad audience (Coombs, 2015).

Finally, the spokesperson must be able to handle difficult questions from the audience. These can include one or more of the following five scenarios:

- *Long and complicated questions.* The spokesperson should ask for the question to be repeated or rephrased.
- *Multiple questions.* The spokesperson should reconstruct the question in smaller parts, perhaps numbering each part so that the audience can follow the explanation better.
- *Tricky or challenging questions.* Difficult inquiries are often designed to make the spokesperson look incompetent. Some questions may not have a clear answer, and the spokesperson will need to point this out.
- *Questions that are based on incorrect information.* The spokesperson must identify erroneous assumptions early on
- *Multiple-choice questions based on alternatives that are limited or unacceptable.* The spokesperson must determine whether the response options are fair or not (Coombs, 2015).

Some "questions" are statements that express a viewpoint or a grievance. When this occurs, a good response might be something like, "This sounds more like a comment, not a question. Perhaps these are some items that can be discussed in a separate venue outside of this session." Indeed, all crisis spokespersons must be aware of the bully questioners and respond to them respectfully, but directly.

When handling difficult questions, a spokesperson must have the ability to remain calm under pressure. During a crisis, the organization may be criticized, often unfairly, by the media, elected officials, or customers. Such was the case for Connective Power Delivery, a distributor of electric power in the mid-Atlantic region, including parts of New Jersey, Maryland, and Delaware. In September 2003, Hurricane Isabel swept through the area and knocked out power to 400,000 customers. Although the company worked hard to restore power quickly, some criticism was received from external stakeholders. Yet, Connective Power Delivery president Tom Shaw took the "high road" and focused on restoring power instead of worrying about unwarranted criticism (Brown, 2003).

The organization should also arrange backup spokespersons if the designated one is not available (Barton, 2001; Coombs, 2015). The organization must still speak with one voice, even if more than one spokesperson is required. Alternate spokespersons may also be needed if the crisis lingers. Also, some experts advocate designating a team of spokespersons from the outset. This situation will occur if the organization's audience is unusually diverse or if extensive expertise is needed to explain the crisis response in a more detailed manner (Gainey, 2010).

Communicating with the Media

Some managers mistakenly assume that members of the media inherently seek to discredit the organization when a crisis occurs (Parsons, 2016; Sherman, 1989). While some in the press harbor a skeptical view of business organizations, the media can help the company reach essential audiences (Weiner, 2006). Members of the media are more likely to misrepresent a situation when they lack the facts. The result often depends on what the organization chooses to say early on. We recommend cooperating with the media as much as feasible, while understanding that journalists are trained to be inquisitive (Barton, 2001; Sherman, 1989; Wailes, 2003). Providing periodic updates to the media and directly through social media is also helpful. When developing the media message, the organizational spokesperson should be trained to deliver the news consistently. In some instances, detractors—and perhaps competitors—will find "experts" who can blame the company. Organizations should be prepared to confront these claims. Crisis communication preparedness includes utilizing third-party experts who can address the media to support the organization's position and endorse its response to the crisis (Wailes, 2003).

News conferences should be arranged and managed by those with expertise in press relations. The following guidelines are offered for the organization's spokesperson in preparing for a news conference (Barton, 2001, 2008).

1. The spokesperson should continually practice and rehearse, based on potential questions asked by the media.
2. The spokesperson should seek to develop rapport and be candid with members of the media.
3. The spokesperson should avoid canned speeches and instead strive for a presentation that is more conversational and spontaneous.

4. Technical experts should be used, if necessary, to clarify to the public details about the crisis. This person can also serve to field technical questions from reporters that may be beyond the scope of the regular company spokesperson's knowledge.
5. The spokesperson should maintain calm and concern, and not become angry over questions from reporters.
6. The spokesperson should always report the truth. No attempt should ever be made to mislead the press.
7. The media should be alerted several hours before a news conference occurs. Late morning or early afternoon conferences are ideal since they give managers ample time to prepare.

One phrase that should be avoided when addressing the media is "no comment." The crisis communication literature is consistent in making this recommendation for several reasons. First, "no comment" raises skepticism and implies that the company is hiding something or is guilty as charged (Parsons, 2016; Vise, 2005). There are some situations where specific information cannot be divulged, at least not initially. For example, there may be an ongoing criminal investigation, and revealing details of the inquiry may damage the case. If there has been an incident where employees or customers have been injured or died, the next of kin must be notified first before revealing their identities publicly. Under these circumstances, the spokesperson must clarify that some information must be withheld until it is authorized for release (Valentine, 2007).

The "no comment" suggests a lack of concern and disrespect to victims and other stakeholders. It also forces journalists to seek information from other sources, including those who view the organization unfavorably (Barton, 2001; Coombs, 2015). When this occurs, the company loses credibility. For example, disgruntled former employees may be more than willing to talk to a reporter about alleged safety problems at the manufacturing facility where they used to work.

Truthfulness is essential, even when all the facts cannot be revealed publicly. Communicating negative facts may be painful, but hiding them usually delays the inevitable and expands the damage.

Communicating with Customers

Customers are the lifeblood of any business because they represent cash flow. They are free to abandon their relationships with the organization at any time. Companies can keep customers' loyalty by being truthful, responding to product or service complaints, and giving them the proper information concerning a crisis. When the facts are properly explained, customers tend to be more understanding. However, when they have not been given an appropriate explanation of a crisis problem, especially if there is a consumer complaint involved, credibility issues arise. They may search for other vendors (Grégoire, Tripp, & Legoux, 2011).

Poor communication with customers can result in unpleasant consequences for any organization. Utility companies are especially aware of customer concerns' importance because they must communicate with frustrated customers without power. Matt (2004) illustrates this dilemma with the story of customers beating a utility truck with baseball bats when power had not been restored after a hurricane.

A mixed-media approach to communication reinforces te company's position. Posting updates on company websites and social media platforms is common and expedient. Press releases can also be archived on the website for all to view. School systems use this approach to alert students and parents about class cancellations due to inclement weather and other factors. Power companies notify customers via text message or phone before, during, and after a significant storm. Although most customers might access updates posted online, some constituencies might not.

Crisis Communications Content

We have explored the communication strategies directed to internal and external stakeholders. We now turn to content. Coombs's (2007) Situational Crisis Communication Theory (SCCT) represents a common response strategy. SCCT provides four categories of responses, which Coombs labels postures: denial, diminishment, rebuilding, and bolstering.

Denial Posture

The **denial posture** attempts to remove the link between the organization and the crisis and includes three response strategies:

- *Attacking the accuser* involves confronting the person or group that has identified the organization with the crisis at hand. The crisis response is to be forceful and possibly retaliate against the accuser.
- *Denial* involves communicating that no crisis exists and explaining why.
- *Scapegoating* involves blaming another person or group for the crisis.

Diminishment Posture

The **diminishment posture** attempts to soften the link between the organization and the crisis. The response does not deny that a crisis exists but downplays the organization's involvement. Two response strategies are in this posture:

- *Excusing* involves minimizing the role of the organization regarding the crisis at hand. Communication may focus on denying that the organization wanted to hurt anyone or by emphasizing its limited control over the crisis.
- *Justification* involves diminishing the crisis's damage by suggesting that things are not as bad as they seem.

Rebuilding Posture

The **rebuilding posture** attempts to improve the organization's reputation. Two response strategies are in this posture:

- *Compensation* represents more of an action than a communication response; in that, the company compensates the crisis victims.
- *Apology* involves publicly apologizing for the crisis and asking forgiveness.

Bolstering Posture

The **bolstering posture** attempts to build a definite connection between the organization and its stakeholders. It may be used in conjunction with one of the other three postures. There are three response strategies associated with bolstering:

- *Reminding* involves pointing out the organization's past good works to stakeholders.
- *Ingratiating* involves praising the organization's stakeholders.
- *Victimage* explains how the organization was also a victim of the crisis.

The second component of SCCT is the identification of crisis types by the level of responsibility. Coombs (2007) identifies three categories, which he calls clusters: victim, accidental crisis, and preventable.

- Crises in the victim cluster have little attribution to the organization, meaning the company is not responsible for what happened; instead, it was also a victim of the crisis. Examples include natural disasters, rumors, workplace violence, and malevolence (e.g. computer hacking).
- Crises in the accidental cluster have some connection with the organization, meaning the company is probably culpable. Examples include challenges from stakeholders and technical-error accidents such as equipment failure.
- Crises in the preventable cluster involve active involvement of blame on the organization's part, meaning the company is directly responsible. Examples include human-error accidents (e.g., an employee causes the accident resulting

in harm), human-error product harm (e.g., a product that can injure or kill a customer), and organizational misdeed (e.g., a company decides to cut expenses results in workplace safety problems).

Given the four postures and three types of crisis clusters outlined above, crisis managers should identify the posture strategies appropriate to the crisis at hand. Table 8.1 summarizes Coombs' (2007) strategy selection recommendations.

Table 8.1 Recommended SCCT Strategies by Crisis Cluster

Posture/Strategy	Best Used For
Denial • Attacking the Accuser • Denial • Scapegoating	**Crises in the Victim Cluster** - when the link between the crisis origin and the organization is weak or nonexistent. The denial strategy is only used for rumors and challenges when the challenge is unwarranted.
Diminishment • Excusing • Justification	**Crises in the Accident Cluster** - when the link between the crisis origin and the organization is present, but not strong.
Rebuilding • Compensation • Apology	**Crises in the Preventable Cluster** - when the link between the crisis origin and the organization is strong.
Bolstering • Reminding • Ingratiation • Victimage	**Supplementing the other strategies on an as-needed basis.** The victimage strategy is only recommended for the victim cluster.

Adapted from Coombs (2007).

Denial strategies are used to address crises in the victim cluster, while diminishment strategies are primarily for crises in the accident cluster. Rebuilding strategies are used to resolve crises in the preventable cluster, while bolstering strategies are employed to supplement the other strategies as needed.

Coombs (2007) offers a caveat to the three clusters regarding how stakeholders perceive the organization's attribution to the crisis. If the organization has a prior history with the crisis, stakeholders will perceive its blame as more severe, what Coombs calls the Velcro effect. Likewise, if the organization already has image problems, then the crisis will have a more severe impact on the company's reputation. In practical terms, this means that a recurring crisis that was poorly managed before may move the company to the next level of higher attribution. Some stakeholders might perceive an accident crisis as preventable.

The SCCT model is one of the most cited and researched frameworks in the crisis communications literature (An & Cheng, 2010). The model focuses on the content of crisis communications messages sent to stakeholders. We now shift our attention from content to evaluating the medium of exchange used in the crisis management landscape. We have addressed legacy media in the first part of the chapter. Next, we examine social media and how it has affected the crisis management landscape.

Social Media and the Crisis Management Landscape

Social media was once considered an alternative communication outlet. Today, it has evolved into a widely used source of news and participation by many stakeholders. It has even been labeled "stakeholder-controlled media" (Hunter, Van Wassenhove, &

Besiou, 2016) for a good reason. Many stakeholders, mostly external, take part in social media attacks on companies. Social media adds three dimensions to crisis management: (1) news travels faster, (2) news travels farther (Gonzalez-Herrero & Smith, 2010), and (3) news shared in social media is often irrational and reactive rather than analytical and reasoning-based (Lambret & Barki, 2018). Because social media content is subject to bias, the concept of sensemaking should be overviewed.

The Concept of Sensemaking

Social media posts are attempts to describe, rationalize, and opine on an event. Social media users must make sense of all posts, including those that are merely reactions to an event, not reasonable assessments (Lambret & Barki, 2018; Stieglitz, Bunker, Mirbabaie, & Ehnis, 2017). Hence, all posts are subject to interpretation, even those that appear objective.

Sensemaking enables the CMT to function more effectively. Reacting to inaccurate news, fake news, or speculations is usually not advisable. With social media, the charge for the CMT is more complicated. Put differently, how does the CMT respond to stakeholder reactions to inaccurate news, fake news, or mere speculations? Thus, sensemaking takes on two dimensions, making sure the CMT is performing the sensemaking function effectively, and helping stakeholders do the same. Evaluating the integrity of social media posts—discerning truth, partial truths, opinions masking as truth, and outright falsehoods—is indeed a challenge.

While most individuals view themselves as rational, they are guided by emotional and irrational biases and take shortcuts in decision-making (i.e., heuristics). As discussed previously, heuristics simplify decision-making by applying decision rules. For example, one heuristic might suggest that something familiar is also safe (Steinmetz, 2018).

Another might suggest that the first items listed in a Web search are the most accurate and relevant, although this is not always true. Because social media is fraught with simple technology and information overload, the typical user must employ various heuristics to process the vast amount of information that is available (Lin, Spence, Sellnow, & Lachlan, 2016). While this approach is efficient, it is not always desirable because people fail to critically evaluate what they see online. The result has been termed "online gullibility," a state whereby people fail to ask important questions about the content they encounter online (Steinmetz, 2018). For example, a heuristic often referenced as the "confirmation bias" suggests that we tend to believe new information or evidence that affirms our existing beliefs while ignoring sound, contrary evidence. This manner of thinking can lead some to believe stories that are really "fake news" (Hou, 2018).

Crisis managers must make sense of the social media bombardment of tweets, blogs, YouTube videos, Facebook posts, and forums and respond appropriately. They also need to remember that their stakeholders follow heuristics and believe fake news, false accounts, and incorrect assumptions about a crisis. Tailoring the crisis response to its intended audience is more challenging than ever in this changing crisis management landscape.

Twitter and Facebook as a Sounding Board

Organizations and individuals can "tweet" or post on Facebook their viewpoints, news items, and share anything they find interesting. Like other social media platforms, news travels fast, far, and wide. A high-profile case at the University of Virginia illustrates the power of Twitter and Facebook (Gruber, Smerek, Thomas-Hunt, & James (2015). On Friday, June 8, 2012, President Teresa Sullivan was asked to resign by the Board of Visitors after serving two years. The board believed she was not leading the university in a strategic manner. In contrast, Sullivan was advocating a more incremental approach to change, a strategy she thought was suitable for an academic environment. However, outside support for President Sullivan was strong, and the battleground for that support occurred primarily in social media via Twitter, Facebook, and YouTube. This support was unanticipated, and under tremendous pressure from stakeholders, the board reinstated Sullivan on Tuesday, June 26, 2012. Posts on Twitter and Facebook contributed to her reinstatement. This example illustrates how information on Twitter, YouTube, and Facebook can inform constituencies about a crisis or create a new one. The impact of social media has intensified ever since.

Blogging

Blogs can convey negative news and opinions and should receive special consideration. Bloggers (i.e., social media influencers) who have significant followings can quickly reach a broad audience. These online audiences can then convey their thoughts and opinions on a topic or event to their online friends and colleagues.

Bloggers are often viewed as citizen journalists, but one need not have any journalistic expertise to circulate an opinion electronically. This situation creates challenges for crisis managers who must distinguish between bloggers who warrant attention and those who do not. The principles of media relations that apply to journalists can also apply to some bloggers. In the past, some public relations professionals created media lists of journalists who were their contact points. Similarly, crisis communicators must now view bloggers as another key stakeholder to establish ongoing two-way communication. Just as traditional media relations strategies revolve around building trust with the media, managers must now earn bloggers' trust (Ziemnowicz, Harrison, & Crandall, 2011).

In an early example of a blogging crisis, well-known blogger Jeff Jarvis wrote about his poor customer service experience with computer maker Dell. The company responded slowly but eventually hired a blog specialist to help the company address the mounting negative publicity. Company founder Michael Dell even caught up with Jarvis at a social gathering and apologized for its poor customer service performance (Conlin, 2007; Flynn, 2009).

In March 2007, Home Depot was the target of an onslaught of negative publicity when MSN money columnist Scott Burns stated that the company was a "consistent abuser" of the customer's time. Within hours, the comment section to MSN was filled with similar stories from customers who were tired of the poor service they received at Home Depot due to staff cutbacks. Altogether, there were more than 10,000 angry emails and 4,000 posts criticizing its poor service (Conlin, 2007). CEO Francis Blake responded by going online and apologizing for the poor showing of the company. He promised to improve staffing and even thanked Scott Burns for his critique. Indeed, negative news on a company can travel quickly even when it originates from a single source. In this event, influential columnist Scott Burns triggered this online media crisis (Ziemnowicz et al., 2011).

Consider the Pink slime case discussed previously. Beef Products Inc. (BPI) manufactures lean finely textured beef, a common low-fat additive to ground beef products. Food blogger Bettina Elias Siegel noticed the term *pink slime* in a news article

 referencing lean finely textured beef. She responded by launching an online petition to ban the federal school lunch program (Gruley & Campbell, 2012). Soon *ABC News* covered the story, and the blogosphere became active as various stakeholders weighed in on the product.

Lean finely textured beef is made by running scraps of meat through a process that eliminates the fat and is treated with ammonia to kill bacteria such as *E. coli* and salmonella. It is used as a filler for ground beef, low-fat hot dogs, pepperoni, frozen meat entrees like meatballs, and canned foods. McDonald's, Taco Bell, and Burger King used lean finely textured beef until 2012 (Bloomgarden-Smoke, 2012). There has never been a health-related crisis associated with the product, which has been available for two decades and is considered safe by the US Department of Agriculture (Gleason & Berry, 2012). Nonetheless, this social media-related crisis hurt the lean finely textured beef industry.

Living in a YouTube World

One of the earliest examples of a major social media-induced crisis occurred on Easter Sunday in April 2009, when two Domino's employees posted a video on YouTube showing one of the employees sticking cheese up his nose and then putting it on a sandwich. The video received nearly 1 million views before it was taken off YouTube the following Wednesday, but not before it earned the infamous name "Boogergate" (York & Wheaton, 2009).

Domino's addressed the crisis by targeting the audience that would be most aware of it, those who learned about it on YouTube. Patrick Doyle, president of Domino USA, responded in a YouTube video stating, "We sincerely apologize for this incident. We thank members of the online community who quickly alerted us and allowed us to take immediate action. Although the individuals in question claim it's a hoax, we are taking this incredibly seriously," he said, also adding that the company is revamping its selection processes so that "people like this don't make it into our stores" (York & Wheaton, 2009, p. 24).

Public relations experts praised Domino's for its tactics in handling the crisis in what was considered a landmark case in crisis management (Beaubien, 2009; Johnson, 2009;

York & Wheaton, 2009). The Domino's incident illustrated the merit in the adage of "learning to fight fire with fire." In this case, Domino's used its own YouTube video to counter a YouTube-induced crisis to best respond to concerned consumers (Zerillo, 2009). This case also illustrates that a public apology on YouTube is now considered part of a company's arsenal in its response to social media crises (Sandlin & Gracyalny, 2018).

The Domino's case underscores how social media can make any firm vulnerable. YouTube offers the viewer a video of almost any adverse event that can be recorded. Many organizational crises have erupted as a result of videos appearing on YouTube. For example, some companies discover a product was defective only when someone aired a YouTube video about it. Consider Kryptonite, a maker of heavy-duty locks for bicycles and motorcycles. In September 2004, unexpected publicity resulted when an online video post revealed that a ballpoint pen could open the company's locks. In just a few days, the company faced enormous negative Internet-generated hype, resulting in a recall of their locks and an estimated $10 million in lost sales (Kirkpatrick, Roth, & Ryan, 2005; Moore, 2005).

In November 2008, Johnson & Johnson (J&J) placed an online ad featuring a voice-over of a mom saying she carries her baby in a sling because it makes a "fashion statement." The ad contained a short cartoon showing how carrying a baby in a sling can be a bonding experience for the mother and child and cause back pain, hence, the need for Motrin pain reliever. However, a small group of online moms complained that the ad was offensive. Some moms vented their outrage by posting their own YouTube videos asking the company to pull the offensive ad. J&J removed it shortly after its airing (Johnson, 2009).

The crisis response by J&J to remove the ad was strategic, even though the negative reaction to it was quite small:

> *Mommy bloggers and Twitterers make up a tiny fraction of the US population, 0.15% in the case of Twitter. It just happens that a large number of that 0.15% work in advertising and media. A not-insignificant number of mommy bloggers have worked in advertising or media. In essence, this was a ready-made media firestorm.*
> *(Wheaton, 2008, p. 12)*

Company mistakes are now going to become very public for quite some time. "It's a transparent world—get used to being seen living in it" (Edwards, 2008).

Crises linked to offensive products and advertisements are common. Consider several examples in 2018. Shortly after Hennes & Mauritz (H&M) launched a children's hoodie sporting the phrase "coolest monkey in the jungle" modeled by a black child, the company apologized and created a new diversity and inclusion team. After a Mercedes-Benz Instagram post quoting the Dalai Lama created a backlash in China—where he is widely viewed as a separatist—the company apologized for the "deeply hurt feelings of the Chinese people." An advertisement in Russia highlighting women's products featured a woman in Adidas workout apparel with the tag line, "move from the pressure of man's approval to a man's face." Parent-company Reebok pulled the ad after some viewers perceived sexual overtones (Germano, 2019).

A famous case involving YouTube concerned an event with United Airlines. In the spring of 2008, Canadian musician Dave Carroll was traveling with his band from Canada to Nebraska when the neck of his guitar was damaged by baggage handlers. Not only was his guitar damaged, but he witnessed the event while waiting on the plane during a connection at Chicago's O'Hare airport. Carroll informed three different United employees in Chicago of the event, but none took any action or responsibility. After the flight, Carroll spent nine months trying to get United to pay for the repair, to no avail. Frustrated over this chain of events, Carroll and his band wrote and performed a song, "United Breaks Guitars," and posted it on YouTube on July 6, 2009. The song eventually amassed 8 million hits and created a vast public relations embarrassment for United Airlines. United finally offered compensation for the repair and changed its operations procedures (Grégoire et al., 2011).

The United case illustrates how a customer can try to resolve a service mistake with a company. Carroll's efforts to fix the problem over nine months were not taken seriously by United. During this time, few knew of the event, which could have been easily remedied by the airline. United's decision to stick with its policies rather than correct an obvious mistake prompted Carroll to become a YouTube whistleblower.

> *Customers typically engage in online public complaining when firms fail to address direct complaints. Such instances are also called "double deviations." That is what happened in Dave Carroll's case. Before he went public, he aimed to solve this problem in direct contact with United Airlines—he even tried for nine months! (Grégoire et al., 2011, p. 28)*

The concept of the **double deviation**, mentioned in the previous quote, makes the United case different from the J&J Motrin ad crisis and the Kryptonite bike lock incident. J&J and Kryptonite both sought to remedy their crises soon after they occurred. On the other hand, United entered a crisis on its own and took several years to resolve it. All three cases illustrate how negative news travels both fast and far on social media.

User Forums and Hidden Crises

Forums are another source of hidden crises for the organization. Forums are typically question and answer sessions on a topic. For example, a car repair forum can help diagnose a problem with a vehicle. Forums can contain a wide assortment of useful and extraneous information. However, when factual statements about product problems are repeated on forums, a crisis can occur.

DuPont Professional Products experienced a product crisis that first surfaced on a user forum. The product was called Imprelis, an herbicide introduced in 2011. However, on the LawnSite.com user forum, news was spreading that the herbicide damages trees adjacent to the treatment area. DuPont had commissioned 400 scientific studies on the product, but crowd-sourced data generated by user forums identified serious product downsides. Users shared photographs and damage reports that even DuPont was unaware of (Hunter, Van Wassenhove, & Besiou, 2016). Eventually, the *New York Times* published a story on the dangers Imprelis could pose to healthy trees (Robbins, 2011). The US Environmental Protection Agency eventually banned the product.

The Imprelis example underscores the importance of information asymmetry in a crisis. Customers who used the product had more experience and, hence, information than DuPont. There are times when social media hides the problem from management, making it a latent crisis that suddenly erupts at an inopportune time.

Social Media and Crisis Communications

Social media has yet to reach its potential as a crisis management communications tool (Lin et al., 2016). Still, there are many lessons to be gleaned from its use. These are discussed next.

Utilize Social Media as a Tool in the Crisis Communications Plan

Many companies now embed social media tools into their websites. Blogs and YouTube videos are apparent additions that can make a company's site more interactive. Also, many organizations have a Facebook page that attempts to reveal a more personal side. Tweeting is also being used more as a communication tool from a company perspective. Whereas social media is dynamic and aimed at the human side of the Internet audience, corporate Web pages, by contrast, are meant to showcase the company's products, services, and, to some degree, its history. Web pages offer only one-way communication and usually an opportunity to purchase something. Social media makes the company more personable by providing two-way communication with its external stakeholders.

The CMT should develop a crisis communication plan that specifies how it will use social media tools during a crisis. Larger companies usually have in-house staff, whereas smaller firms may require help from social media specialists. Three of the companies discussed previously—Dell, Home Depot, and Dominos—utilized social media to counter crises. Conventional media outlets and a positive social media presence are essential. During a crisis, both outlets can disseminate messages to stakeholders. Although Twitter permits only short posts, communicators can use the outlet to link readers to Internet sites providing details of the organization's response (Ziemnowicz et al., 2011).

Social media tools should meet the standards of redundancy and consistency (Morton, 2014). From a social media perspective, redundancy means that multiple social media tools should be used when stakeholders use different outlets. Not all will get the message if just one tool (e.g., Twitter) is employed. Consistency means the same message should proliferate across all social media outlets. Also, when the message is updated, all the tools should be updated simultaneously otherwise stakeholders will have conflicting information at their disposal.

Respond Quickly and Accurately

Publicly responding to an organizational crisis within 24 hours was once considered the standard. Today, the acceptable response time has been reduced to hours or minutes in some instances. It took Domino's more than 24 hours to respond with its now-famous YouTube video of Patrick Doyle speaking on the crisis. Tim McIntyre, vice president of communications for Domino's, commented:

> *So, you post a video on YouTube featuring the president of an iconic brand within 48 hours of a hoax video being posted by two idiots. And the [criticism] of this has been amazing to me—because on one hand, we're lauded for doing something unprecedented, something that had never been done before [posting only a YouTube response]. And yet, we didn't do it fast enough. And yet nobody has been able to answer: How can you do something that's never been done before, but not fast enough? (Jacques, 2009, p. 9)*

The social media world demands that organizations respond quickly, and not commenting online can be interpreted as a "no comment" response from the company (Taylor & Perry, 2005), a taboo that raises suspicion in crisis communications (Gonzalez-Herrero & Smith, 2010). Dominos did not use Twitter when the crisis occurred because it was not used widely at the time. Today that is no longer the case as Twitter is a critical component of organizational crisis communications.

Monitor the Various Social Media Outlets

Organizations should periodically monitor relevant social media to identify potential problem areas with products, services, or company reputation (Eriksson, 2018). The

Imprelis example illustrates the importance of tracking user forums that may be using a specific product. There are user forums that focus on certain products and brands, and these can be a source of invaluable information to management (Hunter, Van Wassenhove, & Besiou, 2016). Research suggests that Twitter is the most important social media tool to monitor (Eriksson, 2018; Gaspar et al., 2014).

Pick Your Battles

When a crisis occurs, some stakeholders will never be satisfied, no matter what the organization does to appease them. It is essential to distinguish between a *dissatisfied customer* (who can eventually be satisfied) and a *troll* (who will never be satisfied). "Dissatisfied customers can be approached personally and want to change their minds about something. Bigger fights only satisfy trolls. Bloggers have learned to ignore trolls...PR professionals must develop the same skill—pick your battles" (Johnson, 2009, p. 24).

Dave Carroll, discussed previously in the United Airlines case, was an example of a dissatisfied customer. He simply wanted United to compensate him fairly for his broken guitar. United lost an opportunity to satisfy a grieved customer. However, some websites and blogs are maintained by trolls. Such websites are sometimes called *rogue sites, sucks sites,* or *anti-websites* (González-Herrero & Smith, 2008).

Evaluating the Success of the Crisis Communication Process

Chapter 9 focuses exclusively on organizational learning that must take place after a crisis. In this section, we briefly address the assessment of the organization's crisis communication responses. The evaluation process provides information and facts that build a knowledge base that promotes learning. This process of evaluation is critical because it determines which actions were effective. Hence, the reality of crisis management (and thus, communications) is that some aspects of implementation may be successful, while others will be unsuccessful (Pearson & Clair, 1998).

In the evaluation phase, crisis managers focus on the successes and failures of the crisis communication process. For example, after the severe hurricane season of 2005, many retail chains began reassessing their crisis communications. The successes and failures in this area have led management to implement changes in communication during a crisis. Some retailers now utilize sophisticated technological applications, including GPS (global positioning systems) and satellite telephones so that they can stay in touch with employees during a crisis (Amato-McCoy, 2007).

Debriefing and Post-Crisis Analysis

After a reasonable interval following the crisis, the CMT should meet to evaluate the organization's crisis response. Written notes should provide an assessment of internal and external communications. They should also include an evaluation of how the company communicated with the media and how the media portrayed the company. Documenting this process and evaluation is essential to retrieve the materials for later referral and continuous learning.

The team should make recommendations for improving crisis communications function. Bovender and Carey (2006) provide a summary of how HCA's (Hospital Corporation of America) Tulane University's hospital assessed its crisis responses and communications after Hurricane Katrina. Key observations made during this hurricane concerning telephone usage included:

- Cell phones may not work after a disaster such as a hurricane.
- Cell phones seeking to call area codes outside of the disaster area might work better than those cell phones calling area codes inside the disaster area.
- Digital phone lines will go down when a building loses power; therefore, some analog phones should be kept on hand.
- Amateur radio operators can often fill the void when other types of technical communication systems fail.
- Communication between headquarters (in this case, HCA is based in Nashville) and the field office (Tulane Hospital is in New Orleans) should be regularly scheduled. In this case, hourly phone calls were made during the most critical period of the crisis.
- Ironically, there were no problems with long-distance calls, but local ones were impossible (Bovender & Carey, 2006).

A case involving the death of a professional wrestler employed by the World Wrestling Entertainment (WWE) illustrates how crisis communications can falter after a tragic event. On Sunday, June 24, 2007, the bodies of WWE wrestler Chris Benoit, his wife, and son were found in their Atlanta home. Benoit was to appear on the WWE's televised *Monday Night Raw* the next day, but due to the tragedy, the event was canceled. Vince McMahon, CEO of WWE, aired a tribute to Chris Benoit instead, out of courtesy to the employees of the WWE and Benoit's family. During the tribute, McMahon eulogized Benoit as one of the greatest wrestlers of all time (Walton & Williams, 2011). At this point in the crisis, though, the exact circumstances surrounding the death had yet to be determined.

Unknown to McMahon or the WWE, police determined that Benoit had murdered his wife and son by asphyxiation before hanging himself. The timing could not have been worse for airing the tribute to Benoit. The WWE was left with an embarrassing situation; the very person they had honored on Monday was considered a murderer on Tuesday, the night of the next WWE broadcast. Furthermore, speculations were now running rampant that Benoit had succumbed to steroid abuse or "'roid rage" (Mosconi, Quinn, & Nichols, 2007). This news item had created a second crisis for the WWE, as critics, including the US Congress, began to question them about its drug policies. In hindsight, an assessment of the WWE's crisis communications concluded that, although the tribute showed respect to his family, employees of the WWE, and the fans, it was aired without having full knowledge of the deaths. It was an honest mistake, but a mistake nonetheless (Walton & Williams, 2011).

In summary, the post-crisis evaluation process should lead to revised plans that can be used in future crisis communication preparations and responses. The evaluation can also indicate where crisis communication training may need to be improved.

Crisis Communication Training

The CMT is responsible for coordinating the training efforts needed to ensure that relevant organizational members have the necessary knowledge of crisis management procedures. Medium-sized and large organizations should take advantage of the training expertise these human resource departments can offer.

When crisis communications training is considered, the burden usually shifts from human resources to the organization's marketing or public relations departments. Staff members in these departments spend their time promoting the company and its products, which prepares them for crisis communications training (Barton, 2008).

Legacy Media Training

Legacy media training prepares a spokesperson to communicate effectively with newspaper, magazine, and television reporters. The company spokesperson should remember that journalists make a living conducting interviews. From this perspective, a company spokesperson is like an amateur taking on a professional (Blyth, 2009). Hence, media training is an absolute must, even for staff with good speaking abilities. One perspective is to approach training through four basic types of instruction: (1) discussion and staging, (2) instruction, (3) simulation and drama, and (4) evaluation (Caponigro, 2000).

Discussion and Staging

This training involves viewing videos and reading news reports with the intention of comparing effective and ineffective spokespersons. The emphasis of this training is to evaluate the effects their comments have on the audiences. There is a famous crisis training video involving a television interview with former Exxon CEO Lawrence Rawl shortly after the 1989 *Exxon Valdez* oil spill in Alaska. The interview took place on the

Good Morning America show with anchor Kathleen Sullivan. It did not go well for Rawl, who was being pushed to answer questions about Exxon's plan to clean up the oil spill. At one point, Rawl accuses Sullivan of creating a public relations nightmare for Exxon (Lentini, 2009).

Instruction

Modules in this segment instruct the participants about the "behind the scenes" activities in a news organization. These lessons help crisis spokespeople understand media needs and the deadlines they must meet. As such, the spokesperson can learn to express what the CMT needs to communicate while simultaneously providing the media with the information they need.

Simulation and Drama

This training typically involves responding to potential questions that may be asked by media representatives. Rehearsing can help the spokesperson become confident with stressful questions (Coombs, 2015). Barton (2008) recommends an approach whereby the CMT develops "the worst 20," the 20 most disturbing questions a spokesperson could be asked after a crisis occurs. This part of the training can also occur in a private television studio where participants become accustomed to the necessary tools and techniques used in a television interview.

Evaluation

This element of the training focuses on areas that need improvement. Learning from past successes and mistakes is an essential part of becoming an effective media spokesperson (Caponigro, 2000).

Spokespersons must learn how to limit comments to a few well-chosen vital messages. Media training instructs the participants to identify those key messages correctly and then to articulate them successfully. Effective training can help representatives confront a succession of different questions that might arise in print and broadcast interviews (Wailes, 2003).

Summary

The crisis management team oversees the function of crisis communications. When a crisis commences, a command-and-control role must be established by the team. Communicating to employees is especially important because they are company ambassadors during the crisis. The organization should not withhold information from employees, as they are the ones who have the most contact with customers and the general public.

Communicating with external stakeholders such as customers, the media, and the public will need to take place at several levels. For formal press conferences or interviews, a spokesperson will need to be designated well in advance of any crisis. This person should be carefully chosen and must display the appropriate traits for being a high-profile representative of the company. Social media outlets should also be considered in the crisis communications strategy. Using the proper outlet—such as the organizational web page, YouTube, Facebook, or Twitter—will help reach the widest audience, including those who may have firsthand knowledge of the crisis.

The effectiveness of the crisis communications function should always be evaluated during the post-crisis stage, where organizational learning needs to occur. Finally, appropriate training can improve crisis communications.

Discussion Questions

1. How can effective crisis communication help organizations manage a crisis more favorably?
2. How does communicating to internal stakeholders differ from communicating to external stakeholders?
3. What problems can occur with crisis communications directed to internal stakeholders (i.e., within the organization)?
4. What examples of the "mushroom analogy" of communication have you witnessed in organizations?
5. What traits should a company spokesperson possess? What examples of poor spokespersons have you seen?
6. How can social media impact a crisis? What examples can you provide beyond those addressed in the chapter?
7. How would you prepare for a news conference if you were the spokesperson and your organization had just experienced a severe industrial accident?
8. How can the crisis management team evaluate the effectiveness of its communications?

Chapter Exercise

This exercise can familiarize you with the various types of crises that are emerging because of social media. This activity can be done in groups if the class is large and time is limited. Otherwise, each student in the class should identify a video about an organizational crisis that has surfaced on YouTube. Each student should answer the following questions:

- Why is this event considered to be a crisis? Remember the book definition of a crisis presented in Chapter 1.
- If this event had not been recorded on YouTube, would it have still been a crisis?
- What is the nature of the comments that accompany the YouTube video? Are they justified? Do you see any patterns in the comments?
- What is the nature of the blame that is being assigned in the videos and comments sections? Is the organization being blamed? If so, is it justified? Is there another party involved that is to blame for the crisis?

Closing Chapter Case: United Airlines Wants you OFF the Plane! - Part 2

Dr. David Dao suffered a concussion, a broken nose, and two broken teeth during his removal from United Express Flight 3411. The violent treatment of Dr. Dao rattled United Airline's CEO Oscar Munoz. Ironically, Munoz was honored in 2017 as "Communicator of the Year" by *PRWeek*, a major communication outlet (Selk, 2017). However, his communication skills were about to be tested with this crisis. Appearing on *Inside Edition*, Munoz noted after the crisis, "We let our policies and procedures get in the way of doing the right thing" (Carey, 2017, p. B1). Munoz later apologized for United's handling of the event and took ownership of the problem: "Things happened in so many places, there was no particular breakdown I can't and shouldn't take ownership of" (Carey, 2017, p. B2).

United Enters Crisis Management Mode

To its credit, United Airlines took the incident seriously and shifted into crisis management mode. CEO Oscar Munoz commented: "I continue to be disturbed by what happened on this flight and I deeply apologize to the customer forcibly removed and to all customers aboard. No one should ever be mistreated this way. I want you to know that we take full responsibility, and we will make it right" (Baker, 2017, pp. 1, 24).

United conducted an internal investigation of its processes and generated an 11-page report of its findings (*United Express Flight 3411 Review and Action Report, 2017*). In the report, United noted the following internal failures:

- The airline had no policies governing practice if a customer refused to depart an aircraft for reasons not associated with security. United had never encountered this type of situation before.
- Gate agents were limited by the amount of compensation they could award a passenger who was being bumped from a flight.

- There was a lack of training on how to help employees manage a situation involving denied boarding situations.

United made sweeping changes in its policies involving overbooked flights in the future. A summary of some of their new policies appears below:

- Law enforcement will not be used to remove passengers unless it is a matter of safety and security.
- Passengers already seated will not be asked to give up their seat involuntarily unless it is a matter of safety and security.
- Compensation incentives for voluntary denied boarding can be as high as $10,000.
- Training for gate agents will be provided to help them address difficult situations.
- An automated system will be implemented that gauges a customer's interest in voluntarily giving up their seat in exchange for compensation.
- Overbooking will be reduced for flights with smaller aircraft and those that are the last flight of the day to a destination.
- Flight crews that are traveling to other destinations will be booked at least 60 minutes before departure. (United Express Flight 3411 Review and Action Report, 2017).

Other airlines learned from the United debacle. Southwest Airlines vowed to eliminate overbooking. In 2016, Southwest had the highest involuntary denied boarding rate of all passenger airlines (Shine, 2017). Delta Airlines increased its compensation for denied boarding to $9950 (Goldstein, 2017), while American Airlines promised not to ask a passenger to depart an aircraft after being seats. American also gave its gate agents more flexibility in offering compensation to those who are denied boarding (Baker, 2017).

Final Aftermath

United reached an amicable settlement with Dr. David Dao, the terms of which were not disclosed (Goldstein, 2017). Two Chicago Department of Aviation security officers were fired as a result of the incident. A department report revealed that the officers mishandled a non-threatening situation and provided misleading statements in their reports documenting the event (Lui, 2017). United recovered from the crisis, however. Although the airline experienced a massive public relations crisis, its stock hit an all-time high within a month after the incident (Huddleston, 2017).

Case Discussion Questions

1. Identify and discuss the positive changes in the airline industry that occurred because of this crisis.
2. Sometimes, governments mandate changes in an industry after a crisis occurs. For example, after the terrorist attacks of September 11, 2001, the US government enacted many new safety regulations regarding air travel. However, in the United Airlines case, airlines responded without government pressure. Why do government mandates occur after some crises but not others?

References

Amato-McCoy, D. (2007). Ensuring continuity. *Chain Store Age, 83*(6), 50.

An, S., & Cheng, I. (2010). Crisis communication research in public relations journals: Tracking research trends over thirty years. In W.T. Coombs, & S. Holladay (Eds.), *The Handbook of Crisis Communication* (p. 65). Boston, MA: Wiley-Blackwell.

Argenti, P. (2002). Crisis communication: Lessons from 9-11. *Harvard Business Review, 80*(12), 103–109.

Baker, M. (2017, May 15). Airlines after David Dao. *Business Travel News, 34*(7),1,24.

Barton, L. (2001). *Crisis in organizations II.* Cincinnati, OH: South-Western College Publishing.

Barton, L. (2008). *Crisis leadership now: A real-world guide to preparing for threat, disaster, sabotage, and scandal.* New York: McGraw-Hill.

Beaubien, G. (2009). Domino's YouTube flap: "A landmark event in crisis management." *Public Relations Tactics, 16*(5), 4.

Berinato, S. (2010). You have to lead from everywhere. *Harvard Business Review, 88*(11), 76–79.

Bloomgarden-Smoke, K. (2012, March 27). "Pink Slime": Health crisis or misunderstood meat product? *Christian Science Monitor.* Retrieved August 31, 2019, from http://www.csmonitor.com/USA/2012/0327/Pink-slime-Health-crisis-or-misunderstood-meat-product

Blyth, A. (2009, February). A word in your ear . . . *Training and Coaching Today,* 10.

Bovender, J., Jr., & Carey, B. (2006). A week we don't want to forget: Lessons learned from Tulane. *Frontiers of Health Services Management, 23*(1), 3–12.

Brown, T. (2003, Winter). Powerful crisis communications lessons: PR lessons learned from Hurricane Isabel. *Public Relations Quarterly,* 31–33.

Caponigro, J. R. (2000). *The crisis counselor: A step-by-step guide to managing a business crisis.* Chicago: Contemporary Books.

Carey, S. (2017, April 27). United cites litany of failures. *The Wall Street Journal*, B1.

Conlin, M. (2007, April 16). Web Attack. *Business Week,* 54–56.

Coombs, W. (2007). Ongoing crisis communication: Planning, managing, and responding (2nd ed.). Thousand Oaks, CA: Sage.

Coombs, W. (2015). *Ongoing crisis communication: Planning, managing, and responding* (4th ed.). Thousand Oaks, CA: Sage.

Edwards, J. (2008, November 17). J&J triggers mommy war with Motrin "anti-baby sling" ad. Retrieved November 13, 2018, from http://www.bnet.com/blog/drug-business/j-j-triggers-mommy-war-with-motrin-8216anti-baby-sling-8217-ad/212

Eriksson, M. (2018). Lessons for crisis communications on social media: A systematic review of what research tells the practice. *International Journal of Strategic Communication, 12*(5), 526-551.

Flynn, M. (2009). First response: The importance of acting within minutes, not hours. *Public Relations Tactics, 16*(4), 13.

Gainey, B. (2010). Crisis leadership for the new reality ahead. *Journal of Executive Education, 9*(1), 33–43.

Gaspar, R., Gorjao, S., Seibt, B., Lima, L., Barnett, J., Moss, A., & Wills, J. (2014). Tweeting during food crises: A psychosocial analysis of threat coping expressions in Spain, during the 2011 European EHEC outbreak. *International Journal of Human-Computer Studies, 72*(2), 239-254.

Gerchick, M. (2013). *Full upright and locked position: Not-so-comfortable truths about air travel today.* New York/London: W.W. Norton and Company.

Germano, S. (2019, February 20). Brands learn to defuse outrage. *Wall Street Journal*, p. B3.

Gleason, S., & Berry, I. (2012, April 3). Beef processor falters amid "slime." Wall Street Journal, p. B2.

Gnage, M., Dziagwa, C., & White, D. (2009). *Community College Journal of Research and Practice, 33,* 948–950.

Goldstein, M. (2017, December 20). Biggest travel story of 2017: The bumping and beating of Dr. David Dao. Forbes. Retrieved, October 27, 2018, from https://www.forbes.com/sites/michaelgoldstein/2017/12/20/biggest-travel-story-of-2017-the-bumping-and-beating-of-doctor-david-dao/#68e906eef61f

González-Herrero, A., Smith, S. (2008). Crisis communications management on the Web: How Internet-based technologies are changing the way public relations professionals handle business crises. *Journal of Contingencies and Crisis Management, 16*(3), 143–153.

Grégoire, Y., Tripp, T., & Legoux, R. (2011). When your best customers become your worst enemies: Does time really heal all wound? *New Insights, 3*(1), 27–35.

Gruber, D., Smerek, R., Thomas-Hunt, M., & James, E. (2015). The real-time power of Twitter: Crisis management and leadership in an age of social media. *Business Horizons, 58*, 163-172.

Gruley, B., & Campbell, E. (2012, April 16). SLIMED: Was a food innovator unfairly targeted? *Bloomberg Businessweek,* 18–20.

Hopper, N. (2017, April 24). United's no good, very bad day – and what it means for all of us. *Time, 189*(15), 22.

Hou, J. (2018, February 6). How to combat fake news to build trust and protect your reputation. *Communication World Magazine*, 1-3.

Huddleston, Jr. (2017, December 15). Shortest-lived existential crisis: United Airlines. *Fortune*, p. 8.

Hunter, M., Van Wassenhove, L., & Besiou, M. (2016). The new rules for crisis management. *MIT Sloan Management Review*, (Summer), 71-78.

Jacques, A. (2009). Domino's delivers during crisis: The company's step-by-step response after a vulgar video goes viral. *The Strategist, 15*(3), 6–10.

Johnson, C. (2009). Social media in crisis: Blog and Tweet your way back to success. *Public Relations Strategist, 15*(2), 23–24.

Kirkpatrick, D., Roth, D., & Ryan, O. (2005, January 10). Why there's no escaping the blog. *Fortune,* 43–50.

Klophaus, R., & Pölt, S. (2006). Airline overbooking with dynamic spoilage costs. *Journal of Revenue and Pricing Management, 6*(1), 9-18.

Lambret, C., & Barki, E. (2018). Social media crisis management: Aligning corporate response strategies with stakeholders' emotions online. *Journal of Contingencies and Crisis Management, 26*, 295-305.

Lentini Jr., A. (2009). After it hits the fan. *Risk Management, 56*(5), 42–47.

Lin, X., Spence, P., Sellnow, T., & Lachlan, K. (2016). Crisis communication, learning and responding: Best practices in social media. *Computers in Human Behavior, 65,* 601-605.

Lui, K. (2017, October 18). The officers involved in a United Airlines passenger's forced removal have been fired. *Time.com,* p. 18. Retrieved November 10, 2018 from http://time.com/4987015/united-airlines-ua-david-dao-passenger-removal-fired/

Madhani, A., & Janega, J. (2007, April 17). Slow reaction spurs anger. *Chicago Tribune,* p. A1.

Maggart, L. (1994). Bowater incorporated: A lesson in crisis communication. *Public Relations Quarterly, 39*(3), 29–31.

Magnuson, S., & Parsons, D. (2014, January). Crisis mass communications to enter new age. *National Defense,* p. 14.

Marquez, J. (2005, October 10). The best-laid disaster plans are merely works in progress. *Workforce Management Online*. Retrieved November 13, 2018, from https://www.workforce.com/2005/10/10/the-best-laid-disaster-plans-are-merely-works-in-progress/

Matt, M. (2004). Crisis communication in the eye of the hurricane. *Electric Light and Power, 82*(7), 30, 39.

McLaren, J. (1994). Bowater's Calhoun Mill at center of fog-related highway pileup dispute. *Pulp and Paper, 68*(8), 79–80.

Moore, A. (2005, Autumn). Are you prepared for the power of the blogosphere? *Market Leader, 30,* 38–42.

Morton, J. (2014). How to warn occupants about active shooters. *Buildings, 108*(9), 44-48.

Mosconi, A., Quinn, T., & Nichols, A. (2007, June 27). Rage roid have him on ropes? Steroids found in house where wrestler, his wife and son died. *New York Daily Times,* p. 17.

Nelson, J. (2004, July). Crisis communication, coordination in the program. *Security, 41*(7), 68.

Parsons, J. (2016, May 9). What should you say when the press calls? *Risk Management,* CBQ10-CBQ12.

Pearson, C., & Clair, J. (1998). Reframing crisis management. *Academy of Management Review, 23*(1), 59–76.

Premeaux, S., & Breaux, D. (2007). Crisis management of human resources: Lessons from Hurricanes Katrina and Rita. *Human Resource Planning, 30*(3), 39–47.

Reilly, A. (2008). The role of human resource development competencies in facilitating effective crisis communication. *Advances in Developing Human Resources, 10*(3), 331–351.

Reynolds, B., & Earley, E. (2010). Principles to enable leaders to navigate the harsh realities of crisis and risk communication. *Journal of Business Continuity and Emergency Planning, 4*(3), 262–273.

Robbins, J. (2011, July 14). New herbicide suspected in tree deaths. *The New York Times,* p. 1.

Sandlin, J., & Gracyalny, M. (2018). Seeking sincerity, finding forgiveness: YouTube apologies as image repair. *Public Relations Review, 44,* 393-406.

Scanlon, J. (1975). *Communication in Canadian society*. Toronto, Ontario: B. D. Singes.

Seeger, M., Sellnow, T., & Ulmer, R. (1998). Communication, organization and crisis. In M. E. Roloff & G. D. Paulson (Eds.), *Communication yearbook* (Vol. 21, pp. 231–275). Beverly Hills, CA: Sage.

Selk, A. (2017, April 10). A man wouldn't leave an overbooked United flight. So, he was dragged off, battered and limp. *The Washington Post*. Retrieved October 30, 2018, from https://www.washingtonpost.com/news/dr-gridlock/wp/2017/04/10/a-man-wouldnt-leave-an-overbooked-united-flight-so-he-was-dragged-off-battered-and-limp/?utm_term=.e349a2fcded0

Sherman, S. (1989, June 19). Smart ways to handle the press. *Fortune,* 69–75.

Shine, C. (2017, April 27). Southwest Airlines will stop overbooking flights, CEO says. *The Dallas Morning News*. Retrieved November 10, 2018, from https://www.dallasnews.com/business/southwest-airlines/2017/04/27/southwest-airlines-ceo-says-company-will-stop-overbooking-flights

Siddappa, S., Rosenberger, J., & Chen, V. (2007). Optimizing airline overbooking using a hybrid gradient approach and statistical modeling. *Journal of Revenue and Pricing Management, 7*(2), 207-218.

Spillan, J., Rowles, M., & Mino, M. (2002/2003). Responding to organizational crises through effective communication practices. *Journal of the Pennsylvania Communication Association* (Pennsylvania Communication Association Annual), *58/59*, 89–103.

Steinmetz, K. (2018, August 20). The real fake news crisis. *Time, 192*(7), 26-31.

Stieglitz, S., Bunker, D., Mirbabaie, M., & Ehnis, C. (2017). Sensemaking in social media during extreme events. *Journal of Contingencies and Crisis Management, 26*, 4-15.

Taylor, M., & Perry, D. (2005). Diffusion of traditional and new media tactics in crisis communication. *Public Relations Review, 31*(2), 209–217.

United Express Flight 3411 Review and Action Report (2017, April 27). Retrieved November 10, 2018, from https://s3.amazonaws.com/unitedhub/United+Flight+3411+Review+and+Action+Report.pdf

Valentine, L. (2007). Talk is not cheap. *ABA Banking Journal, 99*(12), 38–41.

Veil, S., Liu, M., Erickson, S., & Sellnow, T. (2005). Too hot to handle: Competency constrains character in Chi-Chi's green onion crisis. *Public Relations Quarterly, 50*(4), 19–22.

Vernon, H. (1998). *Business and society: A managerial approach* (6th ed.). New York: Irwin McGraw-Hill.

Vise, A. (2005). Going beyond "no comment." *Commercial Carrier Journal, 162*(6), 38.

Wailes, C. (2003). Crisis communication 101. *Business and Economics Review, 50*(1), 13–15.

Walton, L., & Williams, K. (2011). World Wrestling Entertainment responds to the Chris Benoit tragedy: A case study. *International Journal of Sports Communication, 4*(1), 99-114.

Weiner, D. (2006, March/April). Crisis communications: Managing corporate reputation in the court of public opinion. *Ivey Business Journal, 1*–6.

Wheaton, K. (2008, December 1). Middle road in Motrin-gate was right choice. *Advertising Age, 79*(44), 12.

York, E., & Wheaton, K. (2009). What Domino's did right—and wrong—in squelching hubbub over YouTube video. *Advertising Age, 80*(14), 1, 24.

Zerillo, N. (2009). Crisis forces Domino's to revamp social media plan. *PRWeek, 12*(16), 1, 20.

Ziemnowicz, C., Harrison, G., & Crandall, W. (2011). The new normal: How social media is changing the way organizations manage a crisis. *Central Business Review, 30*(1–2), 17–24.

Chapter 9: The Importance of Organizational Learning

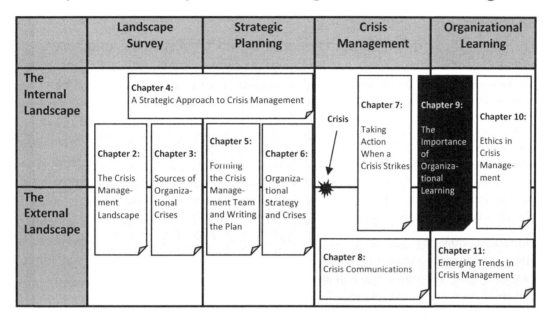

Learning Objectives

After reading this chapter, each student should be able to:

1. Define organizational learning.
2. Differentiate between single and double-loop learning.
3. Identify and describe the five components needed to build a learning organization.
4. Describe the post-crisis learning opportunities that can occur by examining the landscape survey, strategic planning, crisis management, and organizational learning phases of the crisis management framework.
5. Explain what is meant by degrees of success in crisis learning.
6. Identify and describe the barriers to organizational learning.

Opening Chapter Case: Crisis Brews at Starbucks - Part 1

Managing a restaurant is not easy. Many stakeholders are invested in the success of the business, but some can pose a potential threat. Employees can be untrustworthy or dishonest, and at their worst, can bleed the company of inventory, cash, and customer goodwill. A customer can post complaints on social media about the food and service they received, an act that can spread negative news far and wide. A vendor can provide spoiled or contaminated food products that can cause sickness. All of these are industry-specific examples and are potential crises that can disrupt operations and, in some cases, lead to failure.

On April 12, 2018, Starbucks encountered a different kind of stakeholder-induced crisis at its Rittenhouse Square store in Philadelphia, Pennsylvania. Although there was no physical damage or any human injury, the company suffered an unexpected blow to its reputation but, more importantly, prompted the arrest of two innocent young men who were waiting on a friend inside the store. The crisis stemmed from a Starbucks employee's decision to ask the two men, Rashon Nelson and Donte Robinson, to leave the store. Neither Nelson nor Robinson had purchased anything. The men refused, so a store manager called the police, and officers eventually arrested them for trespassing and took them to jail (Joffe, 2018). It is not uncommon for restaurants to deny seating or access to restroom facilities to non-customers. This practice is usually not a concern when it involves only a small percentage of store traffic. Still, Starbucks has developed a reputation as a favorite "hangout," and the growing number of non-customers in some stores had become a problem (Jargon & Feintzeig, 2018a, 2018b). Nonetheless, the optics for Starbucks were not positive.

The arrest was captured on social media and immediately went viral. Many accused Starbucks of racial bias and discrimination for initiating the arrests. However, this explanation was inconsistent with the company's professional, progressive, and inclusive philosophy. Ironically, Starbucks had demonstrated a commitment to racial justice and eliminating any bias in their restaurants (Marszalek, 2018). Still, the constant broadcast and the social media reports seemed to tell a different story.

The public perception of the event evolved into a discourse on race, as some perceived it as an attack on the black community. The Black Lives Matter movement officially condemned the incident as an example of how unfounded fear arises when black males are present in white spaces (Joffe, 2018). Many called for the boycott of Starbucks, and protestors confronted management at the Rittenhouse Square store and demanded that the manager who called the police be fired. This protest resulted in a temporary closure of the restaurant. Indeed, there was trouble brewing at Starbucks.

Case Discussion Questions

1. Starbucks is not the only retailer to restrict restroom access to paying customers only. Many retailers follow a similar practice citing security concerns. From a crisis management perspective, how should an establishment protect the safety of its store, customers, and employees if non-customers are allowed access to the restrooms?
2. When should managers call police about customer behavior?

Introduction

Although it is common to think of a crisis as a negative event, it provides an opportunity for learning and change in the organization (Brockner & James, 2008; Wang, 2008). A crisis should have the capacity to shock an organization out of its complacency (Veil & Sellnow, 2008). New perspectives can be developed that hedge the organization against future crisis attacks. The Chinese concept of a crisis views it as both a dangerous situation and an opportunity for improving (Borodzicz & van Haperen, 2002). Those who do not learn from a crisis may recall the adage that those who ignore history are doomed to repeat it and thus are likely to be visited by similar crises in the future (Elliott, Smith, & McGuinness, 2000).

Unfortunately, human nature seems to prevent some managers from addressing a crisis before substantial damage has already occurred (Nathan, 2000). When a crisis ensues, learning from it can be haphazard at best. The research that addresses crisis learning is limited but growing (Broekema, van Kleef, & Steen, 2017).

What Is Organizational Learning?

Organizational learning is the process of detecting and correcting errors (Argyris & Schön, 1978). It seeks to improve the organization's operation by reflecting on past experiences (Sullivan & Beach, 2012). In the context of crisis management, learning should occur when the organization experiences a crisis. Learning should have both cognitive and action dimensions that promote more effective crisis management (Broekema et al., 2017). However, learning does not always originate from a crisis because some organizations do not learn effectively. A distinction between single-loop and double-loop learning is relevant. Barriers to organizational learning are discussed at the end of this chapter.

Single-Loop Learning

Single-loop learning refers to detecting and correcting an error without changing basic underlying organizational norms (Argyris & Schön, 1978). Suppose you are driving your car in a snowstorm, and you suddenly lose control of your vehicle. You sense your car is now veering left into oncoming traffic. To avoid hitting an oncoming vehicle, you steer the car away from the center lane, but in the process, you sense you are now turning too far to the right and running the risk of going off the road. You set your wheels again, this time to the left, so that you are back on the road. You are careful not to turn your wheels too far to the left lest you head into oncoming traffic again. The process of steering to the right and then to the left is an example of single-loop learning. The corrections were made instinctively by responding to the current driving conditions in the best way possible based on the established norms of driving.

Learning from a Structure Fire

Firefighting is an example of an emergency process that involves single-loop learning. For instance, in fighting a structure fire, one must determine how much water to use. A firefighter should increase or decrease the volume of water and adjust the spray pattern according to the location and size of the blaze. Also, a minimal amount of water will be used to extinguish the fire not to cause excessive damage to the property. If possible,

firefighters will enter the structure and attempt to "push" the fire farther away from the building, meaning they will spray the fire with water in the direction of an open window or door. This type of attack extinguishes the fire more quickly and minimizes property damage but doing so increases the risk of injury to the firefighter entering the burning building. If a structure is hopelessly consumed by the fire and entry into the building is not feasible, then the fire department will launch a defensive attack known as "surround and drown." In this procedure, the firefighters are positioned outside and aim their hoses onto the fire and the structure. In this instance, there is little attempt to save the property, only to extinguish the fire.

In the previous example, firefighting principles are the same regardless of the type of structure fire encountered. Any learning that occurs is based on adjustments made along the way. For instance, if the firefighter thinks more water is needed, they will increase the volume by adjusting the hose's nozzle. Alternately, another hose (called a line) may be utilized to supplement the amount of water on the fire. Firefighting principles do not change in single-loop learning during a fire, only the decisions regarding items such as water volume, pressure, or the type of attack (i.e., interior vs. exterior).

Single-loop learning is illustrated in figure 9.1. In this example, an interior attack is initiated on a fire, which quickly escalates out of control despite the firefighters' best efforts. They learn from the situation that they must exit the building and use a series of more massive lines so that an increased volume of water can be distributed on the fire, thereby extinguishing the blaze. Note that the basic underlying assumptions of firefighting have not changed; hence, it is an example of single-loop learning. In the next section, we employ another example of firefighting to illustrate double-loop learning.

Figure 9.1 – Single-Loop Learning in Fighting a Structure Fire

Underlying Assumptions Used in Fighting a Structure Fire	Actual Strategies Used in Fighting a Structure Fire in Chronological Order	Outcomes in Chronological Order
Increase or decrease the volume of water depending on the size of the fire. Adjust the spray pattern of the water stream: straight stream or fog pattern. Use as little water as possible so that property damage is minimized. Seek an interior attack on the fire as a first strategy. Open the roof so that smoke can escape the structure, and the firefighters inside can see better. Use an exterior (defensive) attack only if an interior strategy is not working or possible.	1. Firefighters use an interior attack with one hose (line).	1. The fire is not suppressed.
	2. Firefighters add a second line on the fire.	2. The fire is not suppressed and, instead, escalates.
	3. Firefighters exit the structure and utilize a larger line outside the building to extinguish the fire.	3. The fire is suppressed partially, but not sufficiently.
	4. Firefighters add a second line on the fire.	4. The fire is extinguished.
	In this example, single-loop learning takes place as the firefighters learn and adapt to the fire. However, no underlying assumptions are changed in the strategies used to fight the fire. The assumptions in the left column remain viable.	

Double-Loop Learning

Double-loop learning involves detecting and correcting an error, but there is also a change in the basic underlying organizational norms (Argyris & Schön, 1978). Such learning usually occurs after a process of thoughtful reflection (Kolb, 1984). This type of learning changes the organizational culture and the cognitive arrangement of the company. "Based on an inquiry or some form of crisis, the organization's view of the world will change and, so, stimulate a shift in beliefs and precautionary norms" (Stead & Smallman, 1999, p. 5). Such a change in beliefs can cause organizational leaders to rethink the "It couldn't happen to us" mentality whereby managers feel immune to a crisis (Elliot et al., 2000, p. 17). As Stead and Smallman point out, this evaluation–rethinking process has come to be known by different terms, including "double-loop learning" (Argyris, 1982), "un-learning" (Smith, 1993), and "cultural readjustment" (Turner & Pidgeon, 1997). When these deeper learning processes are applied to crisis learning, the perception that a crisis cannot occur, and that the organization is invulnerable usually diminishes.

Learning from the Hagersville Tire Fire

Double-loop learning can also take place as a crisis unfolds and escalates. The 1990 Hagersville tire fire in Ontario, Hagersville, illustrates how double-loop learning took place, not only in extinguishing the fire but also in how discarded tires should be managed. Tire fires are difficult to extinguish for several reasons. First, the shape of the tire allows ample airflow that can feed the fire. Second, tires are usually stored in large mounds that may be difficult to reach with conventional fire equipment. Finally, burning tires produce oil, which can ignite and add heat and flames to the existing fire (Mawhinney, 1990).

Traditional assumptions on firefighting had to be adjusted for the Hagersville fire. Simply adding water to the fire was not a workable option because of the complex nature of the blaze. First, the tires were stacked in large mounds, which made access difficult for firefighters. Initially, the strategy was to attack the fire from the perimeter and gradually advance toward the center of the burning tire pile. This strategy continued for seven days, but firefighters were unable to advance to the core of the fire with their hose streams or equipment because of the intense heat. When applying the concept of double-loop learning to this situation, firefighters began separate the tires into smaller batches and extinguish the overall blaze as a series of smaller fires (Mawhinney; 1990; Simon & Pauchant, 2000). Although this strategy worked, water runoff from the tires took oil with it, forming large puddles and threatening to contaminate the underground water supply. Addressing this situation required trenches, and sandbag barriers to direct the runoff water into temporary holding ponds. The oil was skimmed off the runoff water, which was pumped into tanker trucks to be treated at a local water treatment plant while the oil was sent to a refinery (Mawhinney, 1990).

In addition to the fire, a more profound, long-term problem had to be addressed. Should the government regulate the management of used tires? The Ministry of Environment in Canada did not act, except to impose an incineration ban. The local community was also concerned about the environmental aspects of the fire. Smoke produces toxic fumes, and the resulting water and foam from extinguishing a fire are also dangerous because it could seep into the groundwater supply (Simon & Pauchant, 2000). Attention focused on preventing another tire fire. Again, double-loop learning emerged as traditional assumptions on used tire management were being challenged. Figure 9.2 summarizes the discussion on the Hagersville fire and the role of double-loop learning.

Figure 9.2 – Double-Loop Learning in Fighting the Hagersville Tire Fire

Underlying Assumptions That Had to be Changed in Fighting a Tire Fire	Actual Strategies Used in Fighting the Hagersville Tire Fire in Chronological Order	Outcomes in Chronological Order
Perimeter firefighting strategies are the norm but must be changed to a divide-and-conquer approach.	1. Firefighters attempt a perimeter attack to advance to the core of the fire.	1. After seven days, the fire is still not suppressed.
The storage of tires in large piles must be replaced by arranging tires in small mounds.	2. Firefighters break up the massive piles of tires into smaller mounds for easier access with water lines.	2. The fire begins to be extinguished, although the process takes several more days.
Runoff water from a fire must now be managed and contained if it contains toxins.	3. Water and foam are found to be effective in extinguishing the fire.	3. Water runoff from extinguishing the fire contains oil, a substance not usually found in a structure fire but a problem in a tire fire.

In this example, single-and double-loop learning occurs as the firefighters learn and adapt to battling the blaze. Underlying assumptions are challenged and changed in the strategies used to fight the fire. The assumptions in the left column are malleable.

When traditional assumptions do not need to be challenged, then single-loop learning is beneficial. But when an organization enters unchartered territory, double-loop learning may be necessary. For example, Metallinou (2017) documented single and double-loop learning in a series of training exercises in the Norwegian onshore pipeline industry, which improved learning.

Learning from Failure

Learning from failures is another way that organizations have incorporated double-loop learning. Some organizations thrive in environments that should be at high risk for failure and a potential loss of life (Weick & Sutcliffe, 2001). Such organizations have been labeled **high-reliability organizations** (HROs) and include aircraft carrier flight decks, medical facilities, and firefighting incident command systems (Roberts & Bea, 2001). Extensive literature exists on HROs (Bourrier, 2011), and lessons from these organizations have permeated into industries considered less risky. This move is in the spirit of organizational learning, which seeks to improve critical activities and enhance performance based on an analysis of past events (Sullivan & Beach, 2012).

One of the hallmarks of HROs is their obsession with analyzing past failures to prevent future ones. For example, the 1967 accident on the USS *Forrestal* that killed 134 crew members has been studied extensively by the US Navy to prevent a similar catastrophe (Brunson, 2008). The event occurred when a Zuni rocket from a fighter jet accidentally discharged into a group of other aircraft on the flight deck. The resulting fire was a combination of burning jet fuel and detonating bombs from the remaining aircraft on deck. Much was learned from the mistakes made in the firefighting tactics on board that day. First, because some sailors were not trained to respond to this type of accident, mistakes were made fighting the fire, and proper equipment was not appropriately employed. Today, all sailors are trained as firefighters. Second, foam and water were not used effectively. Foam was used to smother the fire, a typical procedure for a fuel fire, but it was later removed by water sprayed by other firefighters. This action caused the fuel and the fire to spread into the bottom compartments of the ship.

Crew members using the foam also had to stop and read the directions on applying it correctly (Brunson, 2008). As a result of the USS *Forrestal* accident, the US Navy has upgraded its firefighting capabilities and has designated the Farrier Fire Fighting School in Norfolk, Virginia. The school is named after Chief Gerald W. Farrier, who died fighting the fire on the USS *Forrestal* that fateful day.

As this example illustrates, organizations should learn from failure and pass the lessons on to future staff and managers. Failure is a byproduct of organizational life and part of operating in a complex and changing world (Cannon & Edmondson, 2005). Confronting failure allows managers to reevaluate their assumptions on how a problem should be solved.

Building a Learning Organization

We cannot discuss organizational learning without acknowledging the work of Peter Senge and how it relates to learning in a crisis management context. Senge (2006) describes the components of the learning organization as systems thinking, personal mastery, mental models, building a shared vision, and team learning. Each of these is described next.

Systems Thinking

From a systems perspective, everything that occurs in an organization is influenced by something else. Likewise, the events the organization initiates influence other items or systems. This interconnectedness forces managers to think conceptually: How does one decision affect future decisions?

As we have seen, a crisis is not merely a random event. Instead, it is caused by many other movements of systems that culminate in a trigger event that initiates the crisis. Recognizing that an organization is part of a more substantial flow of activities helps the manager understand how crises emerge. Crisis events do not just occur; they evolve and are influenced by various systems. In the Hagersville tire example, we saw how the fire influenced several other systems. Smoke from the burning tires affected the air quality in the region. Water used to fight the fire contained oil runoff, which could contaminate drinking water if it seeped into the underground water supply. The fire was a system, affecting other systems as well. As the strategies were planned for fighting the fire, those leading the crisis response had to consider what other systems were being affected by their actions.

Personal Mastery

Personal mastery is the ability to see reality objectively. Without it, learning is not possible. Senge (2006) maintained that personal mastery could be developed. It is also an organizational skill set. Fostering this ability takes time, effort, and a commitment to discovering the truth.

Sensemaking occurs during a crisis as managers seek to assign meaning to events. However, there are times when a crisis is so bizarre that there is a collapse of sensemaking (Weick, 1993). This collapse can be caused by the loss of a frame of reference because nothing similar has occurred in the past. A loss of a frame of reference takes away one's ability to make sense of the world (O'Grady & Orton, 2016). The human response is one of fear and helplessness, the encountering of the fateful cosmology episode that has been discussed elsewhere in this book. As Weick (1993) put it, "I have no idea where I am, and I have no idea who can help me" (pp. 634–635). Nonetheless, decision-makers in charge of responding to a crisis should acknowledge their need to regroup to see the event as objectively as possible. This mindset can help the response to the crisis and begin to let the organization learn from the event.

Mental Models

The sets of assumptions and viewpoints that we carry in our thinking are called **mental models**. They are necessary because they help us make sense of the world. Organizations also have mental models that reflect the collective assumptions of their members. Mental models can be useful when they urge us to think creatively about the problems they face. Indeed, some managers thrive on thinking outside the box because they try to see possibilities behind every problem.

Mental models can also hamper crisis response and, ultimately, organizational learning. When managers insist that a crisis "cannot happen here," they exhibit a mental model of denial. Destructive mental models can exist even when crisis events repeatedly occur in the same organization. For example, scapegoating is a mental model that seeks to shift the blame to some other party. This mental model is a form of denial—not a healthy ingredient in an environment for learning.

Building Shared Vision

Building **shared vision** involves a collective agreement by members of the organization on its mission and goals. It includes a passion that employees show for the projects they work on and the role their company plays in society. Thus, when a crisis occurs, the whole organization is hurt because the collective vision has been attacked. As a result, efforts to confront the crisis and get the organization "back to business" are embraced enthusiastically. This response can explain why some communities immediately move into action when a disaster strikes. Cleanup crews hit the streets quickly, volunteers abound, and government visibility increases as everyone works together to overcome the crisis and return to a sense of normalcy.

When there is no shared vision, a crisis can make an organization highly vulnerable. A fragmented organization will not respond cohesively and may even attack itself as the crisis unfolds. Scapegoating may occur among organizational members. Many professional sports teams experience this type of crisis. The scenario is usually predictable; the team has a bad season or loses a big game, the owners and coaches become confrontational, and the players frequently complain about the owner, the coach, or fellow teammates. Ultimately, some players may demand to be traded. When this type of "venting" occurs, a public relations crisis is born as well.

Team Learning

Senge (2006) described a situation when an average group of managers could produce an above-average company, but the opposite is also true; a group of above-average managers can create a below-average company. Many crises originate because less-than-ideal dynamics occur among a group of otherwise competent professionals.

According to Senge (2006), the key to better team learning is to acknowledge the presence of dialogue. **Dialogue** is a deeper form of discussion through which new ideas originate from the group. In the end, the team becomes the learning unit for the organization and can reach new levels of performance that a group of individual managers might not achieve on their own. Dialogue is the prerequisite for double-loop learning because new assumptions may be required as old ones are discarded.

Dialogue is vital from a crisis management perspective. Crisis management teams (CMTs) are specialized units capable of doing more than just generating a list of potential threats and crisis plans. The crisis team is the unit that protects the organization, its mission, its values, and its reputation. Thus, the CMT is a strategic unit within the organization. Thinking of the CMT as just a committee or a staff department hampers its ability to promote authentic learning and long-term benefits for the organization. The status of the CMT must be elevated to a level at which it can attain strategic importance.

Learning from a Crisis

Learning from a crisis is easiest shortly after it has occurred. Waiting too long to extract lessons from a crisis could cause a sense of urgency for learning to wane (Kovoor-Misra & Nathan, 2000). Also, organizational learning cannot occur unless there is feedback

(Carley & Harrald, 1997). After a crisis, managers should reevaluate use feedback received during the event to reevaluate the CMP. They should determine why specific decisions were made during the crisis. Mechanisms such as debriefings, stakeholder interactions, and technology enable managers to capture and share information with members of the crisis management team. This information can be used in follow-up discussions to learn lessons and develop best practices.

We place organizational learning as the last stage in the four-stage framework. This placement is not to imply that learning does not take place in the early stages. As a formal activity, it is a reflective process that must take place after the crisis has ended. Early crisis management frameworks also posit that learning takes place toward the end of the crisis management process. For example, Pearson & Mitroff (1993) place "learning" as the fifth phase in their five-stage framework. Table 9.1 offers a framework for assessing the learning areas in crisis management. If learning is to be systematic, we must examine the four major categories of the crisis management framework and the internal and external landscapes associated with each one.

Table 9.1 – Potential Learning After the Crisis

	Landscape Survey	Strategic Planning	Crisis Management	Organizational Learning
The Internal Landscape	Were there warning signals missed before the crisis? Are there new vulnerabilities in our organization that we need to consider? Are there new methods of detection that we can use to sense an impending crisis?	Do we need to change the composition of our crisis management team? Are there aspects of the crisis management plan that need to be changed? Is there enough redundancy in the day-to-day operations of the company? Can the organization take advantage of new types of crisis training?	Were resources deployed effectively during the crisis? Did the organization's departments work together effectively? Are any improvements needed in the crisis communications function? Is there an adequate use of paper and electronic recording during the crisis?	Are the post-crisis debriefing meetings effective? Are we building systems that provide feedback?
The External Landscape	Are there new threats in the external environment that could lead to a potential crisis?	Are there additional resources in our industry or government that can help us in our crisis management planning?	How can we better partner with industry and government agencies in managing a crisis?	What can we learn from the best practices other organizations that have encountered similar types of crises?

Landscape Survey

The landscape survey phase of organizational learning focuses primarily on the crisis threats that existed. The following discussion considers the questions relating to the internal and external landscapes.

Were there warning signals missed prior to the crisis occurring?

The internal landscape survey looks inside the organization for emerging crisis vulnerabilities. Perhaps an equipment breakdown brought on the initial crisis. Have repairs on other equipment been overlooked? Maybe the crisis occurred when key personnel left the company, and their replacements were poorly trained, leading to a production accident. In this example, at least two problems are apparent: (1) why employees departed, and (2) why training was ineffective. Issues such as these indicate that human resource issues may require attention.

Are there new vulnerabilities in our organization that we need to consider?

Although not explicit in every crisis, organizational leaders should consider a critical internal vulnerability, the relationship between the organization and its mission. In his analysis of the sexual abuse problem within the Catholic Church, Barth (2010) noted that the protection of the church became more important than its real mission, serving its members. Unfortunately, this self-preservation mentality can hide a multitude of problems.

Are there new methods of detection that we can use to detect an impending crisis?

An analysis of the internal landscape may also reveal that new detection methods should be used to sense an impending crisis. Perhaps new accounting and financial controls are needed to detect potential sources of employee embezzlement and other types of fraud. As mentioned in Chapter 8, monitoring social media can detect problems before they become crises. Depending on the industry, a firm may identify specific ways to use technology to help detect an impending crisis.

Are there new threats in the external environment that can lead to a potential crisis?

The external landscape survey can also signal emerging vulnerabilities. A recent crisis might have been weather-related; in fact, droughts are frequent in the area where the authors reside. This situation has created water shortages and low-running wells. In a highly agricultural area like the southeastern United States, such an event is both a crisis for many organizations and a data point for a future crisis. An influx of new citizens prompted by the growth of a nearby military installation can compound this type of crisis. Fortunately, learning also occurs, and new plans to satisfy water needs are being developed, even if droughts continue in the future.

Strategic Planning

Organizational learning concerning the strategic planning process looks at changes that may be needed with the CMT, crisis management plan (CMP), and training requirements.

Do we need to change the composition of our crisis management team?

Organizational learning in the internal landscape may necessitate changes in crisis response plans. For example, the composition of the CMT may require revision. Some current members may not be suitable, while other employees may be excellent replacements. It may also be necessary to alter the size of the team. All members should be knowledgeable about social media, and at least one member should have expertise in this field.

Are there aspects of the crisis management plan that need to be changed?

The CMP can be revised at any time. Perhaps there are new scenarios that need to be added to the plan. The suitability of the command center should also be evaluated. The team should discuss whether the communication functions were readily available and whether the meeting rooms were suitable. Even a minor detail such as cell phone access is important because some cell phone users may not have access to certain parts of a building, such as a basement.

Is there enough redundancy in the day-to-day operations of the company?

It has been said that "repetition is the mother of learning." The principle of **redundancy** suggests that backup systems should be in place whenever feasible. The practice of redundancy in an organization's processes helps ensure that everyone understands their jobs and that there are backup systems for computers, files, and mechanical devices. Having a spare tire is an example of redundancy, although it might never be needed. At the organizational level, information technology (IT) professionals learned quickly and early that failure to back up their information systems could lead to disaster. The same is true in any organization. While redundancy is not necessary for every function, it is essential in those areas that are difficult to replicate. The organization prepared with backup systems can be resilient.

The same approach is appropriate for crisis management. When a specific process does not function well or at all, managers should have an alternate process that can substitute for the original. The following examples illustrate redundancy in crisis management:

- Methods of contacting the CMT during a crisis should include cell phones, landlines, text messaging, and email.
- The crisis management plan should be printed and made available on backup storage sites. A public institution such as a college, university, or school district may be required to post their plan on their website.
- The command center's primary location should be backed up by a secondary command center, and perhaps even a third site in case the first command center becomes inaccessible during a crisis.
- Alternate crisis team members can be designated if one or more of the original members are unavailable.

Redundancy is a common means of crisis preparation and avoidance. Backup generators may be available when the primary power is offline. Additional counselors may be put on standby after a significant event has occurred on campus, such as the death of a student. Battery-powered lights illuminate in the stairwells when the main power is unavailable. During the Y2K computer crisis, many organizations brought in extra food, water, and sleeping mats, just in case.

Can the organization take advantage of new types of crisis training?

Crisis management training may also need revising. Techniques and assumptions about managing the crisis should be reevaluated during such training. The reevaluation process begins with experience with a previous crisis. Managers reflect and learn from it, and then use it to plan for the next potential crisis. In learning theory, this process is referred to as "assessment," and more specifically, "closing the loop" (Martell, 2007). Striving for this stage is crucial because it facilitates continuous improvement in managing the next crisis.

Are there additional resources in our industry or government that can help us in our crisis management planning?

The external landscape can offer additional training opportunities that can fit the specific needs of the organization. For example, many workshops offered by industry associations and government agencies address workplace violence, a growing area of concern for organizations. In other areas of crisis prevention, various agencies, colleges and universities, and consulting groups are useful because they offer expertise that managers in the company may not possess.

Crisis Management

The crisis management stage addresses the crisis response. Organizational learning in this stage seeks to improve how the organization manages a crisis once it has commenced.

Were resources deployed effectively during the crisis?

Additional human and material resources may be needed to enhance the organization's capacity to respond to a crisis. In the 2007 Virginia Tech massacre crisis, communication was critical. Had more effective communications systems been in place, the number of fatalities might have been reduced (Reilly, 2008). Indeed, since the Virginia Tech massacre, many colleges and universities have updated their real-time communication networks so that faculty and students can be notified of a crisis in a moment's notice.

In another university-related crisis, the deployment of a material resource, pepper spray, was called into question during an Occupy Wall Street Protest at the University of California-Davis in November 2011. Campus police were called in to remove tents occupied by the protesters. During the operation, a group of students sat on a sidewalk and linked arms, refusing to stand. After repeated warnings to disperse by the police, two officers doused them with pepper spray. The event was recorded and appeared on YouTube, causing worldwide attention and creating a public relations nightmare for Chancellor Linda P. B. Katehi. Critics called for her resignation and challenged the campus police department for using pepper spray on a group of otherwise peaceful students (Stelter, 2011).

The pepper spray incident illustrates an ineffective use of resources, a fact later confirmed in a 190-page report by a campus task force. The report described campus leadership as inadequate in handling the event, and "the pepper-spraying incident that took place on November 18, 2011, should and could have been prevented" (Medina, 2012). The incident also highlights the challenges faced by any university president (often called a chancellor). Presidents are influential leaders who must set the strategic direction of their university. They must also reach out to external stakeholders in the area of fund-raising. And yet, the skill set of a president also includes crisis management ability. Some critics will call for a resignation even in the president has no control over the event. In this incident, the campus police department oversaw the command and control process, yet the chancellor was asked to resign. The extent to which she should be held responsible for events such as these is debatable. Nonetheless, the organization's leader has the responsibility to oversee what goes on throughout the university, which is difficult.

Did the organization's departments work together effectively?

Success managing a crisis is often a function of the degree of cooperation and interdependence that exists among various departments within and across organizations (Carley & Harrald, 1997). Interdependence is essential in resolving resource allocation issues and developing teamwork. When a crisis occurs, there should be a unified effort to keep the organization functioning effectively.

A mold outbreak in a university building illustrates the degree of cooperation that must take place. Indeed, the authors have been at two universities where this crisis has occurred. This not-too-uncommon scenario requires the redeployment of all personnel and activities from the building affected:

- The physical plant and maintenance department must set up the initial cleanup of the facility. The work is often contracted to an outsourced firm, but the university department must oversee all work and reconstruction. This department also coordinates any movement of materials, office supplies, and furniture.
- The Registrar's office identifies and assigns new classrooms.
- Deans communicate new location information for classes and offices to the affected students and faculty members.
- The university's public information department can disseminate information to students and faculty. Still, its primary goal is to communicate important news about the crisis to the general public and make sure the university is viewed positively.

Are any improvements needed in the crisis communications function?

Communication and cooperation across departments are important if a crisis is to be managed successfully. If there is any consolation, organizational learning can expose weaknesses in the crisis management practices and then follow-up with corrective action to resolve or eliminate the shortcomings. At that point, learning will be somewhat easier as participants try not to repeat their mistakes.

A classic case where communication messages had to be changed during a crisis involved the company Source Perrier. This French company bottled Perrier water in green bottles and faced a crisis in February 1990. Ironically, the problem was discovered by government inspectors in North Carolina who used bottled water as a diluting agent in its testing of local water samples. As the inspectors were testing the local water supplies, they found traces of benzene in their samples, diluted with Perrier water. Much to their surprise, they eventually discovered that the benzene originated not with the local water being tested, but with the Perrier water.

For Source Perrier, communicating to the general public information about the origin of the problem was a challenge. Two days after the initial detection, the company disclosed that a careless worker had used cleaner laced with benzene on a bottling line. Upon further investigation, a different reason for the problem emerged; carbon dioxide filters used in the bottling process had not been appropriately changed (Brookes, 1990). Benzene is a natural ingredient in carbon dioxide, thereby requiring filtration. Upon this revelation, Perrier revealed that there were *two* sources of their "naturally sparkling" water, not one. The water came from one source, while the gas originated from another. The two were combined during the bottling process. Thus, carbon dioxide was used to add an artificial boost of bubbles to a product that was inappropriately labeled "naturally sparkling." This disclosure forced the company to admit that its product was not what it claimed—natural sparkling water. Source Perrier was later required by the US Food and Drug Administration (FDA) to relabel its US-bound bottles "natural mineral water" ("Perrier relabeled," 1990).

Are the crisis records sufficient?

Most organizations use technology to supplement their traditional paper-based processes. During a crisis, it may be necessary to produce a status report on any aspect of the incident, regardless of whether it concerns people, premises, or press communications. Proper venues for recording information are necessary.

How can we better partner effectively with other firms and government agencies?

The external environment can offer learning opportunities through partnerships with industry and government agencies. At the community level, businesses can work with their local emergency service providers. Training opportunities often exist through which these providers conduct simulation drills at the business location. After a disaster, two or more cities may partner and change their emergency response structures to manage their obligations more effectively. Such was the case after the 1997 Red River Flood in Grand Forks, North Dakota. Timothy Sellnow and colleagues discussed how the flood prompted a reorganization of emergency services between the adjacent cities of Moorhead, Minnesota, and Fargo, North Dakota (Sellnow, Seeger, & Ulmer, 2002). On the positive side, cooperative structures between the two cities emerged after the crisis whereby crisis communication was centralized through Fargo's City Hall.

Crisis learning and subsequent partnerships are taking place in the oil industry after the British Petroleum (BP) Gulf of Mexico oil spill in 2010. Four oil companies— ExxonMobil, Royal Dutch Shell, Chevron, and ConocoPhillips—formed a joint venture to develop a Gulf of Mexico oil spill response and containment system. The four companies created a $1 billion pool to fund new equipment that will help prevent a future spill like the one that occurred to BP (Pfeifer & McNulty, 2011). The oil spill response and containment systems that are used to collect spilling oil were also enhanced.

Organizational Learning

Within the crisis management framework, organizational learning is the fourth stage in which post-crisis analysis takes place. Managers are debriefed, and possible improvements are discussed in this stage.

Are we making good use of post-crisis debriefings?

Within the internal landscape, the organization should learn from the crisis in a constructive manner (Lagadec, 1997). Specifically, how and what is the organization learning, and what changes are being implemented to prevent and mitigate future crisis events? Post-crisis debriefings offer a constructive venue for learning. First responders, consultants, and other outsiders can often help management learn objectively from the crisis.

Are we building systems that provide feedback?

Within the internal landscape, adequate feedback should be provided to others in the organization. Without feedback, learning cannot occur because an accumulation of knowledge that "sits" in a department of the organization cannot be useful in causing a cultural adjustment; it must be fed back to other parts of the organization (Smith & Elliott, 2007). Feedback must be channeled back to the landscape survey, strategic planning, and crisis management phases. The feedback loop brings in a separate but related concept in organizational learning: knowledge management.

Knowledge management is the process an organization uses to manage what it has learned (Alavi & Leidner, 2001). Knowledge must be routed, stored, and retrieved when necessary. Generally, there are two types of knowledge: explicit and tacit. **Explicit knowledge** can be codified and physically stored in databases, whereas **tacit knowledge** comprises individuals' experiences and mental models. This type of knowledge is manifested in the form of specific experiences, individual expertise, and intuition. Both knowledge forms require a feedback process so appropriate stakeholders can utilize them as needed (Racherla & Hu, 2009). Figure 9.3 illustrates the crisis feedback process.

What can we learn from the best practices in other organizations that have encountered similar crises?

Managers can learn from crisis events by observing the failures and crises of other organizations (Ulmer, Sellnow, & Seeger, 2007). The external landscape can yield numerous resources that can be useful to crisis managers. Books and articles on crisis management comprise one such resource. This book offers a framework for learning about crisis management, whereas journal articles and other reports tend to be more specialized and often highlight the best practices of specific companies. Many articles focus on lessons learned from a crisis. In addition to these outlets, some colleges and universities offer courses in crisis communications and crisis management. These have increased in popularity since the COVID-19 pandemic.

Figure 9.3. Crisis Management Feedback

	Landscape Survey	Strategic Planning	Crisis Management	Organizational Learning
The Internal Landscape	The CMT identifies the crisis threats the organization is facing.	The CMT develops the crisis management plan & leads training in crisis management.	The CMT actively manages the crisis when one occurs.	The CMT leads the post-crisis evaluation so that learning can occur.
The External Landscape	Industries and other external organizations identify crisis threats.	Industries and other external organizations engage in crisis management planning.	External organizations respond to a specific crisis.	The organization and other relevant stakeholders engage in learning activities.

Within the external landscape, crises related to safety problems resulting in fatalities will inevitably create regulatory changes. For example, the 2006 Sago Coal Mine accident in Sago, West Virginia, resulted in 12 miner fatalities after methane gas seeping from the mine walls caused an explosion. After the investigation, the Mine Safety Health Administration (MSHA) announced a new standard to increase the required strength of seals used to separate active and inactive sections of coal mines (Madsen, 2009). Unfortunately, one coal mining company, the now-defunct Massey Energy, choose to ignore safety regulations altogether and compromise miner safety. In this example, the company deliberately ignored the learning that had occurred in the mining industry. The Massey example is more a violation of business ethics than a lack of organizational learning. We explore the relationship between business ethics and crises in the next chapter.

Degrees of Success in Crisis Learning

Many organizations experience a combination of successes and failures when responding to a crisis. Table 9.2 depicts three levels of outcomes—failure, midrange, and success (Pearson & Clair, 1998). Each outcome is further distinguished by the degree of learning, future impact on the organization, and strategy posture toward crisis management. Companies that struggle with crisis management often do so because they fail to learn from previous disasters. Many continue to repeat their mistakes each time a similar crisis erupts. Such organizations are reactive, and therefore they are unable to learn because they are always in a state of surprise or, perhaps, nonchalance. Table 9.2 conveys the idea that learning success can vary among several ranges of outcomes.

Some companies will experience limited degrees of success in their crisis management practices and thus show some capacity for learning. A degree of learning is possible, but its applications will be sporadic. Therefore, certain areas in the organization will change for the better, while others might remain the same. In terms of a strategy posture, the firm is still reactive but shows some willingness and ability to learn.

A total learning organization is ideal but not always achieved. The hope is that the learning will enable the organization to respond more effectively to future crises.

Barriers to Organizational Learning

Learning is not a natural outcome of a crisis. Instead, many companies simply choose to return to the status quo as quickly as possible (Canon & Edmondson, 2005; Roux-Dufort, 2000). There are many reasons why this occurs. In the next section, we examine the more common reasons managers resist learning. Barriers to learning are approached from operational and cultural perspectives.

Operational Considerations

Operational considerations focus on issues related to the day-to-day functioning of the organization. This discussion includes an overreliance on programmed decisions, information asymmetry, and the tendency to ignore small failures.

Table 9.2 Levels of Learning Outcomes After a Crisis

	Failure Outcomes	**Midrange Outcomes**	**Success Outcomes**
Degree of learning	No learning occurs.	Learning occurs, but its applications are sporadic.	Learning occurs throughout the organization.
Future impact on the organization	The organization continues to make the same mistakes when similar crises occur.	Some areas of the organization may change for the better, while others remain the same.	The organization changes its policies and procedures. Learning is applied to future crisis events.
Strategy posture toward crisis management	The organization is reactive; unwilling or unable to learn.	The organization is reactive; willing to learn yet ill-equipped to do so.	The organization is proactive; willing to learn and take the knowledge to the next step by applying it.

Source: Adapted from Pearson and Clair (1998), p. 68.

Overreliance on Programmed Decisions

Programmed decisions—those based on some decision rule or prearranged logic—can be useful in many situations. They tend to work well when management decisions are routine and repetitious, such as reordering inventory when levels reach a prespecified number. Programmed decisions have also been built into specific crisis management procedures. For example, many organizations have a prearranged list of processes to follow when there is a bomb threat. These are designed to methodically protect assets and people (usually by evacuating the occupants from the building) while seeking as much information as possible about the person making the threat (e.g., taking note of background noises, extending the conversation with the caller to identify speaking patterns). Such programmed decisions are useful because they are systematic in their application.

Overreliance on programmed decisions can present a problem because it fosters resistance to change (Lester & Parnell, 2007). This situation can occur in companies where programmed decisions are used to promote efficiency. Because programmed decisions work, management may become complacent and fail to consider new approaches. This complacency can bleed into crisis management, especially when crisis planning is either ignored or is left to top management.

At the employee level, programmed decision making can lead to a work routine in which the worker becomes a "mindless expert," meaning they concentrate on the outcome instead of the task (Langer, 1989, p. 20). This dysfunction can result in a workplace accident or missing the cue for a crisis altogether.

Information Asymmetry

Information asymmetry exists when multiple parties (e.g., a manaufacturer and its customers) do not have the same information. It can occur when similar incidents involving the same technology transpire over a wide geographic area (Boin, Lagadec, Michel-Kerjan, & Overdijk, 2003). Moreover, different customers may have access to different information as well. The Therac-25 incidents from 1985 to 1987 illustrate this scenario (Leveson & Turner, 1993).

Therac-25 was a computer-controlled radiation machine that administered prespecified doses of radiation to cancerous tumors. The devices were offered by Atomic Energy Canada Limited (AECL) and were introduced in 1982. The machines operated flawlessly until a period between June 1985 and January 1987. During this period, six incidents occurred when patients received massive overdoses of radiation while undergoing treatment. Several of these patients later died (Leveson & Turner, 1993). What made the crisis especially perplexing was the lack of information transfer among the six medical centers using the Therac-25. Instead, each medical center reported the machine failure directly to the manufacturer, unaware that other medical centers were also experiencing problems. Figure 9.4 illustrates the information asymmetry.

The figure shows four different medical centers affected by overdoses of radiation caused by the Therac-25 machines. The incident that started the Therac-25 crisis occurred at Kennestone Regional Oncology Center in June 1985. The second incident occurred at Ontario Cancer Foundation in July 1985. Yakima Valley Memorial Hospital experienced episodes in December 1985 and in January 1987. East Texas Cancer Center experienced incidents in both March and April 1986. The radiation overdoses resulted in three fatalities and three other patients who suffered severe physical injuries (Fauchart, 2006).

As Fauchart reports in his analysis of the case, communication took place between each medical center and the manufacturer, but not among the four medical centers. Thus, the manufacturer, AECL, had complete information, but the four medical centers did not. Hence, potential learning opportunities at each of the four medical centers were not possible. Fauchart (2006) maintains that this information asymmetry could have been avoided:

> *The manufacturer should have informed all the users that many accidents had occurred, but he did not. Instead, he told every user who asked for information about other possible incidents. He thus used the information asymmetry to pretend that each accident was a fluke, thereby delaying the focus of a learning process aimed at fixing the problem and preventing other accidents from occurring (p. 101).*

Small failures are routinely ignored

Small incidents ignored by managers can lead to more substantial incidents or crises (Cannon & Edmondson, 2005; Smith, 1993; Veil, 2011). Such events can be understood as warning signals of a more significant crisis on the horizon. They can also be likened to an incubation stage when the crisis is growing, mostly unnoticed by organizational members (Seeger, Sellnow, & Ulmer, 2003; Veil, 2011). The BP oil disaster in the Gulf of Mexico that resulted in the deaths of 11 workers was an example of a series of smaller construction-related problems that were routinely ignored.

Figure 9.4 The Problem of Information Asymmetry During the Therac-25 Crisis

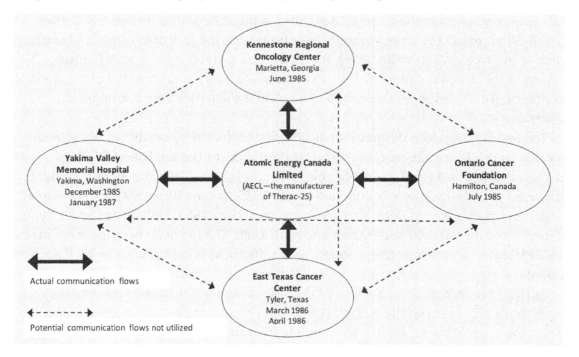

Source: Fauchert, E. (2006). Moral hazard and the role of users in learning from accidents. *Journal of Contingencies and Crisis Management, 14*(2), 97-106.

The crash of a Germanwings airliner in 2015 also illustrates a failure in the system - screening commercial pilots with known psychological problems. On March 24, 2015, co-pilot Andreas Lubitz deliberately crashed his Airbus 320 into the French Alps, killing all 150 onboard. Lubitz was diagnosed with reactive depression during pilot training in 2008 and treated with antidepressants and psychotherapy (Maden, 2017). However, on Germanwings flight 9295, when the captain left the flight deck to use the restroom, Lubitz blocked his return by overriding the access code. He then flew the plane into the Alps.

Although a mental health issue triggered the crash, a procedural factor—the number of people allowed in the cockpit—also contributed to the catastrophe. In the United States, the FAA requires two people in the cockpit. In practice, when a pilot leaves, another pilot or flight attendant must enter the cockpit and remain until the first pilot returns. But this was not a requirement for Germanwings (Ostrower & Pasztor, 2015). However, since the crash, several non-US airlines have adopted the "rule of two" (Firth, 2015). The rule of two started after the 9-11 terrorist attacks to safeguard the flight deck. Entry doors to the cockpit were fortified to be bulletproof and impregnable without an access code. However, the emphasis on cockpit access does come with a cost - the doors themselves have a history of malfunctioning. Regulators in Europe and the US have mandated repairs to hundreds of doors on both Boeing and Airbus aircraft. Case in point, in January 2015, a Delta Airlines co-pilot had to make an emergency landing in Las Vegas without the captain in the cockpit. He had been locked out after the door mechanism failed to work (Ostrower & Pasztor, 2015).

The March 10, 2019 crash of Ethiopian Airlines flight 302 in Addis Ababa killed all 157 people on board, spawning a crisis on multiple levels. The disaster was the second in less than a year involving the Boeing 737 Max 8 aircraft; Lion Air flight 610 crashed on October 29, 2018, killing all 189 onboard. At the time, about 350 Max 8 aircraft were being flown by 52 airlines worldwide, including 34 at American Airlines and 24 at Southwest Airlines. Boeing (like carriers that relied heavily on the Max 8) were caught in a defensive position. Had Boeing accepted responsibility, the company would have faced massive financial liabilities and obvious ethical questions. Boeing defended the airworthiness of the Max 8 in the face of circumstantial evidence, as many travelers wondered why two deadly accidents only months apart involved the same model aircraft. Boeing shares declined 11% during the first two days of trading following the crash (Wall, Tangel & Pasztor, 2019).

Organizational Cultural Considerations

The belief systems within an organization can stifle attempts to learn from a crisis. A track record of success, a scapegoating culture, a status quo culture, and the painful process of looking at failures are deterrents to the learning process.

There is a solid track record of success in the organization

It may seem ironic, but success can ultimately lead to failure (Parnell, Lado, & Wright, 1992). When an organization enjoys success, the result can be an attitude invincibility against crisis events. Success can be defined in many ways, such as consistent revenues, accident-free workdays, or a wealth of positive publicity. Sitkin (1996) noted that some level of failure is needed to encourage organizations to learn. After all, where is the incentive to learn if one does not experience a setback from time to time? A track record of success implies that there is nothing new to learn (Veil, 2011).

The organizational culture at NASA has long been recognized as having a culture of success that has overlooked the potential for failure (Barton, 2008; Gilpin & Murphy, 2008; Tompkins, 2005). Although the organization has had incredible success in its space program, three fatal accidents have occurred.

There is a culture of scapegoating

Scapegoating hinders an organization from learning from a crisis (Elliott et al., 2000). It blames the crisis on another party and deflects attention away from the core source of the problem. There are many pitfalls with scapegoating that ultimately prevent learning in the organization. First, the organization is likely to become even more failure-prone because key issues and warnings are not raised and addressed (Elliott et al., 2000). This scenario is likely because blaming a scapegoat diverts attention away from the issue that needs attention.

Another problem with scapegoating is that it indicates a company's lack of ethics in running the business (Elliott et al., 2000). Scapegoating requires shifting blame even if the company is at fault. Such an ethical stance is a form of denial, hardly a healthy atmosphere for organizational learning. The company's core belief system cannot be changed for the better if managers deny what went wrong at the outset. Instead of displacing the blame to other parties, the organization needs to develop a learning (Argyris & Schön, 1996). This organizational culture shift to learning enables management to make changes that can prevent future crises (Veil, 2011). However, this shift is difficult if there is a status quo–seeking culture in the organization.

There is a status quo culture

A company's core beliefs are the foundation of its organizational culture. If the culture is entrenched in an unwillingness to change, then organizational learning will be virtually impossible (Roux-Dufort, 2000). This type of belief system begins with the attitude that a crisis "cannot happen here" or "it can't happen to us." An organization in denial often becomes more prone to a crisis (Pearson & Mitroff, 1993). When one does occur, the organization must either learn from it or transfer the blame to another party.

Christophe Roux-Dufort studied a 1992 accident involving a French airliner that crashed into the Saint Odile Mountain while making its final approach for landing. He interviewed a vice president for the airline and was surprised to learn that the executive did not consider the event a crisis. He reasoned that the day after the accident, reservations for other airline flights had not changed (Roux-Dufort, 2000). The problem with this mindset is that the crisis is written off as just another event—something that happens when you conduct business—and nothing more. Deep learning and attempts to change the organization's culture are difficult to achieve when a company is in such denial; indeed, analyzing failure is painful.

Analyzing failure is painful

Finally, analyzing a crisis that was the result of human error failure is difficult for those involved. Negative emotions usually surface when individuals examine their shortcomings, resulting in a painful loss of self-confidence and self-esteem. Likewise, managers may find it difficult to focus attention on organizational failures because these failures are an extension of their abilities to govern effectively (Cannon & Edmondson, 2005). After all, if anyone is supposed to exert control in the organization, it is the manager. When a crisis occurs due to the failure of the organization, the manager is ultimately responsible.

Research in organizational behavior has revealed how managers may displace the blame for their failures. **Attribution error** explains how managers attribute responsibility or success when certain organizational outcomes occur. When a manager achieves success, she may attribute that success to her traits as a leader. However, if she fails, she may attribute that failure to external causes. This rationale, the self-serving bias, involves a tendency to make external attributions (i.e., blame the situation) for failures and internal attributions (i.e., take credit) for successes (Hughes, Ginnett, & Curphy, 2012). Hence, managers often hesitate to accept responsibility for a crisis and do not want to discuss it afterward.

Summary

Organizational learning involves the process of detecting problems and then correcting them. Two types of learning can occur. Single-loop learning involves detecting and correcting an error without changing the basic underlying organizational norms. Double-loop learning also involves detecting and correcting an error, but with the changing of organizational norms. Such learning usually occurs after a process of thoughtful reflection. Peter Senge (2006) contributed to our understanding of this process through the concepts of systems thinking, personal mastery, mental models, building a shared vision, and team learning.

   Organizational learning from a crisis should involve evaluating each of the four stages of the crisis management framework. In assessing the organization's response, management should seek improvements in each stage: landscape survey, strategic planning, crisis management, and organizational learning. Barriers to learning should also be examined both from an operational and a cultural perspective.

Discussion Questions

1. Define organizational learning within the context of crisis management.
2. What is the difference between single-loop and double-loop learning?
3. How do Peter Senge's concepts of systems thinking, personal mastery, mental models, building a shared vision, and team learning apply to crisis management learning?
4. How can learning take place within the four areas of the crisis management framework? Specifically, how does it occur in the landscape survey, strategic planning, crisis management, and organizational learning phases?
5. What examples of organizational learning have you experienced at work? Were any of these examples triggered by a crisis? If so, explain how the crisis initiated the learning process.
6. What examples of barriers to learning have you seen where you work? How could these barriers be overcome?

Chapter Exercise

You have been asked to lead the next meeting of the crisis management team of a medium-sized distribution facility located in a growing suburb of a large city. In the meeting, you will discuss an incident that occurred last week in which an armed man entered the production building and threatened to kill his ex-girlfriend. The man in question came in through the back door in the kitchen and entered the employee cafeteria. He was agitated, verbally abusive, and had been drinking. Two security guards restrained the man until police arrived. An unloaded gun was found in his backpack.

The company has a newly formed crisis management team, and it genuinely wants to improve the workplace's safety. You have been asked to facilitate the next meeting of the CMT. During the session, you want to help the new CMT learn from this event and become an effective learning unit. As you plan the meeting, consider the following questions:

1. What can be learned from this event involving the gunman?
2. How can the CMT address learning within the broader landscape survey, strategic planning, crisis management, and organizational learning phases?
3. What barriers to learning should the CMT consider?

Closing Chapter Case: Crisis Cools at Starbucks - Part 2

The arrest of Rashon Nelson and Donte Robinson at the Rittenhouse Square Starbucks in Philadelphia inflicted immediate damage on the company and had the potential for substantial, long-term damage. However, the company's management response was swift and decisive, including an apology from CEO Kevin Johnson and an announcement to close stores for part of a day in the future to provide mandatory racial-bias training.

Many analysts hailed the company's crisis response as appropriate. CEO Kevin Johnson was applauded for immediately accepting full responsibility. Johnson apologized to the individuals publicly and met with them shortly after the incident (Marszalek, 2018). Crisis communications advisor, Jeff Dickerson commented: "I think Starbucks is sending a strong message in doing this ... They're bucking the trend, because ordinarily when large companies find themselves in this situation, they have counsel who will advise them against admitting they'd done anything wrong" (McGregor, 2018).

The second component of Starbuck's response was a May 29 training session on racial bias. This action was noteworthy because it required closing 8,000 stores, including 175,000 employees, costing an estimated $12-16 million in revenues (Marszalek, 2018). The training sent a message that Starbucks was serious about ensuring that the Philadelphia incident did not recur. Crisis communications expert Timothy Coombs viewed the move to close stores as dramatic and extraordinary, adding that the company took corrective action and was willing to forego significant revenue to amend the situation (Marszalek, 2018).

Starbucks' response to the crisis offers an *instructive playbook* for other CEOs facing similar situations (Whitten, 2018), but opinions vary. Some commentators suggested that one day of training was insufficient, suggesting multiple sessions held more often would be preferable. This strategy would ensure that all employees are familiar with and capable of dealing with racial bias if it occurs (Whitten, 2018).

Some analysts pointed out that while Starbucks responded decisively, the company could have moved more quickly. Jamie Izaks, president of All Points Public Relations commented that the company's response was a day late given the fast-paced events occurring with the crisis (Lalley, 2018). Eric Schiffer, chairman of Reputation Management, told CNBC: "The CEO was slow to address race, which remains a big stain on Starbucks' brand trust" (Whitten, 2018). Lateness aside, it does appear Starbucks was trying to get it right by ultimately apologizing for the arrests and designating a training day for racial bias training.

Many large restaurants and stores with thousands of employees must address similar situations every day. Frontline workers are the face of the company's brand. As this crisis demonstrates, a mistake can cost a firm in lost revenues, reputation, or both. Furthermore, it can harm innocent individuals such as Rashon Nelson and Donte Robinson, who still had to spend several hours in jail.

Case Discussion Questions

1. Although not reported in this case, the two men arrested, Rashon Nelson and Donte Robinson, accepted a financial settlement with Starbucks. What were the terms of the agreement? Do these terms influence your interpretation of the case? Why or why not?

2. Some analysts suggested that one day of racial bias training, although a noble gesture, is insufficient to change the entire culture of a company. What can a large organization like Starbucks do to build a more positive culture over the long term?

References

Alavi, M., & Leidner, D. (2001). Review—Knowledge management and knowledge management systems: Conceptual foundation and research issues. *MIS Quarterly, 25*(1), 107–136.

Argyris, C. (1982). *Reasoning, learning, and action: Individual and organizational.* San Francisco: Jossey-Bass.

Argyris, C., & Schön, D. (1978). *Organizational learning: A theory of action perspective.* Reading, MA: Addison-Wesley.

Argyris, C., & Schön, D. (1996). *Organizational learning II: Theory, method and practice.* Reading, MA: Addison Wesley.

Barth, T. (2010). Crisis management in the Catholic Church: Lessons for public administrators. *Public Administration Review, 70*(5), 780–791.

Barton, L. (2008). *Crisis leadership now: A real-world guide to preparing for threat, disaster, sabotage, and scandal.* New York: McGraw-Hill.

Boin, A., Lagadec, P., Michel-Kerjan, E., & Overdijk, W. (2003). Critical infrastructures under threat: Learning from the anthrax scare. *Journal of Contingencies and Crisis Management, 11*(3), 99–104.

Borodzicz, E., & van Haperen, K. (2002). Individual and group learning in crisis simulations. *Journal of Contingencies and Crisis Management, 10*(3), 139–147.

Bourrier, M. (2011). The legacy of the high reliability organization project. *Journal of Contingencies and Crisis Management, 19*(1), 9–13.

Brockner, J., & James, E. (2008). Toward an understanding of when executives see opportunity in crisis. *Journal of Applied Behavioral Science, 44*(7), 94–115.

Broekema, W., van Kleef, D., & Steen, T. (2017). What factors drive organizational learning from crisis? Insights from the Dutch Food Safety Services' response to four veterinary crises. *Journal of Contingencies and Crisis Management, 25*(4), 326-340.

Brookes, W. (1990, April 30). The wasteful pursuit of zero risk. *Forbes,* 160–172.

Brunson, R. (2008, July). Farrier firefighting: A legacy of training. *All Hands,* no. 1096, 12–17.

Cannon, M., & Edmondson, A. (2005). Failing to learn and learning to fail (intelligently): How great organizations put failure to work to innovate and improve. *Long Range Planning, 38,* 299–319.

Carley, K., & Harrald, J. (1997). Organizational learning under fire: Theory and practice. *American Behavioral Scientist, 40*(3), 310–332.

Elliott, D., Smith, D., & McGuinness, M. (2000, Fall). Exploring the failure to learn: Crises and the barriers to learning. *Review of Business,* 17–24.

Fauchart, E. (2006). Moral hazard and the role of users in learning from accidents. *Journal of Contingencies and Crisis Management, 14*(2), 97–106.

Firth, N. (2015). Germanwings crash. *New Scientist, 226*(3015), 1.

Gilpin, D., & Murphy, P. (2008). *Crisis management in a complex world.* New York: Oxford University Press.

Hughes, R., Ginnett, R., & Curphy, C. (2012). *Leadership: Enhancing the lessons of experience* (7th ed.). New York: McGraw-Hill/Irwin.

Jargon, J., & Feintzeig, R. (2018a, June 1). Antibias training left some at Starbucks uncomfortable, *Wall Street Journal*, p. B3.

Jargon, J., & Feintzeig, R. (2018b, May 30). Starbucks takes a break for its antibias training, *Wall Street Journal*, p. B2.

Joffe, Justin (2018). Starbucks' late crisis response offers PR pros a lesson in social listening, *PR News*. Retrieved June 18, 2018, from http://www.prnewsonline.com/starbucks-late-crisis-response-offers-pr-pros-a-lesson-in-social-listening/

Kolb, D. (1984). *Experiential learning: Experience as the source of learning and development.* Englewood Cliffs, NJ: Prentice Hall.

Kovoor-Misra, S., & Nathan, M. (2000, Fall). Timing is everything: The optimal time to learn from crises. *Review of Business,* 31–36.

Lagadec, P. (1997). Learning processes for crisis management in complex organizations. *Journal of Contingencies and Crisis Management, 5*(1), 24–31.

Lalley, H. (2018, October). Righting the ship in a public relations crisis. *Restaurant Business*, 15.

Langer, E. (1989). *Mindfulness.* Cambridge, MA: Perseus.

Lester, D., & Parnell, J. (2007). *Organizational theory: A strategic perspective.* Cincinnati: Atomic Dog Publishing.

Leveson, N., & Turner, C. (1993). An investigation of the Therac-25 accidents. *IEEE Computer, 26*(7), 18–41.

Maden, C. (2017). Extended suicide: Public tragedy. *Criminal behavior and Mental Health, 27*(5), 389-394.

294

Madsen, P. (2009). These lives will not be lost in vain: Organizational learning from disaster in US coal mining. *Organization Science, 20*(5), 861–875.

Marszalek, Diana (2018). Crisis experts hail Starbucks response, but will it work? *The Holmes Report.* Retrieved July 17, 2018, from https://www.holmesreport.com/latest/article/crisis-experts-hail-starbucks-response-but-will-it-work

Martell, K. (2007). Assessing student learning: Are business schools making the grade? *Journal of Education for Business, 82*(4), 189–195.

Mawhinney, J. (1990). The Hagersville Tire Fire—February 12 to 28, 1990. *Internal Report No. 593.* National Research Council Canada. Institute for Research in Construction.

McGregor, J. (2018, April 19). Anatomy of a PR Response: How Starbucks is Handing its Philadelphia crisis. *The Washington Post.*

Medina, J. (2012, April 12). Campus task force criticizes pepper spraying of protestors. *New York Times,* p. 20.

Metallinou, M. (2017). Single- and double-loop organizational learning through a series of pipeline emergency exercises. *Journal of Contingencies and Crisis Management, 26*(4), 530-543.

Nathan, M. (2000 Fall). The paradoxical nature of crisis. *Review of Business,* 12–16.

O'Grady, K. & Orton, J. (2016). Resilience processes during cosmology episodes: Lessons from the Haiti earthquake. *Journal of Psychology and Theology, 44*(2), 109-123.

Ostrower, J. & Pasztor, A. (2015, March 27). Regulators reassess cockpit rules: Germanwings crash stirs debate over planes reinforced doors installed after 9/11. *Wall Street Journal,* p. A6.

Parnell, J., Lado, A., & Wright, P. (1992). Why good things never seem to last: A dialectic perspective of long-term competitive advantage. *Journal of Business Strategies, 9*(1), 62–68.

Pearson, C., & Clair, J. (1998). Reframing crisis management. *Academy of Management Review, 23*(1), 59–76.

Pearson, C., & Mitroff, I. (1993). From crisis prone to crisis prepared: A framework for crisis management. *Academy of Management Executive, 7*(1), 48–59.

Perrier relabeled. (1990). *FDA Consumer, 24*(6), 2.

Pfeifer, S., & McNulty, S. (2011, April 18). Event that changed an industry. *Financial Times,* p. 19.

Racherla, P., & Hu, C. (2009). A framework for knowledge-based crisis management in the hospitality and tourism industry. *Cornell Hospitality Quarterly, 50*(4), 561–577.

Reilly, A. (2008). The role of human resource development competencies in facilitating effective crisis communication. *Advances in Developing Human Resources, 10*(3), 331–351.

Roberts, K., & Bea, R. (2001). Must accidents happen? Lessons from high-reliability organizations. *Academy of Management Executive, 15*(3), 70–78.

Roux-Dufort, C. (2000, Fall). Why organizations don't learn from crises: The perverse power of normalization. *Review of Business,* 25–30.

Seeger, M., Sellnow, T., & Ulmer, R. (2003). *Communication and organizational crisis.* Westport, CT: Praeger.

Sellnow, T., Seeger, M., & Ulmer, R. (2002). Chaos theory, informational needs, and natural disasters. *Journal of Applied Communication Research, 30*(4), 269–292.

Senge, P. (2006). *The fifth discipline handbook: The art and practice of the learning organization.* New York: Currency Doubleday.

Simon, L., & Pauchant, T. (2000, Fall). Developing the three levels of learning in crisis management: A case study of the Hagersville tire fire. *Review of Business,* 6–11.

Sitkin, S. (1996). Learning through failure: The strategy of small losses. In M. D. Cohen & L. S. Sproull (Eds.), *Organizational learning* (pp. 541–578). Thousand Oaks, CA: Sage.

Smith, D. (1993). Crisis management in the public sector: Lessons from the prison service. In J. Wilson & P. Hinton (Eds.), *Public service and the 1990s: Issues in public service finance and management,* pp. 141-170. London: Tudor Press.

Smith, D., & Elliott, D. (2007). Exploring the barriers to learning from crisis: Organizational learning and crisis. *Management Learning, 38*(5), 519–538.

Stead, E., & Smallman, C. (1999). Understanding business failure: Learning and un-learning lessons from industrial crises. *Journal of Contingencies and Crisis Management, 7*(1), 1–18.

Stelter, B. (2011, November 21). California University puts officers who used pepper spray on leave. *New York Times,* p. 13.

Sullivan, J., & Beach, R. (2012). Making organizational learning work: Lessons from a high reliability organization. *International Journal of Business Intelligence Research, 3*(3), 54-61.

Tompkins, P. (2005). *Apollo, Challenger, Columbia: The decline of the space program.* Los Angeles: Roxbury.

Turner, B., & Pidgeon, N. (1997). *Man-made disasters* (2nd ed.). London: Butterworth-Heinemann.

Ulmer, R., Sellnow, T., & Seeger, M. (2007). *Effective crisis communication: Moving from crisis to opportunity.* Thousand Oaks, CA: Sage.

Veil, S. (2011). Mindful learning in crisis management. *Journal of Business Communication, 48*(2), 116–147.

Veil, S., & Sellnow, T. (2008). Organizational learning in a high-risk environment: Responding to the anthrax outbreak. *Journal of Applied Communications, 92,* 75–93.

Wall, A., Tangel, A., & Pasztor, A. (2019, March 12). FAA lets Boeing planes fly after deadly crash in Africa, *Wall Street Journal,* pp. A1, A6.

Wang, J. (2008). Developing organizational learning capacity in crisis management. *Advances in Developing Human Resources, 10*(3), 425–445.

Weick, K. (1993). The collapse of sensemaking in organizations: The Mann Gulch disaster. *Administrative Science Quarterly, 38,* 628–652.

Weick, K., & Sutcliffe, K. (2001). *Managing the unexpected.* San Francisco: Jossey-Bass.

Whitten, Sarah (2018). For CEOs in Crisis, Starbucks offers an "instructive playbook." *CNBC News.* Retrieved July 18, 2018, from https://www.cnbc.com/2018/04/18/for-ceos-in-crisis-starbucks-offers-an-instructive-playbook.html

Chapter 10: Ethics in Crisis Management

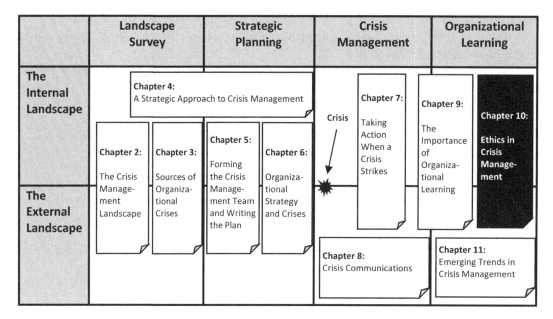

Learning Objectives

After reading this chapter, each student should be able to:

1. Define business ethics.
2. Identify and describe the four components of corporate social responsibility (CSR).
3. Describe how the process of mini steps can lead to unethical and ultimately, illegal behavior.
4. Identify and describe the ethical boulders that can appear during the landscape survey.
5. Identify and describe the ethical boulders that can surface during the strategic planning phase.
6. Identify and describe the ethical considerations that can occur during the crisis management phase.
7. Identify and describe ethical crisis lessons that can surface during the organizational learning phase.

Opening Chapter Case: The Hawks Nest Tunnel

In southern West Virginia, there is an engineering feat known mostly to the locals and the tourists who happen to stop by the small roadside park overlooking the project. It is an underground tunnel about three miles long that carries water from a dam to a small hydroelectric plant perched securely on the side of a mountain. The purpose of the project was to supply electricity to the Union Carbide plant, then located in Alloy, West Virginia, about 6 miles away. The tunnel was built in the 1930s during the Great Depression, mostly by workers who migrated to the area seeking employment (Cherniak, 1986).

The project itself was somewhat ingenious because it solved a problem faced by Union Carbide. Additional electricity was needed to power its new plant, but the prospects of supplying it with hydroelectric power appeared bleak. The New River—one of only a few rivers in the United States that flows north—was (and still is) a slow-moving, narrow band of water that does not have enough force to power a hydroelectric plant in that location. The engineers came up with an intelligent solution: construct a dam to build up water volume and then pitch it in a downward direction to give it force (Cherniak, 1986). They positioned a small hydroelectric building with four turbines where the water forcefully emerged from the tunnel. The result was a facility that makes electricity to this day (Crandall & Crandall, 2002).

Valuing Production over Worker Safety

Unfortunately, there is a dark side to this project. The tunnel contractor, former Virginia engineering firm, Rinehart and Dennis cut corners to reduce project time and expenses. Workers were required to enter the dusty tunnel to begin clearing out the debris shortly after explosives had been detonated. Although engineers were supplied with respirators, laborers charged with cleaning out the tunnel were not. When they encountered silica rock, the workers inhaled the resulting fine dust created by the explosion as they removed debris from the tunnel shaft. As a result, many of them developed silicosis, a debilitating lung disease that eventually caused a slow, agonizing death. This disease is avoidable when respirators are worn.

Rinehart and Dennis also used another cost-cutting measure: dry drilling. Wet drilling should have been used to minimize dust levels. The downside is that wet drilling slows the extraction process, unlike dry drilling, which is faster but creates more dust (Orr & Dragan, 1981; Rowh, 1981). The additional dust associated with the dry drilling, coupled with the lack of respirators, led to the development of silicosis in the tunnel workers.

The number of deaths attributed to the Hawks Nest Tunnel can only be estimated because Social Security records did not exist at the time (Cherniak, 1986). The estimates vary depending on the source of information. Rinehart and Dennis estimated 65 deaths, whereas Union Carbide, the ultimate user of the Hawks Nest tunnel, counted 109. In his account of the Hawks Nest incident, Martin Cherniak estimated a total of 764 deaths. As one might expect, the death estimates become more conservative as the source of information moves closer to the tunnel contractor (Crandall & Crandall, 2002). Even the lowest of these figures is high when considered in light of today's standards of industrial safety.

Some blamed the deaths of the workers on the workers, most of whom were poor and black, and had moved up to the project from the South. To protect the insurance companies that might have to make payouts because of impending lawsuits, some in the medical community discounted the deaths as being a result of unsanitary habits and excessive drinking (McCulloch & Tweedale, 2013).

Aftermath

Although details about the Hawks Nest Tunnel incident are not widely known, many management scholars have studied the event because of the apparent disregard for worker safety. It is a case involving excellent productivity (the tunnel was built in only 18 months), a racial element (many of the workers were poor and black), and a disregard for worker safety (requiring workers to toil in the dusty tunnel without protection for their lungs). Two novels have been written on Hawks Nest. *Hawks Nest*, by Hubert Skidmore (1941), was initially banned because of a potential lawsuit, but has since been republished (Gatlin, 2009). A more recent novel, *Witness at Hawks Nest*, by Dwight Harshbarger (2009), relies on academic research of the events of the time to create the characters for his story.

Because this event occurred nearly 90 years ago, many might assume that serious safety concerns no longer exist, at least in the United States and other developed nations. Unfortunately, this is not always true. Ironically, in 2010, less than 50 miles from the Hawks Nest Tunnel, a mine explosion occurred at the Upper Big Branch mine near Beckley, West Virginia, resulting in the deaths of 29 miners. An independent investigation found numerous safety violations and disregard for employee welfare by then mine-owner, Massey Energy. The investigation also found a workplace culture that valued production over safety, including practices that allowed it to operate in violation of the law (Ceniceros, 2011). This example sadly illustrates that worker safety remains a constant concern.

Case Discussion Questions

1. Why do you think there is so much discrepancy on the number of reported deaths at Hawks Nest?

2. Why would a once-reputable firm such as Rinehart and Dennis fail to take the measures necessary to protect its workers?
3. Both Hawks Nest and the Upper Big Branch mine were underground work locations. Does this have any significance in the hiding of safety violations? If so, how?
4. Why would a modern organization like Massey Energy repeat the legacy of Hawks Nest by compromising worker safety?

Introduction

There is an underlying problem in many of the crisis events discussed in this book. Why do seemingly preventable crises seem to occur again and again? Sometimes the answer can be found with a firm's employees, particularly its managers and top-level business executives, and their desire to gain unfairly at the expense of another party. Put simply, an unabated desire for profits without regard to sound moral principles can trigger an organizational crisis. This problem appears in many forms, but the results are usually the same: an organizational crisis of some type, stakeholders who have been hurt, and a lack of prevention measures that would have cost pennies in comparison to the damage done.

The Hawks Nest Tunnel incident was one of the first major industrial crises in the United States. Although the tunnel was a remarkable success, the human resource tragedy was enormous. The deaths were preventable, but tunnel contractor Rinehart and Dennis decided that breathing protection and other safety measures should be abandoned to maximize profits. It is unclear if the company consciously recognized the seriousness of its decision at the time. Regardless, the contractor did not escape unscathed. Within five years of the project, its assets were liquidated—a victim of bad publicity, lawsuits, and loss of revenue.

So why focus on a human tragedy that occurred more than half a century ago? The Hawks Nest Tunnel incident illustrates the fact that some crises have human roots that can be traced back to unethical or irresponsible behavior by key decision makers. Also, human-induced crises have always occurred and will continue to occur, an inescapable reality. However, some organizations do a better job than others at avoiding these types of crises because they emphasize ethical behavior among their members. This, too, is an inescapable fact and a cause for hope.

In this chapter, we examine human-induced crises more closely, especially those linked to unethical behavior. We begin with an overview of business ethics. We then examine the four stages of the crisis management framework and their relationship to crises that are caused by ethical breaches. We conclude with a note on the relationship of trust to a crisis.

What Is Business Ethics?

Business ethics examines issues of right and wrong behavior in the business environment (Carroll & Buchholtz, 2012). Some business practices can be legal but are not necessarily ethical. Put differently, a business may be acting within the law, but not necessarily doing the "right thing." Such behavior from a callous executive might reveal statements such as, "Well, we didn't break any laws," or "Our job is to maximize profits, period." We consider irresponsible behavior to be unethical as well, although the notion of irresponsibility can be subjective. In our view, ignorance of the law is *usually* a poor excuse.

A related but distinct concept is corporate social responsibility (CSR), which maintains that businesses should seek social benefits for society as well as economic benefits for the business (Post, Lawrence, & Weber, 2002). The concept of CSR is aligned with what has become known as the *stakeholder model,* a viewpoint that seeks to recognize and meet a wide range of groups that have some connected interest in the organization. The goal is to balance the needs of the stakeholders in a way that is both beneficial to the organization and the stakeholders. This thinking is different from the *shareholder model,* which seeks value maximization for the owners of the firm. With the shareholder model, stakeholders are less valued unless they have some bearing on wealth maximization (Berman, Wicks, Kotha, & Jones, 1999).

A simple example illustrates this difference. A firm can allocate its profits in many ways. Under the shareholder model, earnings can be funneled back into the company to increase efficiency and productivity (and hence future profits) or distributed to the owners in the form of dividends. The shareholder model implies that the owners are to receive the top priority in the distribution of these funds. Under the stakeholder model, excess cash might be given to the local community (sponsoring a youth baseball team or a scholarship at a local university), to the employees in the form of a raise or bonus, or perhaps to upgrading the company's technology to reduce emissions. Regardless of one's preference for a shareholder or a stakeholder approach, recognizing the needs of multiple stakeholders can help a firm maximize returns over the long term (Alpaslan, Green, & Mitroff, 2009). For this reason, the CMT should consider how the organization's approach to crisis preparation and response affects all stakeholders.

A popular framework for looking at the two concepts of business ethics and CSR is shown in Table 10.1. In this framework, proposed by Carroll and Buchholtz (2012), CSR is made up of our four parts: economic, legal, ethical, and philanthropic responsibilities. Above all, businesses must meet their economic responsibility by being profitable while operating within the confines of the law.

Table 10.1 – The Components of Corporate Social Responsibility

Component of CSR	Key Thought to Understanding	Manifestations
Economic responsibility	Be profitable.	• Maximize sales revenues. • Reduce operating expenses. • Increase profits. • Maximize shareholder wealth.
Legal responsibility	Obey the law.	• Abide by all legal regulations. • Operate within industry standards. • Maintain all contract and warranty obligations.
Ethical responsibility	Avoid questionable practices.	• Go beyond just obeying the law; abide by the spirit of the law as well. • Avoid practices that may appear to be suspicious, even if they are legal. • Do the right thing and be just and fair to all stakeholders.
Philanthropic responsibility	Be a good corporate citizen.	• Make financial contributions to external stakeholders in the community. • Seek to be a good neighbor in the community by making it a better place to live. • Look for ways to support education, health or human services, and the arts.

Source: Adapted from Carroll and Buchholtz (2012), pp. 37-38.

There is also a realm of business behavior that goes beyond obeying the law. Ethical responsibility seeks to avoid behavior that is questionable though not necessarily illegal. Practically speaking, it is not possible to legally prohibit every unethical business activity. Consider also that many companies sell products or services that are legal but are considered by many to be unethical in some contexts. Hartley (1993) documents the now-infamous PowerMaster Beer controversy in which malt liquor, a legal product, was heavily marketed to poor urban areas, markets in which crime and youth despair were prevalent. This combination created an unethical situation in the eyes of many community stakeholders, who saw this product contributing to even higher crime problems in urban neighborhoods. More recently, the mortgage crisis of the early 2000s that adversely affected an entire industry could have been avoided if individual lenders had simply refused to issue loans with terms that were likely to create a substantial repayment hardship down the road for borrowers. To their credit, several lenders (including BB&T) refused to issue such profitable loans on ethical grounds, a highroad not taken by most in the industry (Parnell & Dent, 2009).

Table 10.2 Ethical Crises Components and Classic Case Flashback

The Basis for an Ethical Crisis	Ethical Crisis Component	Examples of Classic (Early) Crises Note: Some of these examples may not be familiar. These are examined in more detail in the chapter exercise.
Economic: The primary motive is a desire to gain financially, often at the expense of another stakeholder.	**Legal**: These cases involve behavior on the part of company employees that violates the law.	Company misrepresents its accounting statements by hiding debt, overstating profits, or other forms of fraud. Examples: • Tyco (late 1990s to 2002) • Adelphia Communications Corporation (2002) • Enron (2002) • HealthSouth (2002) • Qwest Communications International (2005) • Bernie Madoff (2009) Company knowingly sells a defective product. Examples: • H. Robins Dalkon Shield (1984) • Dow Corning silicone breast implants (1992) Company falsely advertises its product. Example: • Beech-Nut apple juice (1982) Company violates safety standards in the workplace. Examples: • Rinehart and Dennis (1930s) • Warner-Lambert Company (1976) • Film Recovery Services, Inc. (1985) • British Petroleum Texas City explosion (2005) • British Petroleum *Deepwater Horizon* explosion (2010) • Massey Energy (2010)
	Ethical: These cases involve behavior on the part of company employees that is questionable but does not necessarily violate the law.	Company sells a product that is legal but not necessarily beneficial to society. Examples: • Nestlé Infant Formula (1970s) • PowerMaster Beer (1991) • The tobacco industry (ongoing) • Ashleymadison.com (ongoing) Company outsources production to suppliers that impose harsh conditions on their employees (e.g., sweatshops). Examples: • Discount retail chains (ongoing) • Clothing manufacturing companies (ongoing) • Appliance manufacturing companies (ongoing) • Seafood industry in Thailand (ongoing)

Sources: Based on Carroll and Buchholtz (2012); Coombs (2006, 2007); Hartley (1993); Sethi and Steidlmeier (1997).

Finally, some argue that companies have a philanthropic responsibility and the obligation to be good corporate citizens. Some firms seek to fulfill this responsibility by contributing time and money to the communities in which they operate. Many businesses encourage their employees to volunteer in their communities and even compensate these employees for their time invested in civic causes.

Carroll and Buchholtz (2012) maintain that three CSR components—economic, legal, and ethical—are also the most closely tied in with business ethics. Many organizational crises consist of one or more of these components. Table 10.2 provides examples based on the assumption that business ethics crises are motivated by a desire to gain financially at the expense of another stakeholder (Carroll & Buchholtz, 2012; Coombs 2006, 2007; Hartley, 1993; Sethi & Steidlmeier, 1997).

The Process of Mini Steps in Unethical Decision-making

The decision-making process that leads to unethical decisions can be likened to a series of mini steps (see Figure 10.1). Unethical behavior is a breeding ground for organizational crises.

Figure 10.1 - The Process of Mini Steps

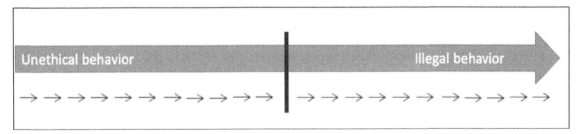

Most illegal behavior does not occur suddenly, instead, it occurs over time in a series of mini steps, as represented by the small errors above.

We posit that unethical business behavior is not illegal, but it is still questionable. Unethical decisions put the decision-maker in dangerous territory, as questionable activities can be viewed negatively by the organization's stakeholders. This process escalates because each unethical decision triggers more serious ones, e. Eventually, decision-making progresses transition from unethical to illegal.

The concept of **normalization of deviance** can help us see how the mini steps in decision making can lead to unethical outcomes. Diane Vaughan (1996) used the phrase "normalization of deviance" to describe how decision making at NASA gradually deviated from acceptable standard. This evolution created a chain of decisions that eventually led to the 1986 launch of the ill-fated space shuttle, Challenger, resulting in a massive explosion and the deaths of 7 astronauts. Normalization of deviance has been utilized in analyzing accidents in the oil and gas industries (Bogard, Ludwing, Staats, & Kretschmer, 2015). Indeed, risk acceptance increases in each successive decision, resulting in the acceptance of greater risk if left unchallenged. The final step is the accident itself, which visibly indicates that too much risk was absorbed in the system.

We propose that unethical decision-making proceeds in the same manner, except that unethical behavior is absorbed into the system until the point is reached whereby damage is inflicted on the organization. The visible damage can be either negative stakeholder fallout from unethical decisions (those to the left of the divide in Figure 10.1) or legal damage as a result of laws being broken (those to the right of the divide in Figure 10.1).

Figure 10.2 shows the progression differently as it passes through the three stages of decision-making. Ethical and legal behavior is depicted at the top, what is commonly called "the high road" in some circles. If one assumes that each arrow is a mini decision, it becomes apparent that between the third and fourth decisions, a slight deviation has taken place. At this point, the decision is still legal and ethical, but it ignites a spiral into unethical decision-making.

The center of the figure is characterized by unethical, but legal behavior. To reach this point, however, a level of unethical risk must be absorbed into the system and then left unchallenged. In other words, each successive decision is a little more unethical than the previous one. For example, service managers at the Sears Auto Centers began to suggest that customers authorize unnecessary repairs (Hartley, 1993). Vehicle repairs are inevitable, but some can be delayed for thousands of miles if a part does not require replacement yet. For example, replacing brake pads prematurely might not unnecessarily burden the customer, but it does increase the revenue of the auto center. Hence, it is still a judgment call whereby the service managers were taking the conservative approach to repairs, "let's replace it now while you are here" versus replacing those same parts later. Technically, the repair advice is legal, but recommending premature brake replacement is unethical.

The bottom part of the figure depicts behavior that has transitioned from unethical to illegal. Indeed, Sears Auto Centers eventually faced a legal fallout as some customers were being required to pay for repairs that they had not authorized. Some of the repairs were unnecessary, placing Sears into the illegal mode of running their auto centers (Hartley, 1993). Sears set stretch sales goals of $147 per hour for store service managers. The decision itself was neither illegal nor unethical, but it began a downward trajectory that would eventually lead the company into unethical decision making.

Figure 10.2 - The Progression of Decision-Making from Ethical, to Unethical, to Illegal Behavior

Type of Behavior	Description of Behavior
Legal & Ethical	Management decisions/behaviors are both legal and ethical. Legal behavior is within the requirements of the law. Ethical behavior goes above what the law requires and strives for decisions that are just and fair. Some observers label this area "the high road". Think of each arrow below as a decision or behavior that occurs in a series. By series, we mean that each decision is affected by the previous decision. *The slide towards unethical behavior has a definite starting point and begins gradually.*
Legal & Unethical	Management decisions/behaviors are still within the law but are deemed unethical. The decisions made reflect questionable behaviors that are not in the best interest of the organization or its stakeholders. Some have labeled this area "the low road". *The path within the realm of unethical behavior still occurs in mini-steps, but its path continues to lead to illegal behavior.*
Illegal	Management decisions/behaviors are totally against the law. The chances of the organization encountering a crisis are greatly increased.

Business Ethics and the Crisis Management Framework

Many of the crises discussed in this section are examples of **smoldering crises**. The Institute for Crisis Management (ICM) notes that these crises start small and can be managed effectively early on, but instead they can fester until they become full-blown crises and known to the public (Institute for Crisis Management, 2018). What makes some smoldering crises ethically induced is that they do not have to occur in the first place. If such a crisis does occur, it can be mitigated through ethical decision making, although not all executives proceed in this manner. Instead, some escalate the crisis by making additional unethical decisions until the crisis spins out of control.

A classic case of unethical decision-making concerned the Beech-Nut apple juice case, a smoldering crisis that should have been stopped early on. During the late 1970s, Beech-Nut Nutrition Corporation found out that it was the victim of a scam when it discovered the supplier of its apple juice concentrate was selling fake apple juice. This discovery was especially troublesome because Beech-Nut advertised its apple juice as "100% fruit juice, no sugar added." Because of the bogus apple juice concentrate from its supplier, this advertisement claim was inaccurate. At that point, Beech-Nut could have reported the incident, pleaded ignorance, and most likely escaped any prosecution because it was an innocent victim ("Bad apples," 1989; Hartley, 1993). However, this supplier was providing its product at 25 percent below the market rate, and the cost savings was too attractive for Beech-Nut executives to pass up.

Beech-Nut chose to continue buying the counterfeit concentrate from its supplier. From 1977 to 1983, Beech-Nut sold its juice as 100% pure when, in fact, it was nothing more than a "100% fraudulent chemical cocktail," according to an investigator close to the case (Welles, 1988, p. 124). What should have been a decision to change suppliers became an ethical misconduct crisis. Beech-Nut president Neils Hoyvald and John Lavery, vice president for operations, were the main parties who instigated the cover-up. When the crisis was over, both men were found guilty of violating federal food and drug laws. Hartley (1993) estimates the crisis that never should have happened cost Beech-Nut $25 million in fines, legal costs, and lost sales.

There are about 550 Pilot and Flying-J truck stops in the US and Canada. On April 15, 2013, agents from the FBI & IRS raided Pilot headquarters in Knoxville, Tennessee, over allegations that Pilot had plotted to cheat trucking customers out of gasoline volume discounts. CEO (and son of the founder) Jimmy Haslam immediately laid off some sales staff and promised to pay any money owed to customers. Although Haslam claimed no knowledge of wrongdoing, several former employees pleaded guilty to crimes and have cooperated with investigators (*Wall Street Journal*, 2013).

Table 10.3 depicts the crisis management framework as it relates to business ethics issues. The next sections develop the four areas of the crisis management process.

Landscape Survey: Uncovering the Ethical Boulders

The landscape survey looks for clues in the organization's internal and external environments that may indicate the presence of an unethical event brewing. Potential crisis indicators include the ethical environment involving the company founder, CEO, and the board of directors; the safety policies of the organization; the economic motives among top executives and management; the degree of industry vulnerability; and the organization's vulnerability globally.

Table 10.3 – The Crisis Management Framework and Business Ethics

	Landscape Survey	Strategic Planning	Crisis Management	Organizational Learning

The Internal Landscape	• The company founder, CEO, and the board of directors
	• The safety policies of the organization
	• The economic motives among top executives and management
	• The disconnect between organizational mission and existence
		• The enthusiasm for crisis management planning and training
		• The ethical culture of the organization
			• The management of internal stakeholders
			  ○ Owners
			  ○ Employees
				• The evaluation of the ethical management process
				• The commitment to organizational learning

The External Landscape	• The degree of industry vulnerability
	• The vulnerability of the organization in the global environment
		• The existence of government regulations
		• The existence of industry standards
			• The management of external stakeholders
			  ○ Customers
			  ○ Suppliers
			  ○ Government entities
			  ○ Local community
			  ○ The media
				• The benefits of industry renewal
				• The inevitability of new government regulations
				• The anticipation of new stakeholder outlooks

The Company Founder, CEO, and the Board of Directors

An organization's approach to ethics an increase or decrease the likelihood of certain crises. The founder of the company wields considerable influence in establishing ethical standards. For example, Enron, WorldCom, Adelphia, HealthSouth, and Tyco have all faced ethical scandals. Their founders were at the helm when each crisis hit (Colvin, 2003).

These companies were also similar in three additional ways. First, they had not learned to question the founder or CEO when required. Second, there was a sense of entitlement coupled with a subtle, but broad disregard for stakeholders. Finally, there seemed to be an insatiable focus on short-term stock prices.

The link between CEO compensation and stock price does not always lead to unethical behavior, but it can. This nexus creates a potential dilemma. Linking CEO compensation and firm performance limits executive pay when they do not generate results, but it also creates an incentive to produce short-term gains at the expense of long-term viability. To resolve this quandary, some firms have introduced a **balanced scorecard** that views performance as a composite of multiple financial and non-financial outcomes (Kaplan & Norton, 2001; Parnell & Jusoh, 2008).

CEO hubris can also be a factor in ethical dilemmas (McManus, 2018). **Hubris** encompasses extreme overconfidence in one's abilities which, ironically, may be based on earlier success (Goel & Thackor, 2008). Success can breed hubris, which can short-circuit future analysis and decision-making. The success breeds overconfidence, which leads to a decision-making style that is more rapid, but less comprehensive (Haynes et al., 2010). As McManus (2018) notes, this thinking leads to less scrutiny into the realm of moral awareness, which compromises the CEO's ethical decision making.

Boards of directors must also be willing to challenge the CEO when necessary (Thorne, Ferrell, & Ferrell, 2003; Zweig, 2010). The crisis at WorldCom was an example of a board that continually gave in to the desires of then-CEO Bernard Ebbers: "As CEO, Ebbers was allowed nearly imperial reign over the affairs of the company with little influence from the board of directors, even though he did not appear to possess the experience or training to be qualified for his position" (Breeden, 2003, p. 1). Two areas of questionable CEO freedom were requested by Ebbers and approved by the board. The first involved the approval of the collection of $400 million in loans and, the second, a rubber-stamping of his request for $238 million to compensate favored executives. The arrangement was made without standards or supervision and allowed Ebbers to pay whatever he wanted to whomever he wished (Breeden, 2003). Ultimately, these schemes, along with others, culminated in a crisis that resulted in one of the largest accounting fraud cases in the United States.

Crisis cases like WorldCom illustrate why boards have to be more than just a rubber stamp for the CEO. In response, some boards are taking a more aggressive approach to hold the CEO accountable for ethical behavior. Boeing's former CEO Harry Stonecipher lost his job after it was revealed he was having an affair with another Boeing executive in violation of company policy (Benjamin, Lim, & Streisand, 2005)

Today, boards of directors are increasingly addressing situations where the CEO has made decisions that may not have been illegal but were still questionable or unethical. Larcker & Tayan (2016) found that 58% of the CEOs were fired when they were involved in a sexual affair, lied to the board over personal matters, used corporate funds for dubious purposes, made public statements that may be offensive to customers or other stakeholders, or engaged in other questionable activities.

The Organization's Safety Policies

The organization's approach to safety is an important part of the ethical climate of the organization. An ethical stance on the part of management promotes an environment in which all stakeholders (particularly employees) are reasonably safe from bodily and emotional harm. However, safety can detract from the bottom line in the short run. In the long run, though, these expenditures can save the company millions and maybe even the company itself.

When investigating industrial accidents, scholars have never concluded that too much was spent on safety (Crandall & Crandall, 2002). Executives who have experienced a safety issue such as an industrial accident resulting in injuries or deaths probably wish they had spent more. For example, in the 1983 Bhopal, India, gas leak incident, Union Carbide and local government officials in India should have focused more on correcting safety problems that had already been widely documented at the plant before the accident (Sethi & Steidlmeier, 1997; Steiner & Steiner, 2000).

Safety measures involve short-term expenses but produce long-term savings by avoiding accidents. Hence, well-crafted remedies are not always costly. Indeed, money spent to prevent employee injury and death can lives, millions of dollars in litigation costs, and a hard-earned reputation. As discussed previously, the Hawks Nest Tunnel contractor, Rinehart and Dennis, could have implemented at least three relatively low-cost measures—better ventilation of the tunnel shaft, wet drilling, and providing respirators for workers—to enhance safety and prevent workers from developing silicosis. While it is difficult to determine the precise cost of these measures, it is clear they would have saved many lives. A focus on safety would have also likely prevented the downfall of the contractor, an event that occurred within five years of completing the tunnel.

The Economic Motives of Top Executives and Managers

Economic motives are often linked to unethical and illegal behavior on the part of top management. The reason for this behavior is easy to see. Management competence is measured by key performance indicators such as sales, profits, and market share, all of which can ultimately drive the price of the company's stock. Boards of directors typically reward the CEO when stock valuations increase because this represents an increase in wealth for the shareholders. At first, this scenario of rewards for stock valuation increases sounds like a win-win situation, but as many recent business crises indicate, abuses can occur that ultimately are not in the best interest of the corporation or its stakeholders. Two examples are hiding debt and questionable cost-cutting measures.

Hiding Debt

Hiding debt creates the illusion that the firm is performing better than it really is, thereby encouraging a false sense of optimism and confidence. The CEO is rewarded for short-term increases in shareholder value. The hidden financial obligations eventually become apparent, creating a crisis for the organization.

This type of downward spiral was apparent at Enron, where debt was hidden through an accounting strategy known as "off-balance sheet" partnerships called special purpose entities (SPEs). These partnerships were allowable under accounting loopholes at the time and were initiated by then-chief financial officer (CFO) Andrew Fastow. The SPEs were joint ventures with various groups of investors, but because they were separate entities, they were not part of the Enron balance sheet. The sole purpose of these SPEs was to remove unwanted assets and liabilities from Enron's balance statements (Boatright, 2012).

The structures of SPEs have trigger mechanisms that require repayment of the debt under certain circumstances (Henry, Timmons, Rosenbush, & Arndt, 2002). It was these trigger mechanisms that began the "visible" crisis at Enron. That crisis became known with the October 16, 2001, announcement that Enron was taking a $544 million after-tax charge against its earnings related to transactions involving its SPEs (Powers, 2002). The result was a third-quarter loss of $618 million and a $1 billion reduction in the company's asset value. From that date, the implosion of Enron was rapid and dramatic. Enron's stock price fell from $33 on October 16 to $15 on October 26. On December 2, Enron laid off 4,000 employees and filed for bankruptcy. Only a year earlier, Enron had been touted as a socially responsible firm leading the way in alternative energy, ranking the seventh largest on the *Fortune* 500 list with a stock price of $90 (DesJardins, 2009). The downfall of Enron later paved the way for the Sarbanes-Oxley Act and other regulations.

Questionable Cost-Cutting

Questionable cost cutting is the other abuse that can arise from unethical motives. Such cost-cutting is the profit motive at work and will cause some managers to do just about anything. Trimming costs deliver dollars to the bottom line but doing so without regard for worker safety has resulted in many examples of industrial tragedies. In 1976, when Warner-Lambert was introducing a new line of chewing gum, it took shortcuts in the manufacturing area by allowing high levels of dust near the machinery. The company could have installed a dust collection system, but the cost was seen as prohibitive. The result was a dust explosion that killed six employees and injured 54 others (Sethi & Steidlmeier, 1997).

Although cost cutting is a healthy and necessary business activity, its irresponsible application was the primary factor in the deaths linked to the Hawks Nest Tunnel. The use of dry drilling to expedite the project cut expenses. The decision not to provide tunnel workers with respirators is especially troubling.

The Hawks Nest incident illustrates the connection between ethical decision making—doing what is just and fair—and protecting worker safety. Perhaps the most famous abuse of worker safety in the United States was the 1911 Triangle Shirtwaist Company fire that occurred on the 10th floor of a factory in New York City. The fire spread rapidly due to the massive amounts of linen and other combustible materials nearby. One hundred forty-six employees died, most of them immigrant women, who were either burned in the blaze or jumped to their deaths. Sadly, the fire escape routes for these employees had been locked by management to prevent theft (Greer, 2001; Vernon, 1998). Some may argue that revisiting cases like Hawks Nest and the Triangle Shirtwaist fire is not necessary today. After all, labor unions, labor laws, safety inspectors, and various watchdog groups discourage this kind of behavior (Shanker, 1992). Unfortunately, history has a way of repeating itself.

On September 3, 1991, a fire erupted at the Imperial Food Products poultry plant in Hamlet, North Carolina. A hydraulic line ruptured, spilling a flammable liquid throughout the kitchen. The vapors from the line were ignited by the gas burners from the flying vats, creating a massive fire in the 30,000-square-foot plant (Lacayo & Kane, 1991). Before the day was over, 25 employees, most of them single mothers, had perished. Critics claimed negligence. "The plant had no sprinkler or fire alarm system, and workers who got to the unmarked fire exits found some of them locked from the outside. Imperial's management was using the same 'loss control' technique as the bosses at Triangle—and with the same results" (Shanker, 1992, p. 27). Many of the victims were unable to open the locked fire exits and died in a cluster by the doorway. Others were found in a freezer where they had sought refuge. The owner claimed that the fire exit doors had been locked to prevent the theft of the chickens.

An $800,000 labor code fine was levied against the company. Fourteen months after the fire, the insurer and claimants reached a $16 million settlement. Plant owner Emmet Roe was sentenced to 20 years in prison after pleading guilty to manslaughter (Jefferson, 1993). Eventually, Imperial went bankrupt. As these examples illustrate, unchecked greed comes in various forms and can hurt other stakeholders in the process.

Implementing Unrealistic Stretch Goals

Managers have employed goal setting as a motivation and productivity tool for many decades. However, goals should be SMART—specific, measurable, attainable, results-oriented, and possess a target date (Locke & Lathan, 1990). Inherent in this philosophy is that goals should be challenging, but not impossible to achieve. Goals that are too easy to attain are not motivating, whereas goals that are too difficult are not motivational because they are impossible to reach. Challenging, but attainable, goals are desirable.

However, a variant of goal setting theory involves the implementation of "stretch goals"—goals that are extremely challenging to achieve, and yet "might" be attainable. Critics of stretch goals maintain an employee or manager may resort to unethical behavior or excessive risk-taking in their efforts to reach the stretch goal (Barsky, 2007; Markovitz, 2012; Ordóñez, Schweitzer, Galinksy, & Bazerman, 2009). The Sears Auto Center case in 1992 offers a frequently cited example of a stretch goal gone wrong. Sears had set a goal of $147/hour for their sales service writers. In theory, the idea was to generate higher sales at the unit level. In practice, it resulted in widespread unethical and illegal behavior in many stores, culminating on June 12, 1992, when the California Department of Consumer Affairs accused Sears of over-charging on auto repairs and prescribing unnecessary service (Hartley, 1993; Ordóñez et al., 2009).

The Disconnect Between Organizational Mission and Existence

The organization's mission should clarify the purpose of the organization's existence (Parnell, 2020). Some organizations seem to lose touch with their mission statements over time, a situation that can lead to ethical breaches.

Schwartz (1990) noted that an organization could exist to do work (its mission), or it can do work to exist. This observation is not just a play on words but has tremendous ethical implications. For example, Barth (2010) notes the Catholic Church operated in this mode early in its crisis concerning priests who were sexually abusing children. The church seemed more interested in protecting its structure than with protecting the children who were victims. Rather than removing the predatory priests, the church chose merely to transfer many of them to other parishes. Whether intended or not, the Catholic Church was communicating that the careers of the priests were more important than the people they were appointed to serve. A disconnect between the organization's mission and the reason for its existence had occurred.

In the business sector, there can be a similar disconnect between a corporation's top management and the firm's shareholders. The result is called the **agency problem** and occurs when managers (i.e., the agents of the shareholders) place their personal goals over those of the owners (Parnell, 2020). For example, Enron's CFO Andrew Fastow benefited financially from his involvement in the SPE transactions. The Special Investigative Committee of the Board of Directors at Enron noted:

Enron employees involved in the partnerships were enriched, in the aggregate, by tens of millions of dollars they should have never received—Fastow by at least $30 million, Kopper by at least $10 million, two others by $1 million each, and still two more by amounts we believe were at least in the hundreds of thousands of dollars. (Powers, 2002, p. 3–4)

Andrew Fastow and Michael J. Kopper were identified as active participants in managing the SPEs. Both benefitted financially as a result of activities that were ultimately detrimental to Enron. Agency theory illustrates how some in top management view themselves as independent contractors, acting in their own interest instead of that of the firm.

The Degree of Industry Vulnerability

Some industries seem to be more crisis-prone from an ethical perspective. For example, professional wrestling and baseball have had a history of steroid use. Professional cycling, particularly with events like the Tour de France, has faced charges of performance-enhancing drugs among participants. The coal mining industry has a long history of safety violations. Indeed, the United Mine Workers of America (UMWA) has a history of being one of the most aggressive unions in existence, due mostly to the abuse of coal miners who have been subject to unsafe working conditions by mine owners. Certainly, coal mining safety has improved in recent years, but rogue coal companies still seem to exist.

Looking through the lens of "ethical rationality" (Snyder, Hall, Robertson, Jasinski, & Miller, 2006), the challenge is to determine whether an industry is more vulnerable to a crisis because of ethical problems. The link between industry-specific factors and unethical behaviors has not been addressed widely, although some attention has been focused on aircraft manufacturers. Both Lockheed and Northrop were found to have made improper cash payments to overseas sales agents in the 1970s to secure contracts to sell aircraft (Securities and Exchange Commission, 1976). In the past, Boeing has been plagued by several ethical problems, perpetuated by what has been called a "culture of silence" by Boeing general counsel Douglas Bain. The culture stems from a lack of speaking up on ethical issues, a problem that has plagued the company for a long time (Holmes, 2006).

The Vulnerability of the Organization in the Global Environment

As a firm expands its international presence, its vulnerability to an ethical crisis may also increase. Three reasons for potential ethical problems include the temptation to make illegal cash payments, the possibility that a defective product will emerge from a foreign country, and potential links to sweatshops.

The Temptation to Make Illegal Cash Payments

Major scandals often result in legislation. The Lockheed bribery scandal led to the passing of the Foreign Corrupt Practices Act in 1977 (Hartley, 1993). The act prohibits offering cash payments to foreign government officials to obtain business. Also, foreign companies whose stock is traded in the United States are subject to review by the Department of Justice (Carroll & Buchholtz, 2012). Critics often complain, however, that the act places American firms at a disadvantage when competing for foreign contracts. This occurs in countries where the legal infrastructure requiring that all companies play by the same rules does not exist. In many parts of the world, bribery is an accepted means of conducting business. To further complicate the matter, the act permits some cash payments, called **grease payments**—smaller amounts of cash used to encourage foreign officials to do what they are supposed to do anyway (Carrol & Buchholtz, 2012). A **bribe**, on the other hand, is a large cash payment used to entice a foreign official or agent to do something not typically done in the course of business, such as buying from a vendor.

As companies expand globally, illegal cash payments can become more tempting. Consider the case of Walmart's expansion into Mexico. A 2012 *New York Times* article broke the case involving bribe payments by Walmart management in Mexico. The trigger point for the crisis was a 2005 email to Walmart headquarters sent by a former Walmart executive who had arranged several bribes to help facilitate the company's development in the Mexican market. The former executive, Sergio Cicero Zapata, had worked for Walmart until 2004 in the company's real estate development department (Barstow, Xanic, & McKinley, 2012).

The Possibility that a Defective Product Will Emerge from a Foreign Country

Two problems result when a defective product emerges from another country. First, the product can pose a danger. Toymaker Mattel discovered this in 2007 when it had to recall more than 22 million toys manufactured in China due to high levels of lead and other toxins (Barton, 2008). What makes this case noteworthy is that Mattel had a long history of safety and social responsiveness. Mattel owned and operated its factories in China. However, one of its plants either violated policy by using the lead-laden paint or a supplier provided the paint unknowingly to Mattel (Hartman & DesJardins, 2011).

Second, a foreign-sourced defective product can lead to negative feelings by citizens in the home country. Because many US manufacturing jobs have been lost to foreign sourced companies, a defective product that emerges on the market is a reminder that it could have been manufactured domestically, presumably without any quality concerns. The result is a public relations crisis for the home country company because citizens may feel resentment for overseas outsourcing in the first place.

Potential Links to Sweatshop Manufacturing and Slavery in the Supply Chain

Companies that outsource processes to overseas vendors may face potential association with sweatshops—manufacturing facilities that pay low wages, employ child labor, have poor working conditions, require extended work hours, and otherwise abuse their workers. Their use has increased as companies seek to lower costs but can engender public relations crises. Walmart, Nike, Liz Claiborne, and Disney are large, high-profile companies that have been linked with sweatshops in the past.

Sweatshops and modern slavery in the supply chain are the ultimate "guilt by association" crisis. Although some progress has been made in recent years to improve working conditions in developing countries, the issue remains. Although a company can "require" its subcontractors to abide by specific working condition standards, enforcing standards through audits has been difficult (LeBaron, Lister, & Dauvergne, 2017). Typically, independent monitors are sent to investigate working conditions in plants that are supposed to be compliant with specific standards. However, this system is not foolproof, as inspectors can be deceived by the very companies they are inspecting. One inspector related how pregnant employees were hiding on the roof of a facility in Bangkok during inspection visits. Another company coached employees on how to answer questions posed by an inspector. The strategy was meant to communicate to the inspector that everything was fine at the plant (Frank, 2008).

Strategic Planning: Confronting the Ethical Boulders

The strategic planning process should generate initiatives to improve the ethical climate of the organization. Improving this climate can reduce the company's vulnerability to an ethics-related crisis. Specific efforts should be directed to generating enthusiasm for crisis management and training, focusing on the prevention of ethical breaches, and abiding by both government regulations and industry standards.

The Enthusiasm for Crisis Management and Training

Neglecting to prepare for a crisis can be viewed as an ethical problem. Unfortunate events can occur to an organization at any time, and the company's stakeholders expect that it will have a plan to meet these crises. The lack of a crisis management plan (CMP) and the subsequent training that accompanies it can engender negative perceptions from employees, suppliers, customers, government agencies, and the general public when a crisis does occur. Stakeholders frown on organizations that were unprepared for a crisis.

Merely forming a crisis management team (CMT) and generating a CMP is not enough. Enthusiasm for the crisis management process and the accompanying training must also be present. For this reason, the organization should seek a crisis management champion from within to help develop an ongoing crisis management program. If the organization is new to crisis planning, an outside consultant can help the CMT write its first plan. Top management should always support the firm's crisis management efforts.

The Ethical Culture of the Organization

The best approach to dealing with an ethical crisis is to prevent it from happening in the first place. An ethical rationality approach seeks to address events in the life of the organization from a morally driven response perspective (Snyder et al., 2006). However, to a great extent the organizational culture dictates how ethical or unethical decision making will be in the company (Heineman, 2007; Vallario, 2007). For this reason, a cultural change in the organization is also necessary to improve ethical decision-making. Changing the culture of an organization requires unseating the deep thought patterns that have prevailed in previous years, particularly if those patterns of behavior are unethical. Even Enron had a code of ethics, but the culture of the company overshadowed the significance of that code. Likewise, the failed accounting firm Arthur Anderson produced an ethics video series once used in US business schools (Fombrun & Foss, 2004).

Effects from the #metoo movement have spilled over into numerous industries. The National Football League (NFL) has been forced to address allegations of sexual abuse and domestic violence more openly. Consider the case of Kansas City Chiefs star running back Kareem Hunt. In a video from February 2018, Hunt appeared to shove a woman, tackle somebody into her, and kick her; police were called, but charges were not filed. It was not until November 30—after TMZ published the video footage—that the Chiefs released Hunt. Fans and critics immediately wondered why action was not taker earlier. When confronted in November, Hunt apologized for the incident but noted that he was never interviewed as part of the NFL's investigation into the matter stemming back to February. Hence, league and team executives felt no sense of urgency about the matter in February but were willing to bar him from playing in November while an internal investigation was underway. This 180-degree shift is problematic in two ways. It suggests not only that the NFL does not take issues of domestic violence and sexual harassment seriously, but also that the league is willing to suspend players immediately—prior to completing a thorough investigation—when videos or serious allegations about player off-the-field wrongdoings surface and threaten the brand.

In 2018, Under Armour ended a longstanding company practice that allowed employees to charge visits to strip clubs on their corporate credit cards. According to founder and CEO Kevin Plank, "Our teammates deserve to work in a respectful and empowering environment. We believe that there is systemic inequality in the global workplace, and we will embrace this moment to accelerate the ongoing meaningful cultural transformation that is already under way at Under Armour. We can and will do better" (Sadfar, 2018a).

There has been a history of questionable activity. Plank's brother, Scott, was a top executive at Under Armour until 2012 when he departed amid sexual misconduct allegations. Co-founder and longtime executive Kip Fulks departed Under Armour in 2017 after he had a romantic relationship with a subordinate, a violation of company policy. The company fired executives Ryan Kuehl and Walker Jones in late 2018. Insiders suggested involvement in corporate spending irregularities, including gifts to athletes and trips to strip clubs expensed to the company (Safdar, 2018b).

Kevin Plank came under scrutiny in 2018 when company emails uncovered an intimate relationship with MSNBC anchor Stephanie Ruhle, who had traveled with Plank and Under Armour staff in his private jet and served as a business advisor. When executives began to suspect that the relationship was more than friendship, they struggled to handle her feedback. Under Armour leases a Gulfstream jet from a company Plank owns, but he also used the jet for private travels. Both Plank and Ruhle were married at the time (Safdar, 2019).

Under Armour's problems have continued. In 2020, The US Securities and Exchange Commission (SEC) issued a Wells notice, an official notification that the regulator intends to bring an enforcement action related to the firm's disclosure and accounting practices in 2015 and 2016. The Wells notice gave Under Armour an opportunity to respond and explain why action should not be taken (Sadfar, 2020).

Changing the culture of an organization is an enormous undertaking; culture is, after all, the prevailing belief system within the organization. Looking the other way when an ethical breach occurs is acceptable in some cultures, while others are committed to ethical standards in any business decision. Employees look to top management for cues to right and wrong behavior in the organization (Trevino, Hartman, & Brown, 2000). Table 10.4 overviews some best practices for companies seeking to promote ethical cultures.

Government Regulations

Flouting government regulations can be catastrophic. Ignoring them is unethical and can create a crisis.

In 1997, the Andrew & Williamson Sales Company sold strawberries grown in Mexico to the US Department of Agriculture (USDA). The USDA distributes food to public school systems, and regulations required that strawberries sold to these school systems be grown in the United States. Andrew & Williamson submitted falsified certificates of origin that indicated the strawberries were grown domestically (Salkin, 1997). Although the company thought it would go unnoticed, a major health crisis soon erupted. Many students in Michigan's public schools were stricken with hepatitis A, and the ailment was linked to the strawberries sold by Andrew & Williamson. Eventually, outbreaks of the hepatitis A strain resulted in 213 cases in Michigan, 29 in Maine, and seven in Wisconsin (Entis, 2007). What started as an illegal scheme to move excess inventory out

Photo by Martin Adams on Unsplash

of the warehouse resulted in a significant crisis across multiple states. When the ordeal ended, Frederick Williamson resigned as president and was sentenced to five months in prison and five months of home detention. The company was also forced to pay $1.3 million in civil damages and $200,000 in criminal penalties (Entis, 2007).

In the Hawks Nest project, Rinehart and Dennis ignored existing regulations that could delay construction of the tunnel. For example, wet drilling was the required practice because this procedure kept dust levels to a minimum (Cherniak, 1986; Tyler, 1975). Testimony before the US Congress revealed that employees were posted to watch for incoming mine inspectors (Comstock, 1973). When the arriving inspectors were announced, wet drilling would begin until the inspectors had left the area. Dry drilling would then resume, expediting extraction.

Existing Industry Standards

Industry standards are often set by associations for their members to follow. The intent is to establish guidelines concerning a practice, such as quality control or safety adherence. Companies then adopt these guidelines in the industry association as the minimally acceptable standard (Vernon, 1998). Such efforts illustrate *self-policing* (Becker, 2006) or *self-regulation* (Hemphill, 2006). Certain professional occupations—including physicians, attorneys, college and university professors, engineers, pharmacists, and accountants—also have standards for their members.

Industry associations can propose guidelines for ethical conduct. For example, Financial Executives International (FEI) requires all its members to review and sign a code of ethics. They also recommend that the financial executive deliver the signed copy to the company board of directors. FEI has become a model for companies seeking to comply with Sarbanes-Oxley and New York Stock Exchange mandates (Vallario, 2007).

Table 10.4 Best Practices for Changing Ethical Cultures

Measures Taken	Description
Installing a code of ethics	Organization-wide ethical principles and behaviors are outlined in a pamphlet or manual. Managers and employees review the code on a regular basis and sign it, indicating their willingness to abide by the code.
Implementing ethics training	Short classes and workshops that highlight ethical issues and how to respond to them are offered to employees.
Providing an ethics hotline	Employees have a person or department within their organization to whom they can report ethical violations. A hotline can also offer guidance on specific ethical issues an employee may be facing.
Requiring that top management articulate and set the ethical example	Executives in top positions in the company—the CEO, president, and vice presidents—need to acknowledge that lower-level managers attain their cues on ethical matters by watching those higher up in the organization. Thus, top managers are encouraged to model the right example.
Requiring managers to attain realistic, but not impossible goals	Goals set for managers are well conceived and realistic. Unrealistic goals encourage unethical decision making because managers may feel they must cut corners to attain the goal.
Disciplining for ethical violations	When an ethical violation is discovered, the company works quickly to correct the situation and punish the person responsible.
Scheduling regular ethics audits	As in a financial audit, the company periodically checks itself in a systematic manner to see if it is following proper ethical guidelines in its business processes.
Appointing of chief ethics officers	Ethics officers who serve in top management are being used in some larger companies. Such officers may report directly to the CEO and the board of directors. Their charge is to promote the ethical standards of the organization and to monitor employee concerns.

Sources: Carroll and Buchholtz (2012); Fombrun & Foss, C. (2004), 284–288; Post et al. (2002).

One caveat should be offered concerning industry standards. Requiring that member companies have a code of ethics is a step in the right direction, but it does not ensure companies have leaders who will always make ethical decisions. For example, Enron's

62-page code of ethical conduct was not embedded in the Enron culture (Becker, 2006). Similarly, many clothing retailers maintain an "ethical sourcing" or "compliance monitoring" link on their company websites, suggesting that they monitor the actions of their foreign suppliers (Frank, 2008). However, compliance can be a game, as one sweatshop inspector noted:

> The simplest way to play [the game] is by placing an order with a cheap supplier and ending the relationship once the goods have been delivered. In the meantime, inspectors get sent to evaluate the factory—perhaps several times, since they keep finding problems—until the client, seeing no improvement in the labor conditions, severs the bond and moves on the next low-priced, equally suspect supplier. (Frank, 2008, p. 36)

According to this sweatshop inspector, some companies can promote ethical sourcing because they use monitors but can continue to purchase from suspect factories, one after another, each time claiming the factory was deficient and severing the tie. With so many substandard factories to choose from, the game need not end.

Further Considerations During an Ethical Crisis

Managerial training is a precursor to ethical crisis management. "Decision-makers who understand the needs of a wide range of stakeholders as part of their strategic decision-making will make more ethical decisions during a time of crisis" (Snyder et al., 2006, p. 376). Thus, ethical rationality is a habit that must be ingrained in the culture and daily operations of the organization (Fritzsche, 2005). Ethical rationality involves the careful management of the organization's internal and external stakeholders throughout the crisis.

Managing Internal Stakeholders

Employees and owners are the internal stakeholders who must be managed with integrity when a crisis occurs. Typically, it is the crisis communication function that should be approached in an honest, straightforward manner. Employees should receive truthful and timely information updates as the crisis progresses.

The owners should acknowledge any potential financial losses. If the shareholders are dispersed geographically, the impact of the loss may not be felt until quarterly reports are distributed months after the crisis commences. In incorporated, public firms, the shareholders, like the employees, may be left in the dark on the details of the crisis at hand. This is unethical. Firms should share with employees and owners the details of the crisis and what is being done to address it.

The organization's website, as well as social media tools, can be used to communicate with these stakeholders. Updates on the state of the crisis should occur regularly. Also, the organization should use its managers and supervisors to communicate the details of the crisis to employees. To supplement this type of communication, an organization-wide memo or letter should be circulated to all employees. In addition, face-to-face meetings with employees are always advisable; these provide opportunities for questions and answers, which in turn, provide information that can clarify misunderstandings or rumors that may be circulating about the crisis.

Managing External Stakeholders

External stakeholders include customers, suppliers, government entities, the community, and the media. As with internal stakeholders, the ethical approach is to ensure honest and timely communication. For example, if a crisis emanates from a false rumor, it should be refuted quickly (Coombs, 2007; Gross, 1990). Again, the organization's website and social media outlets can be a great vehicle for updated information on the latest developments of a crisis. Setting up a link on the website that directly addresses the crisis is a good practice.

Organizational Learning: Lessons from the Ethical Crisis

Recovering from an ethical crisis requires commitment.

Evaluating the Ethical Management Process

During a crisis, sentiments often run against the company, even if it is not to blame. For example, if damaging weather hits a company warehouse and halts operations, some critics will question why the company was not more prepared. Unlike an earthquake, weather event, or other natural disaster where the organization is not viewed as a victim—at least to some extent—an ethical crisis generates little public sympathy.

Every crisis could be interpreted as a sign of a loss of trust even if the organization is not at fault (Bertrand & Lajtha, 2002). Many Americans do not trust business organizations in general and will be critical of a company when it faces a crisis. Other stakeholders might see the crisis from a more realistic perspective. Regardless, managers should assess stakeholder perceptions and communicate accordingly, ensuring each group that the crisis is being addressed in a prudent and ethical manner

The Commitment to Organizational Learning

Chapter 9 focused on the process of organizational learning after a crisis. Once an ethical crisis has been resolved, the organization must commit itself to a learning process that seeks to avoid repeating the mistake. Unfortunately, some companies resort to an unethical "defense-and-attack" mode (Nathan, 2000, p. 3). In a classic crisis management case, the A.H. Robins company used this tactic to discredit the victims who used the Dalkon Shield, a contraceptive device that was inserted surgically into the uterus. When recipients of the Shield became sick, the company resorted to attacking the victims and questioning their sexual practices and partners (Barton, 2001; Hartley, 1993 A.H. Robins paid dearly in the end by enduring an endless onslaught of consumer lawsuits.

In most instances, a company should not publicly attack its suppliers either. While a problem may be traced to a supplier, positioning the company to avoid responsibility only displaces the blame. Some critics may question why the company chose to work with the problematic supplier in the first place. With an ethical crisis, stakeholders are trying to determine if the company is trustworthy. They also expect the company to "get it right" legally and ethically. This learning process may result in new controls and terminations. .

The Benefits of Industry Renewal

Some industries seem to have more ethical challenges than others. This statement may sound odd, given that individuals—not firms or industries—commit unethical acts. Consider the tobacco industry. Many analysts question the ethics of selling a product associated with significant health problems. The tobacco industry maintained for years that cigarettes were not harmful, even though illnesses from tobacco represented a heavy burden on the health care system. In 1998, however, 46 state attorneys general reached an agreement with the five largest US tobacco manufacturers. The settlement required the companies to pay billions of dollars to the state governments each year, ostensibly to alleviate the burden on the state health care systems (Thorne et al., 2003).

In terms of industry renewal, there has been a decline in tobacco advertising aimed at youth and teenagers. Joe Camel was a well-known character that appeared in advertisements in the late 1980s and 1990s for Camel cigarettes, a product manufactured by R. J. Reynolds (RJR). One study found that among children between the ages of 3 and 6, more than half could associate the Joe Camel character with a cigarette (Shapiro, 1993). The Joe Camel campaign lasted from 1987 to 1997, a time during which underage smoking increased. In 1997, the Federal Trade Commission (FTC) asked RJR to remove the character from any venue accessible to children (Carroll &

323

Buchholtz, 2012). RJR complied, thus beginning a period of industrial renewal in the tobacco industry.

The ethical reforms that took place in the pharmaceutical industry in the 1980s were not prompted by governments. Before these reforms, gifts and other incentives were frequently lavished on physicians by representatives advocating the use of their company's drugs (Hemphill, 2006). Using gifts to indirectly influence patient prescriptions is unethical. The American Medical Association (AMA) adopted ethical guidelines in 1990 on gift-giving practices. The initial reactions were positive, but the industry remains prone to criticism.

The Inevitability of New Government Regulations

After a significant crisis, the government may impose new regulations, especially if the company is large and its self-policing efforts have been ineffective. Self-policing can generate positive change without government mandates. Without it, public apathy can generate media attention, public outcry, and ultimately, government intervention (Hartley, 1993). Table 10.5 overviews this progression.

Today, we see numerous examples of how the government seeks to protect society through regulation. The Environmental Protection Act resulted from public outcry against the pollution crises. The Occupational Safety and Health Administration was a government response to safety inadequacies in the workplace. Although the effectiveness of the legislation is often debatable, the links between a widespread and government response is often clear.

Government regulation is currently attempting to address workplace slavery. In the United States, the California Transparency in Supply Chain Act (CTSCA) of 2010 requires companies to disclose on their websites the measures they are taking to rid their supply chains of slavery. The United Kingdom followed with a similar type of disclosure law, the UK Modern Slavery Act of 2015. Both laws suffer from lack of meaningful enforcement penalties for companies that do not comply (Barna, 2018). However, the laws raised awareness about the problem. Additional stakeholder pressure will be required before the issue is completely resolved.

The Anticipation of New Stakeholder Outlooks

Unfortunately, a significant loss of human life often launches a company into immortality. Many baby boomers associate Union Carbide with the Bhopal, India, gas leak disaster that killed thousands in 1983. Indeed, an Internet search with the company name as the search term produces many references to the disaster. Likewise, Hawks Nest Tunnel contractor Rinehart and Dennis is not remembered for successful engineering projects; instead, its name will forever be associated with the needless loss of hundreds of workers who died from silicosis while building the tunnel.

Table 10.5 The Progression from Public Apathy to Government Regulation

	Public Apathy →	**Media Attention** →	**Public Outcry** →	**Government Regulations**
General Description	The general public and companies are not very concerned about a potential crisis in a specific industry.	The media focuses on a crisis event and raises public awareness.	The public reacts to the crisis by asserting that "something must be done".	Government regulations will follow if self-regulation is inadequate.
Example: The Hawks Nest Crisis	The Great Depression is at its height and Americans are searching for work.	In the late 1930s, media attention highlights the abuses of workers who are dying of silicosis.	Public sympathy and concern build momentum as lawsuits and government investigations ensue.	Silicosis legislation is passed in 46 states.
Example: September 11, 2001, Terrorist Attacks	Few stakeholders anticipated that a jet airliner would be used as a terrorist weapon.	The attacks on the World Trade Center and the Pentagon become widely known.	As experience financial shocks, and some eventually go into bankruptcy.	The government responds with the creation of the U.S. Department of Homeland Security and the Transportation Safety Administration (TSA).
Example: Enron Scandal	Few people had heard of Enron since its founding in 1985.	Enron announces a restatement of earnings in October 2001. A month later, the company goes bankrupt.	Thousands of Enron employees lose their jobs and retirement savings. Public outrage occurs.	The Sarbanes-Oxley Act (2002) is passed.
Example: Modern Slavery	Many believe slavery has been eradicated worldwide.	Global supply chains take sourcing to developing nations where debt-bondage work arrangements occur.	Companies are cast in a negative light when slavery is found in their supply chains.	The California Transparency in Supply Chains Act (2010) is passed.

Source: Adapted from Hartley (1993), p. 26.

There is another irony to the Hawks Nest crisis. The company receiving the electricity produced by the tunnel project was Union Carbide. Some critics have speculated that Union Carbide might have played a role in the tunnel crisis (Deitz, 1990; Jennings, 1997).

Nonetheless, name recognition has a strong emotional component. It is associated with quality products and services, but it can also be associated with death.

Other stakeholder outlooks can result from crisis events. Consider the following crisis events and how they changed the viewpoints of many people:

- The September 11, 2001, terrorist attacks in New York City forced air travelers to accept new security measures. The attacks also strengthened the idea that passenger safety is the overriding ethical concern of airliners.
- When manufacturers outsouce production abroad, they lose direct contact with the means of production (Bertrand & Lajtha, 2002). Outsourcing can fuel ethical questions if there are problems with the overseas production. These concerns, coupled with tariffs and supply chain concerns linked to the COVID-19 pandemic, have prompted many firms to rethink outsourcing as a strategy (Ocicka, 2016; Parnell, 2020).
- The climate is always changing. Some scientists link observed shifts in global temperatures to human activity, namely the production of carbon emissions. Prompted by customers and other stakeholders, many firms now view the reduction of emissions as an ethical dilemma.
- Hurricane Katrina and the ineffective government response to the disaster prompted extensive criticism. Many critics cited poor communication and coordination among government agencies, positing that these groups should have been better prepared to manage a storm-related crisis. The ego and turf wars that existed among government agencies were also obvious and invited the scorn of many.

The Problem of a Loss of Trust

Bertrand and Lajtha (2002) have concluded that all crises can be viewed as signs of a loss of trust. If a crisis is viewed as a loss of trust, then the ethical repercussions can be substantial. Consider these examples when the party fault is not included in the blame equation, and yet blame is deflected back onto the organization. The countering questions that follow each event are often raised by critics in the media.

- A recently fired employee walks into his former place of work and kills his supervisor along with several other employees: Why was the employee allowed back on the premises? What did the company do to agitate the employee? Why is the government not doing more to prevent this kind of tragedy?
- An employee is killed on his factory job because she did not follow standard procedures in performing a work task, thus leading to the fatal accident: Why did

the company hire her in the first place? How many similar accidents have occurred at this workplace? Why did the company not enforce its own procedures?

- A young man dies of an opioid overdose, just weeks after being treated at a rehabilitation facility. The victim might have stayed longer but lacked the appropriate insurance. Why is the insurance company so heartless for not extending coverage? Why do large pharmaceutical companies continue to sell dangerous drugs? Can government stop this problem?

Responses like these are common when a crisis occurs. To make sense out of what has happened, many people will cognitively distort the situation and assign an ethical cause to the crisis, even if one is inappropriate. Indeed, a perception can influence behavior more than reality.

Summary

Business ethics examines the morality of behavior in the business world. Unethical behavior can be legal yet damaging to the organization. In practice, all businesses should consider four responsibilities to their stakeholders: (1) making a profit, (2) operating within the law, (3) behaving ethically, and (4) supporting social and community activities that relate to the mission of the firm. The primary motive that triggers a moral crisis is often the desire to gain financially, often at the expense of another stakeholder.

The four stages of the crisis management framework reveal the role of ethics in crisis management. The landscape survey uncovers the ethical weak points that may exist within the organization and its industry. The strategic planning stage promotes what can be done to improve the ethical climate of the business and its industry in general. The crisis management stage examines the ethical behaviors involved when addressing a specific crisis. Finally, the organizational learning stage promotes improving an organization's ethical performance by learning from a crisis event.

Discussion Questions

1. Provide an example of an ethical problem that has occurred in your workplace.
2. Using the crisis management framework (Table 10.3), conduct a landscape survey and determine the status of potential ethical issues in your present organization (the internal landscape) and in the industry in which your company operates (the external landscape).

3. Identify a crisis that involved an organization that violated an ethical standard but did not break the law. How did the organization defend its behavior? What could the organization have done differently?
4. How can the ethical culture of an organization be improved?
5. Why is the example provided by top management instrumental in promoting the ethical culture of the organization?
6. What examples of significant crises illustrate how government intervention can help prevent a similar crisis in the future? Consider Table 10.5 as a starting point in your discussion.
7. Discuss how a crisis can symbolize a loss of trust in the organization?

Chapter Exercise

Select several familiar crisis events from the list provided in Table 10.2. Outside of class, research each case and prepare a one-page summary of what happened and the outcome. Discuss these in class. What crisis did the organization face? How did mismanagement contribute to the crisis? How was the crisis finally resolved? What were the legal implications?

Closing Chapter Case: Facebook Loses Face

Crises emerging from problematic user content are a constant concern for Facebook and other social media firms. Indeed, the high risk of crises linked to misinformation is built into the Facebook business model. Individuals and organizations can post and view information largely unfiltered and without charge, while revenues come to emanate from advertisers and other entities that pay for the opportunity to influence Facebook users. On the surface, this approach resembles traditional media; advertisers sponsor the programming, and consumers can watch or listen free. But the Facebook model is more crisis-prone for several reasons.

First, the nature of social media encourages individuals to post personal information for others to see. When Facebook users post content, they share both private and commercial information entities about themselves, their preferred activities, and their buying patterns. Advances in analytics and artificial intelligence (AI) have enabled organizations to mine and manage this data on a large scale to determine what consumers want, who is most likely to purchase their products, and at what price. Facebook users continuously feed the system with valuable data for which advertisers and other organizations seeking influence are willing to pay.

Second, social media content is posted in real time. Unlike traditional media programming, editors do not have the opportunity to evaluate content before posting.

A current event can trigger millions of posts within hours. Evaluating them one at a time would not only be costly for Facebook but would run counter to the appeal of social media in the first place. Companies like Facebook have no choice but to depend on algorithms to filter unwelcome content before it is posted or reassess it well after it has been viewed widely. Algorithms designed to block only blatant vulgarity and other undesirable material can be easily avoided by perpetrators, while those designed to limit "hate speech" or "fake news" ultimately make value judgments and limit legitimate free expression. Indeed, the platform—as with most other social media entities—is built around the unfiltered exchange of ideas. The problem of dubious content will always exist at companies like Facebook.

Third, social media outlets possess the data necessary to enable advertisers and other organizations to target users in *particular* ways. For example, a luxury carmaker like Mercedes Benz can advertise only to high-income individuals within specific demographic parameters that post certain words or phrases (e.g., Acura, "looking for a new car," etc.). With Facebook, a higher percentage of ad recipients are likely to purchase a given product or service than with traditional media such as radio and television. Entities with ignoble intentions (e.g., to instigate civil unrest or spread "fake news" about a competitor) can do so through "fake posts" or more subtly through paid advertising.

As we can see, crises for social media organizations such as Facebook are inevitable and should come as no surprise when they emerge. Facebook has faced allegations that it was enabling or even promoting "fake news." This problem became a severe crisis when Facebook (and several other large Internet-based firms) became a target of a federal probe into potential influence by Russians and other outsiders launched after the 2016 US presidential election. Facebook's troubles were compounded in 2018 when it was revealed that UK-based Cambridge Analytica obtained access to private data from over 50 million Americans with Facebook accounts as part of a 2016 political campaign designed to influence voters.

Facebook users agree to terms that generally permit the company to use and often sell data to others, but few consumers read the agreements or understand how they can protect parts of their data. Some users viewed this use of data as unethical regardless of any user agreements and demanded a regulatory response (Seetharaman, 2018). To them, the action was both unethical—data should always be protected—and socially irresponsible—Facebook has a responsibility to promote privacy protection in a high-tech world. The company faced a major crisis that engulfed privacy rights, content oversight, and data management.

Epilogue

Facebook's response to the data crisis has been multifaceted. CEO Mark Zuckerberg has recommitted the organization to high ethical standards, while also investing heavily in the political arena to bolster its leadership position in the industry. After investigations identified factually incorrect news reports in users' news feeds in 2017, Facebook invested more than $8.4 million in a team of 36 lobbyists to manage the fallout in Washington, DC, including several new positions dedicated to strategy (Bykowicz, 2017). In response to the debacle, Arizona Senator John McCain proposed legislation to require any social media platform with over 50 million monthly users to monitor political advertisements bought for more than $500. Facebook and Twitter responded with a willingness to work with US legislators to solve the problem of "fake news." David Marcus, the head of Facebook Messenger, also suggested Facebook should vet its new products more carefully and be more cognizant of how advertising can be leveraged to disseminate misinformation (Kuchler & Bradshaw, 2017).

But the social and political upheaval endured. Zuckerberg testified before the US Congress in April 2018 and met with European leaders in May 2018 to address Facebook's response. The Congressional hearings were widely publicized and offered insight into the CEO's thinking and the political nature of the data crisis. For example, when asked if he would be comfortable sharing with the public the name of the hotel where he stayed the night before, Zuckerberg seemed baffled and emphatically said no, a response to which Senator Dick Durbin quipped, "I think that might be what this is all about..." (CBS News, 2010) (see https://www.youtube.com/watch?v=sWDwh5UxWMs). When asked to define hate speech, Zuckerberg suggested that an algorithm should decide (PBS, 2018) (see https://www.youtube.com/watch?v=JPQEIKqt93k). When asked about specific actions Facebook took in some instances, he claimed to know little about the details and offered to investigate them.

As a strategic response, Zuckerberg appears to invite government regulation while influencing the process. Ostensibly, his willingness to "work with Washington" seems to be a means of addressing the crisis, but government control would help cement Facebook's prominent position in the industry by creating compliance costs that potential competitors would be less able to afford. Of course, some problems could be alleviated without any government intervention. For example, companies like Facebook should provide clear user agreements customers understand while safeguarding their data. These concerns have not abated, as critic of Facebook continued through the 2020 election cycle.

Juxtaposing Facebook's response to the data crisis with recent actions outside of the United States gives critics reasons to doubt Zuckerberg's authenticity. Given the market potential in China and the political realities, Facebook seems to have compromised the "free speech" values they extol at home for access to markets elsewhere. For example, Zuckerberg met with Chinese President Xi Jinping and other government officials in 2017 to discuss entering the Chinese market, where the social media platform has been banned since 2009 because it would not censor its content and form a joint venture with Chinese partners (Abkowitz, 2017).

It is noteworthy that Facebook is not the only US-based tech company engaged in such political activity. For example, Apple has argued fervently that the US government has no business demanding access to company data or controlling Internet access. But in 2018, facing fierce competition from Chinese smartphone makers, the company agreed to remove nearly 700 apps that allow Chinese consumers to bypass government restrictions. It also shifted customer iCloud data to servers located on the Chinese mainland, making it vulnerable to government access or even seizure. Apple CEO Tim Cook defended the moves, noting that the company should engage with governments even when they disagree on important issues. Like Facebook, Apple's willingness to compromise its values to obtain access to Chinese markets has drawn criticism from many US analysts (Kubota, 2018).

Case Discussion Questions

1. To what extent should social media outlets be held responsible for user content?
2. What examples of fake news have you seen on Facebook and other social media outlets?
3. How can social media outlets create an environment for a smoldering crisis?
4. How can social media outlets like Facebook mitigate criticism about user content?

References

Abkowitz, A. (2017, October 30). Facebook's Mark Zuckerberg Makes Another Appearance in China. Wall Street Journal. Retrieved July 17, 2018, from https://www.wsj.com/articles/facebooks-mark-zuckerberg-makes-another-appearance-in-china-1509360341?mod=nwsrl_technology&cx_refModule=nwsrl

Alpaslan, C., Green, S., & Mitroff, I. (2009). Corporate governance in the context of crises: Towards a stakeholder theory of crisis management. *Journal of Contingencies and Crisis Management, 17*(1), 38–49.

Bad apples: In the executive suite. (1989, May). *Consumer Reports*, 294.

Barna, A. (2018). Modern slavery in corporate supply chains. *William & Mary Law Review, 59*(4), 1449-1490.

Barsky, A. (2007). Understanding the ethical cost of organizational goal-setting: A review and theory development. *Journal of Business Ethics, 81*(1), 63-81.

Barstow, D., Xanic, A., & McKinley, J. (2012, April 12). Vast Mexico bribery case hushed up by Walmart after top-level struggle. *New York Times*, p. 1.

Barth, T. (2010). Crisis management in the Catholic Church: Lessons for public administrators. *Public Administration Review, 70*(5), 780–791.

Barton, L. (2001). *Crisis in organizations II.* Cincinnati: South-Western College Publishing.

Barton, L. (2008). *Crisis leadership now: A real-world guide to preparing for threat, disaster, sabotage, and scandal.* New York: McGraw-Hill.

Becker, C. (2006). Police thyself. *Modern Healthcare, 36*(41), 28–30.

Benjamin, M., Lim, P., & Streisand, B. (2005, March 28). Giving the boot. *US News & World Report*, 48–50.

Berman, S., Wicks, A., Kotha, S., & Jones, T. (1999). Does stakeholder orientation matter? The relationship between stakeholder management models and firm financial performance. *Academy of Management Journal, 42*(5), 488–506.

Bertrand, R., & Lajtha, C. (2002). A new approach to crisis management. *Journal of Contingencies and Crisis Management, 10*(4), 181–191.

Boatright, J. (2012). *Ethics and the conduct of business* (7th ed.). Upper Saddle River, NJ: Pearson.

Bogard, K., Ludwing, T., Staats, C., & Kretschner, D. (2015). An industry's call to understand the contingencies involved in process safety: Normalization of deviance. *Journal of Organizational Behavior, 35*(1/2), 70-80.

Breeden, R. (2003, November/December). WorldCom: The governance lessons. *Corporate Board,* 1–6.

Bykowicz, J. (2017, October 26). Facebook Steps Up Efforts to Sway Lawmakers. *Wall Street Journal.* Retrieved July 17, 2018, from https://www.wsj.com/articles/facebook-steps-up-efforts-to-sway-lawmakers-1509044190

Carroll, A., & Buchholtz, A. (2012). *Business and society: Ethics sustainability, and stakeholder management* (8th ed.). Mason, OH: South-Western/Cengage Learning.

CBS News (2018, April 10). Senator Durbin asks for name of Zuckerberg's hotel in privacy question. https://www.youtube.com/watch?v=sWDwh5UxWMs.

Ceniceros, R. (2011). Game changer for mine safety? *Business Insurance, 45*(48), 1, 20.

Cherniak, M. (1986). *The Hawks Nest incident: America's worst industrial disaster.* New Haven: Yale University Press.

Comstock, J. (1973). 476 graves. *West Virginia Heritage [Yearbook], 7,* 1–194.

Coombs, W. (2006). *Code red in the boardroom: Crisis management as organizational DNA.* Westport, CT: Praeger.

Coombs, W. (2007). *Ongoing crisis communication: Planning, managing, and responding* (2nd ed.). Thousand Oaks, CA: Sage.

Crandall, W., & Crandall, R., (2002). Revisiting the Hawks Nest Tunnel incident: Lessons learned from an American tragedy. *Journal of Appalachian Studies, 8*(2), 261–283.

Deitz, D. (1990, Fall). "I think we've struck a gold mine": A chemist's view of Hawks Nest. *Goldenseal*, 42–47.

DesJardins, J. (2009). *An introduction to business ethics* (4th ed.). New York: McGraw-Hill.

Entis, P. (2007). *Food safety: Old habits, new perspectives.* Malden, MA: Blackwell.

Fombrun, C., & Foss, C. (2004). Business ethics: Corporate responses to scandal. *Corporation Reputation Review, 7*(3), 284–288.

Frank, T. (2008, April). Confessions of a sweatshop inspector. *Washington Monthly*, 34–37.

Fritzsche, D. (2005). *Business ethics: A global and managerial perspective* (2nd ed.). New York: McGraw-Hill.

Gatlin, J. (2009). An epistemology of the everyday: Occupational health and environmental justice in Hubert Skidmore's Hawks Nest. *Literature and Medicine, 27*(2), 153-174.

Goel, A., & Thackor, A. (2008). Overconfidence, CEO selection, and corporate governance. *Journal of Finance, 63*(6), 2737-2784.

Greer, M. (2001). 90 years of progress in safety. *Professional Safety, 46*(10), 20–25.

Gross, A. (1990, October 11). How Popeye's and Reebok confronted product rumors. *Adweek's Marketing Week, 31*, 27, 30.

Harshbarger, D. (2009). *Witness at Hawks Nest*. Huntington, WV: Mid-Atlantic Highlands.

Hartley, R. (1993). *Business ethics: Violations of the public trust*. New York: Wiley.

Hartman, L., & DesJardins, J. (2011). *Business ethics: Decision making for personal integrity and social responsibility*. New York: McGraw-Hill/Irwin.

Haynes, K., Campbell, J., & Hitt, M. (2010). Greed, hubris, and board power. Effects on firm outcomes. *Academy of Management Proceedings, 2010, (1)*, 1-6.

Heineman, B., Jr. (2007). Avoiding integrity land mines. *Harvard Business Review, 85*(4), 100–108.

Hemphill, T. (2006). Physicians and the pharmaceutical industry: A reappraisal of marketing codes of conduct. *Business and Society Review, 111*(3), 323–336.

Henry, D., Timmons, H., Rosenbush, S., & Arndt, M. (2002, January 28). Who else is hiding debt. *Business Week*, 36–37.

Holmes, S. (2006, March 13). Cleaning up Boeing. *Business Week*, 63–68.

Institute for Crisis Management. (2018). *Annual ICM crisis report: News coverage of business crises during 2017*. Retrieved June 13, 2018, from https://crisisconsultant.com/icm-annual-crisis-report/

Jefferson, J. (1993). Dying for work. *ABA Journal, 79*(1), 46–51.

Jennings, C. (1997, Spring). Was Witt Jennings involved? The Hawks Nest tragedy. *Goldenseal*, 44–47.

Kaplan, R., & Norton, D. (2001). *The strategy focused organization*. Boston: Harvard Business School Press.

Kubota, Y. (2018). Apple's Cook plays along in China. *Wall Street Journal*, p. B4. Retrieved July 17, 2018, from https://www.wsj.com/articles/apples-china-lesson-think-different-but-not-too-different-1519642914

Kuchler, H., & Bradshaw, T. (2017, October 19). Russia ads bill gains bipartisan support in US. Financial Times. Retrieved July 17, 2018, from https://www.ft.com/content/e9ed6836-b441-11e7-aa26-bb002965bce8

Lacayo, R., & Kane, J. (1991, September 16). Death on the shop floor. *Time, 28*–29.

Larcker, D., & Tayan, B. (2016, June 9). We studied 38 incidents of CEO bad behavior and measured their consequences. *Harvard Business Review Digital Articles*, 2-4.

LeBaron, G., Lister, J., & Dauvergne, P. (2017). Governing global supply chain sustainability through the ethical audit regime. *Globalizations, 14*(6), 958-975.

Locke, E. & Latham, G. (1990). *A Theory of Goal Setting & Task Performance*. Englewood Cliffs, NJ: Prentice Hall College Division.

Markovitz, D. (2012). The folly of stretch goals. *Management Services, 56*(4), 34-35.

McCulloch, J., & Tweedale, G. (2013). Anthony J. Lanza, silicosis and the Gauley Bridge 'Nine'. *Social History of Medicine, 27*(1), 86-103.

McManus, J. (2018). Hubris and unethical decision making: The tragedy of the uncommon. *Journal of Business Ethics, 149*, 169-185.

Nathan, M. (2000, Fall). From the editor: Crisis learning—Lessons from Sisyphus and others. *Review of Business*, 3–5.

Ocicka, B. (2016). Reshoring: implementation issues and research opportunities. *Management, 20*(2), 103-117.

Ordóñez, L., Schweitzer, M., Galinksy, A., & Bazerman, M. (2009). Goals gone wild: The systematic side effects of overprescribing goal setting. *Academy of Management Perspectives, 23*(1), 6-16.

Orr, D., & Dragan, J. (1981). A dirty, messy place to work: B. H. Metheney remembers Hawks Nest tunnel. *Goldenseal, 1*(7), 34–41.

Parnell, J.A. (2020). *Strategic management: Theory and practice* (6th ed.). Solon, OH: Academic Media Solutions.

Parnell, J., & Dent, E. (2009). Philosophy, ethics and capitalism: An interview with BB&T CEO John Allison. *Academy of Management Learning and Education, 8*(4), 587–596.

Parnell, J., & Jusoh, R. (2008). Competitive strategy and performance in the Malaysian context: An exploratory study. *Management Decision, 46*(1), 5–31.

PBS (2018, April 10). How does Facebook define hate speech: Zuckerberg dodges question. https://www.youtube.com/watch?v=JPQEIKqt93k.

Post, J., Lawrence, A., & Weber, J. (2002). *Business and society: Corporate strategy, public policy, ethics.* New York: McGraw-Hill.

Powers, W. (2002). *Report of Investigation by the Special Investigative Committee of the Board of Directors of Enron Corp.* Retrieved June 17, 2019, from http://i.cnn.net/cnn/2002/LAW/02/02/enron.report/powers.report.pdf

Rowh, M. (1981). The Hawks Nest tragedy: Fifty years later. *Goldenseal, 1*(7), 31–33.

Safdar, K. (2018a, November 6). Under Armour ends strip-club perk. *Wall Street Journal*, pp. B1, B5.

Safdar, K. (2018b, December 11). Under Armour fires two in marketing over expenses. *Wall Street Journal*, pp. B1, B2.

Safdar, K. (2019, February 22). Under Armour CEO's ties questioned. *Wall Street Journal*, pp. B1, B2.

Sadfar, K. (2020, July 28). SEC readies Under Armour case. *Wall Street Journal*, pp. B1, B2.

Salkin, S. (1997). Attn: School foodservice directors and other commodity purchasers. *Foodservice Director, 10*(7), 82.

Schwartz, H. (1990). *Narcissistic process and corporate decay: The theory of organizational ideal.* New York: New York University Press.

Securities and Exchange Commission. (1976, May 12). *Report on questionable and illegal corporate payments and practices.* Exhibits A and B, submitted to US Congress, Senate, Committee on Banking, Housing, and Urban Affairs.

Seetharaman, D. (2018, March 28). Zuckerberg is expected to testify. *Wall Street Journal*, p. A4.

Sethi, S., & Steidlmeier, P. (1997). *Up against the corporate wall: Cases in business and society* (6th ed.). Upper Saddle River, NJ: Prentice Hall.

Shanker, A. (1992, February 17). The Hamlet, N.C., fire: A postmortem. *New Republic*, 27.

Shapiro, E. (1993, August 11). FTC staff recommends ban of Joe Camel campaign. *Wall Street Journal*, p. B1.

Skidmore, H. (1941). *Hawks Nest.* New York: Doubleday, Doran and Co.

Snyder, P., Hall, M., Robertson, J., Jasinski, T., & Miller, J. (2006). Ethical rationality: A strategic approach to organizational crisis. *Journal of Business Ethics, 63*, 371–383.

Steiner, G., & Steiner, J. (2000). *Business, government, and society: A managerial perspective* (9th ed.). New York: McGraw-Hill.

Thorne, D., Ferrell, O., & Ferrell, L. (2003). *Business and society: A strategic approach to corporate citizenship.* New York: Houghton Mifflin.

Trevino, L., Hartman, L., & Brown, M. (2000). Moral person and moral manager: How executives develop a reputation for ethical leadership. *California Management Review, 42*(4), 128–142.

Tyler, A. (1975, January). Dust to dust. *Washington Monthly*, 49–58.

Vallario, C. (2007). Is your ethics program working? *Financial Executive, 23*(4), 26–28.

334

Vaughan, D. (1996). *The Challenger launch decision: Risky technology, culture, and deviance at NASA.* Chicago, IL: University of Chicago Press.

Vernon, H. (1998). *Business and society: A managerial approach* (6th ed.). New York: McGraw-Hill.

Wall Street Journal (2013, December 27), "Whatever happened to…?" pp. B1, B4.

Welles, C. (1988, February 22). What led Beech-Nut down the road to disgrace? *Business Week*, 124–128.

Zweig, D. (2010). The board that couldn't think straight. *Conference Board Review, 47*(2), 40-47.

Chapter 11: Emerging Trends in Crisis Management

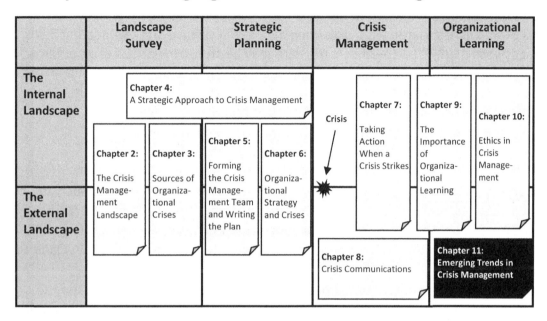

Learning Objectives

After reading this chapter, each student should be able to:

1. Identify and describe the emerging trends in the landscape survey phase of the crisis management framework.
2. Identify and describe the emerging trends in the strategic planning phase of the crisis management framework.
3. Identify and describe the emerging trends in the crisis management phase of the crisis management framework.
4. Identify and describe the emerging trends in the organizational learning phase of the crisis management framework.

Opening Chapter Case: The Emerging Field of Crisis Analytics - Part 1

The closing chapter case discusses crisis analytics, the integration of big data with crisis management. Within crisis management, big data can facilitate the preparation, management, and learning processes involved in addressing organizational crisis events. Hence, crisis analytics has become a sub-field of the crisis management discipline.

Big Data Defined

The term **big data** was first used to describe how multiple datasets can be used to address problems associated with visualizing data in the science and engineering fields (Cox & Ellsworth, 1997). Furthermore, the data may be stored in various geographic locations. The problem for scientists and engineers was how to access smaller segments of the data in a format that facilitated problem-solving. However, local computer capacities may not be able to handle extensive data sets.

More recently, the definition proposed by IBM maintains that big data is characterized by the three Vs: Volume, variety, and velocity (Adams, 2017):

- **Volume** refers to a large amount of data generated across many venues, such as mobile devices, social media, and the Internet of Things (IoT) (Adams, 2017). The concept of volume also implies that the data cannot be processed on a single machine or with traditional computational software (Choi & Lambert, 2017; Qadir et al., 2016).
- **Variety** refers to the nature of the data (e.g., structured or unstructured) and the richness of the data representation (e.g., text format, image, or video) (Emmanouil & Nikolas, 2015). For example, social media data has contributed to the growing level of unstructured data.
- **Velocity** refers to the speed at which data is generated. Some data, such as streaming videos or Tweets are created quickly, while other data, such as inspection forms used to process and predict accidents, accrue more slowly (Bernini, 2017). Velocity can also refer to the speed at which the data is transformed into more useable information (Adams, 2017; Fertier et al., 2016).

Three Vs have been added to augment the definition and characteristics of big data:

- **Veracity** refers to the authenticity of the data. For example, is the data accurate and consistent with reality (Fertier et al., 2016; Qadir et al., 2016)? Data that is not trustworthy presents problems with its ability to help decision-makers.
- **Value** refers to the usefulness of the data. Much of the data within the realm of big data is useless because it is either inaccessible, the dataset is too large, or it lacks integrity.
- **Visualization** refers to the ability to depict big data information in a visual format. Although not a characteristic of big data, it is essential because data that cannot be communicated visually lacks value. An application of visualization would include crisis mapping (Qadir et al., 2016).

Dig Data Described

Describing big data may also prove useful. The Big Data for Development report (UN Global Pulse, 2012) offers several characteristics (Watson et al., 2017):

1. Big data is often digitally generated and does not require human activity. For example, the Internet of Things (IoT) is continually creating data using a series of ones and zeros and, thus, is manipulated by computers and modules.
2. It is a byproduct of digital interactions with service providers.
3. It is collected automatically in IT systems that extract and store it.
4. It is trackable geographically, for example, through smartphone use.
5. It is continuously analyzed, meaning it is being reviewed systematically to ensure human well-being.

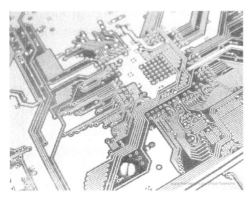

The UN Global Pulse report assumes that data is generated primarily through digital systems. However, others have noted big data can reside in banks of data generated manually, such as safety inspection reports (Schultz, 2015). Also, big data is not always passively produced. Many sources are initiated by customers who buy products or services and then relay experiences via social networking sites (Drosio & Stanek, 2016).

Big Data Sources

Big data emanates from individual, government (public sector), and business (private sector) sources (Watson et al., 2017). However, because these three sources overlap, some have classified big data from their technological roots. In their taxonomy of crisis analytics, Qadir and colleagues (2016) note data sources regarding six techno categories: data exhaust, online activity, sensing technologies, public data, and crowdsourced data. These are described next.

Data exhaust. Much of what is considered big data originates from digital sources with mechanisms that create their data as part of the operating system. Data exhaust describes the process whereby data is a byproduct of a device doing "something" or service rendered, such as processing payments or using a telephone provider (Lokanathan & Gunaratine, 2015).

Online activity. This source is far-reaching in that it includes many venues, including search activity and social media usage. Both activities result in different outcomes with social media encompassing an interaction aspect between senders and receivers. The **deep web** is the dark underbelly which traditional search engines may not reach (BrightPlanet, 2015). Online activity occurs over all three sources of big data, individuals, governments, and business.

Sensing technologies. Sensors gather and communicate data to a central processor. For example, modern automobiles have many sensors that generate data about how the vehicle is running to the vehicle module (i.e., computer), which commands the car's systems. Sensing technologies exist across all three big data sources.

Public data. Governments collect an abundance of data, including census data, birth and death certificates, and personal and socio-economic data (Qadir et al., 2016). Although the government collects a lot of data, much of it is not readily available, and hence, is not very useful.

Crowdsourcing. Data can be collected from large groups of people for specific questions or problems. The rationale is that the collective opinion of a large group of people can be as reliable as the opinions of experts (Qadir, 2016), a phenomenon known as the wisdom of crowds (Surowiecki, 2005).

In addition to the sources noted previously, many companies store data from their day-to-day operations. For example, safety inspection and audit reports can accumulate, both in written and digital forms (Bernini, 2017; Marsh, 2016; Mathis, 2016). Given this backdrop, the links between data analytics and crisis management are clear.

Case Discussion Questions

1. How can the existence of big data create crises in organizations?
2. What potential uses do you see for data analytics in the crisis management field?

Introduction

The opening chapter case illustrates one of the new trends emerging in crisis management, crisis analytics. We examine crisis analytics and other emerging trends through each of the four phases of the crisis management framework. Table 11-1 overviews these trends. As you study each of these phases, consider how they can affect your career.

The Landscape Survey

We examined the crisis management landscape in previous chapters. We now consider trends that may appear on the horizon.

The Internal Landscape

The internal landscape considers the state of the organization and its ability to withstand—or even cause—a crisis. What follows is an identification of emerging internal landscape trends and how you may be affected.

Table 11.1 Emerging Trends in Crisis Management

	Landscape Survey	Strategic Planning	Crisis Management	Organizational Learning
The Internal Landscape	• The SWOT analysis will become an important tool in assessing crisis vulnerability. • The link between organizational crisis and moral failure will strengthen. • Organizations will take advantage of data analytics to assess their crisis vulnerabilities.	• Virtual crisis management plans will become the norm. • Crisis management planning will be integrated into the organization's strategic planning process.	• Contingency responses to specific crisis events will become more common. • The organization's website and social media networks will become the main communication tools during a crisis.	• Organizational learning will provide an important feedback loop necessary for the strategic planning process. • Learning after a crisis will lead to the abolishment of the existing status quo.
The External Landscape	• Victims of crises will become more visible and influential as stakeholders. • A crisis will be viewed as a reason to mistrust an organization.	• Crisis management teams will engage in more planning with crisis teams from outside their organization. • The focus efforts of crisis management will expand to include a broader range of stakeholders. • Sustainable development will become more of an expectation.	• Social media will play a more significant role in determining the outcome of a crisis. • Time will be a critical metric that will be used to evaluate an organization's response to a crisis. • The perceived duration of a crisis will decrease in the minds of external stakeholders.	• Crisis management frameworks and models will become more complex and sophisticated. • Crisis research will continue to use cases but will incorporate more statistical analysis as well. • Crisis research will take on a long-range perspective. • Crisis analytics will become a vital tool in crisis management research.

The SWOT analysis will become an important tool in assessing crisis vulnerability.

In chapter 4, we discussed how SWOT analysis could help managers detect crisis vulnerabilities. We discovered that organizational strengths could precede specific crises. A charismatic CEO (or an athletic coach) with a loyal following can be an incredible asset to the organization. However, left unchecked, such a person may also breach ethical practices and cause a crisis for the organization. Likewise, opportunities, those options external to the organization that can signal new growth, can also lead to crises. Many companies have enthusiastically expanded production and markets to overseas locations, only to encounter crises along the way.

The SWOT analysis not only reveals vulnerabilities but also helps identify the organization's strategic options. By conducting a thorough assessment of its strengths, weaknesses, opportunities, and threats, a business can build a matrix of strategic alternatives that align with its capabilities and limitations (Parnell, 2020). The SWOT analysis should always include input from internal and external stakeholders. Long-term decisions that rely on internal assessments can be shortsighted. Stakeholders, such as employees, suppliers, and business advisory boards, see the organization differently, so their insights can be invaluable.

The link between organizational crises and moral failure will strengthen.

Some have likened crisis events to moral failures on the part of the organization. This thinking is understandable, given the number of ethically related organizational crises over the past three decades. The Institute for Crisis Management has noted that most corporate crises are human-induced, with mismanagement comprising almost 27% of all crises (ICM Annual Crisis Report, 2018). The Institute further classifies 71% of events as a **smoldering crisis**. They start small, emanate internally, and are manageable at the outset, but quickly escalate. Addressing smoldering crises before they become full-blown is important.

In this book, we have discussed smoldering crises that were not adequately addressed by management. Many were due to ethical breaches in the organization. The core problem received inadequate attention, and the situation escalated to a crisis. Based on the nature of human behavior and the record of ethical breaches leading to crisis, such breaches will likely continue despite the best efforts of business schools, religious leaders, and management writers. Top management's example appears to reduce moral shortcomings (Carroll, Brown, & Buchholtz, 2017). It is encouraging that many organizations achieve a high level of ethical integrity in the way they conduct business.

Top managers should set the ethical tone. When they lack direction, employees look one level higher for cues to respond in a situation. Promoting good business ethics can go a long way in preventing an organizational crisis caused by unethical behavior.

Organizations will take advantage of data analytics to assess their crisis vulnerabilities.

As the opening case emphasized, crisis analytics is becoming an emerging trend in the field. Partnerships with tech-savvy companies can operationalize this tool (Crandall, Parnell, Spillan, & Crandall, 2018; Ward, 2017). For example, many companies collect vast amounts of data, particularly in select areas such as accident prevention initiatives. However, the volume of data can become overwhelming as companies do not know how to manage it (Nunan & Di Domenico, 2017; Schultz, 2015). Consider that fleet managers usually have the software installed on vehicles to monitor many variables such as speed and rest times. A vast amount of data can accumulate over time, often in a cloud environment. Analyzing this data requires specialized hardware and software programs. Insights follow the analysis. For example, in the concrete mixer industry, Marsh (2016) reports how on-board cameras have identified pre-accident scenarios.

The takeaway then is that many companies do not leverage the data they have collected. Tech-savvy companies can assist with suitable hardware and software platforms. With any big data collection initiative, there will be additional costs. This realization means that the return on investment for hardware and software must be positive (Poeppelman et al., 2013).

The External Landscape

Within the external landscape, emerging issues focus on two areas: the growing power of victims of a crisis and the eroding trust stakeholders experience when an organization either causes the crisis or is negligent in carrying out its duties during a crisis.

Victims of crises will become more visible and influential as stakeholders.

In the past, victims of crisis events have been acknowledged to some degree but were eventually forgotten. Indeed, individual victims, particularly those of natural disasters, are often poor and marginalized by society. They are also forgotten. Patrick Lagadec (2004) made this observation in examining the fatalities from the killer heat waves in France (2003) and Chicago (1995). In both events, those who died were often the poor, the elderly, and those who were isolated to some degree from society. After Hurricane Katrina struck New Orleans in 2005, victims of the storm began to receive much media attention. One of the reasons these victims were heard was the ineptness of government agencies inadequately responding to this disaster.

Today, social media enhances victim visibility. An Internet search of a crisis event also includes social media videos that are available depicting the event. Videos can be played and replayed, perpetuating the memory of the crisis and its victims. Hence, victims are less likely to be forgotten if they can be viewed on a moment's notice.

A crisis will be interpreted as a reason to mistrust an organization.

A crisis can reflect an issue of trust (Bertrand & Lajtha, 2002). This viewpoint maintains that the organization shares some of the blame for the crisis, either in terms of causing it or managing the crisis response. Even in a natural disaster, the organization or government can lose the trust held by stakeholders if it was not adequately prepared (Akbar & Aldrich, 2017). Hence, stakeholders perceive that organizations get the blame they deserve, and this in proportion to their degree of unpreparedness. While such an attitude does not always seem fair, the onslaught of media attention that accompanies crisis events indeed seeks a party to blame (Boin et al., 2010). Valid or not, this scapegoat mentality does help add meaning to an otherwise chaotic situation. Even if an organization or government is not to be directly blamed, a loss of public confidence is still a likely outcome (Bertrand & Lajtha, 2002).

Management holds a level of trust with its stakeholders. Within the organization, leaders must be trusted to manage the crisis as effectively as possible. Employees also expect that management will not induce a crisis. Such an event would reflect a trust issue if management made ill-advised cuts in say, safety training, or equipment. Should an employee be injured due to a cutback of this sort, employee trust in the organization would be compromised.

External stakeholders also trust the organization to prevent crises when possible and mitigate them when they do occur. As we discussed previously, the media, community, and customers often criticize the organization when it does not manage a crisis effectively. The issue of trust is becoming more critical. If stakeholders lose confidence in the organization, its ultimate survival may be in jeopardy. All stakeholders want to be able to say, "We trust you as an organization to do the right thing."

Strategic Planning

Strategic planning is a proactive stage when management plans for future crisis events. The trends and implications in this crucial area are discussed next.

The Internal Landscape

Virtual crisis management plans will become the norm.

Before the Internet, organizations retained crisis management plans and other standard operating procedures (SOP) in notebooks. Today, most medium-sized and large organizations post their plans online. This approach helps crisis managers evaluate other published plans when formulating or revising theirs. It also makes the plans easier to update.

The organization's information technology (IT) department must be involved in distributing the crisis management plan. This relationship is a welcome one since IT is an integral part of crisis recovery anyway.

Crisis management planning will be integrated into the organization's strategic planning process.

A designated crisis management team has traditionally implemented the plan. In the past, companies with such teams typically had them operate outside of the strategic management process (Preble, 1997). An emerging trend is to incorporate crisis management and strategic planning together (Chong & Park, 2010; Coombs, 2006; Parnell, 2020), a theme consistent with this book. This approach makes crisis awareness an ongoing process that is reviewed alongside other strategic plans and incorporates vulnerability analysis into the SWOT. Management must ensure that the entire crisis management process does not occur in a far corner of the organization, away from the essential players. It should be part of an ongoing strategic planning process, not a separate activity that occurs only occasionally.

The External Landscape

Crisis management teams will engage in more planning with other crisis teams from outside their organization.

Traditionally, one crisis management team (CMT) is organized for each unit in the organization. For example, a large company with several plants may establish one CMT for each manufacturing facility. There may also be an overall team for the entire organization. This type of arrangement works well when the crisis event is localized.

In crises that are more complicated and geographically diverse, organizational crisis management units must interact with similar teams from other organizations. A host of government agencies may also be involved in this network of crisis teams. These interlinking crisis teams have been labeled *hastily assembled networks* (Denning, 2006) and may form during an event such as a natural disaster. The 2005 onslaught of

Hurricane Katrina led to quickly formed networks among aid agencies, crisis management teams, military units, emergency response teams, and local governments.

There may not be a unified chain of command within a local geographic area with a crisis like Hurricane Katrina. What results is a modified chain of command that considers both the various stakeholders that are part of the disaster and the disaster relief efforts. Typically, local governmental agencies coordinate a hurricane response, but in Katrina, the city of New Orleans lacked some essential resources and did not manage others effectively (Berinato, 2010). The result was a network formed quickly and coordinated by multiple agencies.

The implication of this trend is essential. CMT leaders must begin to network with their counterparts in other organizations. There are opportunities for knowledge transfer, as well as the planning of disaster drills. The time to interact with these groups is before the crisis occurs. In this way, crisis team members are familiar with their counterparts and have already developed working relationships.

The focus efforts of crisis management will expand to include a broader range of stakeholders.

The traditional scope of crisis management initially focused on media relations ('t Hart et al., 2001; Marra, 1998). Analysts assumed that a good relationship with the media would help ensure that the public perceives the company in a positive light.

Today, the scope of crisis management outreach is adopting a broader stakeholder approach that advocates meeting the needs of multiple groups with distinct vested interests in the organization (Carroll, Brown, & Buchholtz, 2017). Indeed, employees represent one such stakeholder (Lockwood, 2005). This sometimes-forgotten group needs to know both the good and bad news that occurs during a crisis. Employees are a vital resource. They can help pull the firm through precarious times.

Other stakeholders affected by a crisis include customers and the local communities in which they reside. The response to Katrina by several large private-sector companies in New Orleans and the surrounding areas provides an example. Walmart, Home Depot, and FedEx tracked the hurricane and moved aggressively to meet community needs after the storm hit (Olasky, 2006). While they desired to increase business, these firms were poised to fill a humanitarian role in the aftermath of the storm.

The implication for crisis managers is to expand the scope of organizational response to include helping local stakeholders where possible. Such a strategy is especially welcome when a local geographical area has been affected by a natural disaster. This response will vary according to the type of services offered by the organization. Several applications have become apparent. Foodservice establishments may provide certain products during times when these items may be scarce in the community. Offering products free or at a reduced cost may be feasible. On the other hand, raising prices to reflect scarcity will be viewed by many as inappropriate opportunism and will create community ill will that can last long after the crisis subsides. The community will perceive that the business took advantage of the victims.

Retailers can ensure that adequate supplies of staple items such as flashlights, batteries, and portable stoves will be available. Managers who place orders for these items must be able to anticipate the kind of emergency products that will be needed and order accordingly. Again, opportunistic price increases will create bad feelings in the community. Organizations with access to automotive or van fleets may offer transportation for the elderly or needy. This service could be accomplished by providing pickup and delivery for low-income citizens to local stores, like what a bus service would offer in a city. While providing this type of service may sound absurd to some managers, doing so on a temporary emergency basis will be appreciated and well-received by the community. To summarize, planning for a crisis means considering the interests of the company and the community.

Sustainable development will become more of an expectation.

Sustainable development has been emerging as a trend in recent years, and many organizations are now embracing sustainability as part of their strategic mission. Executives and others must learn more about sustainability issues associated with the use of nonrenewable resources. Governments also play a role. Sustainable development should not be confused with protecting the environment from pollution and avoiding calamities like oil spills, although these incidents indeed squander resources. The former is associated with accidents while the latter concerns everyday business practice. Hence, sustainable development implies that organizations use resources to conserves resources for future generations (Stead & Stead, 2004). In other words, resources that are utilized, such as trees, should be renewable. Nonrenewable resources should be used judiciously. An outgrowth from this movement is that companies must be practicing sustainability and influence their supply chains accordingly.

The relationship between crisis management and sustainable development must also be acknowledged (Crandall & Mensah, 2008). These two areas are closely related because an environmental crisis triggered by an organizational mistake can quickly consume valuable resources. Oil spills are at the forefront of the news when they occur. Consumers become angry when the environment is damaged, and nonrenewable resources are squandered, and public disdain mounts daily for the affected oil companies. But other less obvious examples exist in the crosshairs of crisis and sustainable development. Sustainable development efforts are costly in terms of time and money. A company that ignores sustainable development will soon find itself behind its rivals and potentially in a crisis. Such a scenario can create a public relations problem as the company must explain to its public stakeholders why they have not been embracing sustainability when other companies have been doing so for years.

As discussed in chapter 3, Interface manufactures modular carpet and has been innovating in sustainability since 1994. Modular carpet requires considerable energy resources and capacity to manufacture and significant landfill space for disposal. In its quest to be a leader in sustainable development, Interface created a model that describes the closed loop process it seeks in its manufacturing and disposal processes (Nelson, 2009). The model at Interface builds on a foundation of seven principles:

- Eliminating waste – not just reduce it but remove it altogether in the production process.
- Producing only benign emissions – eliminate all harmful emissions in the manufacturing of its products, and the products themselves.
- Using renewable energy – reduce the use of non-sustainable energy sources (oil) and increase the usage of renewable ones, such as wind, solar, and landfill gas.
- Closing the loop – design the manufacturing process so that waste byproducts are recycled into some aspect of the manufacturing process.
- Using efficient transportation – transport the company's people and products to reduce pollution, greenhouse emissions, and oil consumption.
- Sensitizing stakeholders – educate the company's stakeholders (employees, partners, customers, communities, suppliers, and owners) on promoting a culture of sustainability in the community.
- Redesigning commerce – become a role model for other businesses, supply chains, and industries on incorporating sustainability in business practices (Nelson, 2009).

Interface's strategy is aggressive, to be sure. However, it does give other companies a benchmark to begin their sustainable development initiatives.

Crisis Management

Crisis management is the reactive phase of the four-stage model outlined in this book. Specifically, it is the stage where the organization responds to a given crisis. Emerging trends within the internal landscape are discussed next.

The Internal Landscape

Contingency responses to specific crisis events will become more common.

Conventional crisis planning has typically followed a standardized procedure in addressing incidents. As a result, most crisis plans contain specific procedures to follow during a crisis. For example, bomb threats are frequent crisis events, and strategies for these usually include a step-by-step process for responding. Another example is the evacuation of a building, which should be carried out in an organized, systematic fashion. Responding to complex crises, however, will also involve contingency approaches. This line of thinking maintains that there may not be one best approach to addressing every crisis.

Shrivastava (1993) noted the beginning of a shift from procedures to broader-based crisis skills in the early 1990s, including decentralized decision-making, managerial autonomy, and flexibility. This approach recognizes that organizations need to maintain some flexibility. Bertrand and Lajtha (2002) referred to this ability as the "breaking of inflexible mindsets" or "training oneself to deal with the unexpected" (p. 186).

While becoming more adaptive in its response, an organization may develop greater **resilience**, the ability to recover from an unfortunate event such as a crisis (Linnenluecke, 2017; Sutcliffe & Vogus, 2003). Resilience is not a step-by-step methodology in terms of crisis response. Still, it is more of an inherent trait of the organization that takes advantage of its ability to adapt and improvise when a crisis unfolds (Somers, 2009).

The implications for management are twofold. First, crisis planners need to anticipate specific vulnerabilities and how they should be managed in a step-by-step process if the threat can be addressed in this manner. Second, the crisis response should maintain flexibility in more complex situations. Adjusting along the way is part of contingency thinking, and this is both an art and a science. An effective crisis response includes a set of plans that become the backbone for managing the event. It also requires a degree of improvisation, creating new responses considering further information that the crisis may reveal.

The organization's website and social media networks will become the main communication tools during a crisis.

The organization's web site and social media networks will become the primary communication vehicle to its stakeholders during a crisis. Without redundancy, a crisis can temporarily eliminate an organization's Web presence. Union University, a small private institution in western Tennessee, experienced this in February 2008 when a tornado hit the campus, damaging buildings and shutting down the Web site for several hours. On the other hand, Virginia Tech was able to remain online by loading a simplified "light version" of its Web site after the April 2007 shooting rampage by student Seung-Hui Cho. The Web site became a critical communication device with the public during the ordeal. Following the shootings, the Web site received up to 150,000 visits per hour. It typically transfers 15 gigabytes a day, but the Web server transferred 432 gigabytes on the day of the shooting (Carlson, 2007).

As referenced in chapter 8, social media tools are also being used more in crisis communications. Social media enable firms to disseminate information, even if the organization's Web site becomes inoperable. Such was the case after the Union University tornado. The university's Web site was not operating after the storm, so a blog was set up at blogspot.com to update the damage and recovery.

Crisis managers must educate themselves about the various social networking tools available. Unlike Web sites, which often require individuals with specialized skills to operate, social networking tools are relatively easy to use and manage. However, social media also include the added burden of communicating in a two-way environment, sometimes referred to as Web 2.0. Managers should become proficient with Facebook and Twitter if they have not done so already, as both can be useful for crisis management situations (Crowe, 2010).

The External Landscape

Social media will become more powerful due to its ability to transfer news quickly about a crisis. Three implications of this trend are discussed below.

Social media will play a more significant role in determining the outcome of a crisis.

Social media will continue to exert a more significant influence on the outcome of a crisis. One of the first companies directly affected by an Internet-related crisis was Intel, when its flawed Pentium chip surfaced in 1994. The crisis began rather innocently when Lynchburg College math professor Thomas Nicely discovered a computer error when working on a math problem. He emailed a colleague about the matter, and soon his spreadsheet problem demonstrating an Intel calculation error was widely available on the Internet (Weiss, 1998). Intel had become one of the first victims of substantial negative Internet publicity, a phenomenon known as flaming.

In terms of crisis management, the Internet can transmit information—usually negative—about a company to a broad audience. Social media tools add the ability to communicate in real time using media other than the printed word, through computers and smartphones. Because of this power, social media will also become more pivotal in influencing the outcome of a crisis. We reviewed several cases that were affected by social media in chapter 8.

Time will be a critical metric for evaluating an organization's response to a crisis.

With the influence of social media, organizations are under significant pressure to respond to crises more rapidly. The longer a company waits to respond, the more likely stakeholders will perceive it as either being indecisive or having something to hide. Statements need to appear on the organization's website, Facebook page, and Twitter outlet within a few hours (or less) of the crisis. Waiting more than 24 hours to issue a statement is no longer acceptable. Many stakeholders expect a response in several hours.

The perceived duration of a crisis will decrease among external stakeholders.

One of the ironies of social media is that external stakeholders want to learn about a crisis quickly. That said, the perceived duration of that crisis will diminish as other crisis events will crowd out the attention span of the viewer of social media. The adage, "out of sight, out of mind," rings true. Put differently, today's major crisis is tomorrow's forgotten crisis as other events take over the viewer's attention.

Organizational Learning

Organizational learning ensures that a company's crisis response will improve when the next incident occurs. Learning also helps to prevent certain types of crises from reappearing in the future. The following discussion outlines the importance of establishing a feedback loop in the strategic planning process and abolishing the status quo when necessary.

The Internal Landscape

Organizational learning will provide a valuable feedback loop necessary for the strategic planning process.

Many crisis management scholars have called for a renewed focus on the post-crisis stage, where learning and evaluation need to occur (Deverell, 2009; Nathan, 2015; Racherla & Hu, 2009; Veil, 2011). What is significant about organizational learning is that it initiates the feedback loop (see chapter 9, figure 9-3) necessary for the strategic management framework (Racherla & Hu, 2009).

The implication of this emerging trend is significant and remains a central theme of this book. Indeed, from a landscape survey to organizational learning, the crisis management process needs to be an integral part of the organization's strategic planning process. The days when crisis management consisted of a small, select group of managers who wrote the crisis plan and met occasionally are gone. Crisis events impact strategy in the long run; therefore, planning, managing, and learning from these events must be carried out within the strategic management framework.

Learning after a crisis will lead to the abolishment of the existing status quo.

Returning to business as usual after a crisis has been the traditional mindset of many organizations. However, a crisis offers an opportunity to change or even abolish the status quo. "Crises are, by their very nature, an invitation to abandon standard ways of doing things. They offer an opportunity to think and work laterally and to de-compartmentalize/break down encrusted silos in the company" (Bertrand & Lajtha, 2002, p. 186). Inherent in this mindset is the notion that a crisis can trigger the forces of renewal in an organization (Dynes, 2003; Olshansky, 2006). Some liken the changes after a crisis to a process called "self-organization". This metamorphosis occurs when an organization works through a crisis and transforms into a more adaptable organization (Murphy, 1996).

Consider the Red River Valley flood of 1997 and the subsequent organizational renewal that occurred as analyzed through the lens of chaos theory. The local government of Fargo, North Dakota, emerged as a new leader in that geographic area, taking over the lead in emergency response management from the county, which had formerly carried out this function (Sellnow, Seeger, & Ulmer, 2002). In a similar vein, crisis planning at movie theaters changed forever when James Holmes entered a packed theater in Aurora, Colorado, and shot 70 people on July 20, 2012 (Berzon, Banjo & Audi, 2012).

A cosmology episode can prompt an organization to abolish the status quo. They thrust management into situations that have never been encountered before. As discussed previously, a cosmology episode cannot be explained within the current mindset of management; put differently; there is a collapse of sensemaking and all forms of the status quo must be abandoned for new insights into understanding the crisis and managing it (Weick, 1993). Researchers have examined the cosmology episode dilemma within a crisis management context. Weick (1993) conceptualized sensemaking collapse and used it to explore the Mann Gulch wildfire. More recently, Sherman and Harris (2018) reviewed the GM ignition switch crisis using the sensemaking paradigm. In both cases, significant shifts in the status quo on how to manage a crisis were necessitated. The COVID-19 pandemic also illustrates this phenomenon. For example, many restaurants revised their product lines and service strategies to emphasize online ordering, delivery, and drive-through capabilities (Haddon & Kang, 2020).

The implication for crisis managers and strategic planners is one of hope. Although crises are negative events, they can engender positive change. However, positive change only occurs when the learning process is tied back to the strategic planning process. Managers need to understand their roles as potential change agents in their organizations.

The External Landscape

Outside of the organization, an abundance of learning on crisis management is continually taking place. This area includes the work of crisis scholars. The following are emerging trends in the field of crisis management research.

Crisis management frameworks and models will become more complex and sophisticated.

Frameworks of crisis management have traditionally been simple, with most depicting a sequential format for understanding the evolution and resolution of a crisis. The most basic framework consists of a pre-crisis, crisis, and post-crisis sequence, as overviewed in Chapter 1. Smith (1990) and Richardson (1994) utilized this approach in their studies. Four- and five-stage frameworks also exist (see Fink, 1996; Hosie & Smith, 2004; Myers, 1993; Pearson & Mitroff, 1993); this book also employs a four-stage approach. Crisis frameworks have also been offered for types of crisis categories and crisis management communication strategies (see chapter 8).

Although frameworks offer a general approach to understanding the components of crisis phenomena, models are designed to examine the different variables that interact before and during a crisis. Some progress has occurred in the area of organizational crisis model building. Shrivastava, Mitroff, Miller, and Miglani (1988) offered one of the first industrial crisis models. Sheaffer, Richardson, and Rosenblatt (1998) studied the 1995 collapse of Barings, a conservative and once stable British bank, and proposed a crisis–causal antecedents' model and an early-warning-signals model. Pearson and Clair (1998) proposed a success–failure outcomes model. Elsubbaugh, Fildes and Rose (2004) developed a crisis preparedness model using data from the Egyptian textile industry. Jin and Liu (2010) developed a blog-mediated crisis communication model for public relations professionals.

Crisis research will continue to emphasize case studies and best practices but will incorporate more statistical analysis.

Case studies have dominated crisis management research. Indeed, much can be gleaned from examining a past crisis in detail. In the 1980s, Union Carbide's Bhopal disaster, Johnson & Johnson's Tylenol cyanide sabotage, and the Exxon Valdez oil spill are well documented. Many high-profile events made valuable case studies in the 1990s, including the bombing of the Alfred P. Murrah Federal Building in Oklahoma City, the crash of ValuJet Flight 592 in Florida's Everglades, and the Luby's Cafeteria massacre in

Killeen, Texas. Since the beginning of the millennium, the September 11 toppling of the World Trade Center Towers, Hurricane Katrina, the Asian tsunami of December 2004, and the 2008 China earthquake (also known as the Great Sichuan Earthquake) have been subjects for case studies. The late 2000s and early 2010s brought three more events that will undoubtedly be studied intensely as case studies, the BP Deepwater oil spill, the Toyota recall, the Colorado movie theater crisis, and the Boeing 737 Max crisis. The COVID-19 pandemic that evolved in 2019 and 2020 has radically changed how business leaders view crisis planning.

Crisis research will take on a long-range perspective.

Crisis management research has traditionally focused on short-term, single-event crises. The study of these events includes analyzing the various phases of the crisis from the pre-crisis the learning. However, the long-term effects of these crises have not been widely evaluated. Revisiting the sites and stakeholders involved in a crisis to determine what learning and policy changes have been implemented is often appropriate ('t Hart et al., 2001). A long-term view of a crisis also looks at the precursors of these events. Analyzing variables such as the organizational culture and other mini-steps that led to the crisis can yield useful information to both researchers and managers.

Research data are drawn from the activities and experiences of practicing managers whose organizations are engaged in crisis management. In the future, you may be asked to participate in a research study about organizational crises. Your participation will help scholars learn how organizations can respond more effectively to a crisis.

Crisis analytics will become a vital tool in crisis management research.

We have mentioned that crisis analytics will be a tool for management in the future. It will also be of use for researchers. However, crisis analytics follows different assumptions from traditional scholarly research. It seeks to follow and understand data rather than testing theory. In big data analytics, the goal is to gather as much data as possible and look for patterns (Mayer-Schönberger & Cukier, 2013). Hence, in big data analytics, correlation is very important even if researchers cannot explain causality. The way crisis researchers approach big data will necessitate changes in the way they approach their statistical assumptions.

Summary

This chapter examined the emerging trends in the field of crisis management. One of the key trends mentioned is also a central theme of this book—that crisis management should be an integral part of the strategic management process. In the past, much of what we call crisis management existed in a vacuum, separate from strategic management. Successful companies are integrating the two domains.

Discussion Questions

1. Why do you think crisis management has not always been emphasized in the strategic management process?
2. Hastily formed networks are an emerging trend in crisis management, particularly in disaster management. If a major storm were to hit your local area, what groups do you think should be part of the network to coordinate crisis and disaster relief?
3. Sustainable development is a trend in many organizations. What efforts at sustainability do you see at your college or university? What is occurring where you work to implement sustainable development? What changes do you recommend?
4. How have organizations leveraged crises emanating from the COVID-19 pandemic to strengthen their firms?
5. Why do you think ethical violations continue to be a source of crises in organizations today?
6. Crisis management research is a developing field. What areas not addressed in this chapter might also require additional research?
7. What trends do you see in big data and crisis management practice?

Chapter Exercise

Many organizational crisis management plans are now available online. Locate your college or university's CMP online. As an alternative, locate plans in companies where students work or at a prominent organization in your community. Evaluate each plan as a class and consider the following:

- How long is the CMP? Do you think it is too short, or perhaps too long?
- What items are omitted from the plan and should be included?
- Do the plans present ALL potential crisis vulnerabilities that the organization may face?
- Do the plans acknowledge the presence of potential environmental crises that may occur?
- Do the plans include provisions for post–crisis debriefing? In other words, are their opportunities for organizational learning to occur?

Closing Chapter Case: The Emerging Field of Crisis Analytics - Part 2

As referenced in part 1 at the beginning of the chapter, crisis analytics merges big data with organizational crisis management. In the discussion that follows, we offer recent applications of crisis analytics.

Crisis Analytics Applications

Applications of crisis analytics are relatively new. The discussion below shows examples from crisis mapping, accident prevention, crowdsourcing, the opioid crisis, and river level modeling.

Crisis mapping. From a historical perspective, crisis mapping may be the first documented use of big data in a humanitarian situation (Qadir, et al., 2016). The year was 1854 in London, England, and a severe cholera outbreak had overtaken the city. Physician John Snow published a map of the epidemic using data that included the number of deaths by geographic location. These findings were mapped, and he argued that the deaths were caused by a water pump on Broad Street in the Soho area of London. While these findings may seem logical today, Snow challenged an entrenched theory of the time, the idea that cholera was spread through the air and not by water (Koch & Denike, 2010).

From these humble beginnings, crisis mapping has advanced to the use of sophisticated software to track events on a geographical plane. For example, in 2008, post-election violence in Kenya occurred, causing more than a thousand fatalities. Kenyan activists produced a "live-map" showing geographically where human rights abuses were taking place. Anyone with an Internet or mobile phone connection could report these abuses in real-time and, thus, provide support documentation of the atrocities which would have gone unreported in the past (Meier, 2012).

In 2010, the earthquake in Haiti produced more applications of crisis mapping. Using data from Twitter, text messages, Facebook, and mainstream media, live open-sourced maps were constructed using Ushahidi software to locate survivors who needed food, water, and healthcare (Twarog, 2017). The amount of data was so overwhelming that over 100 volunteers through Tufts University in Boston, Massachusetts were trained to input the data. The resulting map provided the most up-to-date information available for use by the humanitarian community. The US Marine Corps and the US Coast Guard saved hundreds of lives by using the map (Meier, 2012).

During the COVID-19 pandemic, crisis mapping helped governments and medical professionals identify areas where infections were expanding. Resources diverted to these hot spots saved lives.

Accident prevention. Big data safety analytics has yielded impressive results, including reducing injury rates, lost workday rates, insurance fees, and worker's compensation fees (Schultz, 2015).

Accident prevention data can originate from other sources, including digitally generated photographs from video cameras and smartphones. In the railway industry, video cameras have become popular to monitor train rails (Li & Ren, 2012). The aspiration is that images from the video cameras can help predict future problems. For example, Jamshidi and colleagues (2017) proposed a framework to predict rail defects by analyzing the physical length of squats (i.e., physical cracks on the rail) that can lengthen and eventually lead to structural failure.

Crowdsourcing. New product ideas can be evaluated more thoroughly when both internal experts and diverse crowd members are involved in the process. This type of vetting can lessen the risk of myopia and groupthink that engulfs many firms when decisions are made without external input. Coca-Cola's disastrous launch of reformulated "New Coke" in 1985 illustrates this problem. While Coca-Cola spent millions of dollars on research and taste tests that included over 200,000 people, executives—concerned with the firm's attrition in market share—overlooked the intangibles. Building pressure for change prompted Coca-Cola to test the new formula in such secrecy. Unfortunately, issues such as loyalty and emotional attachment to a brand were discounted (Carfagno & Parnell, 2016). Crowdsourcing could have provided independent opinions and diversity from a wide range of participants to balance internal specialists (Chan, 2013; Surowiecki, 2005).

The Opioid crisis. Drug overdoses are killing thousands of people in the United States annually. In 2016, 64,000 people died from this epidemic (Kelly, 2017). Big data is now being used to combat the crisis. With a robust quantity of both objective and subjective data available for analysis, companies can use this information to target areas of high and severe usage of the drug. In one example, the state of Missouri used data solutions from Xerox to eliminate prescription monitoring gaps that led to significant intervention and reduced the loss of life. The aggregation of data sources (i.e., big data) can help health professionals analyze patterns of impact and develop intervention plans to ameliorate or eliminate problems (Kelley, 2017).

Big data to analyze and solve the problem of opioid abuse in the US. The challenge has been to gather data from various, disjointed data silos across the state and merge them into something useful. The state of Indiana has upgraded its information gathering and coding capabilities and created a new Management Performance Hub. Initially, the hub was designed with reducing traffic crashes in mind, but now, efforts are underway to use it to create crisis mapping tools to show where drug treatment centers should be placed (Russell, 2017).

Modeling river level behavior. Floods from France's longest river, the Loire, have been common over the years. In France, 74 percent of the cities are at risk from flooding each year, and over 80 percent of the destruction from natural disasters are caused by flooding (Fertier et al., 2016).

Modeling the river behavior can be beneficial to stakeholders along the river who could be affected by flooding. Fertier et al. (2016) proposed a project that utilizes stakeholders and crisis cells that provide critical information for decision-making before and during the flooding. The cells centralize and facilitate collaboration among the stakeholders in the regional areas along the river. Managing the information sharing and collaboration from a geographical perspective requires sophisticated data management. More essential data becomes available over time. The need to understand and transfer data from stakeholders becomes crucial to make timely decisions. Automation of big data helps filter and aggregate the data for effective decision-making. Because more data sources are constantly added, the situation models can become more accurate, reducing the damage, suffering, and loss of human life.

Assessing Big Data and Crisis Analytics

Big data presents numerous opportunities for crisis managers. Indeed, the potential gains from crisis analytics are immense. Data is powerful. When analyzed properly, it can help decision-makers visualize crisis events before they occur. As such, it offers the most significant potential for crisis prevention.

There are many challenges. First, data must be analyzed before it can generate insight. Managers often have more data available than they have time to analyze. Projects such as the Global Database of Events, Language, and Tone (GDELT) offer substantial promise but are still emerging.

Second, big data lends itself to paralysis by analysis, a state whereby decision-makers cannot navigate the wealth of available data efficiently and hence, fail to act. Crisis managers seek to satisfice. They are trained to make quick, workable (but not optimal) decisions under uncertainty (Parnell & Crandall, 2017). Satisficing decisions may be required. The first satisfactory course of action is often selected (Fox, 2015). Crisis analytics is primarily useful in the pre-crisis stage—when time is not at a premium—but is only useful during a crisis when data can be analyzed quickly and efficiently.

Finally, crisis analytics requires extensive training and a new approach to decision-making. Practitioner models based on intuition and experience do not harness the power of the data. Also, the academic model of hypothesis testing augmented by peer review is also impractical. Statistical tools such as SmartPLS provide an intuitive, more flexible, prediction-oriented approach to data analytics and modeling (Hair et al., 2012). Applying such tools, along with a more practical approach to data analysis, is required.

Case Discussion Questions

1. What applications of crisis management analytics have you seen where you work?
2. What is a specific problem or crisis scenario that could benefit from crisis analytics?

References

Adams, M. (2017, April). Big data and individual privacy in the age of the Internet of Things. *Technology Innovation Management Review, 7*(4), 12-24.

Akbar, M., & Aldrich, D. (2017). Determinants of post-flood social and institutional trust among disaster victims. *Journal of Contingencies and Crisis Management, 25*(4), 279-288.

Berinato, S. (2010). "You have to lead from everywhere." *Harvard Business Review, 88*(11), 76-79.

Bertrand, R., & Lajtha, C. (2002). A new approach to crisis management. *Journal of Contingencies and Crisis Management, 10*(4), 181–191.

Berzon, A., Banjo, S., & Audi, T. (2012, July 23). Suspect's rapid descent. *Wall Street Journal*, pp. A1, A4.

Boin, A., 't Hart, P., McConnell, A., & Preston, T. (2010). Leadership style, crisis response and blame management: The case of Hurricane Katrina. *Public Administration, 88*(3), 706-723.

BrightPlanet, (2015). Strengthen your risk management framework. White Paper. Retrieved October 12, 2017, from http://bigdata2.brightplanet.com/strengthen-your-risk-management-frame-work

Carfagno, K., & Parnell, J.A. (2016). Crowdsourcing: Organizations using social media for meaningful crisis management. *Presentation at the 2016 Academy of Management Conference*, Anaheim, CA, August 8, 2016.

Carlson, S. (2007, August 3). Emergency at Virginia Tech shows the power of the Web, says campus official. *Chronicle of Higher Education, 53*(48), 28.

Carroll, A., Brown, J., & Buchholtz, A. (2017). *Business & society: Ethics sustainability, and stakeholder management* (10th ed.). Mason, OH: South-Western/Cengage Learning.

Chan, J.C. (2013). The role of social media in crisis preparedness, response and recovery. *Vanguard: An In-Depth Analysis of Emerging Issues and Trends. RAHS Think Centre*. Retrieved November 22, 2017, from www.oecd.org/governance/risk/The%20role%20of%20Social%20media%20in%20crisis%20preparedness,%20response%20and%20recovery.pdf

Choi, T., & Lambert, J. (2017). Advances in risk analysis with Big Data. *Risk Analysis, 37*(8), 1435-1442.

Chong, J., & Park, J. (2010). A conceptual framework and research propositions for integrating TQM into crisis planning. *Review of Business Research, 10*(2), 69-74.

Coombs, W. (2006). *Code red in the boardroom: Crisis management as organizational DNA*. Westport, CT: Praeger.

Cox, M., & Ellsworth, D. (1997). Managing Big Data for Scientific Visualization. *ACM SIGGRAPH*, (August), 5-1 to 5-17.

Crandall, W., & Mensah, E. (2008). Crisis management and sustainable development: A framework and proposed research agenda. *International Journal of Sustainable Strategic Management, 1*(1), 16–34.

Crandall, W., Parnell, J., Spillan, J., & Crandall, R. (2018). Crisis analytics: When big data and crisis management collide. *Proceedings* of the North American Management Society, Chicago, Illinois.

Crowe, A. (2010). The social media manifesto: A comprehensive review of the impact of social media on emergency management. *Journal of Business Continuity & Emergency Planning, 5*(1), 409-420.

Denning, P. (2006). Hastily formed networks: Collaboration in the absence of authority. *Communications of ACM, 49*(4), 15–20.

Deverell, E. (2009). Crises as learning triggers: Exploring a conceptual framework of crisis-induced learning. *Journal of Contingencies and Crisis Management, 17*(3), 179-188.

Drosio, S., & Stanek, S. (2016). The Big Data concept as a contributor of added value to crisis decision support systems. *Journal of Decision Systems, 25*(S1), 228-239.

Dynes, R. (2003). Noah and disaster planning: The cultural significance of the flood story. *Journal of Contingencies and Crisis Management, 11*(4), 170–177.

Elsubbaugh, S., Fildes, R., & Rose, M. (2004). Preparation for crisis management: A proposed model and empirical evidence. *Journal of Contingencies and Crisis Management, 12*(3), 112–127.

Emmanouil, D., & Nikolaos, D. (2015). Big data analytics in prevention, preparedness, response, and recovery in crisis and disaster management. *Recent Advances in Computer Science*, 476-482. ISBN: 978-1-61804-320-7

Fertier, A., Montarnal, A., Barthe-Delanoë, A., Truptil, S., & Bénaben, F. (2016). Adoption of big data in crisis management toward a better support in decision-making. *Proceedings of the ISCRAM 2016 Conference*, Rio de Janeiro, Brazil, May.

Fink, S. (1996). *Crisis management: Planning for the inevitable.* New York: American Management Association.

Fox, J. (2015, May). From "Economic Man" to behavioral economics: A short history of modern decision-making. *Harvard Business Review,* 79-85.

Haddon, H., & Kang, J. (2020, June 26). Grocers, restaurants push pickup. *Wall Street Journal*, p. B3.

Hair, J., Sarstedt, M., Pieper, T., & Ringle, C. (2012). The use of partial least squares structural equation modeling in strategic management research: A review of past practices and recommendations for future applications. *Long Range Planning, 45*(5-6), 320-340.

't Hart, P., Heyse, L., & Boin, A. (2001). New trends in crisis management practice and crisis management research: Setting the agenda. *Journal of Contingencies & Crisis Management, 9*(4), 181–188.

Hermann, M., & Dayton, B. (2009). Transboundary crises through the eyes of policymakers: Sense making and crisis management. *Journal of Contingencies and Crisis Management, 17*(4), 233-241.

Hosie, P., & Smith, C. (2004). Preparing for crisis: Online security management education. *Research and Practice in Human Resource Management, 12*(2), 90–127.

Institute for Crisis Management. (2018). *Annual ICM crisis report: News coverage of business crises during 2017.* Retrieved May 13, 2018, from https://crisisconsultant.com/icm-annual-crisis-report/

Jamshidi, A., Faghih-Roohi, S., Hajizadeh, S., Núñez, A., Babuska, R., Dollevoet, R. Li, Z., & De Schutter, B. (2017). A big data analysis approach for rail failure risk assessment. *Risk Analysis, 37*(8), 1495-1507.

Jin, Y., & Liu, B. (2010). The blog-mediated crisis communication model: Recommendations for responding to influential external blogs. *Journal of Public Relations, 22*(4), 429-455.

Kelley, J. (2017, October 2). Using big data medical analytics to address the opioid crisis. *Forbes.* Retrieved September 9, 2018, from https://www.forbes.com/sites/forbestechcouncil/2017/10/02/using-big-data-medical-analytics-to-address-the-opioid-crisis/#335be849142c

Koch, T., & Denike, K. (2010). Essential, illustrative, or … just propaganda? Rethinking John Snow's Broad Street Map. *Cartographica, 45*(1), 19-31.

Lagadec, P. (2004). Understanding the French 2003 heat wave experience: Beyond the heat, a multi-layered challenge. *Journal of Contingencies and Crisis Management, 12*(4), 160–169.

Li, Q., & Ren, S. (2012). A real-time visual inspection system for discrete surface defects of rail heads. *IEEE Transactions on Instrumentation and Measurement, 61*(8), 2189-2199.

Linnenluecke, M. (2017). Resilience in business and management research: A review of influential publications and a research agenda. *International Journal of Management Reviews, 19,* 4-30.

Lockwood, N. (2005). Crisis management in today's business environment: HR's strategic role. *SHRM Research Quarterly, 4,* 1–9.

Lokanathan, S. & Gunaratine, R. (2015). Mobile network big data for development: Demystifying the uses and challenges. *Digiworld Economic Journal, 97*(1), 75-94.

Marra, F. (1998). Crisis communication plans: Poor predictors of excellent public relations. *Public Relations Review, 24*(4), 461–474.

Marsh, D. (2016). Big data mining advances safe mixer truck operations. *Concrete Products, 119*(11), 20.

Mathis, T. (2016). The magic pill called "Big Data". *EHS Today, 9*(9), 8-9.

Mayer-Schönberger, V., & Cukier, K. (2013). *Big data: A revolution that will transform how we live, work and think.* London: John Murray.

Meier, P. (2012). Crisis mapping in action: How open source software and global volunteer networks are changing the world, one map at a time. *Journal of Map and Geography Libraries, 8,* 89-100.

Murphy, P. (1996). Chaos theory as a model for managing issues and crises. *Public Relations Review, 22*(2), 95–113.

Myers, K. (1993). *Total contingency planning for disasters: Managing risk . . . minimizing loss . . . ensuring business continuity.* New York: John Wiley.

Nathan, M. (2015). E-Learning's indispensability in crisis management education. *Global Education Journal, 3,* 82-88.

Nelson, E. (2009). How Interface innovates with suppliers to create sustainable solutions. *Global Business and Organizational Excellence, 28*(6), 22-30.

Nunan, D., & Di Domenico, M. (2017). Big data: A normal accident waiting to happen? *Journal of Business Ethics, 145,* 481-491.

Olasky, M. (2006). *The politics of disaster: Katrina, big government, and a new strategy for future crisis.* Nashville, TN: W Publishing Group.

Olshansky, R. (2006). Planning after Hurricane Katrina. *Journal of the American Planning Association, 72*(2), 147–153.

Parnell, J. (2020). *Strategic management: Theory and practice (6th ed.).* Solon, OH: Academic Media Solutions.

Parnell, J., & Crandall, W. (2017). The contribution of behavioral economics to crisis management decision-making. *Journal of Management & Organization,* 1-16. doi:10.1017/jmo.2017.60

Pearson, C., & Clair, J. (1998). Reframing crisis management. *Academy of Management Review, 23*(1), 59–76.

Pearson, C., & Mitroff, I. (1993). From crisis prone to crisis prepared: A framework for crisis management. *Academy of Management Executive, 7*(1), 48–59.

Poeppelman, T., Blacksmith, N., & Yang, Y. (2013). "Big Data" Technologies: Problem or solution. *The Industrial Organizational Psychologist, 51*(2), 119-126.

Preble, J. (1997). Integrating the crisis management perspective into the strategic management process. *Journal of Management Studies, 34*(5), 769–791.

Qadir, J., Ali, A., ur Rasool, R., Zwitter, A., Sathiaseelan, A., & Crowcraft, J. (2016). Crisis analytics: Big data driven crisis response. *Journal of International Humanitarian Action, 1*(12). Retrieved October 13, 2017, from https://jhumanitarianaction.springeropen.com/articles/10.1186/s41018-016-0013-9

Racherla, P., & Hu, C. (2009). A framework for knowledge-based crisis management in the hospitality and tourism industry. *Cornell Hospitality Quarterly, 50*(4), 561-577.

Richardson, B. (1994). Socio-technical disasters: Profile and prevalence. *Disaster Prevention & Management, 3*(4), 41–69.

Russell, J. (2017). Using big data to attack epidemic. *Indianapolis Business Journal, 38*(14), 6, 42.

Schultz, G. (2015). Don't drown in Big Data: Use it to reduce injuries and save lives. *Industrial Safety & Hygiene News, 49*(6), 52-53.

Sellnow, T., Seeger, M., & Ulmer, R. (2002). Chaos theory, informational needs, and natural disasters. *Journal of Applied Communication Research, 30*(4), 269–292.

Sheaffer, Z., & Mano-Negrin, R. (2003). Executives' orientations as indicators of crisis management policies and practices. *Journal of Management Studies, 40*(2), 573–606.

Sheaffer, Z., Richardson, B., & Rosenblatt, Z. (1998). Early-warning-signals management: A lesson from the Barings crisis. *Journal of Contingencies and Crisis Management, 6*(1), 1–22.

Sherman, W., & Harris, R. (2018). Crisis? What crisis? Strategic crisis management, and the GM ignition switch crisis. *SAM Advanced Management Journal, 83*(1), 41-49.

Shrivastava, P. (1993). Crisis theory/practice: Towards a sustainable future. *Industrial & Environmental Crisis Quarterly, 7*(1), 23–42.

Shrivastava, P., Mitroff, I., Miller, D., & Miglani, A. (1988). Understanding industrial crises. *Journal of Management Studies, 25*(4), 285–304.

Smith, D. (1990). Beyond contingency planning: Towards a model of crisis management. *Industrial Crisis Quarterly, 4*(4), 263–275.

Somers, S. (2009). Measuring resilience potential: An adaptive strategy for organizational crisis planning. *Journal of Contingencies and Crisis Management, 17*(1), 12-23.

Stead, W., & Stead, J. (2004). *Sustainable strategic management*. Armonk, NY: ME Sharpe.

Surowiecki, J. (2005). *The wisdom of crowds*. New York: Anchor Books.

Sutcliffe, K., & Vogus, T. (2003). Organizing for resilience, in Cameron, K. (ed.), *Positive Organizational Scholarship*, San Francisco, CA: Brerrett-Koehler Publishers Inc.

Twarog, D. (2017). Data-driven disaster response: How advanced crisis mapping and big data can improve Coast Guard incident response. *US Naval Institute Proceedings,* 0041798X, October, 143(10).

UN Global Pulse (2012). *Big data for development: Challenges and opportunities, United Nations, New York.* Retrieved November 14, 2017, from http://www.unglobalpulse.org/sites/default/files/BigDataforDevelopment-UNGlobalPulseJune2012.pdf

Veil, S. (2011). Mindful learning in crisis management. *Journal of Business Communication, 48*(2), 116-147.

Ward, J. (2017). Boiling down the benefits of big data. *Automotive Logistics,* 54-56. Retrieved 10/15/2017, from https://automotivelogistics.media/intelligence/advanced-analytics-boiling-benefits-big-data

Watson, H., Finn, R., & Wadhwa, K. (2017). Organizational and societal impacts of big data in crisis management. *Journal of Contingencies and Crisis Management, 25*(1), 15-22.

Weick, K. (1993). The collapse of sensemaking in organizations: The Mann Gulch disaster. *Administrative Science Quarterly, 38,* 628-652.

Weiss, J. (1998). *Business ethics: A stakeholder and issues management approach.* Fort Worth, TX: Dryden.

Appendix - Crisis Management Plan Template

Name of Company Goes Here

Company Logo Goes Here (Optional)

Crisis Management Plan

Last Revision Date

Contents

- Purpose of the Crisis Management Team (CMT)
- Definition of a Crisis
- Activating the CMT
- Command Center Location
- CMT Members and Contact Information
- CMT Role Responsibilities
- Responses to Specific Types of Crises
- Worksheet 1 – SWOT Analysis
- Worksheet 2 – PEST Analysis
- Important Contact Information

Purpose of the Crisis Management Team (CMT)

- The CMT identifies the crisis threats the organization may encounter.
- The CMT develops the crisis management plan.
- The CMT leads training in crisis management.
- The CMT actively manages the crisis should one occur.
- The CMT leads the post-crisis evaluation so that learning can occur.

Definition of a Crisis

A *crisis* is an event that has a low probability of occurring, but should it occur, can have a vastly negative impact on our organization.

The causes of the crisis, as well as the means to resolve it, may not be readily clear; nonetheless, its resolution should be approached as quickly as possible.

Finally, the crisis impact may not be initially obvious to all the relevant stakeholders of our organization.

Activating the CMT

- In the event of an emergency or crisis, any member of the CMT can activate the team by notifying one or more of its members.
- Upon activation of the CMT, the remaining team members will be notified of the crisis in the most expedient manner possible.
- The CMT will meet at the primary command center. If this location is not operational, the secondary location will be utilized.
- The CMT will meet to discuss strategies for managing the specific crisis at hand. Other meetings will be called as necessary until the crisis is resolved.

Command Center Location

Primary Command Center Location

This location is where the CMT meets when a crisis is present, and a meeting needs to be held. Our primary command center location is:

Building   _____

Room   _____

Secondary Command Center Location

If the primary command center is not available, perhaps due to fire or a weather event, the secondary command center location will be used. Our secondary command center location is:

Building   _____

Room   _____

CMT Members and Contact Information

Name	Cell Phone	Work Phone	Email	Other

Extend this list as necessary.

CMT Role Responsibilities

Two key roles need to be determined within the CMT:

1. The leader of the team, and
2. The individual designated to talk to the media.

In our organization: The CMT leader is: _____.

The CMT member who talks to the media is:
_____.

The CMT members who advise on social media communications are:
_____
_____.

In larger organizations, the members of the CMT are usually selected from the major departmental areas. In smaller organizations, the CMT often consists of the owner, the managers, and other designated employees. Regardless of the size of the organization, the two key roles above should be designated before a crisis occurs.

Responses to Specific Types of Crises

The types of crises our organization may encounter are listed in this section. For each potential crisis, there is a short summary of how we will respond and begin to address that crisis. Use Worksheets 1 and 2 to assist in compiling a list of potential crises.

Example - Evacuation of a building.

Provide bullet points how to address the crisis.
Continue your explanation with as many points as needed.

Worksheet 1: SWOT Analysis

Company Strengths Include:	Crises That Could Result from Those Strengths Include:
Company Weaknesses Include:	Crises That Could Result from Those Weaknesses Include:
Company Opportunities Include:	Crises That Could Result from Those Opportunities Include:
Company Threats Include:	Crises That Could Result from Those Threats Include:

Worksheet 2: PEST Analysis

Crises That Could Result from the Political/Legal Environment Include:
Crises That Could Result from the Economic Environment Include:
Crises That Could Result from the Social Environment Include:
Crises That Could Result from the Technological Environment Include:

Important Contact Information

Contact information should also be included in cell phones.

Emergency Management Providers		
Name	Phone	Other Contact Information
Emergency Services	911	
Fire Department		
Police Department		
Ambulance Service		
Power Company		
Telephone Company		
Internet Service		

Employees			
Name	Email	Phone	Other Contact Information

Important Contact Information (continued)

Suppliers and Key Industry Contacts			
Name	**Email**	**Phone**	**Other Contact Information**

Stakeholders: List other contact information for parties who have some type of vested interest in the organization.		
Name	**Phone**	**Other Contact Information**
Radio Station		
Television Station		

About the Authors

William "Rick" Crandall, Ph.D., is a Professor of Management at the University of North Carolina at Pembroke. He earned a Ph.D. degree from the University of Memphis and previously taught for eleven years at Concord College in Athens, WV, where he developed an interest in crisis management and served on the college's crisis management team. Dr. Crandall's articles on crisis management have appeared in *SAM Advanced Management Journal, Internal Auditing, Business Horizons, International Journal of Sustainable Strategic Management, Security Management, and the International Journal of Asian Business and Information Management.* He has addressed audiences on crisis management in the United States, Austria, China, Germany, Poland, and the United Kingdom. Before entering higher education, Dr. Crandall worked in management for ARA Services (now ARAMARK), a service management firm based in Philadelphia.

John A. Parnell, Ph.D., is a Professor of Management and Eminent Scholar of Business at the University of North Alabama. He is the author of over 250 research articles, published presentations, and cases in strategic management and related areas. His work appears in numerous journals, including the *Journal of Business Ethics, Academy of Management Learning & Education, Management Decision, Journal of Management Education,* the *European Journal of Management,* and *Strategic Change.* Dr. Parnell earned the B.S.B.A., M.B.A., and M.A. degrees from East Carolina University, the Ed.D. degree from Campbell University, and the Ph.D. degree in Strategic Management from The University of Memphis. He is the author of a current strategy textbook, *Strategic Management: Theory and Practice,* and has lectured in many countries, including China, Mexico, Peru, and Egypt. His current research focuses on issues related to crisis management, competitive business strategies, nonmarket strategy, and ethics.

John E. Spillan, Ph.D., is a Professor of Management at the University of North Carolina at Pembroke. His research interests include international business, crisis management, and entrepreneurship with a specific interest in Latin America and Eastern Europe. Dr. Spillan's work has been published in such outlets as the *International Journal of Marketing and Marketing Research, Journal of Teaching in International Business, Journal of World Business, Journal of Small Business Management,* and the *Journal of Global Marketing.* He has authored multiple books, including *Navigating Commerce in Latin America: Options and Obstacles* and *Doing Business in Ghana: Challenges and Opportunities.* Dr. Spillan has traveled and lectured extensively in Europe, Latin America, and the Middle East.

Made in the USA
Coppell, TX
11 January 2022

71414262R00214